P9-DEM-374

PAUL LE BLANC is Professor of History at La Roche College in Pittsburgh, and has lectured in Australia, Brazil, Britain, Canada, China, France, India, the Netherlands, and South Africa. Among his books are: *Work and Struggle: Voices from U.S. Labor Radicalism* (2011), *Marx, Lenin and the Revolutionary Experience: Studies of Communism and Radicalism in the Age of Globalization* (2006), *Black Liberation and the American Dream* (2003), *A Short History of the U.S. Working Class* (1999), *From Marx to Gramsci* (1996), *Lenin and the Revolutionary Party* (1990). Since the 1960s he has been active in struggles for racial justice and economic justice.

MICHAEL D. YATES is Associate Editor of *Monthly Review* and Editorial Director of Monthly Review Press. For many years he taught economics at the University of Pittsburgh at Johnstown and has taught working people in Labor Studies programs around the country. He is the author of *Why Unions Matter* (2nd edition, 2009), *The ABCs of the Economic Crisis* (with Fred Magdoff, 2009), and editor of *Wisconsin Uprising* (2012). After retiring from full-time teaching, Yates took up the life of an itinerant radical economist and documented his travels in *Cheap Motels and a Hot Plate: An Economist's Travelogue* (2007).

A FREEDOM BUDGET FOR ALL AMERICANS

Recapturing the Promise of the Civil Rights
Movement in the Struggle for Economic Justice Today

Paul Le Blanc and Michael D. Yates

MONTHLY REVIEW PRESS

New York

Copyright © 2013 by Paul Le Blanc and Michael D. Yates
All Rights Reserved

Library of Congress Cataloging-in-Publication Data

Le Blanc, Paul, 1947–
  A freedom budget for all Americans : recapturing the promise of the civil
rights movement in the struggle for economic justice today / Paul Le Blanc
and Michael D. Yates.
    pages cm
  Includes bibliographical references and index.
  ISBN 978-1-58367-360-7 (pbk. : alk. paper) — ISBN 978-1-58367-361-4
(cloth : alk. paper) 1. United States—Economic policy—20th century. 2.
United States—Social policy—20th century. 3. Economic security—United
States—History. 4. Poverty—Government policy—United States. 5. Civil
rights—United States—History. 6. Equality—United States—History. I.
Yates, Michael, 1946- II. Title.
  HC106.6L385 2013
  330.973—dc23
                            2013021619

Monthly Review Press
146 West 29th Street, Suite 6W
New York, New York 10001

www.monthlyreview.org

5 4 3 2 1

CONTENTS

ACKNOWLEDGMENTS

I MUST EXPRESS GRATITUDE for a sabbatical granted by La Roche College, allowing me to focus on this book, and to my many students there with whom I have shared information about the Freedom Budget. The several-year experience of coordinating the award-winning "Global Problems, Global Solutions" conferences associated with La Roche College also contributed to keeping the Freedom Budget very much in my consciousness.

An early commitment from Monthly Review Press was essential for this project to move forward, and the labor of its dedicated staff was no less essential to its completion. In the same vein, I must acknowledge the kindness and help of the staffs of the Tamiment Library and the Library of Congress.

Thanks are due to many others, including:

Participants who granted interviews or offered correspondence: Rick Congress, Joel Geier, Norman Hill, Velma Hill, Rachelle Horowitz (who subjected portions of the manuscript to a valuable critique), David McReynolds, and Walter Naegle (who also graciously supplied a summary version of the Freedom Budget);

Knowledgeable friends who read through one or another draft of the manuscript, in some cases more than one draft, offering helpful challenges, suggestions, and information: Brian Jones, Russell Pryor and, of course, my co-author, Michael Yates;

Friends and colleagues who offered encouragement and feedback, too numerous to mention, though perhaps an exception should be made in regard to one of the most loyal and thoughtful of collaborators on an accumulating number of projects—Immanuel Ness, an outstanding figure in the field of labor studies. On second thought, I must also express warm appreciation for the good fellowship, wine and munchies, and stimulating comparing-of-notes provided by two current fellow Pittsburghers, David Garrow and Darleen Opfer. Jibran Mushtaq, a brilliant former student and principled activist, also deserves special thanks for help in conceptualizing the cover design for this book.

I especially want to acknowledge the support of my sisters, Nora Le Blanc and Patty Le Blanc, of my sons, Gabriel Le Blanc and Jonah McAllister-Erickson, and of my dearest companion, Nancy Ferrari; and also the inspiration of fellow activists in and around Occupy Pittsburgh, Pittsburghers for Public Transit, the Thomas Merton Center, and the Pittsburgh-area labor movement (particularly Fight Back Pittsburgh, an innovative affiliate of the United Steel Workers), all of whom continue the struggle for economic justice.

—PAUL Le BLANC

FIRST, LET ME THANK Paul Le Blanc, without whose hard work and knowledge of the history of the Freedom Budget and the civil rights movement this book would not have been written. Thanks go also to Karen Korenoski, my partner, traveling companion, and editor, who has helped to teach me that good content is often lost without quality writing. As always, I thank my comrades at Monthly Review Press, especially Martin Paddio and Scott Borchert. And thanks to Erin Clermont, our copy editor, who has done her usual outstanding job, catching errors and omissions we missed and greatly improving the style.

—MICHAEL D. YATES

1. INTRODUCTION

INSEPARABLE FROM THE GOALS projected by the historic 1963 March on Washington for Jobs and Freedom, *A Freedom Budget for All Americans* was advanced in 1966 by A. Philip Randolph, Bayard Rustin, and Martin Luther King Jr., central leaders of the activist wing of the civil rights movement in the 1950s and '60s. It promised the full and final triumph of the civil rights movement. This was to be achieved by going beyond civil rights, linking the goal of racial justice for African Americans with the goal of economic justice for all Americans. If implemented, it would have fundamentally changed the history of the United States. In this introductory chapter, we will first give attention to that larger sweep of U.S. history, and a consideration of the relevance to this of capitalism and socialism, before focusing on the civil rights movement, which—in more than one way—so sharply posed questions of reform and revolution in the American experience.

What Might Have Been and What Was

The Freedom Budget proposal could be seen, and by some was seen, as related to the twentieth-century liberalism that was ascendant in U.S. politics from Franklin D. Roosevelt's New Deal to Lyndon B. Johnson's Great Society. But its dimensions and implications were far more radical. It projected the elimination of poverty within a ten-year period, the creation of full employment and decent housing, health care, and education for all people in our society as a matter of right. This was to be brought into being by rallying massive segments of the 99 percent of the American people in a powerfully democratic and moral crusade embracing the civil rights movement, the labor movement, progressive-minded religious communities, students, and youth, as well as their elders.

The defeat of this effort helped set the stage for a historic defeat for all of these constituencies. The crises of the twenty-first century's first two decades cannot be separated from these defeats—just as keys to the positive resolution of those crises may be found in an exploration of what the Freedom Budget was, where it came from, what it might have done, and why it was defeated.[1]

This defeat was related, in part, to a well-financed and steady (and soon accelerating) conservative onslaught that culminated in the right-wing triumph of the Reagan-Bush years. If the Freedom Budget had been successful, a majority of the voters would not have responded positively to candidate Ronald Reagan's challenge to Democratic incumbent Jimmy Carter when the conservative hopeful asked the American people, at the conclusion of a televised 1980 debate: "Are you better off than you were four years ago? Is it easier for you to go buy things in the stores than it was four years ago?"[2]

The 1980s victory for "free market capitalism," embraced by most conservative Republicans and by many Democrats in succeeding years, has made things worse for the great majority of the people over the four decades that followed, although certainly not for the wealthiest and most powerful 1 percent. Living standards, health, education, welfare, public transit, urban and natural environments, working conditions, job satisfaction, and more have dramatically declined.[3]

For many U.S. residents in the 1960s, this future was unimaginable. Since the 1930s, capitalism had yet to face another global downturn, and the common wisdom was that there would not be another. U.S. politics had been more or less dominated by a relatively generous social-liberalism since the coming of President Franklin D. Roosevelt's New Deal during the Great Depression, maintained to a significant degree by Republicans as well as Democrats.

In 2008, many hoped the presidency of Barack Obama would bring us back to that better, more hopeful, more generous world (personified in the minds of many by John F. Kennedy), and do it in a way that would be even more inclusive and more than what had been possible in the 1930s and 1940s of FDR's America. Obama's enemies cursed this darkly as "socialism"—and for some of his supporters, that *s* word seemed not so horrible after all. But the realities of the Obama administration never matched his rhetoric, and even his rhetoric fell far short of what Roosevelt eloquently expressed during the Second World War as his vision of the postwar future of the United States.[4]

Capitalism and Socialism

Roosevelt's administration had been characterized by aggressive and expansive support for labor rights, encouragement of the formation of powerful industrial unions, generous social programs, and government challenges to conservative business interests. In 1960, Afro-Caribbean cultural critic and revolutionary C. L. R. James commented:

> That was the great contribution of Roosevelt to American capitalism, others will say to American democracy. It was a tremendous political feat, and Mr. Roosevelt and his wife [Eleanor Roosevelt] together have a place in American history and the minds of the American people which will never be forgotten. Before Roosevelt and the New Deal, free enterprise and independent action by yourself for everything reigned as the unchallenged ideology of the United States. When Roosevelt was finished, that was finished. The Government was now held responsible for those who were in difficulties owing to the difficulties of capitalist society. In most of the countries of Western Europe, this had been carried out directly or indirectly by proletarian or labor parties of one kind or another. Roosevelt carried it out in the United States through the Democratic Party.[5]

It should be added that Roosevelt himself was an upper-class reformer who was simply seeking to save U.S. capitalism in the 1930s decade of economic collapse and radical insurgency, but willing to denounce as "economic royalists" those members of his class who attacked him as being "socialistic" because of his sweeping social reforms and support for workers seeking to organize unions. Though he was happy enough to switch from being "Dr. New Deal" to "Dr. Win-the-War" in 1941, his rhetoric veered even further leftward in his efforts to explain and mobilize popular support for the U.S. war effort during the Second World War. In 1941, Roosevelt's State of the Union address advanced a "four freedoms" orientation designed to rally the American people and U.S. allies in the global struggle against the Axis Powers of Nazi Germany, fascist Italy, and Imperial Japan:

In the future days, which we seek to make secure, we look forward to a world founded upon four essential human freedoms. The first is freedom of speech and expression—everywhere in the world. The second is freedom of every person to worship God in his own way—everywhere in the world. The third is freedom from want—which, translated into world terms, means economic understandings which will secure to every nation a healthy peacetime life for its inhabitants—everywhere in the world. The fourth is freedom from fear—which, translated into world terms, means a worldwide reduction of armaments to such a point and in such a thorough fashion that no nation will be in a position to commit an act of physical aggression against any neighbor—anywhere in the world.[6]

In his State of the Union address of 1944, Roosevelt expanded on the "freedom from want" theme by outlining what he called a Second Bill of Rights:

It is our duty now to begin to lay the plans and determine the strategy for the winning of a lasting peace and the establishment of an American standard of living higher than ever before known. We cannot be content, no matter how high that general standard of living may be, if some fraction of our people—whether it be one-third or one-fifth or one-tenth—is ill-fed, ill-clothed, ill-housed, and insecure.

This Republic had its beginning, and grew to its present strength, under the protection of certain inalienable political rights—among them the right of free speech, free press, free worship, trial by jury, freedom from unreasonable searches and seizures. They were our rights to life and liberty.

As our nation has grown in size and stature, however—as our industrial economy expanded—these political rights proved inadequate to assure us equality in the pursuit of happiness. We have come to a clear realization of the fact that true individual freedom cannot exist without economic security and independence. "Necessitous men are not free men." People who are hungry and out of a job are the stuff of which dictatorships are made.

In our day these economic truths have become accepted as self-evident. We have accepted, so to speak, a second Bill of Rights under which a new basis of security and prosperity can be established for all—regardless of station, race, or creed. Among these are:

- The right to a useful and remunerative job in the industries or shops or farms or mines of the nation;
- The right to earn enough to provide adequate food and clothing and recreation;
- The right of every farmer to raise and sell his products at a return which will give him and his family a decent living;
- The right of every businessman, large and small, to trade in an atmosphere of freedom from unfair competition and domination by monopolies at home or abroad;
- The right of every family to a decent home;
- The right to adequate medical care and the opportunity to achieve and enjoy good health;
- The right to adequate protection from the economic fears of old age, sickness, accident, and unemployment;
- The right to a good education.

All of these rights spell security. And after this war is won we must be prepared to move forward, in the implementation of these rights, to new goals of human happiness and well-being. America's own rightful place in the world depends in large part upon how fully these and similar rights have been carried into practice for all our citizens. For unless there is security here at home there cannot be lasting peace in the world.[7]

Roosevelt's expansive rhetoric did not result in the implementation of an "Economic Bill of Rights," but a number of New Deal social programs were preserved, in some cases expanded, in the years after the defeat of the Axis Powers. His successors, engaged in a new Cold War confrontation with Communism,[8] were especially concerned to prove to U.S. workers that the American status quo was pro-labor and capable of providing a decent life for most working people.

The end of the Second World War had opened into a period of prosperity, buttressed by the social safety nets and modest government regulation of the corporate capitalist system, initiated under Roosevelt. As we have noted, this was maintained, more or less, by Democratic and Republican administrations alike from 1945 through 1980. There were frictions and fissures, however, that pushed against this liberal predominance, especially: (1) an anti-union conservatism permeating the South (where the white and segregationist Democrats ruled), and (2) intense conservative dissatisfaction among some Republicans, highlighted by the 1964 Goldwater insurgency and post-1964 ferment.

Many analysts at the time viewed such dissonance as constituting last gasps of the past, not the wave of the future. They were not alert to the migration of the formidable forces that changed the South's racist Democratic Party into a rightward-moving Republican Party, whose evolving ethos and policies replicated much of what had dominated so much of southern politics of earlier years: low taxes, low wages, a non-union labor force, minimal social services, buttressed by an extreme social and cultural conservatism.

In the face of a decline in U.S. power and profits in the global political and economic arena, the so-called Reagan Revolution was initiated in the 1980s. A succession of presidents—Ronald Reagan, George H. W. Bush, Democrat Bill Clinton, and finally George W. Bush—proceeded to cut away more and more of the social safety net, push back and break the power of unions, dismantle government regulations, and give free rein to big business corporations.[9]

The impact of the conservative triumph has persisted through the Obama years, helping to galvanize an all-too-often frenzied right (and intimidate would-be liberals) on the issue of opposing Obama's presumed "socialism."[10] Of course, there is nothing socialist about the policies of the Obama presidency; Obama is opposed, as have been all U.S, presidents, to the essence of socialism: *the social ownership and democratic control of the economy, and its utilization to meet the needs of all people in society.* Nor does he appear to be motivated by the principle enunciated by Karl Marx that "the free development of each would be the condition for the free development of all."[11] Obama's orientation tacks significantly rightward from Franklin D. Roosevelt's policies. Like Roosevelt, he is an unapologetic partisan of the capitalist system. Unlike Roosevelt, however, he has not chosen to advance significant efforts either to regulate the market or to put forward a far-reaching program of social reforms beneficial to America's working-class majority.

The Radicalism of the Civil Rights Movement

Genuine socialists have played a substantial role in helping to shape the history of the United States, particularly in the 1950s and 1960s. The present study will demonstrate that *those leading what was often referred to as "the Civil Rights Revolution" had a socialist orientation.* This is glossed over in popular accounts of the movement. The fact is that the civil rights movement would not have been successful without the active involvement of conscious and organized socialists.

Jacquelyn Dowd Hall, in her magnificent survey of the scholarship covering the complex and multifaceted story of what she calls the "long civil rights movement," has noted that both conservative and liberal defenders of the social-economic-political status quo have done much to dilute and "sanitize" what really happened. Martin Luther King Jr. is presented as "this narrative's defining figure—frozen in 1963, proclaiming 'I have a dream' during the march on the Mall." Selective quotes, repeated over and over and over, result in his message losing its "political bite":

> We hear little of the King who believed that "the racial issue that we confront in America is not a sectional but a national problem" and who attacked segregation in the urban North. Erased altogether is the King who opposed the Vietnam War and linked racism at home to militarism and imperialism abroad. Gone is King the democratic socialist who advocated unionization, planned the Poor People's Campaign, and was assassinated in 1968 while supporting a sanitation workers' strike.

Hall by no means calls for a simplistically radical counter-narrative, but she does insist on truthful accounts of what was felt, thought, advocated, and struggled for by activists who won and lost the various battles that made up the movement's history. If there is a bias in what she argues for, it is that those telling the stories of the civil rights movement be true to what these magnificent human beings were actually about. "Both the victories and the reversals call us to action, as citizens and as historians with powerful stories to tell," she concludes. "Both are part of a long and ongoing civil rights movement. Both can help us imagine—for our own times—a new way of life, a continuing revolution."[12]

This spirit informs our effort in this book to utilize the *Freedom Budget for All Americans* as a prism through which to gain a useful perspective on the history of the civil rights movement, as well as the history of the United States—and maybe its future.

The Freedom Budget that was advocated from 1966 to 1968 was explicitly *not* a program for socialism. However, it was developed and advanced most effectively by socialists. It was seen by them as not only promising a realization of civil rights goals and of improvements in the quality of life for all Americans but also as a pathway that could help lead to a democratic socialist transformation of U.S. society.

The Freedom Budget could be seen as an expansion of the social-liberal orientation of the New Deal, and some of its supporters (and its critics) certainly saw it in that way. Yet there are some on the right as well as the left who would argue that just as capitalism necessarily involves the exploitation of labor in order to generate wealth, so will society-wide efforts to overcome poverty and inequality necessarily damage a system that requires a certain level of unemployment, or "reserve army of labor," and cannot do without periodic devastating economic downturns to ensure the health of the market economy.[13] The Freedom Budget had the potential, however, to seem quite reasonable and desirable to masses of people living in capitalist America. A popularly supported Freedom Budget, if it turns out capitalism cannot accommodate it, could have revolutionary implications, if the capitalist system proved incapable of realizing such reasonable, desirable goals and projections.

One key to understanding what happened in the victories and defeats of the civil rights movement has to do with the questions of organization and leadership. Masses of oppressed people, given their humanity, do not spontaneously or telepathically come up with collective plans of action based on shared analytical perspectives. This comes about through complex social and political processes: individuals and small groups develop analyses and strategies and tactics, which are communicated from a few people to more, and finally many more people; and then there are the steps necessarily proceeding from ideas to implemented realities—all of which involves leadership and organization. All of this is part of how history is made and society is changed.

In their fine study *Poor People's Movements*, Frances Fox Piven and Richard Cloward argue that "protest movements are shaped by institutional conditions [in the larger society], and not by the purposive efforts of leaders and organizers."[14] But this does not explain the victories of the Montgomery Bus Boycott of 1955–56, for example, or the Memphis sanitation workers strike of 1968, which marked the beginning and the end of Martin Luther King Jr.'s life as a civil rights leader. The fact that he and others like him (for example, Bayard Rustin) happened to be in both places is directly related to the existence of these powerful protests, whose eruption, trajectory, and triumph cannot be reduced simply to popular discontent over "conditions." It turned out, as we will show, that leaders, organizers, and cadres who were animated by socialist perspectives were also a key element in all that happened, from beginning to end.

Reform or Revolution?

Of course, not all socialists were the same. Some who claimed to favor socialism were prepared to embrace dictatorship, and those closest to the democratic spirit of Marx denounced this as not socialist at all. Another important difference that developed among those claiming to favor socialism involved approaches to reform and revolution.

In the world socialist movement, as the nineteenth century was turning into the twentieth, an important debate opened up between some (for example, Eduard Bernstein) who believed that the negative features of capitalism could gradually be reformed out of existence, and others (for example, Rosa Luxemburg) who believed that it would take a socialist revolution to end capitalism's oppressive and destructive dynamics.[15] The Bernstein-Luxemburg debate, waged inside a massive working-class party of that time, the Social-Democratic Party of Germany, is relevant to our understanding of the Freedom Budget, and more generally to understanding the dynamics of social movements and social change.

In his book *Evolutionary Socialism* (a series of articles begun in 1896, published as a book in 1899), Bernstein argued that Marx's revolutionary orientation was now out of date. According to Bernstein, capitalism was proving to be more stable, with less inequality, and more open to positive and democratic change than had seemed evident in Marx's time. Great gains were being made through trade unions, social legislation, and democratizing the German state. The Social Democratic movement could and should focus on piling up more and more reforms to gradually bring about, in the capitalist here-and-now, the kinds of improvements that socialism was supposed to bring. Rather than working-class revolution, Bernstein insisted, the Social Democratic Party "strives after the socialist transformation of society by the means of democratic and economic reform."[16]

In her polemic *Reform or Revolution* (1899) Luxemburg insisted that Bernstein's rosy prognosis for capitalism was unrealistic, which in retrospect seems a reasonable criticism given what happened in Germany and the world over the next half century (two horrific world wars bookended a devastating global economic depression, along with the rise of fascism and Hitler). Yet she also insisted that reforms—positive changes within the capitalist here-and-now—must be supported by all serious socialists. Reform struggles would not by themselves eliminate what was wrong with capitalism; only a revolution for *social ownership and democratic control of the economy* (socialism) could do that. Reforms could, however, provide life-giving improvements for masses of people in the present, and she supported them. At the same time, the natural dynamics of capitalism would work to erode those gains in the future, she noted, in order to enhance the power and profits of the capitalists.

However, Luxemburg believed that reform struggles could also help the working-class majority to organize and learn practical political skills. Reform struggles could give workers a sense of their potential power and help them actualize it. Reform struggles could help more and more workers gain a sense of the actual dynamics and limitations and destructiveness of capitalism. All of this added up to a revolutionary class-consciousness that would sooner or later result in the active commitment of the working-class majority to replace the political and economic power of the capitalists with its own—a socialist revolution. "The daily struggle for reforms, for the amelioration of the condition of the workers within the framework of the existing social order, and for democratic institutions, offers to the Social Democracy an indissoluble tie," Luxemburg insisted. "The struggle for reforms is its means; the social revolution, its aim."[17]

On the basis of further experience, Luxemburg advanced a "mass strike" concept, which emphasized various forms of working-class mass action—or as she put it, "the process of the proletarian mass struggle"—that she saw as "the natural means to recruit, organize and prepare the widest proletarian layers" for reforms ("to contain capitalist exploitation"), and also "as the means to undermine and overthrow the old state power." This could not and should not be carried out "under the conductor's baton of a party executive," but would assume, often spontaneously or semi-spontaneously, innumerable local forms, "pulsating life" that "must surely react upon deeper layers, and ultimately draw into a stormy economic struggle all those who, in normal times, stand aside from the normal trade union struggle." It was from this process that there would be the growth of trade unions and from which "the political process would always derive new impetus and fresh strength."[18]

Luxemburg's radicalism was in stark contrast to Bernstein's reformism, which frankly held that "genuine parliamentarianism, based upon universal suffrage, represents in modern industrial society the most effective tool for implementing profound, step-by-step reforms without bloodshed." Placing the blame for bloodshed on the repressive defenders of the old order, Luxemburg believed that mass action of the oppressed was sometimes the best defense—as well as the best way—to move the struggle for social justice forward. And though, "as will always be the case in mass movements and stormy times," there would sometimes be only partial successes and sometimes setbacks, the mass action perspective was nonetheless a revolutionary "quickstep, against the leisurely gait of peaceful development within the framework of bourgeois parliamentarism." The nature of capitalism precluded the success of Bernstein's gradualism.[19]

When the Freedom Budget was put forward, some on the left saw it as pure reformism. This is too narrow a view. The question is, how is something like the Freedom Budget to be used—in a reformist or a revolutionary way? Rustin and King both believed, in the early 1960s, that militant mass struggle is necessary to bring about certain major political and social reforms. Of the two, Rustin was perceived as being more radical. "Rustin had acquired the reputation of being a radical and rather dangerous socialist," Manning Marable has noted. "In October 1960, Rustin's invitation to attend a SNCC conference in Atlanta 'was withdrawn when a union sponsoring the conference objected to [his] radical reputation.'" Yet King, albeit less openly, shared Rustin's socialist orientation.[20] Both saw the Freedom Budget as a key aspect of moving the struggle for civil rights in a socialist direction. Rustin also framed the discussion, as late as 1963 and even 1964, in "mass struggle" terms reminiscent of Luxemburg's conceptualization.

The question soon arose of what should one do if some of the forces of the capitalist status quo offer to "work with you" to help you realize some of your goals. Alternatively, what if those same forces are unwilling to go along with what you are attempting to accomplish? Different responses are possible, some going in the direction of Luxemburg, others consistent with the example of Bernstein. This poses challenges for activists who hope to learn from and utilize something like the *Freedom Budget for All Americans* in struggles for a better future, just as it posed challenges to the activists of the 1960s.

IN WHAT FOLLOWS we will look at the battle for civil rights in the United States, the different dynamics and facets of racism, and at "The Strategy" that some socialists developed for overcoming racism. We will also touch on the role that socialists played in the civil rights struggle and in its 1963 culmination in the March for Jobs and Freedom. We will explore how the Freedom Budget came out of that context, what it was, what it was meant to accomplish, and the economics of how it was meant to work. We will then look at the efforts to advance it, at factors that resulted in the defeat of those efforts, and at the aftermath of that defeat. This volume will conclude with an exploration of the political economy of a New Freedom Budget.

2. THE BATTLE FOR CIVIL RIGHTS

THE FREEDOM BUDGET AROSE organically out of the activist wing of the civil rights movement: activists associated with black trade union leader A. Philip Randolph and those involved in the Southern Christian Leadership Conference (SCLC), the Congress of Racial Equality (CORE), and the Student Nonviolent Coordinating Committee (SNCC). Often glossed over, however, is that these men and women were influenced by conscious and organized forces that favored a socially owned and democratically controlled economy, one in which production would be for the benefit of all—in a word, socialism.[1]

In this chapter a survey of the broader historical trends leading to the rise of the civil rights movement of the 1950s and 1960s [2] will be followed by a consideration of essential elements in the more or less commonly shared civil rights strategy, which arose from the multifaceted socialist movement. We will conclude with an exploration of views shared by two key figures, A. Philip Randolph and Martin Luther King Jr., on which the Freedom Budget was based.

Historical Context of the Civil Rights Movement

After more than two centuries of slavery, the Civil War of 1861–65 finally brought an end to this brutal and horrific "peculiar institution." Many historians see this as an "irrepressible conflict" between what were increasingly incompatible social-economic systems: it involved a greater loss of American lives, and more devastating social and economic destruction on U.S. soil, than any other war in the history of the United States. The war was not simply over the institution of slavery, of course, but over the divergent needs (from the standpoint of economic development policies enhancing the profits of contending economic elites) of an industrializing economy based on free labor versus an agricultural economy based on slave labor. From 1863, when Lincoln's Emancipation Proclamation declared an end to slavery in the rebellious South, through the Reconstruction years, designed in part to facilitate advances in the status and well-being of the ex-slaves, the democratic commitment of the triumphant North was intertwined with a program of industrial progress. These were developments so radical that some historians have tagged this "the Second American Revolution."[3] But what would happen if there was a choice to be made between the requirements for accumulating capitalist profits and the issue of human rights for African Americans? The way this question was answered is indicated in Tom Kahn's brilliant pamphlet of 1964, *The Economics of Equality* (corresponding to insights developed by such Marxist-influenced historians as W. E. B. Du Bois, C. L. R. James, and George Rawick):

> The Great Lesson of Reconstruction is that political and social freedom is inseparable from economic freedom. Democracy may be written into the law books, but if it is not also built into the way men earn their bread and the way they relate to each other in the process, legal rights become mere abstractions, if indeed they survive at all.
>
> The Civil War freed the slaves, and the Fourteenth and Fifteenth Amendments defined their citizenship rights. Armed with the ballot, Negroes wielded political power in the Reconstruction governments. Congress in 1875 passed a sweeping civil rights act outlawing discrimination in public accommodations.
>
> But, rejecting the Radical Republican slogan of "40 acres and a mule," the federal government refused to break up the large plantations into small farms on which the freedmen could establish themselves as independent farmers. Having no other livelihood, they returned to the plantations, but as sharecroppers, and often to their former masters. Before long, they were marched to the polls to help reinstall Dixiecrat political power [i.e., local and state governments ruled by southern white-racist Democrats]. The original intent of the Amendments was warped or gutted, the ballot taken from the Negro, and the Civil Rights Act of 1875 declared unconstitutional by the Supreme Court eight years later. By the turn of

the century the Negro was disenfranchised and segregated. The counter-revolution was complete. . . .

On the verge of a new economic order launched by the victory of Northern industrial capitalism over the Southern agrarian slavocracy, the nation had been called upon to decide a crucial question: What is to be the Negro's place in the new order? The decision was to relegate him to a semi-feudal agrarian status only once removed from slavery—that of a sharecropper. It meant precisely that he was to be excluded from the new industrial order, and from the political and social rights which that order conferred.[4]

One might ask why the racist system in the South persisted as long as it did. After all, the years from approximately 1900 to 1920 are often characterized as the Progressive Era, in which social reform movements were initiated to improve the human condition and advance human rights. There were struggles around labor rights (including a dramatic expansion of the socialist movement), immigrant rights, women's rights. It was in this period that W. E. B. Du Bois and others established the National Association for the Advancement of Colored People (NAACP). But it was only in the 1950s and 1960s that a movement would come into being that proved powerful enough to overcome the system of legalized racism in the South. What changed between 1909 when the NAACP was formed and 1954, when the modern civil rights movement crystallized after the Supreme Court's *Brown v. Board of Education* decision declaring racial segregation in public education to be unconstitutional?

One piece of the answer can be found in a single word: cotton. This had been central to maintaining the slave-labor system and later to the sharecropping system after the Civil War. "King" of the South's economy and, in some respects, the entire U.S. economy in the first half of the nineteenth century, it remained quite profitable later in the century and became even more so from 1900 through the First World War. In the 1920s, however, the cotton economy began to falter, and it collapsed in the Depression years of the 1930s. New Deal farm policies contributed to fundamental changes in the rural economy as white landowners were encouraged to mechanize by shifting from mules to tractors, increasing agricultural productivity. The result was that there was no longer a need for so many black families, or white ones for that matter, to work the land. Urban and industrial development in the South and beyond during the Second World War finished the job. The rural basis of white supremacy in the South, largely grounded in the economics of cotton, increasingly lost its "material basis" in the decades after the Progressive Era.[5]

There were other major factors as well, but some of them cannot be found if we focus only on what was happening in the South. Thomas Sugrue has recently commented that conventional histories of the civil rights struggle "focus on the South and the epic battles between nonviolent protestors and the defenders of Jim Crow during the 1950s and 1960s," often presented as "a morality play, one that pits the forces of good (nonviolent protestors) against evil (segregationist politicians, brutal sheriffs, and rednecks). It is a story of suffering and redemption, with larger-than-life martyrs and prophets." As he points out, in order to understand it all we need to extend our view well before and well after the 1950s and 1960s: we have to see racism in a nationwide context, and we have to give considerable attention to what was happening among anti-racist activists in the North and on how "northern and southern activists influenced one another."[6]

There was, first of all, the Great Northern Migration, sparked by labor shortages hitting industrial centers of the North beginning in 1916, and due to the combination of war-related expansion of industrial production and the cutting off of European immigration. An increasing number of African Americans found themselves in a politically freer atmosphere in the North, and they gained access to somewhat improved economic conditions. This gave greater strength to black organizations. In the wake of the First World War, as the migration continued, the National Urban League crystallized into a unified force, joining with the NAACP to promote the advancement of African Americans in northern cities. There was also the militant black nationalism represented by Marcus Garvey's United Negro Improvement Association (UNIA), as well as the radical labor, socialist, and communist movements represented by such figures as Hubert Harrison, A. Philip Randolph, Claude McKay, Ben Fletcher, and Cyril Briggs. The dramatic African American influx into urban and industrial centers also created a potential voting base in the North that could create greater pressure on elected officials than was possible in the Jim Crow South. Moreover, an incredible and multifaceted artistic and cultural flowering developed, symbolized by, but hardly restricted to, the Harlem Renaissance.

The Depression decade of the 1930s hit the country hard, but African Americans, already on the bottom, were hit twice as hard. Many shifted their allegiance away from the party of Lincoln when the Republicans seemed to offer little more than pro-business conservatism, whereas Franklin D. Roosevelt's Democrats seemed to promise a New Deal for the working-class majority. At the same time, growing numbers developed organizational skills and political education in the burgeoning movement of the militant unemployed and in some, though hardly all, unions, especially among those affiliated with the Congress of Industrial Organizations (CIO), which advanced a vision of black-white unity in the struggle for economic and social justice. Left-wing groups drew a minority of whites and blacks together to oppose racism in the North and South as part of a broader struggle for fundamental social change. These included the Socialist Party, the Communist Party, revolutionary socialist followers of Leon Trotsky, and others unaffiliated with any specific group but favoring the replacement of capitalism with socialism. The recollection of this period, by someone who was a radical black activist as the 1930s were about to give way to the 1940s, is worth considering:

> Between the union movement and the Roosevelt tradition that was coming in and the right of labor to organize and the little things that Mrs. Roosevelt did to have the President's ear about this issue of racism, and Marian Anderson singing and Joe Louis punching out these cats with great regularity. All of that gave one optimism despite the cold-bloodedness of the insult of segregation.[7]

The Second World War that began in 1939 brought an end to the Depression. Although partly a repeat of the First World War—in which the world's "Great Powers" were prepared to kill many millions in violent competition for markets, raw materials, investment opportunities—it was also seen by many as a "people's war" against Hitler's super-racism, and a defense of democratic values that would embrace all of humanity. As the United States was preparing to enter the conflict in 1941, A. Philip Randolph, socialist militant and longtime leader of the all-black Brotherhood of Sleeping Car Porters, explicitly challenged the discriminatory racial practices permeating war-related industries as well as the thoroughgoing racial segregation in the U.S. military. Threatening a march on Washington, Randolph forced far-reaching concessions from the Roosevelt administration (an executive order with teeth, banning racist hiring and promotion practices in war-related industries) as the price for calling off the march. Added to this was the popularity among many African Americans of a "double-V" campaign: victory over Nazi racism overseas, victory over racism here at home. All of this had a powerful impact on black consciousness throughout the United States. But it also had an impact on the consciousness of many whites, who began to reflect on the practical meaning of racism as manifested in Hitler's new order.

Sentiment for liberation from racist oppression was sent soaring after the war by the proliferating anti-colonial revolutions that swept through Asia and Africa, which confronted and defeated white racist power structures and created an increasing number of new independent nations of colored peoples. More than this, the U.S. political and economic leadership felt mounting pressures on the global terrain, in which the balance of nation-states was becoming predominantly non-white. Between the late 1940s and on into the 1950s and 1960s, this pressure became more urgent due to the U.S.-led Cold War with an expanding Communism and the competitive struggle for "hearts and minds" among the colored peoples of the new independent nations.[8]

Manning Marable, surveying the devastating impact of "The Cold War in Black America," sees a decade-long setback for the civil rights movement, speculating: "The democratic upsurge of black people which characterized the late 1950s could have happened ten years earlier." An incredibly fierce Cold War anti-Communism demolished much of the radical insurgency of the 1930s and early 1940s, in which labor struggles and anti-racist struggles were pushing toward a civil rights breakthrough. Yet as Nikhil Pal Singh comments, the relationship of the Cold War and civil rights "cut both ways—it set certain limits on black political activity and public rhetoric, but it also provided new opportunities to frame long-existing forms of black exclusion as violations of liberal norms and to define practitioners of racist violence and exclusion as 'enemies of democracy' and supporters of totalitarianism."[9]

By the 1950s, this convergence of dramatic changes created a reality that was qualitatively different from that of 1909. It was the context within which the modern civil rights movement came into being. The NAACP and the Urban League had actually begun during the Progressive Era, and they would continue to be forces for the advancement of civil rights in the years to come, but other groups arose as the years unfolded that were more in touch with the new moods. The first of these was the Congress on Racial Equality (CORE), formed in 1942 by a religious-pacifist organization, the Fellowship of Reconciliation led by A. J. Muste, with the active participation of Socialist Party members such as black activist James Farmer, who led the new organization in a more militant direction.

In 1955, a local NAACP activist named Rosa Parks was arrested in Montgomery, Alabama, for refusing to obey a segregation law requiring her to give up her bus seat to a white man. E. D. Nixon, a local leader of the Brotherhood of Sleeping Car Porters and the NAACP, helped to organize a coalition to boycott the buses, but the most famous figure to emerge from this victorious struggle was Rev. Martin Luther King Jr. (In the North, A. Philip Randolph helped mobilize support, as did a modest but important entity he helped bring into being called In Friendship, led by Ella Baker, Bayard Rustin, and Stanley Levison.) It is worth noting that Parks, Nixon, and King all had contact with the radically oriented Highlander Folk School, and also with the left-leaning Southern Conference Educational Fund led by Carl and Anne Braden.[10]

In 1956, King and others formed another key organization, the Southern Christian Leadership Conference (SCLC). In addition to a large number of African American ministers, several women, such as longtime NAACP activist Ella Baker and Highlander's Septima Clark, played important roles in making this an effective organization. Influenced by the independence movement in India led by Mohandas Gandhi, King and others advanced the tactic of nonviolent direct action to challenge unjust laws, minimize violence, help win public support, and pressure the U.S. government to compel the southern states and local governments to stop violating the Fourteenth Amendment of the U.S. Constitution.

By 1960, a new organization came into being, started by black college students (soon joined by some white students as well) who organized lunch-counter sit-ins to desegregate eating facilities, first in Greensboro, North Carolina, and then elsewhere. The new group was called the Student Nonviolent Coordinating Committee (SNCC). But the other groups also continued to mount anti-segregation efforts. SCLC waged desegregation campaigns in Albany, Georgia, and elsewhere, and then launched an important campaign in Birmingham, Alabama. In 1961, CORE, largely a northern organization, initiated "Freedom Rides," modeled on similar efforts of twenty years earlier, which involved black and white civil rights activists boarding Greyhound buses destined for the South, where they would maintain desegregated seating arrangements on the buses and also desegregate bus station facilities. In some cases they met with beatings and bus burnings.

Ella Baker explained the difference she found between the moderate older groups and the more radical newer ones. "The NAACP, Urban League, etc., do not change society; they want to get in," she noted, whereas for a group like

SNCC, "It's a combination of concern with the black [equal rights] goal for itself and, beyond that, with the whole society, because this is the acid test of whether the outs can get in and share in equality and worth." She added: "By worth, I mean creativity, a contribution to society."[11]

While the NAACP and Urban League continued to work with (though sometimes complain about or compete with) CORE, SCLC, and SNCC, these three—often with backup from the prestigious A. Philip Randolph—together represented what could be called the activist wing of the civil rights movement. It is hardly the case, however, that their radicalism was defined simply by a willingness to engage in vigorous actions, to organize mass demonstrations, and sometimes go to jail for committing civil disobedience. To be *radical* means to go to the root of something. Their radicalism flowed from their deep analysis of racism and a strategic orientation for overcoming it, which envisioned not superficial changes but a fundamental restructuring of society.

"The Strategy"

For purposes of clarity and succinctness, throughout this book we will make use of the term "The Strategy" when referring to the analysis and orientation outlined here. The term was not used in this manner in the 1960s; activists did not go around referring to something they called "The Strategy."

The activist wing of the civil rights movement, whose most respected representatives were probably A. Philip Randolph and Martin Luther King Jr., developed a strategic orientation that was based on a specific understanding of racism. Racism consists of more than racial prejudice or discrimination based on race. It consists of an interactive mix of what one might call *personal racism* and *institutional racism*, and each of these broad categories consists of a spectrum of manifestations.[12] King and others were determined to eliminate all manifestations of racism, "lock, stock and barrel." At the same time, they realized that this would have to be the result of a process, and to understand how they envisioned this process—this *strategy*—for eliminating racism, it will be helpful to explore the different components of personal and institutional racism they saw and experienced.

Personal racism involves a complex of attitudes and practices on the part of individual human beings. It involves prejudging people based on their race or ethnicity, with consequent behaviors and actions, but it operates on two levels, conscious and unconscious.

On the conscious plane, personal racism varies between the extremely aggressive and the relatively passive. A member of the Ku Klux Klan or the American Nazi Party may be vocal and explicit that "we" must stand up for "our race" and for the supremacy of "our race," and that "we" must achieve that by any means necessary, including force and violence. Members of the White Citizens Council (set up throughout the South in the 1950s to combat racial integration) who are not Klan members may have the same goal, just as explicitly stated, but may reject "force and violence" and insist that "we" must use peaceful and legal means. Some conscious racists may choose not to participate in organized efforts to maintain racial segregation and white supremacy, but to live, more quietly, a lifestyle consistent with those goals.

This shades into more or less unconscious racial prejudice—a conscious rejection of any explicitly racist notions, but various forms of inconsistency, anxiety, and awkwardness concerning racial matters and relationships that suggest unresolved issues. It can also involve a more or less consistent tolerance or lack of awareness of a subordinate position, and its related oppression and humiliation, endured by members of another race. Given the depth and centrality of racism in the history and culture of the United States, it may be impossible for anyone who has grown up in our society, certainly up through the twentieth century, to be absolutely free from all psychological influences and effects associated with racism.

Institutional racism also has two levels—racism enforced by law (*de jure*) and racism not enforced by law but existing in fact (*de facto*). The most obvious example of de jure racism in U.S. history consists of the rich variety of state and national legislation and executive decisions, plus portions of the U.S. Constitution and Supreme Court decisions that defined and upheld the enslavement of African Americans. In the same period, a wealth of laws enforced the second-class citizenship of free blacks, as well as laws designed to preserve "racial purity." After the Civil War brought an end to slavery (with a consequent revision of the Constitution), such legalized second-class citizenship persisted in many areas, and it increased and intensified especially in the South after the obliteration of Reconstruction policies that had been designed to provide citizenship rights and advance the well-being of the ex-slaves. In the 1880s and 1890s, when many small farmers, sharecroppers, and laborers, black as well as white, flocked into the radical Populist movement before it was defeated, a stronger impetus than ever kept the races apart. As the nineteenth century faded into the twentieth, a systematic implementation and enforcement of the so-called Jim Crow laws in the South established a system of rigid racial segregation, dividing blacks from whites in a wide variety of contexts, and also eroding and eliminating the right to vote for African Americans through the imposition of poll taxes, grandfather clauses, and often selectively applied literacy tests.

The de facto racism institutionalized in American life has also taken different forms. Of course, the beating and murder of blacks by white mobs and the prevalence of lynching during the Jim Crow era, though systematic and existing "in fact," were not condoned by law. But the terms de facto racism or de facto segregation are more generally utilized to refer to less violent practices and policies. For example, as large numbers of African Americans moved north during the Great Northern Migration, local politicians worked with real estate companies to funnel the non-white newcomers into specific, largely run-down sections of Boston, New York, Philadelphia, Pittsburgh, Cleveland, Detroit, Chicago, and other cities. Laws were not passed to make it so, but policies were nonetheless systematically carried out to ensure segregated housing patterns.[13] In employment, black labor was much needed and widely utilized in many industries, but there were limitations, with more skilled, secure, and higher-paying jobs invariably going to whites, not according to law but according to company policy.

The historical accumulation of racist discrimination helped to create a new variant of de facto racism, one that was not necessarily intentional. By the 1960s certain long-term patterns had become clear. Overall income of whites tended to be twice as high as that of blacks; unemployment tended to be twice as high among blacks as it was among whites; and though a majority of those living in poverty were white, twice as many blacks as whites lived in poverty. Housing among blacks tended to be inferior; educational levels tended to be lower; health tended to be inferior; and infant mortality tended to be significantly higher. In his 1962 classic *The Other America*, Michael Harrington commented that these facts about African Americans were "the expressions of the most institutionalized poverty in the United States, the most vicious of vicious circles," elaborating:

If all the discriminatory laws in the United States were immediately repealed, race would still remain as one of the most pressing moral and political problems in the nation. Negroes and other minorities are not simply victims of a series of iniquitous statutes. The American economy, the American society, the American unconscious are all racist. If all the laws were framed to provide equal opportunity, a majority of the Negroes would not be able to take full advantage of the change. There would still be a vast, silent, automatic system directed against men and women of color.[14]

According to Tom Kahn's 1964 analysis in *The Economics of Equality*, racial inequalities were being sustained by two factors: "the weight of centuries of past discrimination combining with portentous economic forces that are themselves color-blind." Most decisive were the ominous yet "impersonal" economic forces. In a sense, according to Kahn's analysis, the northward migration of African Americans from the First World War up to the 1960s constituted the last great wave of "immigration" into the industrial North. The earlier immigrant waves from Europe had been absorbed into the U.S. economy during a period of industrial development. But economic changes were now resulting in closing off such possibilities for African Americans.

Between 1940 and 1953, blacks had made genuine economic gains and had begun to close the gap between blacks and whites (for example, the unemployment gap between the two dropped from 25 to 13 percent). But technological innovations and other shifts in the economy were leading to a gradual erosion of the relatively good-paying unskilled and semiskilled jobs that had provided substantial employment and income for much of the working class in earlier times. Thus, whereas in the relatively prosperous postwar period the unemployment rate among blacks was about 60 percent higher than the white rate, between 1954 and 1964 it had become at least 200 percent higher. In the absence of the "radical programs for the abolition of poverty and unemployment," Kahn warned, "persistent economic inequalities will undermine the drive toward legal and social equality."[15]

From the standpoint of Randolph, King, and their co-thinkers, racism in all of its manifestations had to be eliminated. Yet they sought to begin the struggle at racism's weakest link. A victorious struggle at that particular point could help to create a body of experience, resources, support, and a vital momentum that would enable the activist wing of the civil rights movement and its allies to press forward in the struggle for total victory.

For a variety of reasons, the Jim Crow system in the South was the most vulnerable component of the multifaceted racist reality in the United States. The economics of the South, including the growth of industry and the mechanization of agriculture, had considerably eroded the economic motivations and under-pinnings of the Jim Crow laws. So had the Great Northern Migration, which enhanced the ability of northern blacks to organize and to vote. These develop-ments, combined with their integration into the labor movement and the larger political process, helped to create a qualitatively new political reality in the United States. The pressures of U.S. foreign policy—in an international arena in which nations and governments were increasingly non-white and in which the blight of Jim Crow was a serious liability in the Cold War competition with world Communism—also caused the powerful elites defending the global inter-ests of U.S. capitalism to see racist segregation and the denial of voting rights to African Americans as practices the United States could ill afford.

This contributed to a new split in U.S. ruling circles: some, especially in the South, remained rooted in the "old ways," and others were inclined to respond to new political pressures by favoring change. This would be key in this phase of "The Strategy." There was now the potential for support from decisive ele-ments within the nation's elite for ending the Jim Crow system, if sufficient popular pressure could be mobilized.

The Jim Crow system, politically vulnerable as it was, and standing in clear violation of the intentions of the Fourteenth and Fifteenth Amendments to the U.S. Constitution, was the obvious first target for a movement dedi-cated to the elimination of racism in the United States. The nonviolent but unrelenting assault on one of the pillars of institutional racism, in an extended campaign employing moral, religious, and democratic rhetoric so central to the culture and history of the United States, would be able to mobilize consid-erable popular support.

This strategy would intensify the personal racism of some individuals, bringing it out into the open and consequently making it easier to address and deal with than if it remained submerged. For others, all of this would cause them to examine and move away from aspects of their own personal racism, and in many cases to commit themselves to the popular struggle to overcome the racism that had been so central to American society for so many years.

The consciousness and momentum of this crusade against the Jim Crow system could stand as a preliminary stage for confronting the other aspects of institutional racism, which would require a more fundamental social and eco-nomic transformation.

This transformation could only be realized effectively by attacking racism's underlying economic roots, which in turn could only be done effectively by developing a broader program for economic justice: decent jobs, housing, education, and health care for all, as a matter of right. Though such a program would be initiated by blacks, it would be powerfully relevant to a majority of whites. The resulting interracial coalition for economic justice would have the dual function of eliminating the roots of institutional racism and creating an atmosphere of idealism and common struggle that would help to further push back various forms of individual racism. If there was abundance and a decent life for every person, then the fearful competition for scarce resources, an essential breeding ground and one of the material bases of racism, would be eliminated, and this would strengthen the sense of interracial solidarity generated through the shared struggle for a better life for all people.

One way to restate "The Strategy" is to note that it projected (1) a mass struggle against segregation and second-class citizenship; and (2) tackling issues of economic justice, channeling the struggle against the Jim Crow system into an even more massive struggle (through a coming together of the anti-racist and labor movements) for jobs for all, an end to poverty, and democratic regulation of the economy, which would involve a transition from capitalism to socialism. The issue of the Democratic Party was not essential to this basic orientation (Randolph himself voted only for socialist candidates until 1964), although in the 1960s it became an essential—some would argue fatal—"tactical" decision strongly advocated by some key partisans of "The Strategy."

It should be added that this strategic orientation was not a grand blueprint developed by some conference of civil rights activists and carried out in a conscious and self-confident manner by all involved. For many there was a sense of personal urgency, of moral decision, independent of political strategizing or revolutionary intentions. Given the complex nature of the human condition, multiple contingencies and accidents, unforeseen opportunities and dilemmas, and innumerable individual choices were not and could not be thought through politically. It was not the case, for example, that Rosa Parks, E. D. Nixon, Rev. Martin Luther King Jr., and others decided to initiate the Montgomery Bus Boycott in 1955 as a first step toward socialism.

But as organizers and activists began doing their work, and as they continued to move the struggle forward, they formulated an orientation that drew from already existing political perspectives. The civil rights strategy outlined here, which was the general framework within which the Freedom Budget was developed, was by no means simply the brainchild of an A. Philip Randolph or a Martin Luther King Jr. Its elements were part of the shared insights and common wisdom of a broader socialist movement. Before focusing on the specifics that led to the emergence of the Freedom Budget, it is worth considering the diverse and sometimes divergent forces that gave rise to the orientation we have traced.

Forces for Socialism and Democracy

Often acknowledged in the development of the civil rights movement's activist wing is the influence of the pacifist-oriented Christian socialism associated with A. J. Muste's Fellowship of Reconciliation (FOR), which made essential contributions, especially in the 1940s and early 1950s.[16] But in some ways more important, by the 1960s, was the Socialist Party of America (SP) and its youth group, the Young People's Socialist League (YPSL, generally pronounced "yipsel"), and that influence will necessarily receive special emphasis in this account. The historic leader of the SP since the 1930s was Norman Thomas, who represented a relatively "moderate" and reformist-oriented way of understanding socialism.[17] There were also indirect influences from other components of the left—those associated with the "mainstream" of the Communist movement, and also those associated with dissident split-offs.[18]

Historically, the U.S. Communist Party (CP) had played a pioneering role in the struggle against racism. Referring in 1968 to a record of more than forty years, Communist Party leader Henry Winston commented: "For years, almost alone, it led the struggle in the Deep South, under conditions comparable to those faced in Hitler Germany, for full freedom, for the right of black people to vote, to organize, to have equal access to all public places, for the repeal of the poll tax, and for an end to lynching." This was not an idle boast, nor was Winston's assertion that many Communists, "Negro and white, gave their lives in those early battles."[19] Anne Braden, a knowledgeable veteran from the Southern Conference Educational Fund, in a 1965 survey of the movement, went out of her way to stress:

Yet another force which was impinging on the Southern police state, although many people don't want to admit it now, was the work [in the 1930s and 1940s] of radical political groups, especially the Communist Party. In the nation as a whole, ideas were freer then than they are today, and no one was stopping Communists from speaking. In the South, they faced the danger of jails and mobs, but so did the CIO and NAACP organizers, and Communists were not considered any more outlaw in the South than these were. Furthermore, since the risks of organizing any protest in the Deep South were great, even as they are now, there was a need for very dedicated people. Dedication comes most often in people who have their eyes fixed beyond immediate suffering to a vision of a new world—and this many Communists of that day, both white and black, had. Thus they often faced dangers in the South that others would not. Often the CIO sent its Communist organizers into the South because they were the only ones who were willing to go and risk getting their heads beat in. This was before either the labor movement or any other institution trying to change America had let itself be divided by the notion that the test of a man is his anti-Communism rather than his devotion to the task at hand. Thus Communists moved and worked freely in the South, and their attack on the economic causes of Negro oppression opened new doors of thought for many people and contributed to the general ferment.[20]

Communists were active in the fight for racial equality in the North as well, often through the Civil Rights Congress, the "mass organization" it helped establish in 1946 (and which some charged was a "Communist front"). Yet the CP suffered a dramatic marginalization and disintegration in the 1950s, in part through government repression and Cold War anti-Communism, in part because of revelations about the horrific, murderous crimes of the Stalin dictatorship in the Soviet Union that caused idealistic members to leave in droves.[21] It continued, nonetheless, to have a residual and sometimes significant influence among those who were associated with the civil rights struggle. In 1965, Irving Howe offered this description, unsympathetic but not fundamentally inaccurate, of the substantial milieu of former Communist activists:

Those who left the party or its supporting organizations because they feared government attack were often people who kept, semiprivately, their earlier convictions. Many of them had a good deal of political experience; some remained significantly placed in the network of what might be called conscience organizations. Naturally enough, they continued to keep in touch with one another, forming a kind of reserve apparatus based on common opinions, feelings, memories. As soon as some ferment began in the civil rights movement and the peace groups, these people were present, ready, eager; they needed no directives from the Communist Party to which, in any case, they no longer (or may never have) belonged; they were quite capable of working on their own, *as if they were working together*, through a variety of groups and periodicals like the *National Guardian* [an independent left-wing newsweekly that maintained more or less friendly ties to the CP]. Organizational Stalinism declined, but a good part of its heritage remained: people who could offer political advice, raise money, write leaflets, sit patiently at meetings, put up in a pleasant New York apartment visitors from a distant state, who, by chance, had been recommended by an old friend.[22]

Also playing a key role in the movement were activists who had been involved in historic split-offs from U.S. Communism. Certain civil rights stalwarts had in the 1930s been associated with Communist Party Opposition, the so-called Lovestoneites, although the group (after various name changes) had dissolved in 1940, and some of its central leaders had evolved in conservative directions. The fact remains that highly respected activists had origins in this current, including Ella Baker, Pauli Murray, Ernest Calloway, and Maida Springer, as well as Charles Zimmerman, who headed up civil rights work for the International Ladies Garment Workers Union.[23]

Individuals originating from various Trotskyist and ex-Trotskyist currents also played a role: the Socialist Workers Party (SWP, the mainstream Trotskyist group), the "Cochranite" American Socialist Union, the Correspondence Publishing Committee around C. L. R. James, Marxist-Humanists associated with Raya Dunayevskaya, and especially the group led by Max Shachtman, which split from the SWP in 1940 to form the Workers Party, renaming itself the Independent Socialist League in 1949, and finally dissolving into the Socialist Party in 1958.

The "Shachtmanites" included Michael Harrington, Tom Kahn, Norman Hill, Rachelle Horowitz, Paul Feldman, and others. Since they were a substantial and influential force in the Socialist Party and in the activist wing of the civil rights movement, particularly after their recruitment to the Socialist Party, that group is important in this account. This is especially the case because they were able to win Bayard Rustin to their ranks, and to their orientation.

All of the socialist forces in this brief survey shared certain things in common. One was the influence of Marxism, whose discovery, A. Philip Randolph once commented, was "like finally running into an idea that gives you your whole outlook on life."[24] (Further discussion of the Marxist perspectives that influenced the civil rights activists discussed here can be found in the appendix to this chapter.) Such elemental aspects of the socialist outlook, as influenced by Marx, constituted much of the intellectual toolbox that a variety of left-wing organizations and activists utilized to make sense of the racism that afflicted U.S. society, and in developing strategies and tactics for overcoming it.

We have already considered "The Strategy" that came from people influenced by this orientation. In the next chapter, we will see key figures associated with this outlook who were central to the 1963 March on Washington for Jobs and Freedom that, in its immediate aftermath, pointed the way to the Freedom Budget. But first we must give attention to the civil rights movement that provided the context for the March and Budget, and to the central figures of the civil rights movement's activist wing, Randolph and King.

Civil Rights Upsurge

Many on the left were, of course, alert to what veteran Communist Abner Berry referred to as "thunder in the South" in 1956. "The effect of the [1954] Supreme Court ruling against segregation, and the tremendous effort at popularizing it done by the NAACP, has left its mark on the Southern Negroes," Berry commented. "They move into battle against segregation now with the knowledge that jim crow laws have been declared illegal." He added: "The vigor of the Negroes' drive for enforcement of the nation's laws has spilled over into the church bodies of all denominations. In turn, the Negro movement has stimulated the churches to act, and the labor movement, turning from its old economism, is developing a program geared to the social and political demands of the Negro people." Although he didn't mention the Communists' old Socialist rival A. Philip Randolph in this regard, he did give very honorable mention to Rev. Martin Luther King Jr., who was leading the Montgomery Bus Boycott to victory, particularly King's internationalist comment: "It is part of something that is happening all over the world. The oppressed peoples are rising up. They are revolting against colonialism and imperialism and all other systems of oppression."[25]

"Negro students throughout the South began their sit-in movement in February of 1960," wrote Tom Kahn in the first major civil rights pamphlet produced during the same year. When students from a black college in Greensboro,

North Carolina, sat at a "whites-only" lunch counter at a Woolsworth's five-and-ten-cent store, and refused to leave when not served, they sparked other sit-ins, plus picket lines and demonstrations throughout the South, with student-led sympathy actions throughout the North. "Their immediate challenge was directed against segregated lunch counters," he noted. "But they left no doubt that their aim was the abolition of the entire Jim Crow system." The impact was dramatic. "It was the Negro student revolt of 1960 that turned the Southern civil rights movement into a Southwide mass movement," Anne Braden observed. "Many people refused to believe that the sit-in movement growing from Greensboro was spontaneous, but it was, and nobody active in the civil rights movement would have predicted it. In fact, the constant lament among adult activists in that period was, 'Where is the younger generation?' " The nationwide mobilization of students opened an era that would fundamentally alter the politics of the United States. "College students, most of them part of the 'apathetic' generation of the Fifties, suddenly began to act," Kahn reported. "They picketed, raised money, sent wires of sympathy, and organized Northern stores of the national chains which discriminated in the South." What the black students of the South had carried out was "a profound social act" with "tremendous social implications for every institution in American society—above all, for a political party system that has managed to blur over the civil rights for decades."[26]

Just as the Montgomery Bus Boycott generated the formation of SCLC, so the sit-ins brought into being yet another activist formation, SNCC. Meanwhile, CORE began initiating Freedom Rides in 1961, with black and white activists getting on Greyhound buses in the North, intent on challenging segregated accommodations in the bus stations of the South. Many were beaten by mobs, and some of the buses were torched. Yet the movement continued to grow.

Interesting insights can be culled from a document that was probably read by a relative handful of young activists, the 1961 Civil Rights Resolution of the Young People's Socialist League, authored by Tom Kahn and Rachelle Horowitz. The resolution declared: "As an organization of students and young people, we are especially proud of the lead that Southern students have taken in the struggle. Placing their bodies where others have long directed only pronouncements, Negro students and their white supporters have rejuvenated the entire civil rights movement and stimulated assaults on new racial barriers." Hailing the lunch-counter sit-ins throughout the South, the resolution continued that "YPSL is also proud of the role that its members have played in developing support of the Southern movement in various parts of the country and in initiating direct action assaults against Jim Crow in non-Southern cities. Our members have suffered violence at the hands of racists and they have been imprisoned. They have sat-in, knelt-in, and waded-in. In cities from coast to coast, they have organized picket lines and protest meetings." Kahn and Horowitz pointed out that black student and youth activists had "turned to a technique of which we took note in our Civil Rights resolution of 1959: direct mass action executed outside of the framework of the two political parties."[27]

The resolution explained that similar tactics were being utilized in other fields of protest, such as protests defending civil liberties against the House Un-American Activities Committee, and that new tactics, such as the Freedom Rides, were posing new challenges. The global dimension of the youth radicalization was acknowledged: "Like students of Japan, Poland, Turkey, Hungary, and South Korea, the Negro students have taken the lead in the struggle for democracy." Indicating continuing support for the NAACP, the resolution focused enthusiastic attention on the more activist-oriented groups—SCLC, CORE, SNCC—and also the Negro American Labor Council (NALC, initially headed by A. Philip Randolph). Favoring the expansion and continued militancy of civil rights direct action, with a commitment to "tactical nonviolence," the resolution cautioned against "elitist developments," insisting that "our aim must always be to broaden the base of the movement and to stimulate mass action. The vast potential of the movement will not be fulfilled until the great mass of unorganized working-class Negroes are actively mobilized."[28]

The resolution noted that "at present only the Negro American Labor Council appears to be cognizant of the necessity for developing a mass action program aimed at the bread and butter needs of the working-class Negro community." The resolution also insisted that "despite all its faults and short-sightedness, the labor movement [which historically had been predominantly white] has been the major white ally of the Negro in his struggle and has, because of its very social nature, goals and interests parallel to those of the Negro. Indeed, though the wedge of race prejudice may unfortunately come between the Negro and the white worker, their common welfare transcends the color line, which has been dimming with the growth of unionism." In addition, "Because their interests are parallel, the Negro and labor movements have been attacked and frustrated by the same enemy: the coalition of conservative Republicans and Southern Dixiecrats." The resolution concluded with a hopeful though somewhat ambiguous speculation about "the potential for political realignment in America."[29]

At the same time, the perspective of such activists as Kahn and his comrades—for all their acceptance of tactical nonviolence—was one of unrelenting activism and militant radicalism:

Where does the power reside which can advance the movement for Negro liberation? As we saw clearly during the Montgomery Bus Protest and the lunch-counter sit-ins, it lies in mass action by the Negro people. This is not merely a matter of numbers, though they are important. It is a matter of human solidarity, of the social power that is generated when people who had been fragmented individuals, because they accepted inferior status, are transformed by their common demand for freedom. It is the power which suddenly causes an imposing structure of custom, law, authority and force to crumble because people unitedly stop respecting it and conforming to it. . . .

Large demonstrations serve to arouse mass support, to give notice of strength, to culminate campaigns; but demonstrations cannot take the place of constant, organized grassroots activity, which involves the great mass of the Negro people on a day-to-day basis, which becomes part of them, part of their own movement. That is the lesson and meaning of the Montgomery Bus Protest. And this is the experience, too, of the American labor movement. The parallel is not superficial. It is profound in its implications. For both movements, there were very few friends indeed on the court benches, in the government, in the ruling circles; and for both movements victory came through social dislocation, a withdrawal of support from those agencies that deprived them of their just rights. In Montgomery, the Negro population stayed off the buses until the bus companies realized that the cost of *protested* segregation was greater than the cost of integration. . . . In like manner does the laborer withdraw himself from the production lines by conducting sit-down strikes, picket lines and boycotts. For both, the principle of victory has been this: shift the cost of inequality and injustice from the backs of the exploited and oppressed to the backs of the exploiters and oppressors! . . .

The *essence* of revolution is the coming into action of the masses of people; this is what differentiates it from a "coup" or "palace revolt." . . . Today the building of a heightened and broader mass action movement must be the *primary* task. Without it we can look forward only to a relapse of gradualism in one shape or another. But, though it may not be at once apparent, the very logic of the movement will lead to a transformation of economic and political structures in the United States.[30]

This was the general orientation of an essential and influential core group within the new wave of activists who led the civil rights movement forward in the early 1960s. But it happened to be consistent as well with the orientation of the movement's most prominent two figures.

Randolph and King

Over the next several years, generalities became specific and speculation was transformed into action. A substantive strategic package was developed, bookended by the 1963 March on Washington for Jobs and Freedom and the projection of a massive campaign around the *Freedom Budget for All Americans*. It reflected the general orientation and clearest conceptualizations of the left-wing, activist-oriented components of the mass movement for civil rights, a collective product developed through a multifaceted process involving hundreds and thousands of people, and reflecting the experiences of millions. Nonetheless, it was articulated and coordinated by a smaller number of unusual people. In 1963, two of their number most dramatically represented their common project.

A. Philip Randolph stands as one of the most remarkable figures in the socialist, labor, and civil rights movements. He had a complex and multilayered history fraught with ambiguities, but his political efforts ultimately yielded an impressive body of accomplishments. Born in 1889, he moved to New York City in 1911, where he became part of what W. E. B. Du Bois referred to as "the talented tenth" of African American intellectuals. But he had no interest in remaining ensconced in an intellectual elite. Among what was referred to as the radicalizing "New Negroes," he was drawn to the Socialist Party of America, which projected a coming together and empowerment of the laboring masses, of all races and ethnicities. "When no profits are to be made from race friction," he reasoned, "no one will longer be interested in stirring up race prejudice." He found kindred spirits in a young intellectual from North Carolina named Chandler Owen and a socialist-minded widow and businesswoman in Harlem named Lucille Campbell Green, whom he soon married.[31]

Beginning in 1917 they published *The Messenger*, combining culture and revolutionary politics. They denounced Republicans and Democrats while promoting the Socialist Party and Industrial Workers of the World (IWW); they denounced imperialist war while hailing the Russian Revolution; they denounced the anti-black race riots of 1919 while publishing Claude McKay's fiery poem "If We Must Die." Attorney General A. Mitchell Palmer of "red scare" fame denounced Randolph and Owen as "the most dangerous Negroes in America"; indeed, they were seen by some as the Lenin and Trotsky of Harlem. Yet *The Messenger* has also been hailed as a vital element within the Harlem Renaissance and was a political and cultural magnet among black intellectuals, artists, and activists.[32]

In the early 1920s, having attracted the attention a number of African American service workers employed by the railroad companies (predominantly porters on the Pullman cars), Randolph was drawn into years-long efforts to create a union, the Brotherhood of Sleeping Car Porters. He gathered a cadre of shrewd and dedicated working-class militants, moderated his own revolutionary rhetoric, converted *The Messenger* into a tool for union organizing, and slowly but surely, with plenty of compromises and retreats along the way, accomplished by 1935 the seemingly impossible task of making the Brotherhood the recognized bargaining agent for black railroad workers. He also led his organization into the almost all-white American Federation of Labor, where he was a consistent voice against the white racism permeating many of the Federation's union affiliates, insisting on solidarity among workers of all racial and ethnic backgrounds. More than other African American leaders, Randolph had "a comprehensive understanding of the vast conquests of modern industry and the grand movement of labor to keep abreast of it," wrote Claude McKay in the late 1930s, "and he is aware that the Negro group is in a special position and has a special force. . . . He takes a long, balanced view of men and affairs," seeing that "the mainspring of the Negro group lies within itself."[33] In an appreciation written years later, his protégé Bayard Rustin gave additional sense of his outlook and significance:

> A. Philip Randolph . . . has maintained a total vision of the goal of freedom for his people and of the means for achieving it. From his earliest beginnings as a follower of Eugene V. Debs and a colleague of Norman Thomas [Socialist Party leaders], he has understood that social and political freedom must be rooted in economic freedom, and all his subsequent actions have sprung from this basic premise. . . . While he has felt that Negro salvation is an internal process of struggle and self-affirmation, he has recognized the

political necessity of forming alliances with men of other races and the moral necessity of comprehending the black movement as part of a general effort to expand human freedom. Finally, as a result of his deep faith in democracy, he has realized that social change does not depend upon the decisions of the few, but on direct political action through the mobilization of masses of individuals to gain economic and social justice.[34]

As a central spokesman in the country for black rights and economic justice for all, he was one of the founding members of the National Negro Congress in 1936, and he became its president. The new organization was a united front of diverse political forces, including Communists, Socialists, and liberals, and it had a reputation for being more inclusive and more socially radical than the NAACP. The united front broke apart in 1939, and Randolph denounced what remained of the organization when Communist members insisted that it support the Stalin-Hitler nonaggression pact. But Randolph was by no means inclined to withdraw from radical activism. In 1941, he built an effective March on Washington Movement to protest racial discrimination in the armed forces and war industries. This forced President Roosevelt (as a condition for calling off the march) to sign an executive order banning discrimination in war industries, government training programs, and government industries. A Fair Employment Practices Commission (FEPC) was established at the same time to help ensure the implementation of this agreement. During the Second World War, he prominently campaigned against racism in the military, particularly in situations where black servicemen were victimized by white racist "superiors." In 1948, Randolph led a successful effort to force the end of racial segregation in the armed forces.[35]

Throughout the 1950s and into the 1960s, Randolph distinguished himself as someone who labored to overcome the racist practices prevalent in some segments of the labor movement. "Only a strong labor organization is the answer to labor exploitation," he argued. "A labor organization can be strong only if it brings within its fold all workers in the trade, craft, class or industry. Racially segregated local unions are as morally unjustifiable and organizationally indefensible as racially segregated public schools, housing, recreation or transportation."[36] In the same spirit, he played an essential role in helping to build support for early civil rights efforts in the South, particularly with the development of the Montgomery Bus Boycott of 1955–56 that catapulted Martin Luther King Jr. to national attention.

Many on the left have a false conception of Martin Luther King Jr., portraying him as a well-meaning if naïve liberal, a moderate, who gradually became increasing radical under the impacts of the anti-racist struggle and the Vietnam War, finally coming to see—in his final years, before he was tragically cut down—that some variant of socialism might be necessary to overcome the problems facing the United States and the world. It is worth contrasting this with information provided by one of King's most capable biographers, David Garrow. In 1968, King emphasized that in dealing with issues of economic justice, pursuing "substantive" rather than "surface" changes by dealing with "class issues . . . that relate to the privileged as over against the underprivileged," the movement must move in the direction of realizing that "there is something wrong with the economic system of our nation . . . something is wrong with capitalism," and that "there must be a better distribution of wealth, and maybe America must move toward a democratic socialism."[37]

Garrow went on to add that Marxist intellectual C. L. R. James later recalled a conversation with King voicing radical economic views to him in private conversation, saying: "You don't hear that from me from the pulpit, but that is what I believe." According to James, "King wanted me to know that he understood and accepted, and in fact agreed with, the ideas that I was putting forward—ideas which were fundamentally Marxist-Leninist. . . . I saw him as a man whose ideas were as advanced as any of us from the Left, but who, as he said to me, could not say such things form the pulpit. . . . I saw him as a man with clear ideas, but whose position as a churchman, etc. imposed on him the necessity of reserve." [38]

James is not asserting that King was a "closet Leninist," but simply that he was conversant with, and in agreement with, the socialist ideas that James was putting forward (and which James identified with his own Marxist and Leninist orientation).

King's widow, Coretta Scott King, later noted that "within the first month or so of our meeting," in 1952, King "talked about working within the framework of democracy to move us toward a kind of socialism," arguing that "a kind of socialism has to be adopted by our system because the way it is, it's simply unjust." She commented that "democracy means equal justice, equity in every aspect of our society," and that King "knew that the basic problem in our society had to do with economic justice, or . . . the contrast of wealth between the haves and the have-nots. Believe it or not, he spoke these words to me when I first met him. It wasn't something that he learned later and developed." She added: "I think Martin understood from the very beginning that this goal could not be accomplished all at once . . . I had enough training and background myself to appreciate where he was in his thinking."[39]

Before he met Coretta Scott, King attended Crozer Theological Seminary in Chester, Pennsylvania, from 1948 to 1951. It was clear to one of his teachers and closest associates there, Rev. J. Pious Barbour, that King "believed Marx had analyzed the economic side of capitalism right" and that "the capitalistic system was predicated on exploitation and prejudice, poverty, and that we wouldn't solve these problems until we got a new social order."[40]

More than Marx, of course, this pastor-in-training immersed himself in the works of Protestant theologians, of whom, he noted more than once, Walter Rauschenbusch and Reinhold Niebuhr were the most important to him. Both were authors of decidedly left-wing works. Rauschenbusch, whose 1907 *Christianity and the Social Crisis* reveals a powerful Marxist influence, proclaimed that "the working class is now engaged in a great historic class struggle which is becoming ever more conscious and bitter," and that "socialism is the ultimate and logical outcome of the labor movement." Rauschenbusch argued that "the new Christian principle of brotherly association must ally itself with the working class if both are to conquer," since "the force of religious spirit should be bent toward asserting the supremacy of life over property." Niebuhr, whose 1932 classic, *Moral Man and Immoral Society*, critically integrates not only Marx but even more the "brutal realist" Lenin into what was (in that period) a radical version of the "Christian realist" synthesis, approvingly quoted from Lenin's *State and Revolution:*

> In their sum, these restrictions [of bourgeois democracy] exclude and thrust out the poor from politics and from active share in democracy. Marx splendidly grasped the essence of capitalistic democracy, when, in his analysis of the spirit of the commune, he said the oppressed are allowed, once every few years, to decide which particular representatives of the oppressing classes are to represent and repress them in politics.

According to Niebuhr, "a certain system of power, based upon the force which inheres in property, and augmented by the political power of the state, is set against the demands of the worker." In his opinion, "conflict is inevitable, and in this conflict power must be challenged by power." One could also point to the significant influence on King of A. J. Muste, of the Fellowship of Reconciliation, a radical pacifist with deep, Marxist-influenced

Christian-socialist convictions. It is instructive to consider Muste's insistence on "a necessary connection between pacifism and democracy," and his comment that "to argue, as has in effect often been done, that democracy has only been imperfectly realized, much so-called democracy is camouflaged dictatorship of a class, therefore we must get rid of democracy and embrace some kind of dictatorship . . . is neither good logic nor good politics." A better logic and politics, presumably, would be to "base ourselves on democracy as it already exists" and to struggle "for a complete and manifold realization of all democratic forms," culminating in the economic democracy of socialism. This was certainly the approach of Muste and King (although these last-quoted words happen to be from an article by Lenin two years before the Russian Revolution).[41]

Throughout the 1950s and 1960s, King worked closely with activists whose thinking was similarly shaped by Marxist perspectives—A. Philip Randolph, Bayard Rustin, Ella Baker, former Communist Party members Stanley Levison and Jack O'Dell, among others.[42] These included some of his most intimate advisors. His 1958 bestseller *Stride Toward Freedom* articulated a labor solidarity perspective that all of them would have embraced. "Both Negro and white workers are equally oppressed. For both, the living standards need to be raised to levels consistent with our national resources." He projected a class-based struggle for economic justice:

> Strong ties must be made between those whites and Negroes who have problems in common. White and Negro workers have mutual aspirations for a fairer share of the products of industries and farms. Both seek job security, old-age security, health and welfare protection. The organized labor movement, which has contributed so much to the economic security and well-being of millions, must concentrate its powerful forces on bringing them together in social equality.[43]

There are simply no grounds for the notion that King's radicalism was a newfound product of his final years. For him, it blended naturally with the revolutionary conceptions inherent in the teachings of Jesus:[44]

> I want to say to you as I move to my conclusion, as we talk about "Where do we go from here," that we honestly face the fact that the Movement must address itself to the question of restructuring the whole of American

society. There are forty million poor people here. And one day we must ask the question, "Why are there forty million poor people in America?" And when you begin to ask that question, you are raising questions about the economic system, about a broader distribution of wealth. When you ask that question, you begin to question the capitalistic economy. And I'm simply saying that more and more, we've got to begin to ask questions about the whole society. We are called upon to help the discouraged beggars in life's marketplace. But one day we must come to see that an edifice which produces beggars needs restructuring. . . .

Now, when I say question the whole society, it means ultimately coming to see that the problem of racism, the problem of economic exploitation, and the problem of war are all tied together. These are the triple evils that are interrelated. . . .

One night, a juror came to Jesus and he wanted to know what he could do to be saved. Jesus didn't get bogged down in the kind of isolated approach of what he shouldn't do. Jesus didn't say, "Now Nicodemus, you must stop lying." He didn't say, "Nicodemus, you must stop cheating if you are doing that." He didn't say, "Nicodemus, you must not commit adultery." He didn't say, "Nicodemus, now you must stop drinking liquor if you are doing that excessively." He said something altogether different, because Jesus realized something basic—that if a man will lie, he will steal. And if a man will steal, he will kill. So instead of just getting bogged down in one thing, Jesus looked at him and said, "Nicodemus, you must be born again."

He said, in other words, "Your whole structure must be changed." A nation that will keep people in slavery for 244 years will "thingify" them— make them things. Therefore they will exploit them, and poor people generally, economically. And a nation that will exploit economically will have to have foreign investments and everything else, and will have to use its military might to protect them. All of these problems are tied together. What I am saying today is that we must go from this convention and say, "America, you must be born again!"[45]

Far from stumbling into something that could be seen as having revolutionary implications, King knew exactly what he was saying. These words did not reflect recently-arrived-at insights, but rather, long-held political convictions.

[APPENDIX]

Marxist Perspectives

Karl Marx (1818–1883) and his close co-thinker and comrade Frederick Engels (1820–1895), developed the basic ideas and theoretical approach associated with what is now called Marxism, but which they called *scientific socialism*. This involved a fusion of what became the separate social science disciplines of economics, sociology, political science, anthropology, and history, undergirded by a philosophical orientation influenced particularly by G. W. F. Hegel and Ludwig Feuerbach, and by perspectives of the Enlightenment and Romanticism. They were no less influenced by the ideas and examples of a wave of democratic revolutions (especially the French Revolution) and the momentous Industrial Revolution, as well as the emergence of the working-class and labor movement.[1]

With a grand philosophical sweep that comprehends reality as an evolving and dynamic interplay of matter and energy, Marxism projects reality as a vibrant totality in which amazing qualities of humanity—creative labor, community, the quest for freedom—have generated technological advances, economic surpluses, and consequent inequalities that, in turn, generate struggles against oppression. This way of seeing history perceived a succession of economic systems nurturing different social structures and cultures. Since the rise of civilization, all the social-economic systems (whether ancient slave civilizations or feudalism or capitalism) have involved powerful minorities enriched by the exploitation of laboring majorities. But sometimes the oppressed laborers fight back and demand a better life—more food, genuine community, freedom—with their exploiters striving to keep them in their place.[2]

While all history has been marked by such class struggles, capitalism is unique, generating technological innovations and spectacular increases in productivity, ultimately producing enough wealth to provide a decent life for all people—if the economy can be made the common property of all. Capitalism's distinctive economic expansionism naturally transforms a majority of the people into workers, who can make a living only through selling their ability to work (labor power) for payment from the capitalist employer as their labor creates the actual wealth that makes society possible and their life activity allows for the functioning of society.

Marxists see this working class as the key to creating a socialist future. The working-class majority must organize to make it so: build large, inclusive trade unions for better wages and working conditions; build powerful social movements to bring changes for the better (reforms); build political power of the working-class majority "to win the battle of democracy" and bring about a transition from capitalism to socialism, which they saw as the extension of "rule by the people"—democracy—over society's economic life, providing for the dignity and free development of all.

The relevance of Marxist thought to the struggle against racism in the United States is highlighted if we consider Marx's own analyses of U.S. realities. The young Karl Marx, in examining the revolutionary potential of the working class in this most democratic of capitalist republics, had concluded that the obvious radicalism of the early working-class movement there had little hope of being triumphant as long as slavery continued to exist[3] and as long as the "safety-valve" of Western lands remained available to the discontented of the industrializing Northeast. By 1877, however, small farmers of the West were coming under greater corporate-capitalist pressure; slavery had ended but the democratic promise to blacks had been betrayed by the federal government's corrupt abandonment of Reconstruction; and the growing working class had responded to insult and injury by a violent nationwide insurgency aimed especially at the all-powerful railroad corporations. Writing to Engels, Marx speculated on the possibility of the predominantly white working-class movement merging with struggles of black agricultural labor in the South and hard-pressed small farmers in the West might set the stage "for a serious labor party in the United States." Such themes would be repeated among U.S. followers of Marx in later years. Most obvious, as Marx scholar August Nimtz has noted, "Marx and Engels understood the ability of the working class to carry out its historic mission depended on it being able to overcome the divisions that capital promoted among the toilers."[4] Whether or not it was derived directly from Marx, this commonsense notion was clearly present in the outlook of Randolph, Rustin, and King.

Historically, there have been deep dividing lines among socialists in regard to general perspectives of how to bring about the transition from capitalism to socialism. One of the biggest we noted in the first chapter: those who believe capitalism can gradually be reformed out of existence, and those who believe that only a revolutionary transfer of power from capitalist elites to working-class majorities can bring a democratic and socialist future. The Russian Revolution of 1917, led by V. I. Lenin and his Bolshevik organization of revolutionary socialists (which in 1918 changed the name of their organization to "Communist"), was originally animated by this super-democratic vision. But then, in the chaos of civil war and devastating foreign assault that followed, a "temporary" one-party dictatorship was established in Russia. Unfortunately, following Lenin's death, the dictatorship became permanent as Joseph Stalin rose to power, jailing and killing many of the original revolutionaries in the process, and carrying out a brutal "revolution from above" to modernize Russia's backward economy. In the world Communist movement there was a new way of defining "socialism," replacing actual "rule by the people" with a presumably benevolent one-party dictatorship.[5]

One of the reasons that Leon Trotsky and his followers (such as Max Shachtman) had broken away from the Communist mainstream was because they insisted that workers' democracy, which Lenin himself had favored, was central to any genuine socialism. But Shachtman and others around him, dissatisfied with what they perceived as rigidities in Trotsky's outlook, sought a path they felt would be more democratic, more revolutionary, more relevant. By the 1950s this caused them to merge, still with a *revolutionary* self-perception, into the reformist Socialist Party of Norman Thomas. Even after this, Shachtman and his co-thinkers were inclined to defend the democratic honor of Lenin and Trotsky, but they also agreed fully with Thomas's absolute rejection of the Communist mainstream.[6] Tom Kahn described Shachtman's views, many years later, in this way:

> Freedom and democracy—they were not abstractions; they were real and could therefore be destroyed. Communist totalitarianism was not merely a political force, an ideological aberration that could be smashed in debate; it was a monstrous physical force. Democracy was not merely the icing on the socialist cake. It was the cake—or there was no socialism worth fighting for. And if socialism was worth fighting for here, it was worth fighting for everywhere: socialism was nothing if it was not profoundly internationalist.[7]

It can be argued that Shachtman and Kahn ended up interpreting all of this in ways that their younger selves would not have accepted. The fact remained that socialism, democracy, and freedom were inseparable for Marx and all those who embraced his actual orientation, which separated them absolutely from both Stalin and the U.S. Communist Party. And an uncompromising belief in freedom and democracy had profound implications for those confronted by the oppressive and anti-democratic realities of systematic racism in twentieth-century America.

Ironically, U.S. Communists and former Communist Party members, even as they often made "socialist" apologies for dictatorships in Communist countries, were definitely inclined to join Thomas, Shachtman, and other Socialist Party members in defending "freedom and democracy" in capitalist America, and like them they also favored economic justice for the working-class majority and defended solidarity among workers regardless of racial or ethnic differences.[8]

Marxist perspectives—in varied forms and with varying interpretations, often muted, sometimes masked—exercised a significant influence within most of the major social movements of the twentieth century in the United States, the civil rights movement no less than others. It should be noted that there was also a tendency to see one's own group as the exclusive repository of virtue and the other groups as beyond the pale. For example:

A. The Socialist Party members 1) never hid their politics; 2) always emphasized that these politics were secondary to the demands and politics of the civil rights movement. That was not true of the Communists, who were acting on behalf of Soviet policy, nor of the Trotskyists, who were there to foment a revolution.

B. The Communist Party members 1) saw racism and imperialism as central to capitalism; 2) refused to compromise with racism even in the labor movement. That was not true of the Socialists, who subordinated the movement to U.S. foreign policy and a racist labor bureaucracy, nor of the Trotskyists, who were anti-communists posing as revolutionaries.

C. The Trotskyists 1) refused to subordinate anti-racist struggle to the liberal politics of the Democratic Party; 2) believed the anti-racist struggle had revolutionary potential. That is not true of the Socialists or the so-called Communists, who have both embraced the Democratic Party and sought to block the revolutionary potential of the struggle.

Regardless of the truth or falseness in any of these views, one or another of these standpoints was more or less held by many who saw themselves as Marxists in the United States from the 1930s onward. Yet impressive contributions can be found in what people from each of the above-defined currents brought to the struggle to oppose racism. And these currents did not by any means encompass all existing currents.[9]

The comparatively small group of Trotskyists concentrated in the Socialist Workers Party often demonstrated a capacity to work well with others and help accomplish broad goals while raising challenging ideas.[10] There is now little controversy that the contributions of the Communist Party were entangled with the terrible destructiveness of Stalinism, although Jack O'Dell, who combined impressive practical organizing abilities with no less impressive historical and political analyses grounded in Marxism, has commented that, among black comrades, "I never met anyone who joined the Communist Party because of Stalin or even because of the Soviet Union. They joined because the Communists had an interpretation of racism as being grounded in a system, and they were with us."[11]

Despite important political differences among them, all were inclined to embrace the basic outlines of "The Strategy" for challenging and overcoming racism in the United States. The focal point of this particular study, of course, involves efforts of those in and around the Socialist Party, who played such a central role in the civil rights movement, culminating in the March on Washington for Jobs and Freedom and in the Freedom Budget.

3. FOR JOBS AND FREEDOM

THE YEAR 1963 is generally seen as a high-water mark for the civil rights movement, the year of the great March on Washington for Jobs and Freedom, which drew at least 250,000 (some insist the number was twice that many) to march for civil rights. But the march was for more than civil rights—as was highlighted not only by the official title of the event, but also by a significant and important conference, organized by the Socialist Party, taking place on the heels of the march. In fact, the combined march and conference set the stage for the opening of the second phase of the activists' radical civil rights strategy, "The Strategy," leading up to the development of the Freedom Budget.

Taken together, A. Philip Randolph, Martin Luther King Jr., Bayard Rustin, Max Shachtman, Michael Harrington, and Tom Kahn represent a collectivity that advanced a general strategic perspective culminating in the interrelated March on Washington for Jobs and Freedom and the *Freedom Budget for All Americans*. We have already examined the perspectives of Randolph and King. Before seeing how the march paved the way for the budget campaign, we must turn our attention to the other figures essential in the playing out of this dramatic scenario.

Strategists, Organizers, Cadre

The general political orientation of King was almost indistinguishable from that of Bayard Rustin, although Rustin "got there first" (born in 1912, he was seventeen years King's senior), and he felt free to be more open about his socialism.

Stokely Carmichael (who, after moving to Africa in 1969, took the name Kwame Turé) has been quoted by Rustin biographer Jervis Anderson as saying: "Bayard was one of the first I had been in direct contact with [of whom] I could really say, 'That's what I want to be.' He was like superman, hooking socialism up with the black movement, organizing blacks."[1] In his autobiography, recalling his high school days, Carmichael/Turé elaborated even more vividly on his first contact with Rustin in the late 1950s:

A handsome man, he was turned out in an elegant, eye-catching way. He may not have been wearing anything so dramatic as a cape, but in manner and gesture he *looked* as if he should have been. Part of the dramatic effect was because, as he paced deliberately and confidently to the front, that voice was marshaling his arguments with a laser-like precision. Then he turned to face us and delivered an address, part admonition, part analysis, and part gentle scolding. It was eloquent and effective and displayed an easy mastery of the vocabulary, issues, and arguments of the left, all delivered in this clipped, British accent. He kept throwing out daring strategies for direct action and engagement at points where the system seemed vulnerable to pressure. Clearly this man was a radical activist, an intellectual *and a strategist* who apparently commanded the respect of the room.

I sat up. "Who the hell is *that?*" I asked Gene.

"Why," he said, "that's Bayard Rustin, the socialist."

"That's what I'm gonna be when I grow up," I whispered exultantly.[2]

Born in the urban North, Rustin grew up in his grandparents' household, in which literature, music, and ideas were taken seriously. The influence of the NAACP was strong and helped propel him toward activism. His musical talents earned him scholarships at Wilberforce University and Cheney State Teachers College, but his interests tended at least as much toward the political as the cultural. Although much of his family was involved in the AME (African Methodist Episcopal) Church, his grandmother was strongly influenced by Quakerism, which she passed on to him. Shortly after receiving activist training conducted by the American Friends Service Committee, he attended classes at City College of New York, where he connected with and became a leader of the Young Communist League in 1936.

In considering the alternative offered by the Socialist Party of the 1930s, Rustin had been put off by what he perceived as their notion that "only when you changed the economy into a socialist economy would blacks automatically get their civil rights." Not inclined to wait, he was drawn to the Communist movement. "The Communists were passionately involved and I was passionately involved," he later commented, "so they were ready-made for me." In the mid-1930s the Communists were in the forefront of struggles that championed labor rights and the struggles against racism and fascism in the name of democracy. In 1939, when the governments of the Soviet Union and Hitler's Germany signed a non-aggression pact, however, anti-fascism was dropped and replaced by an emphasis on opposition to U.S. imperialism and military preparations for the Second World War, and Rustin helped to lead a campaign against racist segregation in the U.S. armed forces. Two years later, when Germany attacked the Soviet Union, the Communist Party line was reversed yet again to a pro-war position, and Rustin's desegregation efforts were quickly scuttled. He angrily concluded that "the Communists' primary concern was not with the black masses but with the global objectives of the Soviet Union," as defined by the Stalin dictatorship, which "were bound to conflict with the necessities of the racial struggle."[3]

Definitively breaking from the Communist movement, Rustin's Marxist outlook remained intact—even as late as 1966 he was encouraging social work students to learn about the world by reading the *Communist Manifesto*—and his activism, if anything, became more radical.[4]—Working with A. Philip Randolph's 1941 March on Washington Movement (and sharply criticizing Randolph from the left for calling off the march), he served on the staff of the Fellowship of Reconciliation, where he was mentored by A. J. Muste, and later the War Resisters' League, among other groups. His abilities as a speaker and organizer, his accumulation of rich experience, his effectiveness in recruiting and leading young activists in struggle, and also his willingness more than once to be arrested for his convictions gave him considerable credibility, as did the international experience and contacts he developed as part of the radical pacifist movement.

In 1955, through A. Philip Randolph, Rustin made contact with the Montgomery Bus Boycott and became a close and influential advisor to Martin Luther King Jr. Unfortunately, his past ties with the Young Communist League and also his homosexuality (revealed through an arrest for "immoral conduct" after an incautious tryst several years earlier) forced him to stay in the background, and even to leave Montgomery, although his close political ties with King continued, and his connection as a trusted aide to Randolph facilitated his ability to play an important role in the evolving civil rights movement. In the late 1950s, Rustin coordinated early civil rights rallies and activities in the North. "The Washington rallies that Rustin organized in these years had a continuing impact," writes biographer John D'Emilio. "The [1957] Prayer Pilgrimage and youth marches served as training grounds for students and young adults yearning to express idealistic impulses in a decade when anti-Communist fervor squelched most forms of progressive activism."[5]

As Rustin was assuming increasing importance within SCLC, however, he was subjected to fierce red-baiting and gay-bashing attacks by Congressman Adam Clayton Powell, and was quickly marginalized. He was to have company in the marginalization process. A friend he had introduced to King was Stanley Levison, a lawyer and businessman particularly adept at fund-raising and writing, who had left the Communist Party in 1957. Like Rustin, he had become a trusted advisor. Ironically, Levison (along with King, for a time) backed away from Rustin after the vicious 1960 attack by Powell. Within a year, Levison helped bring Jack O'Dell onto the SCLC staff.[6]

There was much O'Dell had in common with Rustin, although aspects of their story were different. Twelve years Rustin's junior, he had been a Communist almost twice as long, from 1950 to 1959, and had been an experienced organizer. Nikhil Pal Singh comments that he "learned early on that community organizing along racial lines and labor organizing across racial lines were parallel and complementary tracks . . . for defeating Jim Crow," and felt that to make any genuine contributions to the struggle, "you had to find forms of organization that allowed you to be something else other than [simply] somebody who believes in socialism." Like Rustin, O'Dell emphasized that "the struggle for black equality involves the question of gaining a just share of the economic and political decision-making power in the country." But soon the FBI focused hostile attention on Levison and O'Dell, orchestrating attacks on them by liberal "friends" of SCLC in and around the Kennedy administration, causing them to be marginalized as well, although all of them—Levison, O'Dell, and Rustin—continued to have influence with King until the time of his death.[7]

Still enjoying A. Philip Randolph's backing, Rustin became a magnet for the radicalizing young activists who would become major figures in the activist wing of the civil rights movement in the 1960s, particularly those who would become leaders of SNCC and CORE. He also connected with a young activist-intellectual from the religious-pacifist community named Michael Harrington, involved in the Catholic Worker movement when he befriended Rustin in 1951. By 1954, Harrington had been drawn to the revolutionary Marxism of the Socialist Youth League, associated with Max Shachtman's International Socialist League. Other young followers of Shachtman were teenagers Tom Kahn and Rachelle Horowitz, whom Harrington introduced to the charismatic Rustin in 1956, resulting in a set of political partnerships that would last for many years.[8]

After the 1958 merger of the Independent Socialist League with the Socialist Party-Social Democratic Federation, Kahn, Horowitz, and Harrington drew Rustin into their milieu. And they pressed Max Shachtman to plug into this partnership. Horowitz later recalled: "Bayard was in the real world. Bayard was Max's connection to what was really going on in the world." According to biographer D'Emilio, "From Rustin, Shachtman absorbed an appreciation of the dynamism of the black freedom struggle, the depth of the discontent and the potential for mobilization in Southern communities, and the implications it might have for a revolutionary politics in the United States."[9] Peter Drucker, in his biography of Shachtman, captures important aspects of the old maverick-Trotskyist's perspective at this time:

> Shachtman was enthusiastic about the civil rights movement from its earliest years. The rhetoric of equality it relied on in the 1950s fit in with the approach to African-American rights he had advocated since the 1930s. Even more important to him, the civil rights movement fit into the strategy he had been developing since 1949 of aggravating contradictions inside the Democratic Party to hasten the emergence of a labor party. The civil rights movement threatened the Democratic Party alliance of northern Cold War liberals, big-city machines, and union leaders with southern segregationist "Dixiecrats." Shachtman began using the word "realignment" to describe the transformation of U.S. politics that he thought could be brought about by uniting the labor and civil rights movements with their liberal allies in a party that labor would dominate.[10]

Shachtman, born in 1904 and the product of a working-class immigrant household, one of the many of Russian Jews who found refuge in the United States from tsarist Russia. had started out as a teenager in the left wing of the Socialist Party in its heyday as a mass organization led by Eugene V. Debs. After the Russian Revolution, he became a youth leader in the early Communist Party.

Closely aligned with James P. Cannon, an older working-class militant prominent in the Communist Party, he worked with Cannon to build the impressive International Labor Defense (a civil liberties and legal defense group for workers) and was centrally involved in the ill-fated campaign to save the convicted anarchists Sacco and Vanzetti.[11] He also joined with Cannon to oppose the Stalinist degeneration of the Communist movement, rallying to the defense of Leon Trotsky, with whom Shachtman became intimately acquainted. A young Trotskyist from the Socialist Workers Party of the 1930s, Julius Jacobson, later offered these recollections:

> How we respected Max! . . . We respected James P. Cannon, too. But we knew him as Cannon, Shachtman was Max. We could joke and banter with him. And when Max spoke at a "big meeting" at Irving Plaza or Webster Hall we were always there. It was not merely that we were entertained by his razor-sharp wit, his polemical skills, his sense of irony, his robust humor but primarily we were clearly in the presence of an exceptional political intelligence. Even back then, in his ability to integrate Marxist theory, political history and specific events, he had few peers in the American socialist movement. . . . Max was the theoretician, the writer, the one with greater appeal to the young and the intellectuals within the Party and its periphery, Cannon was the organization man, the proletarian oriented leader and magnificent orator. Of the two, Shachtman was clearly the more thoughtful and independent personality.[12]

For Jacobson, this greater thoughtfulness and independence was reflected in Shachtman's break with Trotsky. The Russian revolutionary viewed the Soviet Union under Stalin as a "degenerated workers' state" that should be liberated by a democratic workers' revolution to overthrow Stalin (Shachtman agreed with this) but which also retained progressive features that were worth defending in any confrontation with capitalist and imperialist powers. By 1939, Shachtman disagreed, seeing the Soviet Union as a totalitarian "bureaucratic collectivist" order that was no better than capitalism. (In later years he would conclude that it was worse, which, as we shall see, had important political consequences.) The outcome was an organizational split in 1940, which resulted in a Workers Party led by Shachtman. Nine years later, it renamed itself the Independent Socialist League (ISL), and nine years after that it merged into the then-withering Socialist Party-Social Democratic Federation.[13]

Aspects of Shachtman are captured in the recollections of a younger comrade for whom he was a father figure: "He was a passionate man—passionate in his iron socialist faith, passionate in the brilliant theoretical writings, passionate in his unforgettably resounding speeches, passionate in his devastating polemics, passionate in his convulsing humor, and, most painful to remember, passionate in the bear hug warmth of his friendship." So wrote Tom Kahn at the time of his mentor's death. Julius Jacobson, who had broken with the same mentor when Shachtman was shifting rightward in the early 1960s, has different memories: "He was not a candid man nor was he a generous man. Indeed, in politics he possessed a sort of vindictiveness belied by his surface bonhomie. When he felt 'crossed,' even on a relatively minor issue, he often retaliated with a kind of meanness that could shock his closest supporters. He was a combination of callous bureaucrat and sentimentalist."[14]

At the time of the 1958 merger of Shachtman's ISL with the Socialist Party, the youth organizations of the two groups—the Young Socialist League (YSL) and the Young People's Socialist League—also merged, but the new YPSL experienced rocky beginnings in part because much of the leadership of the YSL politically disagreed with the merger. The YSL eventually broke away to form a different group, the Young Socialist Alliance, which formed ties with the more "mainstream" Trotskyist Socialist Workers Party. Nonetheless, the new YPSL was soon revitalized by an influx that was part of an initial wave of the 1960s youth radicalization.[15]

Involved in this influx was a bright young socialist activist named Joel Geier, who in 1961 became an energetic YPSL national secretary, helping to build the organization into a dynamic entity that expanded from roughly 150 members to about 1,100 in an eighteen-month period. He had joined YPSL only a year before, and it was the civil rights movement that had "convinced him at a gut-level that social change from below was possible." The intensity of Geier's own political growth under the impact of the civil rights experience involved developing "an understanding of activism and theoretical coherence," and becoming persuaded "of the possibility of revolutionary, of working-class self-emancipation, of socialism as workers' democracy." This was reflected in the experience of many of the other new recruits who got involved in the struggle.[16]

A number of YPSL members, particularly those influenced by Shachtman, could be termed *cadres*. This is a term often associated with Leninist politics, but it definitely has a broader applicability, and it is quite relevant to some of the specifics of movements for social change in this period. It refers to experienced activists, educated in political theory, analytically oriented, with practical organizational skills, who are able to attract and train new recruits and contribute to expanding efforts in broader movements and larger struggles. As we will see, fissures among some of these experienced activists would have significant political consequences.

The political orientation of Geier and some of the other YPSLs was definitely rooted in Shachtman's revolutionary stance of the 1940s, which castigated both Democrats and Republicans as representing capitalism and called for a labor party to represent the working class. This would soon grate against the new "realignment" perspectives (and the tilt toward Cold War anti-Communism) that marked the subsequent evolution of Shachtman and his closest protégés. However, this was not fully evident in 1961.

Shachtman-influenced YPSLs have been described by one perceptive historian as "people with political skills, a sense of mission, and a willingness to devote long hours to the movement," and their impact was felt throughout the organization. One female recruit, Betty Denitch, recalled: "They really identified with the Bolshevik tradition. They knew that you could start with a very small group and when a critical moment came, if you had your act together, you could play a role entirely disproportionate to your size." A non-YSPL activist on the West Coast observed in 1961 that socialist groups were "reporting a high degree of interest in their programs," and that the YPSLs, "blessed with highly skilled leadership, have been particularly successful of late." A number of these activists, black and white, became active in CORE, and in both the rank and file and central leadership of SNCC, among whose leading cadre both Rustin and Kahn had considerable influence. As Michael Harrington later recalled, the new recruits included "some of the most important militants of the second generation of the SNCC leadership—Stokely Carmichael, Courtland Cox, and Ed Brown [older brother of H. Rap Brown]," among others. Their discussions took up such questions as "why our various struggles would have to converge someday into the battle for socialism itself."[17]

Harrington (b. 1928) had been recruited to YPSL in the early 1950s, and then to the Shachtmanites, becoming a prominent figure and the head of their youth group, the Young Socialist League (YSL). Through the 1950s, biographer Maurice Isserman has noted, Harrington became "an effective writer and a charismatic speaker, echoing Shachtman in style and inflection." Paul Feldman, a one-time comrade from both the Shachtman group and the Socialist Party, later referred to him as "a Catholic radical who not only was the boy genius of American Marxism, but who also understood Proust, Stendhal and Freud, and could talk about these subjects at the drop of a hat. Not only that, he was a wine connoisseur and knew Irish revolutionary songs." Harrington's thoughtful and well-written articles began appearing not only in Shachtmanite publications, but also in *Commonweal*, *Partisan Review*, *Commentary*, *The New Republic*, and *Dissent*, and he developed a reputation "as an up-and-coming freelance thinker to whom it was worth paying attention." An increasingly prominent presence on the intellectual scene, and an appealing public figure, he wrote and spoke tirelessly on behalf of the Socialist Party. He helped to launch its well-produced biweekly paper, *New America*, became immersed in various aspects of the civil rights movement, and focused especially on issues related to poverty.[18]

In 1962, Harrington's *The Other America* became a bestseller. He stunned thousands of readers by his informative and sensitively written account of "the other America" in which 40 million to 50 million people lived in poverty, close to a quarter of the people in the United States. What he had to say had powerful impact:

> To be sure, the other America is not impoverished in the same sense as those poor nations where millions cling to hunger as a defense against starvation. This country has escaped such extremes. That does not change the fact that tens of millions of Americans are, at this very moment, maimed in body and spirit, existing at levels beneath those necessary for human decency. If these people are not starving, they are hungry, and sometimes fat with hunger, for that is what cheap foods do. They are without adequate housing and education and medical care.[19]

According to Harrington, "Poverty is a culture, an interdependent system," and therefore "one cannot deal with the various components of poverty in isolation, changing this or that condition but leaving the basic structure intact." He insisted that "a campaign against the misery of the poor should be comprehensive. It should think not in terms of this or that aspect of poverty, but along the lines of establishing new communities, of substituting a human environment for the inhuman one that now exists." Pointing to "the coalition of Southern Democrats and conservative Northern Republicans" that defended existing power structures against the demands for racial and economic justice, he stressed "the friends of the poor are to be found in the American labor movement and among middle-class liberals." The book ended with a call to arms, reflecting the general activist-oriented civil rights orientation—"The Strategy"—articulated in the framework of Shachtman's realignment perspective:

> The other America cannot be abolished through concessions and compromises that are almost inevitably made at the expense of the poor. The spirit, the vision that are required if the nation is to penetrate the wall of pessimism and despair that surrounds the impoverished millions cannot be produced under such circumstances.
>
> What is needed if poverty is to be abolished is a return of political debate, a restructuring of the party system so that there can be clear choices, a new mood for social idealism. . . . The means are at hand to fulfill the age-old dream: poverty can now be abolished.[20]

To help advance this perspective, Harrington and his comrades would soon make use of an old educational front-group of the Socialist Party, established in 1905, called the League for Industrial Democracy (LID), "dedicated to increasing democracy in our economic, political, and cultural life." According to right-wing publicist Philip Crane, the LID was a "fluid power clique" whose influence "in molding public opinion" was related to "its important role as an idea factory," enhanced through contact and interaction with major trade unions and liberal politicians. In fact, Crane, warning against the LID as a gradualist-socialist threat, was working with somewhat out-of-date information in his 1964 study; the changes generated in that year, when bestselling author Harrington became Chairman of the Board, would have horrified him. (A year later, Alan Stang of the right-wing John Birch Society, did incorporate some of the new information, and was indeed horrified.) Added to the Board of Directors were illustrious academics, prominent liberal/left-inclined trade unionists, civil rights figures from the activist wing of the movement, and some new student radicals associated with the LID's suddenly growing youth group, Students for a Democratic Society (SDS).[21] And Harrington drew into the position of hands-on Acting Executive Secretary the energetic former YPSL militant Tom Kahn.

In addition to being a key socialist influence among young civil rights activists and, for a time, a partner of Bayard Rustin, Tom Kahn (born in 1938) in YPSL was a skillful spokesman, organizer, and capable factional in-fighter. One of his factional opponents referred to him matter-of-factly as "evil." But more than one person in the know has also referred to his fine analytical mind, permeated (in the Shachtman mold) with Marxist sensibilities, that could boldly engage with new realities and give voice to the results in a clear and forceful manner. His writings were studied by early student activists and had significant influence.

His lifelong friend Rachelle Horowitz has given special emphasis to Kahn's early civil rights pamphlet, *The Unfinished Revolution*, published by the Socialist Party in 1960. The pamphlet was composed while Kahn was busily campaigning for the American Committee on Africa and for the 1959 hospital strike of the New York Drug and Hospital Workers Union, as well as helping with preparations for protests at the Democratic and Republican party conventions. "The start of the sit-in movement in February 1960 gave the pamphlet new urgency," notes Horowitz. "Kahn drew heavily on Rustin's experiences in the civil rights movement, A. J. Muste's thinking on nonviolence, Michael Harrington's socialist perspective, and George Rawick's historical analysis— but *Unfinished Revolution* was pure Kahn."[22]

He offered a vivid, passionate description of the activist upsurge of 1960, but also pushed for a broadened strategic orientation capable of bringing about positive reforms and a fundamental power shift in society. Linking the struggles for racial justice with the necessity of fighting for economic justice, *The Unfinished Revolution* pressed for an alliance of the civil rights and labor movements. "The Negro without a vote and without a union card has little to say about his wages and is up against a take-it-or leave-it proposition," he wrote. "In addition, the presence of a politically disenfranchised and economically uprooted Negro population represented a threat to the poor whites because if the latter sought to improve their economic status, their bosses could always threaten to turn them out and give the job to Negroes who, in desperation, would work for less." He envisioned civil rights forces and struggles associated with A. Philip Randolph and Martin Luther King Jr. joining with unions to help lay the basis for a mass political party of labor, "committed to the fight of the Negro for equality, of the workingman for improved living conditions, of the farmer for the fair share of his produce."[23]

The pamphlet was graced by a laudatory foreword by Socialist Party icon Norman Thomas, but more significantly another foreword was written by James Lawson (a militant black minister leading the nonviolent struggle in Nashville, and a close ally of Martin Luther King), who commented:

In the heat of the struggle, it often happens that the deepest implications of a mass movement are not understood. Historically, the marriage of action and analysis has been difficult to forge. . . . This pamphlet, written by a young man who has worked on the Youth Marches for Integrated Schools and in a number of other important civil rights projects, makes a unique contribution in filling this void. . . . I highly recommend this pamphlet to all who want really to understand the changes which must be made in our political, social and economic way of life if civil rights are to be won in full, and who seek the most effective means of advancing our common cause.[24]

This pioneering pamphlet, the resolution Kahn and Rachelle Horowitz wrote for the YPSLs in 1961, and his exceptional 1964 pamphlet *The Economics of Equality,* seem somewhat at odds with Horowitz's description of her friend as "primarily a staffer functioning behind the scenes, ghost-writing speeches, developing strategies, organizing events, and supporting the elected leadership" within the socialist, civil rights, and labor movements. A different way of viewing the matter can be traced to a politically hostile characterization, in 1963, by Stanley Levison: "Tom Kahn is the Lenin of the Socialist Party . . . and Bayard is absolutely manipulated by him. This was Bayard's downfall years ago." Stokely Carmichael (and other young activists) saw things differently than Levison's contemptuous remark: "Tom was a shrewd strategist with by far the most experience of us all in radical political organizing, having, as it were, studied with Rustin."[25] Another young activist from this circle of future SNCC leaders at Howard University (which Kahn attended from 1959 to 1961), Michael Thelwell, elaborated:

Tom represented a socialist collaboration with the nonviolent black movement. Politically, he was far more sophisticated and experienced than any of us. Though shy and reticent, he taught us a great deal about politics and the techniques of radical action; and as we grew close to him, he introduced us to the polemical style of sectarian socialist discourse in New York City. It was all very fascinating and exotic to us.[26]

Indeed, in the early 1960s, Kahn was seen by those in the know as a dynamic force on the left. Horowitz recounts that "Kahn and Harrington broadened the LID's reach," setting the stage "for the LID to be the bridge among the civil rights movement, the labor movement, and liberal intellectuals—a place where new programs could be developed and problems worked out." Yet for some on the left, as we shall see, aspects of the "new programs" would prove to have highly problematical qualities.[27]

In 1960 Kahn had joked about the need to "just keep repeating the formula: . . . increased tension within the Democratic Party—split in the Democratic Party—formation of Labor Party—Labor Party under influence of mass socialist left-democratic foreign policy," but as one year led to the next in the 1960s, he became convinced that instead the Dixiecrats should be driven out of the Democratic Party while labor and civil rights forces should stay in, with socialists blending together with liberals. This was the position that Max Shachtman was developing. Kahn and Rachelle Horowitz were like family members to Shachtman (he spoke of the two as "my children"), and Kahn helped lead the charge in YPSL of "realignment" forces, marginalizing those still adhering to the old Labor Party position. Kahn would continue to play the role of uncompromising polemicist, one might almost say a factional hitman, against others on the left at odds with his Shachtmanite "realignment" perspective.[28]

These "others" included some of his own comrades in the Socialist Party and YPSL who were not in agreement with that perspective, as factional disputes flared around such things as realignment and questions regarding U.S. foreign policy. In the context of internal struggles in YPSL, he honed analytical and organizational qualities that would come into play in the broader movement. On a legal pad in 1962, a period in which YPSL was still growing significantly, although realignment influence had declined, Kahn sketched out the following:

The last convention revealed
1) The decline of the political realignment position and of the influence of the national leadership associated with it.
2) The proportional increase in the delegate strength of the [Tom] Condit and "Labor Party" factions—the former reflecting infantile radicalism among new members not integrated into serious political tendencies within the YPSL or into mass arena work, the latter [associated with Joel Geier] reflecting dissatisfaction with the political-intellectual level of the organization and the functioning of the national leadership.
3) A growing rift with the party and particularly with the adult Shachtmanites.

CONCLUSIONS:

1) The failure of the realignment forces to organize has left a vacuum which could *conceivably* result in a Condit victory at a convention in the near future. This would mean the end of the YPSL as a serious political force in the youth movement.

2) Though a majority victory for the Landyites, already the largest tendency, would not be so apparently catastrophic, they have *as a faction* proved incapable of building the YPSL. The problem is not with their theoretical position so much as with the attitudes, approaches, moods and practical disabilities that take cover under it. They are a tendency in transition, hence unable to give organizational leadership.

OBJECTIVES:

The creation (or re-creation) of a youth cadre around the realignment position.

There is a distinction between a caucus and a cadre. While a majority caucus is the goal, the immediate problem is to develop a cadre—i.e., a *politically* and *organizationally* trained group who can *build* a caucus. The emphasis of cadre is on self-education. Also the development of a cadre is a more organic, informal process than the organization of a caucus. *There is no question whether a cadre is secret or open as there is with a caucus.* The aims of a cadre should be:

1) Socialist self-education. The fact is that, however intuitively "correct," the present leadership lacks adequate background in socialist *theory* and *history*. This may be a private affair for the individual, but a spirit and set of standards have to be adopted to motivate members of the cadre-to-be. The convention defeat should be that stimulus.

2) Critical and detailed evaluation of the Realignment position in terms of both its general political validity for the current American scene and its relevance to *every facet of our practical political activity*. This means that every member of the cadre be required to write an article for YSR. This is the only way to get ideas and positions concretized and challenged. Articles ought to be presented and discussed critically in advance.

3) The development of leadership and organizational skills. The emphasis here is not on licking stamps but on speaking and the orderly, cogent presentation of ideas. Also how to speak to contacts and weak members; how to engage in *persuasive* dialogue. As the cadre develops and grows

it should be thinking about training its members as national secretary and field secretary types.

4) A comradely relationship with the best realignment people in the party, particularly Max.[29]

The toughened cadre that Kahn sought to develop, in 1962, would be guided by the view that although "a Democratic Party free of the Dixiecrats would not be a socialist party, it would have substantially the same composition as the 'labor party' advocated by the [Joel] Geier Resolution [presented to the YPSL convention], and would provide a vehicle through which the civil rights, peace, and labor movements could achieve a more nearly unified political purpose and in which socialists, as socialists, would function as a left wing."

At the same time, he was still emphasizing his belief that there should be "the concentration of YPSL and party activity in the mass movements for civil rights, peace, and in trade unions and not within either of the two political parties as presently constituted." As a key player in the activist wing of the civil rights movement, Kahn's attention was focused far more on civil rights protest than on electoral politics. In an introduction, dated June 18, 1963, to Kahn's pamphlet *Civil Rights: The True Frontier*, Bayard Rustin eloquently gave a sense of the spirit of this historical moment:

The Negro community is now fighting for total freedom. It took three million dollars and a year of struggle simply to convince the powers that be that one has the right to ride in the front of the bus. If it takes this kind of pressure to achieve a single thing, then one can just as well negotiate fully for more, for every economic, political, and social right that is presently denied. That is what is important about Birmingham: tokenism is finished.

The Negro masses are no longer prepared to wait for anybody: not for elections, not to count votes, not to wait on the Kennedys or for legislation not, in fact, for Negro leaders themselves. They are going to move. Nothing can stop them from moving. And if that Negro leadership does not move rapidly enough and effectively enough they will take it into their own hands and move anyhow. . . .

Birmingham has proved that no matter what you're up against, if wave after wave of black people keep coming prepared to go to jail, sooner or later there is such confusion, there is such social dislocation, that white people in the South are faced with a choice: either integrated restaurants or no restaurants at all, either integrated public facilities, or none at all. And the South then must make its choice for integration, for it would rather have that than chaos.[30]

As Kahn put it, "We are achieving the declared goals of liberalism but we are not doing it in the liberal way. There's the rub." He noted that "against this background, the [Kennedy] Administration's efforts to veer the movement away from direct action and toward 'political action' are suspect. They are the most sophisticated means yet devised for obtaining a 'cooling-off' period." Indeed, "the Kennedy policy represents an attempt to capture the civil rights movement for the Democratic Party." Kahn added that there would be "nothing wrong with this" if the Dixiecrats were not part of the Democratic Party then it would be "a political vehicle that would make our movement more powerful." In any event, the uncompromising struggle against the Jim Crow system, against racial segregation and against the denial of the right to vote, continued to move forward. "Thus, the pressing need for a democratic transformation of the South, the greatest political obstacle to social progress in modern American history, looms with a magnitude unprecedented in this century as a realizable possibility."[31]

Kahn and his comrades thus had a shared commitment to "The Strategy," envisioning a transition from the initial phase of the struggle against the Jim Crow system to the more radical struggle for economic justice. "We are socialists," he affirmed. "Ultimately, we believe, the elimination of all forms of prejudice, of all the subtle, psychological and emotional products of centuries of racism, awaits the creation of a new social order in America—a social order in which political democracy passes from shibboleth to reality, and in which economic democracy guarantees to each individual that he shall be judged as a person, not as a commodity. This, we are convinced, is a democratic socialist order." But his focus was on the here-and-now: "To those who reject our socialist vision we therefore reply: Very well, but at least live up to your own vision. . . . Give all moral and material support to the Negro struggle for equality," because "the elimination of Jim Crow, with all its legal, administrative and political supports, is an immediate possibility." He concluded: "To those whose commitment knows no compromises we pledge our full, vigorous and loyal cooperation."[32]

Looking back on the YPSL involvement in the civil rights movement from the standpoint of 1980, Kahn commented: "It is no exaggeration to say that we were there first and immersed ourselves in it more deeply than did any other largely white youth group." Noting that "YPSLs were the backbone of the 1958 and 1959 Youth Marches for Integrated Schools," he added that they "helped staff numerous defense committees, played an important role in CORE, participated in direct action projects, marched in the South, and went to jail." In sum, "Out of our efforts, in large part, came the 1963 March on Washington."[33]

March for Jobs and Freedom

The strategic orientation that led directly to the development of the Freedom Budget was inseparable from the 1963 March on Washington for Jobs and Freedom, and was dramatically reflected in a conference organized by the Socialist Party immediately afterward.

The earliest beginnings of the March on Washington arose among socialist activists clustered around A. Philip Randolph. It is likely that the idea was never far from the consciousness of Randolph himself (who in the 1940s had projected four different marches on Washington, and cancelled them each time). As early as 1961, in the Negro American Labor Council (NALC), created by several thousand black trade unionists and headed by Randolph, discussion was initiated around the idea of a march on Washington. In the autumn of 1962, left-wing union organizer Stanley Aronowitz, who had been active in civil rights efforts, quietly surveyed labor circles on Rustin's behalf. The purpose was to gauge support for a mass demonstration, focused on the issue of jobs, to be held in Washington during the centennial year of the Emancipation Proclamation. Discussions between Randolph and Bayard Rustin crystallized, in December 1962, on the conception of a mass action in Washington to advance this aspect of the civil rights strategy. The old trade unionist asked Rustin to develop a detailed proposal. The experienced organizer reached out to some of his closest young Socialist Party comrades to develop it—Tom Kahn and Norman Hill, a seasoned African American socialist, associated with the Shachtman tradition, active in the leadership of CORE. By January 1963, Rustin was able to present Randolph with a finished proposal.[34]

The document called for what would initially be tagged an Emancipation March for Jobs, prefaced by an economic analysis, concluding that "the dynamic that has motivated Negroes to withstand with courage and dignity the intimidation and violence they have endured in their own struggle against racism, in all its forms, may now be the catalyst which mobilizes all workers behind the demands for a broad and fundamental program for economic justice." The initial proposal envisioned two days of militant nonviolent action in June, described in this way:

a) Friday in June—a mass descent on Congress and a carefully chosen delegation to the White House. The objective in Congress would be to flood all Congressmen with a staggered series of labor, church, and civil rights delegations from their own states so that they would be unable to conduct business on the floor of Congress for an entire day. Just as these delegations would present, in part, our list of legislative demands, so would the White House delegation seek to put before the President, as leader of his party and as Chief Executive, our proposals for both legislative and executive action.

b) Saturday in June—a mass protest rally with the twofold purpose of projecting our "Emancipation Program" to the nation and of reporting to the assemblage the response of the President and Congress to the previous day.

The proposal concluded with a list of organizational steps to draw together the organizations and forces in a way that would make the generalities specific.[35]

Randolph was pleased, secured adoption of the proposal by the Negro American Labor Council, and then sought support from King's Southern Christian Leadership Conference and SNCC, as a prelude to seeking participation from the NAACP and the Urban League. For various reasons, King's initial reaction was lukewarm. The NAACP and the Urban League were noncommittal. The projected date was shifted to October, and Randolph reached out to the AFL-CIO. Its president, George Meany, exasperated by Randolph's criticism of racist policies in some unions, had complained during the 1959 AFL-CIO convention: "I would like Brother Randolph to stay a little closer to the trade union movement and pay a little less attention to outside organizations that pay lip service rather than real service." At the same convention he exploded: "Who the hell appointed you as the guardian of all the Negroes in America?" Distancing himself from the March several years later, Meany said that it was "an unwise legislative tactic" and rejected the proposal for AFL-CIO endorsement. The liberal ex-socialist head of the United Auto Workers, Walter Reuther, was the only member of the AFL-CIO executive board to respond positively.[36]

A succession of events in the first half of 1963 changed the landscape within the civil rights movement, and caused King to become a strong advocate. "Birmingham was a turning point in the Southern struggle; it eventually changed the face of the South and awakened the nation," Anne Braden observed. "The immediate objectives of the Birmingham campaign were a beginning on desegregation of public accommodations and a beginning on opening up job opportunities." The arrest of Martin Luther King, which resulted in his eloquent "Letter From a Birmingham Jail," was part of a larger phenomenon in which "thousands joined the movement and went to jail," and even "the children of Birmingham became involved." Police Commissioner Bull Connor, who "had been breaking up integrated meetings since the 1930s," remained true to form. He did not hesitate to bring out "the police dogs, clubs, and fire hoses." In contrast to previous years, however, now it was televised and widely reported in the national and international media. "The nation and the world were shocked and moved to action."[37]

A firestorm of protests swept through the South. "No state remained untouched. In a single month, there was mass direct action in at least 30 cities," according to Braden. "Some surveys placed the figure at 100 communities for that entire hot summer of 1963." The backlash of white racist violence assumed murderous proportions, most dramatically with the assassination of the outstanding NAACP leader in Mississippi. "The nation was horrified by the assassination of Medgar Evers in Mississippi and the fire-hosing of children in Birmingham, Alabama," as Rachelle Horowitz has recounted. "President John F. Kennedy was forced to introduce civil rights legislation."[38]

It was now an entirely new situation, and the thinking of King and his advisors shifted dramatically. "We are on a breakthrough," King insisted. "We need a mass protest." A decision was made to contact A. Philip Randolph and work out a common perspective. One agreement was that civil rights must be co-equal with economic justice. The name of the March was changed to "for Jobs and Freedom."

The young militants of SNCC, with whom Horowitz and Kahn were, at this point, closely aligned, were on board with this. Increasingly frustrated with and critical of the failure of the Kennedy administration to provide clear support on either issue, or adequate protection for civil rights activists in the South, they were especially eager for militant action in the nation's capital. Along with Rustin, they envisioned the march as a massive and radical flashpoint of protest. Cleveland Sellers, one of a number of leading SNCC activists drawn into helping to organize the action, recalls the way Rustin outlined it to them:

The march, which was [to be] sponsored by SNCC, CORE, SCLC, the NAACP and the Urban League, was being conducted to emphasize the problems of poor blacks. It was to be a confrontation between black people and the federal bureaucracy. Rustin told us that some people were talking about disrupting Congress, picketing the White House, stopping service at bus and train stations, and lying down on the runways at the airports.[39]

One of Rustin's biographers has emphasized that he saw the Gandhian method of civil disobedience as being "near the heart of [the march's] conception," without which the action would be "little more than a ceremonial display of grievance." And as he himself put it, the Washington action would be followed by "mass demonstrations continuing in this country for the next five years, covering wider and wider areas, and becoming more intense."[40]

Things turned out somewhat differently. It was a one-day action—August 28, 1963—with the civil disobedience, the confrontations, and most of the explicit radicalism combed out as a condition for the support of the NAACP, the Urban League, the Catholic clergy, Kennedy supporters, and other liberals. There are many detailed accounts of the March on Washington. Here we can touch on only a few key points.

There is the fact, already stressed, that Rustin and the Socialist Party were central both to the conceptualization and organization of the march. There had been concerted efforts—because of Rustin's explicit radicalism, his homosexuality, and his former membership in the Young Communist League—to prevent him from playing the role of directing the march. A. Philip Randolph had no tolerance for this exclusion, believing that "Rustin is Mr. March-on-Washington himself," and he maneuvered skillfully and successfully to ensure his central organizing role. Randolph assumed the position of director of the march, and then appointed Rustin as his deputy director.[41] Rustin, in turn, appointed trusted members of the Socialist Party as his key aides, and they drew together to assist with their organizing work in Washington and in cities throughout the country a substantial network of activists in or near the Socialist Party. These included the YPSLs; members of Students for a Democratic Society (the youth group of the LID); staff members of the Socialist Party–linked Workers Defense League; SNCC activists and members of CORE, a number of whom were in and around YPSL and the Socialist Party.[42]

One of those not involved in the march was Michael Harrington. In a five-page letter from Paris to Max Shachtman, dealing mostly with theoretical questions, he confessed: "I picked a hell of a year to take off." He wondered: "Are the Negroes going to make a revolution in my absence?" Writing back on August 20, Shachtman responded to the theory but also wrote critically, in referring to Socialist Party comrades in opposition to his "realignment" perspective, that "most of the people think entirely in internal terms," with factional axes to grind rather than devoting themselves to "servicing" the civil rights movement, which he characterized as "the latest and most dramatic development" in the U.S. scene.[43]

Yet this gives a skewed picture. *New America* ran a major article by Harrington himself in its August 31 issue on "Socialists and Civil Rights," which began with a historical survey of the positive role of socialists in the anti-racist struggle, although he took a swipe at what he described as a less admirable role played by the Communists. He then advanced and elaborated on the Socialist Party perspective that "there can be no social justice for the majority if it is paid for at the expense of civil rights for the minority. And conversely, civil rights can only be achieved as part of an integrated movement for justice for all." He went on to argue for a political realignment: the gathering of civil rights and labor and liberal forces into a single party, "a second party," independent of conservative Republicans and Dixiecrats. "We socialists are and have been committed to being in the midst of the struggle as militants," he concluded. "We want one privilege and only one from the civil rights movement: to fight against racism. Beyond that, we believe that our vision is relevant to the common battle for freedom and jobs." And that involved "a political movement for realignment for a second party in the United States."[44]

The perspectives of the Socialist Party were also advanced in lengthy congressional testimony by Norman Thomas, reprinted in a special March on Washington supplement of *New America*, emphasizing the need to strengthen President Kennedy's proposed civil rights legislation by including provisions for full employment and fair employment to wipe out poverty and economic inequalities. The same issue of the paper included a statement by A. Philip Randolph, lauding the Socialist Party's platform, and adding: "The revolution for Freedom Now has moved into a new stage in its development. Its demands have necessarily become not only the end of all discrimination against black

Americans, but for the creation of a new society—a society without economic exploitation or deprivation."[45]

There were, of course, more moderate elements drawn, finally, into support for the March on Washington. The NAACP, led by Roy Wilkins, which had made countless contributions to the civil rights struggle over the years, had actually been started by socialists (including the great African American historian, sociologist, and educator W. E. B. Du Bois), and included in its ranks some of the outstanding civil rights activists in the recent period (Rosa Parks, E. D. Nixon, Medgar Evers being only some of the better known). But as an organization, it favored a moderate stance, not only veering away from radical and socialist ideology, but also preferring legal and educational pathways, and working with establishment politicians and tending to look down on protest demonstrations. The National Urban League, led by Whitney Young, had embraced an even more moderate orientation, and had consequently enjoyed an even closer relationship with the Kennedy administration.

Urban League sponsorship meant that a greater aura of "respectability" would be associated with the action, which meant little to some, but much to many others. And the NAACP—with its massive membership, significant resources, and dense network of branches throughout the country—had a capacity to mobilize large numbers. Yet if these organizations were to support the march, they would insist on much greater moderation than the initial organizers had projected. There is ample evidence that they did just that.[46]

Although Wilkins and Young did not always get their way (for example, they intended to block Rustin from being the central organizer of the march), they were able to force the weeding out of one radical aspect of the initial plan after another. Rustin aide Rachelle Horowitz "regarded the compromise as a terrible sellout. . . . Roy Wilkins and Whitney Young weren't going to join anything that would be embarrassing to John F. Kennedy, because they were very close to the President. I was in a funk for days." Even Martin Luther King Jr. was dismayed over dropping each and every possibility of civil disobedience. Rustin saw things differently: "The march will succeed if it gets a hundred thousand people—or one hundred fifty thousand or two hundred thousand more—to show up in Washington," he insisted. "Bayard always knew we would have to trade in militancy for numbers," Norman Hill suggested later. "He probably let us put in militant actions [in the original plan] so he could trade it away. Four things mattered—numbers, the coalition, militancy of action, and militancy of words. He was willing to give up militant action for the other three."[47]

As it turned out, even the militancy of words was contested terrain when major forces of the march leadership insisted on the censorship of the speech of John Lewis of SNCC. The speech had been a collective product of the young militants who had considered themselves to be "Bayard Rustin people." Rachelle Horowitz had loved the initial draft, and Tom Kahn had worked with SNCC leaders to help sharpen it. There are indications that the Kennedy administration had gotten a copy of it and applied pressure on moderate elements to have the speech killed. Washington archbishop Patrick O'Boyle, who had agreed to deliver the invocation at the beginning of the march, threatened to pull all Catholic clergy out of the event. Walter Reuther and even King joined forces with Wilkins and Young to demand either a rewrite or yanking Lewis from the speakers' list. Randolph and Rustin ran interference for the indignant SNCC activists, but also persuaded them to cut and soften the speech. Much of its radicalism remained, and, according to some, was even covertly sharpened, but it is instructive to ponder some of what was left out:[48]

> We are now involved in a serious revolution. This nation is still a place of cheap political leaders who build their careers on immoral compromises and ally themselves with open forms of political, economic and social exploitation. What political leader here can stand up and say, "My party is the party of principles?" The party of Kennedy is also the party of Eastland. The party of Javits is also the party of Goldwater. Where is *our* party? . . .
>
> The revolution is a serious one. Mr. Kennedy is trying to take the revolution out of the streets and put it into the courts. Listen, Mr. Kennedy. Listen, Mr. Congressman. Listen, fellow citizens. The black masses are on the march for jobs and freedom, and we must say to the politicians that there won't be a "cooling-off" period.
>
> All of us must get in the revolution. Get in and stay in the streets of every city, every village and every hamlet of this nation until true freedom comes, until the revolution is complete. In the Delta of Mississippi, in southwest Georgia, in Alabama, Harlem, Chicago, Detroit, Philadelphia and all over this nation, the black masses are on the march![49]

Given its now iconic place in the history of the twentieth century, it is all too easy to forget the intense hostility and fear that powerful forces felt in regard to the march. The prestigious *Herald Tribune* voiced the view of many of these forces when it editorialized: "If Negro leaders persist in their announced plans to march 100,000-strong on the capital . . . they will be jeopardizing their cause. . . . The ugly part of this particular mass protest is its implication of uncontained violence if Congress doesn't deliver. This is the kind of threat that can make men of pride, which most Congressmen are, turn stubborn."[50]

Even greater hostility was felt, covertly but powerfully, from J. Edgar Hoover and his Federal Bureau of Investigation. A Justice Department lawyer of the time later commented: "Everything you have read about the FBI, how it was determined to destroy the movement, is true." Accounts indicating that "the Bureau and its Director were openly racist," and that "the Bureau set out to destroy black leaders simply because they were black leaders" have been carefully investigated and frankly corroborated by historian David Garrow, who adds: "The Bureau was strongly conservative, peopled with many right-wingers, and thus it selected people and organizations on the left end of the political spectrum for special and unpleasant attention." Pulitzer Prize journalist Russell Baker has commented that Hoover was "a terrifying old tyrant whose eyes and ears were everywhere," who explained to a skeptical Attorney General Robert Kennedy that "the brains of black people were twenty percent smaller than whites'," and who gloated—once tapes were secured about Martin Luther King's "amatory" indiscretions—that "this will destroy the burrhead." According to Charles Euchner's book-length study of the March on Washington, "The FBI attempted to exploit fears about violence and Communist infiltration of the civil rights movement—fears that were partly the result of J. Edgar Hoover's long campaign against the movement." Hoover quite simply had no sympathy for civil rights. "The Negro situation," he reported in the 1950s, "is being exploited fully and continuously by Communists on a national scale." FBI activities in part reflecting such attitudes and in part reflecting a need to find justification for continued funding, found ample justification for investigating, spying on, and at times attempting to disrupt or discredit the activities of protest groups and leaders such as Martin Luther King Jr. and Bayard Rustin. "Bureau officers exchanged information about African American protest with local police in the South," writes John D'Emilio. "The practice sustained an atmosphere in which Southern sheriffs who suppressed demonstrations knew they had friends in the Bureau, while FBI agents saw the protection of civil rights activists as outside their mission." Over a thousand civil rights activists, including Rustin, were tagged as security threats by the FBI. "With the knowledge it secretly acquired, it could disrupt events, sow dissension in organizations, ruin relationships, and destroy the credibility of individuals."[51]

The suggestion that there was not significant Communist involvement in the March on Washington was unacceptable to the FBI director. "We are right now in this Nation involved in a form of racial revolution," one of his aides assured him at the time of the March on Washington. "The time has never been so right for exploitation of the Negroes by communist propagandists." This is what the Chief wanted to hear, and to share with various government authorities. Terming South Carolina segregationist senator Strom Thurmond "one of our strongest bulwarks in the Congress," the FBI shared with him a tremendous amount of information on Bayard Rustin's political past, radical beliefs, and sexual history, as well as a considerable accumulation of negative judgments, to be used in a full-scale attack on the march on the Senate floor. Fed similar material, Attorney General Robert F. Kennedy viewed the upcoming march as "very, very badly organized," with "many groups of Communists trying to get in."[52]

As it turned out, the march was brilliantly organized, and participation was incredibly broad and "respectable." The element of truth in Hoover's vicious interpretation of the march, however, is that central to the entire effort was an influential core of socialists who sought, as they themselves more than once asserted, a revolutionary, nonviolent transformation of society. The social-ist element was reflected in Randolph's opening remarks, which hailed the demonstrators as "the advance guard of a massive moral revolution" aimed at a social transformation where "the sanctity of private property takes second place to the sanctity of the human personality." The veteran radical emphasized the traditional socialist linkage of racial justice and economic justice: "Yes, we want all public accommodations open to all citizens, but those accommoda-tions will mean little to those who cannot afford to use them." This linkage was a running theme in speeches throughout the rally.[53]

The question remains, to what extent did the march live up to the revo-lutionary hopes and expectations that animated its key organizers? To what extent had that been compromised away? The most unrelenting criticism came from Malcolm X, in his "Message to the Grassroots":

The same white element that put Kennedy into power—labor, the Catholics, the Jews, and liberal Protestants—the same clique that put Kennedy in power, joined the march.

It's just like when you've got some coffee that's too black, which means it's too strong. You integrate it with cream, you make it weak. But if you pour too much cream in it, you won't even know you ever had coffee. It used to be hot, it becomes cool. It used to be strong, it becomes weak. It used to wake you up, now it puts you to sleep. This is what they did with the march on Washington. They joined it. They didn't integrate it. They infiltrated it. They joined it, became part of it, took it over. And as they took it over, it lost its militancy. It ceased to be angry, it ceased to be hot, it ceased to be uncompromising. Why it even ceased to be a march. It became a picnic, a circus. Nothing but a circus, with . . . clowns leading it, white clowns and black clowns. . . .

No, it was a sellout. It was a takeover.[54]

Whether or not one agrees that the March on Washington was a sellout, the fact remains that Malcolm X had put his finger on one aspect of "The Strategy": the decision by a significant sector of those with power in the United States, whether one calls it the power structure or ruling class or power elite, to support the elimination of the Jim Crow system. Legalized institutional racism had become a liability to them, given political shifts domestically and the emergence of new global political realities following the Second World War. The activist wing of the civil rights movement, intensely aware of this, was determined to take advantage of it. SNCC leader Robert Moses has emphasized this in discussing the interplay, the political dance, that existed between the Kennedy administration, later the Johnson administration, and the most radical wing of the civil rights movement in the Deep South. There were, in fact, behind-the-scenes relationships with *some* sectors of the government (not the FBI!) that provided some resources and protection at dangerous moments. The radical militants of SNCC were serious and sincere in their uncompromising challenge to the white power structure in the South, and clear about and critical of the ties between it and the white power structure in the North, both of which had a historic interest in maintaining the subordination of black Americans. A SNCC leader could make a telephone call to contacts in the federal government that might sometimes blunt or undermine local segregationist assaults. This was neither hypocrisy nor sellout. Movement allies in the government were not going to do the dangerous organizing, but they became part of the equation. "The movement was really a coalition of the bottom and the top," Moses noted. "In order for the top to listen—the executive or the judiciary or the Congress—you needed the pressure from the bottom."[55]

"I came to recognize that the decision to scale down the militancy of the march was a sensible one," Rachelle Horowitz later commented. "After all, we wanted the demonstration to be as broad-based as possible, reflecting a coalition of American conscience. We couldn't have achieved that objective if we had insisted on a program of radical confrontation with the government." One might argue that this Rustin aide had to talk herself into such acceptance, but at least some revolutionary socialists from other groups (for example, Barry Sheppard of the Socialist Workers Party), while noting the tight controls, also had a positive take: "The turnout emboldened black people and white fighters for equal rights too. It was the largest action I had ever participated in, and I could feel the power of ordinary people when we unite and organize for our rights and needs. It was exhilarating."[56]

The march, however, involved, as Malcolm X emphasized, an accommodation with the U.S. government (insisted on by the march moderates), which in some cases, ranging from an agreed-upon post-march meeting with President Kennedy to vital last-minute assistance in repairing a sabotaged sound system for the rally, eased over into a degree of government assistance, which some argued finally meant a high degree of government control. Indeed, A. Philip Randolph, Martin Luther King Jr., James Farmer, Roy Wilkins, Whitney Young, and Walter Reuther met with President Kennedy on June 22 to iron things out and secure his support. Initially, Kennedy sought to compel them to call off the march. Persuaded that this was impossible, but assured that these leaders were committed to keeping the action moderate and not antagonistic to his administration, he indicated his tacit support. "Once Kennedy agreed," Tom Kahn confided to Stokely Carmichael, "all kinds of liberal support miraculously appeared. The morning after, it was like a different world." Carmichael's own comments were sour:

> Bayard had his coalition, but there would be a price. From now on everything, but everything, would have to be approved by them, or indirectly by "representatives" of the White House: the program, the speakers, the route of the march, the slogans, the signs to be carried, and of course, the speeches. . . . Which is not to say that Bayard and Mr. Randolph do not deserve credit. They surely did. For their initiative and persistence had forged that alliance that made the march possible. And the march itself? It was a spectacular media event . . . a "political" event choreographed entirely for the television audience.[57]

Of course, the fact that millions of people throughout the United States and the world were watching an unabashedly pro-civil rights spectacle in 1963, when powerful legal and extralegal forces were fighting to save the racist Jim Crow system by any means necessary, had a profound impact on the course of events. It was obvious that not only the Kennedy administration, but the entire "white liberal establishment" and the moguls of the mass media wanted to tame and co-opt this event. As Charles Euchner suggests, however, maybe "the march organizers co-opted the co-opters." [58] Also important is an additional comment by Cleveland Sellers. He shared much of Carmichael's sourness over the de-radicalization of the march, and especially over the heavy-handed reaction to and censorship of John Lewis's speech, although he notes that "despite the deletions his speech was very good." He concluded:

> The people who got the most out of the march were the poor farmers and sharecroppers whom SNCC organizers brought from Mississippi, Alabama, and Southwest Georgia. The march was a tremendous inspiration to them. It helped them believe that they were not alone, that there really were people in the nation who cared what happened to them. [59]

I. F. Stone, a shrewd left-wing maverick whose independent journalism had considerable influence in radical and liberal milieus, echoed this in regard to himself, his own "special moment," standing in the early morning inside the Union Terminal and watching "the thousands pouring in from New York and Pittsburgh and Chicago, and suddenly to feel no longer alone in this hot-house capital but as if out in the country people did care." He added caustically that "the price of having so many respectables on the bandwagon was to mute Negro militancy." Noting the censorship of John Lewis's speech, he felt that "the rally turned into one of support for the Kennedy civil rights program. Somehow on that lovely day, in that picnic atmosphere, the Negro's anguish never found full expression." [60]

Then there were the novelists. Norman Mailer caught what he saw as the negative, non-revolutionary aspect: "It was an agreeable afternoon, but it had a touch of the cancerous to it— the toxic air of totalitarianism. . . . Yes, the seed of dialectics was stirring again, a shade of Marx, the ghost of Lenin. Many . . . came to Washington expecting danger, looking secretly for an historic issue that day. And they were disappointed. . . . The iron word had gone out: no violence today! And there was none. That took its toll. That put the hand of powerful depression into the agreeableness of the afternoon." James Baldwin caught the challenge: "The day was important in itself, and what we do with this day is even more important."[61]

Randolph, Rustin, and their socialist comrades were by no means inclined to settle for a pleasant afternoon—their concern, precisely, was *what to do with the day*. Their plan all along had been to utilize the momentum of the march, the coalition it represented, and the militant grassroots struggles against Jim Crow that it reflected, to move forward on a revolutionary path.

Civil Rights Revolution

The game plan of the Socialist Party was to draw a number of activists into a major conference that would map out and help propel forces into the future of the civil rights struggle, a future that would fundamentally change the structures of power in U.S. politics and in the economy.

A special tri-fold flyer was mimeographed and distributed, inviting those interested to a Conference on the Civil Rights Revolution, to be held in Washington, D.C., for two days following the March on Washington. The speakers highlighted in the brochure were James Farmer, A. Philip Randolph, Bayard Rustin, left-liberal Democratic Congressman William Fitts Ryan, and Norman Thomas.[62] The sponsor was the Socialist Party—with a 50-cent registration fee, with the unemployed to be admitted for free.[63]

According to *New America*, over 400 people attended this conference whose purpose was to engage in "discussions of the strategy and politics of this unfinished revolution," with the participants including "many young civil rights activists from the North and the South."[64]

The independent journalist I. F. Stone was impressed:

Far superior to anything I heard at the monument [the Lincoln Memorial, where the march's speeches were given] were the discussions I heard the next day at a civil rights conference organized by the Socialist Party. On that dismal rainy morning-after, in a dark union hall in the Negro section, I heard A. Philip Randolph speak with an eloquence and humanity few can achieve. . . . He reminded moderates that political equality was not enough. "The white sharecroppers of the South have full civil rights but live in the bleakest poverty." One began to understand what was meant by a march "for *jobs* and freedom." For most Negroes, civil rights alone will only be the right to join the underprivileged whites. "We must liberate not only ourselves," Mr. Randolph said, "but our white brothers and sisters."

The direction in which full emancipation lies was indicated when Mr. Randolph spoke of the need to extend the public sector of the economy. His brilliant assistant on the March, Bayard Rustin, urged an economic Master Plan to deal with the technological unemployment that weighs so heavily on the Negro and threatens to create a permanently depressed class of whites and blacks living precariously on the edges of an otherwise affluent society. It was clear from the discussion that neither tax cuts nor public works nor job training (for what jobs?) would solve the problem while automation with giant steps made so many workers obsolete. The civil rights movement, Mr. Rustin said, could not get beyond a certain level unless it merged into a broader plan for social change.

In the ill-lighted hall, amid the assorted young students and venerables like Norman Thomas, socialism took on fresh meaning and revived urgency. It was not accidental that so many of those who ran the March turned out to be members or fellow travellers of the Socialist Party.[65]

"In days of great popular uprising—like today's civil rights revolution—with their tensions, tumult, and fermentation," Randolph intoned, "the frontiers of freedom, equality, social justice, and racial justice can be advanced." Emphasizing the centrality of demonstrations for forcing the drafting and passage and implementation of civil rights legislation, Randolph argued that there was a necessity for deeper change, that to solve the economic issues related to racism, "the public sector of the economy must be expanded, the private sector of the economy must be contracted," and that "we need some organization in the country that will carry on and maintain sound exposition of the economic qualities that are to obtain in the nation, and this can only be done by . . . the Socialist Party, which is dedicated to democracy, and which believes that political democracy requires economic democracy, and that the two must go hand in hand."[66]

Another black trade unionist speaking at the conference, Cleveland Robinson, the secretary-treasurer of the left-wing District 65 of the Retail, Wholesale and Department Store Union (RWDSU), coming from a somewhat different tradition, did not beat the drums for the Socialist Party, but concurred on the need for discussion among working people on how to create a political structure meeting the needs of the present moment in history. Commenting that "the March on Washington, if anything, has only laid the beginning, the foundation for a great upsurge," he echoed Randolph that "there must be profound changes to make our political and economic structure more democratic." He said that "the power structure of our nation today is in the hands of people whose stated interests are [maintaining] great profits and power," and that "no significant changes will occur unless there is an uprising of the people."[67]

Stressing the revolutionary nature of the civil rights movement, Bayard Rustin clarified: "Its byproducts are revolutionary. There are few revolutionary Negroes in this country. It's the implications of their struggle, it's when Negroes touch basic economic problems that touch all men, when they use their dynamic for the changing of the whole society, that it becomes revolutionary." Emphasizing the need for a coalition of the labor and civil rights movements, he turned a critical eye to the top leadership of the AFL-CIO. "I do not blame Meany for not supporting this march. Why should I blame a man who says he's never been on a picket line for not supporting the march? The problem is that the executive council of the AFL-CIO is not representative of the elements which make up the labor movement. . . . But I have not lost faith in the alliance between Negroes and white workers. It will come from the streets and from that movement which emerges from the streets." He predicted that such pressure could force even people like Meany to adapt to more radical perspectives. Rustin concluded: "What I want people to do is accept the fundamental ideals of American society, democracy and equality, and try to work out an economic and social system that fits them."[68]

Two of the central leaders of the Socialist Party addressed the conference. The comments of Norman Thomas—lauding the march, emphasizing the importance of young activists wrestling with the problems facing society, and repeating that "the ideals of socialism still provide the best framework for approaching these economic problems in a humane way"—certainly generated no controversy among his comrades of the Socialist Party. There had been, however, an acrimonious controversy within the organization over the decision to have Max Shachtman give a presentation on his "realignment" orientation that would link the struggle with, and funnel activists into, the Democratic Party (ultimately freed, to be sure, from the Dixiecrats). Arguing that Shachtman's views did not reflect those of the Socialist Party as a whole, some members of the organization's National Administrative Committee argued in favor of a panel, including Shachtman, to present different points of view on the matter.

The argument against this, which ultimately prevailed, was that Shachtman could present his views as his own, not those of the party as such, and that a panel "displaying inner-party controversy" would not be desirable at such a conference. At this point, the YPSL leadership, dominated by forces disagreeing with Shachtman's perspective, voted not to cosponsor the conference.[69]

In his remarks, Shachtman hailed the March on Washington as "a spectacular triumph," which he saw as "our triumph, as it is for all people who cherish freedom, democracy, and human equality." He went on to echo the call for economic change, particularly the creation of a jobs program, connected with a housing program, a medical care program, a schools program, and the like. "All important steps of progress in the U.S. today, insofar as they depend upon government enactments, government initiatives, are stalled today, as yesterday, by the existence of the power of the great anonymous party in the U.S.," Shachtman argued. "That anonymous party, which although it submits no candidates formally to the electorate, is . . . the Dixiecrat-Republican coalition." He called on civil rights activists, trade unionists, genuine liberals, and socialists to consolidate their coalition in a campaign to drive the Dixiecrats out of the Democratic Party and make it their own political force to advance the progressive agenda for racial and economic justice. "I hope it goes without saying that I'd consider my remarks an utter failure—a failure of communication—if you understood by this idea that the demonstrations now going on should be in some way suspended. Not in the least. The pressure should not be relaxed for a moment," Shachtman reassured his listeners. "Without that pressure this coalition would mean nothing except that the Negroes are sold into voting slavery again as they have been many times before, that they would lose their political independence and power." Yet he concluded the point somewhat equivocally: "This political coalition must be supplemented and reinforced by the demonstrations."[70]

Perhaps unintentionally, a tension arose between the political coalition within the Democratic Party and the independent power of mass demonstrations. Did the demonstrations exist simply to "supplement" and "reinforce" the Democratic Party coalition? The tension is highlighted if we compare and contrast statements of two prominent followers of Shachtman, articulated decades after Shachtman's speech.

At the conclusion of a tribute to longtime civil rights activist Norman Hill, in the *New York Sun* in 2005, Gary Shapiro wrote:

Mr. Hill spoke about how he was influenced and guided by both A. Philip Randolph and Bayard Rustin. He spoke of the five principles that served as the undergirding for their labor and civil rights activities: These were, firstly, a commitment to a society in which racial equality and economic justice would prevail; secondly, development of a majoritarian strategy that would include coalition politics to pursue racial equality and economic justice; thirdly, that the initiative for change should come from those who are mistreated, exploited, and discriminated against (such that they gain strength, awareness, and confidence); fourthly, a commitment to mass action, whether it be through demonstration, rally, march, picket line, or boycott, and finally, that the commitment be to nonviolent mass action.[71]

The stress in the comments from the late 1990s by Paul Feldman, former editor of *New America*, appears to be differently placed, with an initial stress on the leadership of Max Shachtman:

We followed [him] and gave up our revolutionary romanticism an inch at a time. Max's persuasiveness, combined with the real struggle of the civil rights movement, moved us deeply. A Democratic Party orientation made sense, because we were convinced that if the southern blacks got the vote they would unseat the Dixiecrats, and there was at that time a major struggle over civil rights between the liberal-labor wing of the Democratic Party on one side and the Dixiecrats and other conservatives on the other. So we could see some connection between getting involved in civil rights and the Democratic Party. Our people even worked out a novel strategic conception called realignment, whereby the liberal-labor wing of the Democratic Party would replace the Dixiecrats and [the relatively corrupt urban political] machines. Our opposition to the Dixiecrats and our civil rights work were right on target, but the efforts to break up the machines didn't work out exactly as expected. The machines, bad as they were, had a decent relationship with the labor movement. . . . At the time, we believed in our ideas and rhetoric more than anything else.[72]

Setting aside the later disillusionment that Feldman experienced over the failure of the realignment strategy to "work out exactly as expected," his comments reflect Shachtman's 1963 stress on the hoped-for labor–civil rights coalition in the Democratic Party, with demonstrations being supplementary. In Norman Hill's comments, we see a greater stress on the demonstrations that Randolph and Rustin were projecting in 1963. In a literary snapshot of the Socialist Party milieu in 1966, it seems that the reformist element is predominant:

> In some important instances serious changes have been brought about through the coalition of liberals and radicals that Bayard Rustin now calls for building on a great scale. Rustin, Michael Harrington, Irving Howe, Tom Kahn, and Robert Pickus—to cite a few of the democratic socialists who hold this view—believe it *is* possible to better the lot of the American people by putting left pressure on the government from within the political system. And they believe a plurality of power *does* exist in America, that there are levels of government which can be influenced by reason or humanitarian arguments. So they participate, to varying degrees, in traditional day-to-day politics.[73]

But there was certainly room, in the framework of "The Strategy," and within the general framework of the post–March on Washington conference organized by the Socialist Party, for a different balance to be struck, one more consistent with the revolutionary approach reflected, for example, in Rosa Luxemburg's orientation (touched on in chapter1). The tension between the two aspects of the orientation articulated at the conference was not made explicit or resolved. Among many of the radical young activists present, the dominant themes could have been interpreted as:

- the radical linkage of the struggles for racial justice and economic justice;
- the need for a comprehensive program to focus and advance the linked struggles;
- the progressive coalition represented by the March on Washington taking on the edge of an interracial alliance of all sectors of the working class; and
- the dynamic and revolutionary deepening of democratic change into socialist change.

Politics of Mass Action

It is interesting to consider the thinking of Bayard Rustin in the spring of 1964 regarding the way to advance this orientation. The thinking is shared in comments he offers in a discussion involving the editorial board of *Dissent* magazine (the best known being Irving Howe and Michael Harrington) and Rustin, Norman Hill, Rachelle Horowitz, and Tom Kahn. Rustin is clearly the central figure in the discussion, and it is he who articulates first and most clearly "the important point . . . that the civil rights movement, because of its limited success, is now confronted with the problem that major Negro demands cannot be met within the context of the civil rights movement." Hill backs him up with the observation that "the usual tactic of direct action which here and there has produced an integrated lunch counter does not seem to be answering the demands of larger numbers of Negro people." Rachelle Horowitz chimed in that since the March on Washington "the Negro in the street has not seen one gain." Rustin focused on jobs, which he defined as one of the key "problems of the whole society." He emphasized that "the labor movement . . . is itself unable to provide jobs for the people enrolled in the unions." He argued that "the only way labor can handle this thing is if it allies with the Negro in a bigger struggle." He emphasized that he was talking about "trade union people," clarifying: "I certainly do not look for any alliance which would include the AFL-CIO per se." The political program to unite these forces, Rustin noted, would need to be "around questions of total employment, limited planning, work training within planning, and a public-works program."

Rustin argued that the civil rights movement must do two things. "First, stay in the streets," he insisted, "winning little victories, and sometimes none, but stay, for the very reason that you stimulate other segments of society, limitedly, to move." But the second necessity would be "to carry the question which I discussed earlier under full employment, planning, training, and so forth. They must carry that message into the streets." This was interwoven with the conception of organizing a "sit-down in front of the building trades" and other direct action. He expanded on this at length later in the discussion:

> I think we've got to have a political movement, in the sense that the civil rights movement is now a political movement. It's a matter of broadening that. Regardless of people's politics, regardless of what church they belong to, or union, thousands and millions of people are contributing to the civil

rights movement, are getting into the streets. They came to the March on Washington. This is the kind of movement I see as a political movement, around such things as full employment, some planning, training within that planning, a public works program. I think without setting up a political structure or a party we can carry this to the people and get the kind of enthusiasm you now get around the civil rights bill, or that we got around the March on Washington.

Rachelle Horowitz commented that "there are things which are intrinsic to people in motion," concluding, "Something wonderful happens to people when they are somehow determining their own destiny and beginning to control and change their own conditions."[74]

This way of understanding politics and of conceptualizing "The Strategy," while envisioning a labor–civil rights alliance, was not constrained by George Meany's leadership of the AFL-CIO. As Tom Kahn later commented, "The sit-in generation" saw that as "an over-bureaucratized and complacent institution, itself tainted by racism."[75] Nor did it focus on the electoralism stressed in Max Shachtman's remarks at the Socialist Party's 1963 conference in Washington. It seemed more akin to the politics represented by Rosa Luxemburg. But this would change.

4. A FREEDOM BUDGET FOR ALL AMERICANS

IN THE FIRST DECADES of the twenty-first century, there has been a sort of Bayard Rustin revival. He is a forgotten hero, a "lost prophet" being rediscovered by new generations who are fascinated, and in many cases inspired, by the amazing person he was. A beautifully made full-length documentary, *Brother Outsider: The Life of Bayard Rustin* (2003), has won much deserved recognition and awards.[1] Yet, as one of Rustin's close friends and comrades has pointed out, important parts of the story are missing.

Velma Murphy Hill, the spouse of Norman Hill but a seasoned activist in her own right, stresses that "with all its indisputable value, *Brother Outsider* is a flawed work, because it does not fit Rustin's civil and human rights activities into the context of his broader political and social philosophy." Indeed, for the average viewer of the film it is not clear that Rustin was a dedicated socialist. Also "fundamentally missing" is the quality of Rustin's relationship with A. Philip Randolph. And it "does not mention the *Freedom Budget for All Americans*, a comprehensive legislative program developed with Leon Keyserling and other economists and proposed to Congress in the late 1960s."[2]

The Freedom Budget was inseparable from what Rustin and his mentor Randolph had been doing for many years in the cause of civil rights, labor, and socialism. Its glowing promise and tragic failure, so reflective of these two champions, have much to teach those who remain committed to the radically democratic ideals to which they gave voice. Progressive journalist John Nichols has speculated that had Senator Robert F. Kennedy not been killed in 1968 as he was starting to win presidential primaries, had he "survived to be nominated and elected, it is not so difficult to think that a Freedom Budget might have been enacted—and with it an advance toward the democratic socialism which Randolph had championed."[3] This seems highly unlikely for reasons that will be elaborated later on. The fact that it is a thinkable thought and that Nichols could make a case for it reinforces Velma Hill's insistence that the Freedom Budget is an essential part of Bayard Rustin's story and, related to that, a key element in the story of the U.S. civil rights movement.

Far from simply being the construct of socialist ideologues, the Freedom Budget was designed to address problems that were arising within the ongoing struggle for civil rights in the wake of the 1963 March on Washington. This was highlighted in a talk by Norman Hill three months later. One of the leaders of CORE, Hill pointed to what he saw as a crisis flowing from the very success of the March on Washington. There was now "the potential for all kinds of new people to come into the movement to broaden its base, but the question now is—for what?" A lack of clarity on programmatic specifics needed to be overcome in order to move forward on broad goals of civil rights, and this, he suggested, could only be achieved by moving to "a deeper level."

Around housing, Hill argued, it was necessary "to attack not only the interests which controlled the housing market, but also to begin to develop a program which meant moving politically to create support for a massive crash program for housing, especially for low-income housing."

Around education, it was necessary to struggle not only against segregation, but "to couple our demands for integration with demands that there be a crash program to raise the entire quality of the educational system."

Around jobs, he noted, "the March on Washington has helped to raise the question, 'What do you do about jobs for Negroes in an era of automation, in which there are not enough jobs to go around for all workers?'" He concluded: "I think it's the particular role of those who have thought through the problem of unemployment, and who have a long range perspective—the particular contribution, I would hope, of socialists—that they help put this discussion in some kind of economic and political framework."[4]

The Vision of Randolph and King

A "Freedom Budget" for All Americans that addressed these and other issues was endorsed by over two hundred prominent civil rights, labor, social activist, and academic figures, but the two most prominent figures in the civil rights movement who were most closely associated with it were certainly A. Philip Randolph and Martin Luther King Jr. It represented a culmination of their strategy to win civil rights for African Americans and to overcome racism in the United States.

On November 18, 1965, at a White House conference on civil rights titled "To Fulfill These Rights," Randolph and those around him were among those who challenged the limitations of Johnson's Poverty Program. "Advanced tokenism," was how CORE representatives termed it. Describing poverty and unemployment as the equivalent of "increasingly explosive socio-racial dynamite in the black ghettoes," Randolph proposed the remedy as being "the creation of a vast 'freedom budget,' a nationwide plan for the abolition of the ghetto jungles in every city, even at the cost of a hundred billion dollars." Asserting that in 1965 "we have both the resources and the know-how" to end unemployment and poverty, he commented that "the millions of unemployed and the more than thirty million living in poverty take on the aspects . . . of a national crime." Randolph announced that "in the near future, I shall call upon the leaders of the Freedom Movement to meet together with economists and social scientists in order to work out a specific and documented 'Freedom Budget.'" According to historian Thomas Sugrue, "Randolph's proposal created a real buzz."[5] One year later, the Freedom Budget was presented to the world through the auspices of the recently created A. Philip Randolph Institute.

The Randolph Institute's initial "Prospectus" projected an alliance of "labor, both Negro and white," and it asserted that "united, we can win the social reforms which America needs." It projected "mobilizing the intellectual resources of the Negro, Labor, academic and professional communities with the object of expanding and intensifying their participation in day-to-day work of the civil rights movement as it seeks to develop strategies and meet concrete problems." The institute's premise was "that to go beyond the achievement of civil rights would require a movement which sought basic, far-reaching institutional changes in the nation's social and economic structures." Its executive director was Bayard Rustin, soon to be joined by Norman Hill. The primary focus of the institute was to oversee the finalization of the Freedom Budget and the campaign to make it a reality.[6]

Randolph and others presented the Freedom Budget at a special conference on October 24, 1966. The aging activist described it as being dedicated "to the full goals of the 1963 March." He elaborated on the

Freedom Budget's specifics (involving a ten-year federal expenditure of $180 billion) and its meaning:

> The "Freedom Budget" spells out a specific and factual course of action, step by step, to start in early 1967 toward the practical liquidation of poverty in the United States by 1975. The programs urged in the "Freedom Budget" attack *all* of the major causes of poverty—unemployment and underemployment; substandard pay, inadequate social insurance and welfare payments to those who cannot or should not be employed; bad housing; deficiencies in health services, education, and training; and fiscal and monetary policies which tend to redistribute income regressively rather than progressively. The "Freedom Budget" leaves no room for discrimination in any form, because its programs are addressed to *all* who need more opportunity and improved incomes and living standards—not just to some of them.

Randolph explained that such programs "are essential to the Negro and other minority groups striving for dignity and economic security in our society," but that "the abolition of poverty (almost three-quarters of whose victims are white) can be accomplished only through action which embraces the totality of the victims of poverty, neglect, and injustice." He added, "In the process everyone will benefit, for poverty is not an isolated circumstance affecting only those entrapped by it. It reflects—and affects—the performance of our national economy, our rate of economic growth, our ability to produce and consume, the condition of our cities, the levels of our social services and needs, the very quality of our lives." In Randolph's opinion the success of this effort would depend on "a mighty coalition among the civil rights and labor movements, liberal and religious forces, students and intellectuals—the coalition expressed in the historic 1963 March on Washington for Jobs and Justice."

The Freedom Budget was an 84-page document, complete with statistics, charts, graphs, and a discussion of methodology. A popularized 20-page summary was prepared that contained an introduction by Martin Luther King Jr., who believed that "the ultimate answer to the Negroes' economic dilemma will be found in a massive federal program for all the poor along the lines of A. Philip Randolph's Freedom Budget, a kind of Marshall Plan for the disadvantaged." The introduction he provided dovetailed with Randolph's, and expressed a special urgency:

After many years of intense struggle in the courts, in legislative halls, and in the streets, we have achieved a number of important victories. We have come far in our quest for respect and dignity. But we have far to go.

The journey ahead requires that we emphasize the needs of all America's poor, for there is no way merely to find work, or adequate housing, or quality-integrated schools for Negroes alone. We shall eliminate slums for Negroes when we destroy ghettoes and build new cities for *all*. We shall eliminate unemployment for Negroes when we demand full and fair employment for *all*.

This human rights emphasis is an integral part of the Freedom Budget and sets, I believe, a new and creative tone for the great challenge we yet face.

The Southern Christian Leadership Conference fully endorses the Freedom Budget and plans to expend great attention and time in working for its implementation.

It is not enough to project the Freedom Budget. We must dedicate ourselves to the legislative task to see that it is immediately and fully achieved. I pledge myself to this task and will urge all others to do likewise. The Freedom Budget is essential if the Negro people are to make further progress. It is essential if we are to maintain social peace. It is a political necessity. It is a moral commitment to the fundamental principles on which this nation was founded.[7]

Putting the Program Together

A "Freedom Budget" for All Americans was a collective work, coordinated by Rustin, with input from a number of individuals, including Gerhart Colm (a prominent economist who had held various posts in the Roosevelt and Truman administrations), Paul Feldman, Herbert J. Gans (Professor of Sociology at Columbia University), AFL-CIO economists Woodrow Ginsburg (Director of Research for the AFL-CIO's Industrial Union Department), Nathaniel Goldfinger (Director of the AFL-CIO's Economics Department), Michael Harrington, Vivian Henderson (an economist and civil rights activist who was president of the historically black Clark College), Tom Kahn, Hylan Lewis of Howard University, Max Shachtman (who came up with the name *"Freedom Budget" for All Americans*), Don Slaiman (Director of the AFL-CIO's Civil Rights Department), Elizabeth Wickenden from the National Social Welfare Assembly, and, especially, economist and lawyer Leon Keyserling.[8]

The Freedom Budget benefited greatly from Keyserling's participation. He had entered government service in 1933, participating in drafting various New Deal initiatives, including the National Industrial Recovery Act, the Social Security Act, and the National Labor Relations Act. In the throes of the Depression years of the 1930s, he had quietly shared with intimates some socialist sympathies ("without revolution which transfers power to the workers and sets up a socialized state, little will be gained," he mused in a letter to his father), but the thrust of his thinking and of his considerable activities was very much in the direction of New Deal liberalism. In 1946 Keyserling became a member of President Harry Truman's Council of Economic Advisers, and in 1950 served as its chairman. In later years, he consulted with Congress on a variety of economic issues, practiced law, and both founded and presided over the Conference on Economic Progress. Bringing much more than his reputation and professional credibility to the project, Keyserling was the central figure in working out the methodology and specifics of the document. As historian David Garrow pointed out years later, with this "ambitious Freedom Budget," Randolph and Rustin sought to "transform the civil rights agenda into a broad and fundamental program of economic justice," with specific proposals "for improving the lives of America's poor and dramatically increasing their incomes that made President Johnson's uplifting 'War on Poverty' look miserly."[9]

Keyserling was passionate in his advocacy of the Freedom Budget, whose underlying principles he had been pressing for decades. "My years of interest and efforts on behalf of translating the Employment Act of 1946 into what it was intended to be, the uniting of our economic resources with the fulfillment of our social needs, did not originate with the 'Freedom Budget,'" he emphasized. A designer of this full employment bill of the Truman administration, Keyserling was animated by the New Deal idealism of his younger years. Like Franklin D. Roosevelt, he believed in a variant of the capitalist economy in which the government would ensure this "uniting" of economic resources with social needs. Again and again, he used the terms *neglect* and *moral lapse* when this failed to happen. "This neglect has been persistent all along, and the reasons for it have been moral and political rather than economic and financial. Federal Budget outlays in ratio to GNP have trended downward, in the main, since 1947."[10]

He argued that "it is true that there are now very serious shortages of teachers, doctors, nurses, etc., but these shortages were accruing at a serious rate . . . even prior to the Cold War, and they have been accruing because we have not adopted the policies needed to allocate to the public sector the resources which would call forth the rapid expansion of these types of personal services." The "gross neglect" was to be found in Republican and Democratic administrations—"not only during the Eisenhower administration but for all practical purposes from 1961 forward. The enormous tax reductions conceived in 1961 and effectuated in 1964 represented in my view a deliberate decision to distribute our resources in the wrong direction on purely economic grounds, with consequences now beginning to be apparent, and this distribution through the tax cuts did violence to all of our great social priorities."[11]

The policies of Franklin D. Roosevelt during the Second World War demonstrated what could be done: "The organizing resources required to fight World War II were infinitely more varied and complex than what would be required to do the job proposed in the 'Freedom Budget.' The real question is whether we take a war against want half as seriously as we took a war against external enemies." He was prepared to challenge the privileges of the wealthy elite, if need be: "Even if the growth estimates in the 'Freedom Budget' are 'too high,' it insists that we should then use progressive taxation and other measures to restrain the superfluous in order 'to afford' the essential." Keyserling's view, also consistent with the message of Randolph and Rustin (and with "The Strategy" as well), was that "this is not just a 'Freedom Budget' for Negroes or poor people but for the benefit of all Americans." In fact, it was a new incarnation of Roosevelt's Economic Bill of Rights. And yet it also dovetailed with the needs of the second phase of "The Strategy." In Rustin's opinion, Keyserling "created a realistic, complex and highly developed Freedom Budget and at the same time made it comprehensible to the people in the ghetto."[12]

Rustin oversaw an effort to secure 207 prominent endorsers. At the special conference launching the Freedom Budget, Randolph, Rustin, and Keyserling were joined by Donald Slaiman (a veteran Shachtmanite now in the upper circles of the AFL-CIO), the NAACP's Roy Wilkins, and representatives of several religious organizations. Generating major articles in the *New York Times* and *Washington Post*, it also received coverage, in some cases on the front page, in a number of other papers. According to the *AFL-CIO News*, the gathering drew "several hundred people in the civil rights, trade union, social welfare, education, and religious organizations." It summarized the program in this way:

- Restore and maintain full employment.
- Guarantee a minimum adequate income to all who cannot be so employed.

- Assure adequate income for all employed.
- Wipe out slum ghettoes and provide a decent home for every American family.
- Provide modern medical care for all Americans.
- Provide educational opportunities for all within the limits of their ambition, ability, and means.
- Wipe out other examples of neglect, including air and water pollution, transportation snarls, and inadequate use of our great natural resources.
- Correlate full employment with sustained production and economic growth.[13]

The *Wall Street Journal* was aghast. "In an atmosphere of uncalled for enthusiasm, a coalition of civil rights, religious, and labor leaders is launching a drive to 'end poverty' in the next ten years," it reported. "Without questioning their motives, we have no hesitation in saying that their approach appears to reflect a poverty of thought." And concluded: "We believe intelligent and private policies can provide further assistance to the poor. But not utopian talk of literally ending poverty, talk which bespeaks a rare innocence of human nature. Those who demand action on that basis delude not only themselves but the very people they profess to want to help." And *New America* reproduced this plus the *AFL-CIO News* piece under the overarching headline: "Freedom Budget—Class Struggle."[14]

Campaign and Legislation

The strategy to advance the Freedom Budget that Rustin and his co-thinkers developed was similar to the model for the 1963 March on Washington: (1) find liberal friends in Congress willing to hold hearings on and put forward legislation that would implement the program of the Freedom Budget, and (2) build what Rustin's biographer John D'Emilio calls "a populist campaign to pressure both Congress and the White House." This would require "enthusiastic backing from growing numbers of 'movement' people who were both the conscience and foot soldiers propelling Rustin's political vision forward."[15]

Copies of *A "Freedom Budget" for All Americans* were sent out to elected officials, religious leaders, and civil rights figures throughout the country. The League for Industrial Democracy, under Harrington's and Kahn's leadership, published its own edition and became a prime sponsor in the liberal community, joined by an enthusiastic Americans for Democratic Action. The AFL-CIO's Industrial Union Department published a labor edition that was distributed to union officers. The popularized 20-page version was prepared for even wider distribution. Of the longer version, 50,000 copies were distributed by early 1967, along with 70,000 copies of the more popular version; by the beginning of 1968 the respective figures were 85,000 and 100,000. Articles on the budget and excerpts from it were printed in trade union papers and magazines, the publications of sponsoring organizations, and elsewhere. There was talk about organizing study groups.

Speaking tours were developed, featuring Rustin, Harrington, Kahn, and others. Keyserling debated conservative Milton Friedman, the icon of laissez-faire capitalist economics, drawing a crowd of 3,000 at UCLA on March 4, 1967, as part of his swing to promote the Freedom Budget at about twenty difference colleges and universities around the country. Ad hoc committees in support of the Freedom Budget were formed in various cities (such as Detroit, Cleveland, Pittsburgh, Philadelphia, Boston), and efforts were begun to organize broad-based meetings and conferences in different parts of the country. Proposals in support of the Freedom Budget were presented to a number of student and youth organizations, bringing positive initial responses and endorsements, including from the United States Youth Council and several of its affiliates (the youth division of the NAACP, the campus ADA, in some areas the College Young Democrats, and, of course, YPSL).[16]

Legislation to implement the Freedom Budget was discussed and developed, in consultation with friendly lobbyists and politicians. But the key would be mass pressure to force through such legislation. Two detailed seven-page study guides were produced by the A. Philip Randolph Institute, and another was developed by the U.S. Youth Council. Rustin developed and sent out a memo (also seven pages) to community leaders detailing what they could do to build mass support for the Freedom Budget. Of course, much more than this would be needed to make the Freedom Budget a reality. Yet "it appeared for a moment," writes Thomas Sugrue, looking back on it with a historian's eye, "to be a revival of the proletarian turn of the Depression and World War II years, when a broad swath of activists found common ground challenging the intertwined problems of racial and economic inequality."[17]

Indeed, in an introduction to a Spanish-language edition of the popularized twenty-page edition of the Freedom Budget, César Chávez of the United

Farm Workers proclaimed: "Now is the time in the history of the United States that the poor people—Mexican-Americans, Negro or white, the prisoners of poverty—must organize to overcome and eradicate injustice, prejudice and the inhumanity of man to man."[18]

Yet one of the ingredients that had at one point been projected by Rustin and some of his comrades as being a key to the success of the Freedom Budget—militant direct action and deep-going mass struggles—never materialized. Amid all of the efforts around endorsements and educational efforts, and all-too-modest legislative efforts, the rhetoric and conceptualization of mass protest and mass action seemed to have evaporated. There would certainly be protest, militancy, and mass action very much in evidence from 1966 through 1968, but it seems that such things were organized by others, around issues to which the Freedom Budget had not been connected.

Problematical Context of the Freedom Budget Launch

The actor and activist Ossie Davis has succinctly and engagingly sketched the context within which the Freedom Budget was put forward, beginning with the aftermath of the March on Washington:

> The euphoria that followed the great success of the March on Washington was well deserved. Two hundred fifty thousand people moved into and out of Washington, D.C., in perfect peace and harmony. The doomsayers' dire pronouncements that chaos, disorder, and even bloodshed would occur had not prevailed. The unfinished civil rights revolution had become the number one item on the national agenda and our efforts had put it there. . . .
>
> Martin's "I Have a Dream" speech was still ringing victoriously in all our ears. We all had a dream! But the dream was not to last. Nineteen days later, on a Sunday morning in Birmingham, Alabama, the South struck back: Four little girls were killed by a bomb placed in a church. And as if that wasn't tragedy enough, on November 22, 1963, President John F. Kennedy was killed in Dallas, Texas.
>
> Then it was Lyndon Johnson's turn and we were a bit surprised. Johnson seized on the grief of a shocked, frightened, and guilty country and used it to political advantage. In 1964, the Civil Rights Act passed, and in 1965, the Voting Rights Act was passed. Then Johnson issued an executive order

calling for affirmative action to encourage and promote Negro business, and he declared a War on Poverty, instituting programs, reminiscent of FDR's New Deal, for rebuilding our cities, guaranteeing jobs—the kinds of jobs we desperately needed—for everybody for years to come. The call for jobs and freedom that had brought us to Washington in 1963 had finally been answered. Or so it seemed for one brief, shining moment. Johnson had seized the initiative and was ahead of the pack running the ball down the field.

But then came Vietnam, and little by little, the dream turned into a nightmare.[19]

The issue of Vietnam would become central to what happened to the Freedom Budget, and we will return to it. Here, it is worth noting that by no means did the war originate under the Johnson presidency. In his book about the March on Washington, Charles Euchner reports that on the very day of the march, shortly before John F. Kennedy met with the leaders of the march, he had been involved in a key meeting with his foreign policy advisors to discuss the intensification of the already substantial U.S. involvement in Vietnam. They were discussing the fact that the dictator they had been supporting and funding all along, Ngo Dinh Diem, was becoming increasingly unpopular, and his generals were preparing a coup that would soon overthrow his regime and kill him. A decision was made to tell the generals that the Kennedy administration would support their coup. A year later, most of the same people (with Johnson replacing Kennedy) would end up moving to the next logical step, dramatically escalating U.S. military involvement.[20]

More than one knowledgeable person has pointed out that Vietnam was not simply a result of mistakes made by the Kennedy and Johnson administrations. As Daniel Ellsberg commented, "The quagmire myth, the notion that presidents had been misled at critical turning points by unrealistic optimism in their civil and military advisors," is untenable in the face of the facts (for example, those gathered in the Pentagon Papers), which reveal that this war flowed from fundamental strategic policy decisions sustained by presidents of both the Democratic and Republican parties going back to Harry Truman and Dwight D. Eisenhower.[21] Historian William Appleman Williams has described how the Vietnam War was inseparable from "the pattern of intervention . . . ineradicably entwined with other inequitable and destructive aspects of American society" going back to much earlier days of the U.S. capitalist republic, connected with the dynamics shaping the Open Door Policy, which has in various forms shaped U.S. foreign policy for generations, especially for the benefit of corporate-business elites.[22]

The failure of Rustin and many of those closest to him to consider the implications this might have for their efforts, and to factor this into their strategic orientation, was to have serious consequences. In a letter adding his endorsement on August 31, before the Freedom Budget's formal launch, Norman Thomas cautioned: "I don't see how we can avoid reference to what effect the Vietnam War may have on the Budget. There is already a 'real' as well as a psychological strain on the economy due to the war." (Thomas publicly commented on this to the news media at the Freedom Budget's formal launch two months later.) The same concern was raised by Jerome Davis, writing from the organization Promoting Enduring Peace on September 4, before the budget's formal launch, in a friendly letter to A. Philip Randolph urging that "we need to think of what we are doing in Vietnam," referring to U.S. violations of the 1954 Geneva Agreements and the United States "murdering men women and children and spending billions of dollars." Randolph was evasive in his response, referring to his own antiwar credentials and personal thoughts, but concluding, "The civil rights leaders have no mandate from the Negro masses, in view of the crucial crisis of disaster proportions now plaguing the Negro freedom movement, to carry on any broad, massive movement to end the war in Vietnam."[23]

But the issue would not go away. Immediately after the Freedom Budget's formal launch on October 26, in a friendly but critical letter to Randolph on the same day, African American economist Robert S. Browne argued that "although there is admittedly a Herculean task to be performed in the way of winning broad acceptance for the principle of the Freedom Budget, the first obstacle to the realization of the Budget's goals is the burgeoning war spending, and it may be irresponsible to fail to point this out. One risks raising hopes quite falsely." The same concerns were again raised by Norman Thomas, in a December 14 letter to Keyserling, who responded to both the Browne and Thomas letters in similar terms. To Thomas he emphasized that "We may, whether we like it or not, face a very high defense budget and one small war or another for many years to come," and "I could not possibly agree—and I know you could not—that we should lie low with respect to our imperative domestic needs until the whole world is as we would want it to be." Making the same point to Browne, Keyserling added: "The task for those who recognize the imperatives of the 'Freedom Budget' is to work all the harder toward its accomplishment, through the process of education and appropriate pressures, just because the task is so difficult for all of the reasons you state."[24]

Many other developments were part of the context, but two in particular would powerfully influence the fortunes of Freedom Budget efforts. One involved the "Freedom Summer" campaign of SNCC to win voting rights in the Deep South, which was in fact a radical implementation of the realignment strategy. The other involved a dramatic deepening of the commitment on the part of the bulk of the Socialist Party to support the Democratic Party, accelerated by the conservative takeover of the Republican Party by forces around presidential candidate Barry Goldwater.[25] Although these may have seemed two sides of the same coin, they exacerbated the contradiction embedded in the realignment strategy: Were freedom struggles and protests central to the realignment orientation (understood as a fundamental tilt in national politics toward a powerful combination of the civil rights and labor movements) or were they simply a supplement to building up the "liberal-labor" Democratic Party?

In Mississippi hundreds of civil rights staffers and volunteers, black and white, some from the South and others coming down from the North, had committed their lives to the Mississippi Freedom Summer project—focused on voter registration, but combined with community organizing and Freedom Schools. Many were threatened and jailed, some were beaten, and some were killed. But they had succeeded in building with courageous black residents throughout the state a Mississippi Freedom Democratic Party (MFPD).

The all-white contingents of the regular Democratic Party in the South, the Dixiecrats, were absolutely opposed to blacks being allowed to vote, and to the pro-civil rights program of the national Democratic Party. They now threatened to bolt in support of conservative Republican Barry Goldwater.[26] The MFDP mobilized to send a large contingent to the 1964 Democratic Party convention in Atlantic City, demanding that the MFDP delegation replace Mississippi's "regular" Dixiecrat delegation. SNCC staffer Cleveland Sellers explains the perspective, which appeared to be right out of the realignment handbook of Shachtman, Kahn, and Rustin:

> We would prove that the MFDP's delegates were more loyal to the stated goals of the national party than the state's regular delegation and, therefore, deserved to be seated in its place. We were scrupulous in our attention to

detail. There was no way for anyone to claim that the MFDP's delegates were not legally and morally entitled to the seats. It was time for the national party, as they say in the black ghettoes, "to shit or get off the pot."

We were thinking far beyond Atlantic City. If our venture there was successful, we intended to utilize similar tactics in other Southern states, particularly Georgia and South Carolina. Our ultimate goal was the destruction of the power of the Dixiecrats, who controlled over 75 percent of the most important committees in Congress. With the Dixiecrats deposed, the way would have been clear for a wide-ranging redistribution of wealth, power and priorities throughout the nation.[27]

If this democratic radicalism went far beyond the comfort zone of many Democratic Party regulars in the North, it was utterly unacceptable to the party's central leaders and key strategists, President Lyndon B. Johnson most of all. Himself a Southern Democrat and particularly adept at speaking the language of (and cajoling) his fellow southerners in the party, Johnson was by no means committed to driving the Dixiecrats into the Republican Party. The powerful machinery and resources of this presumed "liberal-labor" party were mobilized to blunt and deflect such challenge. The MFDP strategy had been dependent upon some degree of support at the national level from that party, but instead, as Sellers put it, "they ignored principle and offered the MFDP delegates a compromise—two non-voting seats beside the regular delegation."[28]

The MFDP delegation was overwhelmed by an avalanche of prominent liberal, labor, civil rights, and religious leaders, with a message vividly described by Stokely Carmichael:

For the party. For the president. For the *country* . . . We gotta have unity. . . . All depends on you . . . the most important decision of your life . . . a great victory . . . be *political*. You gotta accept. For God's sakes, don't blow this . . .

Some—Dr. King, Dr. [Robert] Spike, maybe even Bayard—say, "Here's what we think, but finally, it's not our decision, it's yours." But mostly I remember unrelenting pressure: "You simply can't afford to make a serious mistake now."[29]

The SNCC staffers, repelled by the proposed compromise, stood aside and emphasized that only the actual grassroots delegation should deliberate and decide. The result was later symbolized in a poem by SNCC staffer Jane

Stembridge,[30] describing the comments of the legendary local organizer Fannie Lou Hamer:

Mrs. Hamer

The
revolutionary
element
remained
intact:
they
simply
stood.
She said
"No, sir,
        (for emphasis)
we didn't come
for no two
seats"

since
all of us
is tired.

Of course, Lyndon B. Johnson was reelected president anyway, and back in Mississippi the MFDP ended up endorsing and campaigning for him. But especially among the young civil rights cadres who had been close to Rustin and Kahn, and in some cases had been in or around the Socialist Party and YPSL, a fissure had opened and was beginning to widen.[31] For some, the black nationalist critique articulated by Malcolm X had growing resonance.

Greater credibility was given to an increasingly critical view of Rustin and what was seen, by many radicalizing activists, as the "civil rights establishment"—or "liberal establishment" or "white liberal establishment"—when in late July 1964 Rustin and Randolph put together and presented a public statement, with leaders of the NAACP, the Urban League, CORE, and SCLC, calling on the entire civil rights movement "voluntarily to observe a broad curtailment, if not total moratorium, of all mass marches, mass picketing and mass demonstrations until after Election Day." Instead, there should be "political action," by which they meant exclusively *electoral* action, such as massive voter registration and get-out-the-vote efforts. This was not accepted by SNCC, and very quickly radical members of CORE caused their organization to pull back as well. For many of his erstwhile followers and protégés, Rustin was now coming to represent something different from the principled and uncompromising revolutionary in whom they had believed. The centrality of mass action to his politics, emphasized in his discussion with *Dissent* editors only two months earlier, seemed to have slipped away. "I think he just flip-flopped," commented central SNCC activist Robert Moses, who had led the Mississippi Freedom Summer project. "The civil rights forces just had to move with the common people. And Bayard was moving with [liberal Democrat Hubert] Humphrey and the [Johnson] Administration."[32]

Also taking issue with Rustin was Eleanor Holmes (later Eleanor Holmes Norton), who was a longtime activist from the YPSL and Socialist Party milieu, a veteran of CORE, and a lawyer for SNCC during the Atlantic City confrontation. She warned: "We will lose the extremely important activist wing of the civil rights movement and risk turning the politics of the movement over to politicians who have no protest perspective whatsoever, unless we can convince today's activists that politics can be protest, and that it is they who must lead such a political movement just as they have led a great protest movement." The compromise Rustin and others pushed in Atlantic City, she argued, went in exactly the wrong direction.[33]

In a friendly debate with her, Rustin advanced key points that would now define his perspective on "protest and politics." Rustin's first point was the significance of "the appearance of Goldwater and the mobilization of the Right to maintain the status quo or to force us backwards comes during a period of technological revolution," resulting in poverty amid plenty. "Negroes are hardest hit but millions of whites suffer from the obstacles in our political and economic structure to effective remedies." In this context it would be necessary to move beyond simple protest in order to "develop a broader perspective of building and strengthening a political movement in this country to solve these problems." Defeating the Goldwater challenge and mobilizing black voting power "will give greater meaning to whatever protest action needs to be carried on." At the same time, "it is necessary to go beyond thinking of protest in purist ways," and work seriously to "liberalize a major political party." As a minority, African Americans must form a coalition with "others, including forces of the liberal and labor community that share with us certain mutual interests" that can best be done by "driving out the racists and reactionaries." And "although all the groups are moving in the same progressive general direction, each have their own interests to protect, their own political base, and they are responsible to their own membership" meaning that they cannot "go along merely in the way that one of the elements in the alliance might like to see things happen." Rustin went on to argue: "We have to look at political parties differently than we look at other institutions like segregated schools and lunch counters, because a political party is not only the product of social conditions, but an instrument of social change as well."[34]

Rustin went on to emphasize that the decade of protests by the civil rights movement had in fact been highly political, and that "the distinction I make is not that protest should not be carried on—I think protest in many, many forms must be carried on—but the nature of protests within political institutions is not chanting slogans, is not picket lines." Rather, one's effectiveness is maximized to the extent that "one develops a political program of social change and gets into that institution and fights for that position," at the same time "bringing sufficient other elements within that political structure to the point where they have also to fight for it." He also mapped out a perspective for the post-election period:

> I am convinced that the Johnson forces have a strategy for this election that the civil rights movement must turn to its benefit. Johnson plans to move to the left on economic questions and stand where he is on civil rights questions. I think that is going to be his game vis-à-vis Goldwater. If we handle things right we can push him very far to the left on economic questions, bearing in mind that to the degree that we push him to the left on economic questions we are essentially answering for the nation the basic civil rights questions—jobs, slums, poverty, etc.[35]

Very much in line with this, after Johnson's landslide victory, the Socialist Party's paper, *New America*, offered a running critique of Johnson's War on Poverty and on his projection of "the Great Society," with the obvious hope of helping to generate pressure for pushing him "very far to the left."[36]

In an initial evaluation of Johnson's projection of a Great Society in his 1965 State of the Union address, Michael Harrington noted two aspects: "On the one hand the President promised to extend some important welfare state programs and deepen some existing priorities. . . . And on the other hand there was some vague rhetoric about a new kind of society, but one which would be achieved within the present institutional framework in American society." Harrington's lengthy analysis of the practical proposals concluded with this summary: "In short, the immediate proposals made by the President are something of a mixed bag. The gains are in education and in some traditional but good proposals. The question-mark is over the assumption that consensus politics can solve the housing problem. And the failure to develop a real full employment budget—which is immediately possible and not in the far distance—is a disturbing augury for the Great Society." Of course, this is precisely what the Freedom Budget, which Harrington was helping to develop, was designed to overcome.[37]

On the visionary rhetoric of the Great Society, Harrington offered a critical note that actually could be seen as having a troubling relevance regarding the "liberalization" of the Democratic Party advocated by him, Rustin, Shachtman, and others:

> The broad definition of the Great Society is in keeping with the vision which has inspired every utopian movement of the past, and of the socialist movement of the past and the present: "Ahead now is a summit where freedom from the wants of the body can help fulfill the needs of the spirit." Yet at the same time, the President sees no need to question or challenge any of the present institutions of American society. The Great Society presumably will be the creation of business, labor, the consumer, the religious believers, the atheists, and so on. There are many elements that go into this amalgam.[38]

But would the resulting "consensus" be able to solve the actual problems? In a follow-up article he posed the question: "Is it true that conflict has essentially been banished from the United States, that the electoral alliance between Walter Reuther and Henry Ford behind LBJ can become a permanent thing?" He insisted that there continued to be "deep-going problems that cannot be wished away, of possibly greater difficulties in the future, and of conflict reactions to them," presumably based on major differences of interest between, for example, capital and labor. (But was there not such a "consensus" and "electoral alliance" within the Democratic Party itself?)[39]

A discussion of the War on Poverty, offering different points of view, was presented in *New America*, with S. M. Miller seeming to take a middle ground

between Hyman Bookbinder's positive view that "the war on poverty represents the kind of concern about the poor that permits much development and
hope" and Harrington's more critical insistence that "the government is not
doing enough to generate jobs." Miller suggested that "no one measure—economic, educational or welfare—will help all of the diverse poor," nor was he
convinced that "spending a great deal of money on public goods (which I am
very much in favor of) will generate enough jobs for all who want to work."
On the other hand, a far more critical Paul Jacobs questioned the relevance
of any of this in regard to the actual War on Poverty: "No, this anti-poverty
crusade is not yet a crusade, nor a war. It's not even a battle. It's more like a
reconnaissance by a patrol into the enemy territory. And the patrol would have
to withdraw very quickly when it discovered, as it would if this was a war on
poverty, that there were real enemies, identifiable enemies: the men who have a
personal interest in keeping people poor."[40]

Also relevant for understanding the context, and reflected in the columns
of *New America*, were ghetto uprisings from Harlem to Watts, and the development of radicalization and rage among various components of the hoped-for
realignment coalition—all caused by rising expectations being frustrated by the
continuation of oppressive realities.[41]

From Protest to Politics

In 1965, Rustin presented "From Protest to Politics," perhaps his
most widely read essay, published in the February issue of the then-liberal
Commentary, summarizing what he saw as the basic political framework within
which the Freedom Budget, which he and his comrades were still developing,
would become a practical and transformative reality.

Rustin argued (making positive reference to Freedom Summer and the
Freedom Democratic Party in Mississippi) that now "direct-action techniques
are being subordinated to a strategy calling for the building of community institutions or power bases." He went on to assert that the civil rights movement
was now, logically and necessarily, evolving into a broader social movement
"concerned not merely with removing barriers to full *opportunity* but achieving the fact of full *equality*." Noting that "Michael Harrington has said that a
successful war on poverty might well require an expenditure of $100 billion,"
he asked where the forces were "to compel such a commitment." In fact, "the

Negroes' struggle for equality in America is essentially revolutionary," he stated, because even though most "seek only to enjoy the fruits of American society as it now exists, their quest cannot *objectively* be satisfied within the framework of existing political and economic relations." Such change, however, requires that the civil rights movement connect with allies: trade unionists, liberals, religious groups, which were mobilized in the March on Washington in 1963 but which also "laid the basis for the Johnson landslide" in 1964. This landslide not only defeated "Goldwaterism," but provided an expression "of a majority liberal consensus." This could provide the mass base and the political power to force through the revolutionary changes that were needed. The coalition of progressive forces, "including hitherto inert and dispossessed strata of the population," could make the Democratic Party a vehicle for radical change (envisioning the departure from the Democrats of Dixiecrat and Big Business "elements which don't belong there"). Rustin emphasized: "We must see to it that the reorganization of the 'consensus party' proceeds along lines which make it an effective vehicle for social reconstruction."[42]

Here we can see powerful insights blended with what, some would argue, were the fatal conceptual flaws destined to undermine the campaign for the Freedom Budget's realization, yielding a devastating defeat for Rustin's version of "The Strategy." Yet as political scientist Adolph Reed perceptively noted, Rustin's essay was composed just *before* the U.S. escalation of the Vietnam War and the spread of ghetto uprisings, when it was unclear how far the Johnson administration could (and could not) be pushed toward a radical agenda, and while the progressive coalition of 1963–64 (despite stresses and strains) was still basically intact. It reflects what Reed terms a "strategic ambivalence." It contains divergent elements—a possibility for moving toward a deepening radicalism, in line with some of the formulations we find in the essay itself, and also a possibility for moving in a direction of far-reaching compromise.[43]

In February 1965, U.S. military escalation in Vietnam made it clear that Johnson's 1964 campaign promise of "no wider war," when he ran against Goldwater, was a lie. In the name of fighting Communism, the Johnson administration committed itself to a brutal war to maintain an unpopular military dictatorship. This was followed by a massive military invasion by U.S. Marines in the Dominican Republic, in support of a military junta about to be overthrown by a popular insurgency, one that was attempting to put a democratically elected and militarily deposed Juan Bosch, a socialist-oriented radical, back into the presidency. This put Rustin's essay in a new light.

An influential polemic in the summer of 1965, by radical historian Staughton Lynd (who had coordinated the Freedom Schools during the Mississippi Freedom Summer project), lamented that Rustin had abandoned his long-held radicalism, asserting that "1) the coalition he advocates turns out to mean implicit acceptance of [Johnson] Administration foreign policy, to be a coalition with the marines; 2) the style of politics he advocates turns out to mean a kind of elitism . . . in which rank-and-file persons would cease to act on their own behalf and be . . . 'merely represented'" by Democratic Party politicians. The approach "subordinates foreign to domestic politics, which mutes criticism of American imperialism."[44]

Rustin's supporters, and Rustin himself, were incensed over the "coalition with the marines" accusation. Nor was it clear, in 1965 and even when the Freedom Budget was launched a year later, that the trajectory Lynd argued against was, in fact, the path Rustin would follow. It was still possible to align what the essay said with the radical elements remaining in Rustin's outlook, and also, as Martin Luther King Jr. was about to show, with open opposition to the Vietnam War. Indeed it seemed that Rustin himself was not far from taking that path, and from giving his "protest to politics" orientation that radical twist.

This is suggested in an article by Dave McReynolds in the June 18, 1965, issue of *New America*, pushing in the direction of "Militant Protest, Then Politics." McReynolds headed the War Resisters League, with which Rustin had been associated for many years, and he was working with Rustin's former mentor, A. J. Muste, to build opposition to the war. Rustin had spoken at an antiwar rally several days before, and McReynolds wrote: "Just now we need even more militant protest, as Rustin pointed out in his Madison Square Garden speech at the June 8 Vietnam Protest Rally. It was on that occasion that Rustin urged the peace movement to learn from the civil rights movement, and to 'get out of the public halls and into the public streets.'" McReynolds similarly called for the kind of mass protests that made the civil rights movement a powerful political force. "Let us carry it, finally, into the halls of the Pentagon, the State Department, and the White House—not as a polite gesture of radicalism that can be ignored, but as a force of hundreds and thousands of nonviolent but determined protestors who seek to jam the wheels of the military machine with their very bodies," he urged. "Let us seek to do this now—because such an effort, and only such an effort, will bring to life a radical politics able to cope with the Johnson Administration."[45]

As it turned out, there were elements among Freedom Budget endorsers and supporters whose inclinations went in the direction suggested by McReynolds, but there was a significant diversity, some of which suggested significant divergences in orientation.

Dubious Allies, Activist Projections

Left-wing critics of Rustin's "From Protest to Politics" essay have often overlooked the radical thrust of its underlying analysis. "The very decade which has witnessed the decline of legal Jim Crow has seen the rise of de facto segregation in our fundamental socioeconomic institutions," he argued. This fact called for a transition within the civil rights movement: "At issue, after all, is not civil rights, strictly speaking, but social and economic conditions." The many civil disorders in black urban ghettoes, he insisted, "were not race riots; they were outbursts of class aggression in a society where class and color definitions are converging disastrously." Adding that "we are moving into an era in which the natural functioning of the market does not by itself ensure for every man with will and ambition a place in the productive process," which affected the entire working class, not just black workers, Rustin argued that "the civil rights movement is evolving from a protest movement into a full-fledged social movement—an evolution calling its very name into question." The problems facing a majority of African Americans "are more deeply rooted in our socioeconomic order; they are the result of the total society's failure to meet not only the Negro's needs but human needs generally."[46]

Flowing from this, Rustin and other key architects of the Freedom Budget, as Norman Hill observed, advanced a primary focus on class. "The Freedom Budget would have undergirded the power of workers and the poor, it had a redistributive aspect, and it had revolutionary implications," Hill commented. Regardless of any formal endorsement, however, "the civil rights leaders [associated with such organizations as the NAACP and Urban League] had a problem in making the transition called for in 'From Protest to Politics.' The Freedom Budget raised the problems of race and class, combining them, and the old-line leaders had a problem with taking on the issue of class."[47]

In their outstanding survey of the African American struggle for civil and economic equality, Dona Cooper Hamilton and Charles V. Hamilton found that with the Freedom Budget, "for the first time in the history of the civil rights movement, a comprehensive and specific economic proposal had been put before the country, a proposal initiated by the movement itself." They added: "The Freedom Budget represented the civil rights movement's general consensus on basic goals and principles—if not on every projection and statistic." However, "many people doubtless signed the document out of respect for Randolph and not because they necessarily agreed with every item in it."[48]

One such endorser of the Freedom Budget was Whitney Young, the highly respected social worker who served as executive director of the National Urban League, often viewed as the most moderate and "respectable" of the major civil rights leaders. In supporting the budget, he commented that he himself had "a few years ago" called for a "domestic Marshall Plan," suggesting that the Freedom Budget was based on a similar principle, offering "a 'blueprint' for what must be done to eliminate poverty." And yet there was a fundamental difference between what Young had articulated previously and the underlying principle of the Freedom Budget. In his "Marshall Plan" speech during the March on Washington, he had called for the replacement of impoverished, overcrowded, unsafe ghettoes with "residential areas dispersed throughout our city . . . established training centers . . . high occupations commensurate with our skills . . . health and welfare centers . . . well-equipped integrated [educational] facilities throughout the city . . . newly opened areas in the parks and recreation centers." And as a close advisor to the Kennedy, Johnson, and even Nixon administrations (in ways that Randolph, Rustin and King would never be), he would powerfully influence policy along the lines of "the agenda that would change the American landscape for generations to come," as Charles Euchner put it, although his policies and programs were put into place piecemeal, not as part of a grand radical crusade as projected by the Freedom Budget's architects. But Euchner put his finger on another essential in Young's perspective: "As the civil rights debate advanced in 1963, Young became the leading voice for the most controversial solution to the race problem, this side of Malcolm X's call for separatism. Young wanted to guarantee blacks a quota of jobs, positions in schools and colleges and unions."[49]

The Hamiltons succinctly and clearly summed it up:

Young called for a "special effort" to help Negroes, denied for so many years. He believed that in order for Negroes to take advantage of the new opportunities being slowly opened to them, they needed "special" attention from the public and private sectors in the form of programs specifically targeted to increase their educational and job skills. He compared this approach to America's foreign aid Marshall Plan after World War II. This was necessary, he reasoned, to close the gap of deprivation between blacks and whites caused by decades of denial. He frequently talked of "correcting historical abuses. . . ."

In speeches and in his book *To Be Equal*, he suggested that "the best schools and the best teachers" be placed in Negro communities, and that jobs be provided preferentially to Negroes "where two equally qualified people apply" and especially if a company had never before hired Negroes. Without question, he was calling for "preferential" treatment, although he tried to suggest otherwise. He argued: "The nation should not be misled by sloganeers of dubious motivation who conjure up fright phantoms by waving trigger phrases such as 'preferential treatment,' 'reverse discrimination,' 'indemnification,' and 'reparation' before unsuspecting, unthinking, and uninformed Americans." . . .

Young attempted to show that if anything less than such a special, crash program was launched, there would be dire socioeconomic consequences.[50]

In stark contrast to this, Martin Luther King's approach, initially, was consistent with the underlying principle of the Freedom Budget. In responding to a 1964 proposal for "A Negro Bill of Rights," King argued: "It is my opinion that many white workers whose economic condition is not too far removed from the economic condition of his black brother, will find it difficult to accept a 'Negro Bill of Rights,' which seeks to give special consideration to the Negro in the context of unemployment, joblessness, etc. and does not take into sufficient account their plight (that of the white worker)."[51]

The issue was also aggressively taken up in the pages of *New America* by Tom Kahn. Referring to "the conservative nature of the National Urban League's philosophy," combining "urgent indignation" over racial inequalities with "an orientation toward the corporate structure," he quoted Young as saying that the Negro civil rights movement "differs from many revolutions inasmuch as it is an attempt by an underprivileged element of society not to change the fabric of that society, but to revolt into partnership with it." Kahn insisted that capitalist corporations are primarily committed to ensuring "soaring profits" rather than such human needs as decent jobs, public education, or decent housing for all. "Moreover, while expanding sections of the private economy may be willing to apply preferential treatment in acquisition and training of skilled personnel, even they are not concerned with creating new jobs." Kahn observed that "the demand for labor in the total private economy has remained virtually static in recent years," and argued that a struggle for full employment ensured by the government was necessary. Preferential treatment for African Americans would not solve the problems facing the majority. "Used functionally in negotiations with certain employers, preferential treatment can be advantageous," he conceded, but "broadcast as a central slogan, it drives a wedge between Negroes and those whites who stand most to gain from a political alliance for economic reform." He added:

> The technological revolution, it has been said, is creating two Americas— "the affluent society" and "the other America." It is also dividing the Negro community, offering glittering rewards to the cream of the crop. The Negro technocrat may emerge as a social type—a new perch on a narrow reality (but a reality all the same). Meanwhile the majority of Negroes—trapped in ghettoes, undereducated, unemployed, underemployed or unemployable— will be subject to new disintegrative forces, to new forms of racial-economic separation and alienation.

Kahn insisted (in 1964, before the appearance of the Freedom Budget) on the need for a master plan to provide full employment, jobs for all that would eliminate poverty. "Preferential treatment yes—but as A. Philip Randolph declares, preferential treatment for all the unemployed and poor, the sick, the aged, the disadvantaged youth—for the other America."[52]

Hyman Bookbinder, an old socialist friend of Randolph and Rustin, was himself dubious about the Freedom Budget concept. A strong partisan of President Johnson's policies, and an experienced lobbyist with the American Jewish Committee, he saw the Freedom Budget as "utterly unrealistic," for reasons elaborated by historian Daniel Levine. Rustin "showed no appreciation for the political process and for what was politically possible. Even with good ideas, simply presenting them in one hundred thousand copies distributed all around the country is not the way to proceed toward any political goal." A similar point of view was advanced by AFL-CIO legislative director Andrew Biemiller, who had been a key force in advancing the Civil Rights Bill of 1964, but who had no enthusiasm for introducing the Freedom Budget as a bill to Congress. "He was interested in pushing this or that aspect of labor's or AFL-CIO's economic program," Norman Hill noted later. "But he never really focused on introducing something as comprehensive as the Freedom Budget." Hill added that "aspects of the AFL-CIO's program" could actually "be subsumed under the Freedom Budget," but standard "practical politics" would involve smashing the budget's proposals into distinct bits and pieces of legislation, to be debated, amended, haggled over, and passed in diluted form or defeated, piece by piece.[53]

In his introduction to the Freedom Budget, A. Philip Randolph had insisted, in contrast, that "the abolition of poverty ... can be accomplished only through action which embraces the totality of the victims of poverty, neglect, and injustice. Nor can the goals be won by segments; or *ad hoc* programs alone; there is need for welding such *programs* into a unified and consistent *program*." He was sharply critical of "the pessimists and the tokenists" who "counsel 'gradualism' and those who urge piecemeal and haphazard remedies for deep-rooted and persistent evils." Randolph's response: "Here again, 'gradualism' becomes an excuse for not beginning or for beginning on a base too small to support the task, and for not setting goals; and the scattered, fragmented remedies, lacking priorities and coordination, often work at cross purposes."[54]

It was the central component of full employment and the elimination of poverty that was seen by practical politicians as being "utterly unrealistic." Senator Joseph Clark—a pro-civil rights, pro-labor liberal Democrat from Pennsylvania, who co-chaired a Senate subcommittee with Jacob Javits (a pro-civil rights, pro-labor liberal Republican from New York)—politely listened to the testimony of a strong Freedom Budget endorser, Dr. Arthur Logan, then made the point quite bluntly:

> Let me say, Dr. Logan, that I have had a look at the [Freedom] Budget and I think in the best of all possible worlds, it would be a wonderful thing, but as a matter of pragmatic politics, it seems to me utterly unrealistic. . . . I don't want to prolong the argument, but we do, after all, live in a democracy and in the end Senator Javits and I have to represent our constituents and I don't think our constituents are anywhere near ready for that budget.[55]

This kind of response makes sense on several levels. The constituents of Clark and Javits included many people: poor blacks and whites and Hispanics, union members of various racial and ethnic backgrounds, owners of small businesses, professionals, corporate managers and their numerous assistants, super-rich and powerful families such as the Mellons and the Rockefellers, and more. Most of them had not heard of the Freedom Budget and therefore had no opinions about it. This was a constituency that certainly was not ready for the Freedom Budget; they would have to hear about it and be won over to support it. Segments of the constituency, especially among the rich and the powerful, would never "be ready" for the Freedom Budget. They would oppose it and fight it, even some who had been ready for the elimination of the South's Jim Crow system (as discussed in chapter 2). Some among the powerful elite would prove to be more open to proposals of Whitney Young, which did not raise questions about their economic power. Quite plausibly, other segments of the constituency of Senators Clark and Javits, maybe a very substantial majority, might "be ready" for the Freedom Budget, and perhaps with great enthusiasm, if an energetic campaign was organized to win them over.

Some supporters of the Freedom Budget envisioned such a campaign when they signed on to it. A. Philip Randolph spoke of restructuring and revitalizing the old civil rights coalition in order to "transform the civil rights revolution into a social revolution." Leon Keyserling warned: "We must get away from the idea that the Freedom Budget can be enacted under the present conception of consensus." Paul Feldman, editor of *New America*, explained that "the [Lyndon] Johnson consensus which extends from Walter Reuther to Henry Ford is breaking down and dividing over economic questions such as wage guidelines and tax policy." Even as the Freedom Budget was being finalized, Michael Harrington, in an article that foretold its coming, had commented that "the financing of a massive war on poverty will require change and struggle in the United States," pushing "beyond the Johnson consensus and the reactionary Keynesianist subsidizing of the very rich."[56]

Martin Luther King Jr. projected plans for national demonstrations to support the Freedom Budget. Courtland Cox of SNCC, speaking of the laboring poor of the South, asserted that "the Freedom Budget is something that we can begin to look at and use because the present poverty program is so inadequate." His perspective was to see that "the people who are poor get behind the budget and say not, 'Please give us a handout,' but make it impossible for the country to function if it does not put the Freedom Budget into action."[57]

These activist projections were entirely in the spirit of the underlying thrust of the Freedom Budget orientation and of "The Strategy," the general civil rights strategy we have examined. But we have seen that there was an ambiguity, illustrated in slightly divergent expressions of "The Strategy" in 1963–64 among Max Shachtman and his co-thinkers, on whether its keystone was mass action or the Democratic Party. One year later, we saw that this played itself out during the 1964 challenge to the Democratic Party convention posed by the Mississippi Freedom Democratic Party. For many, the realignment/Democratic Party perspective became central to "The Strategy." In 1965, Tom Kahn was writing that "those democratic socialists . . . who have this view considered this strategy in the context of hastening the tendency toward fundamental political realignment in America," adding: "In this process, they believe, the Democratic Party can be transformed from an amalgam of New Dealers and Slave Dealers into the political instrument of the labor, civil rights, and peace movements—and of the poor."[58]

The notion that such a coalition would take control of the Democratic Party was utopian, according to a longtime comrade of Shachtman who broke with him around the realignment strategy, Julius Jacobson. "No such coalition is going to capture the Democratic Party," he commented. "The Democratic Party has its own coalition, a network of hardened political machines which is not going to permit itself to be taken over by the Freedom Budget visionaries or permit the Party to be torn apart, with its consequent loss of political power, prestige, patronage, and so on."[59]

At the very heart of the realignment conception was the emphasis on the necessity of a working-class orientation, and of the alliance of the civil rights and labor movements. Here too an ambiguity was creeping in.

We have seen, in Bayard Rustin's comments about AFL-CIO president George Meany at the Socialist Party's 1963 civil rights conference, cited in the previous chapter, that he was a relatively conservative labor bureaucrat and that the key to the alliance would be in black and white workers, civil rights and labor activists, joining in struggles "in the streets." In late 1963, however, Rustin's comrade Tom Kahn was expressing second thoughts about that in a letter to Rachelle Horowitz: "I can't quite seem to drive out the negative that characterizes my worldview these days. Everything points me more and more into an alliance with George Meany against intellectuals and radical moralists."[60]

Related to this is Michael Harrington's description of his and his comrades' evolving point of view. "We were perfectly aware that most Left theorists had written off Meany and his friends as conservatives and that some even regarded Reuther as too moderate," he recalled. "But we had determined to be truly radical: to involve ourselves with the leaders elected by the workers themselves, rather than with those imaginary figures who should have been leading a revolutionary proletariat that did not exist." Max Shachtman's biographer has traced this view to "Shachtman's version of Marxist orthodoxy," noting that he "saw the AFL-CIO apparatus as the incarnation of the U.S. working class."[61]

As this comment from Shachtman's biographer suggests, the actual working class did not elect George Meany to be the president of the AFL-CIO. The great majority of workers did not even belong to that labor federation or any union. Even those who were members of unions affiliated to the AFL-CIO did not elect Meany. He was selected through consultations and negotiations by key figures in bureaucratic machines running unions (in many cases not especially democratically) that belonged to the AFL-CIO and was elected every few years (with no opposition) by delegates attending a succession of AFL-CIO conventions. Meany and those around him had a distinctive ideology, which they were not inclined to debate democratically within the AFL-CIO, and which they sought to impose on the labor movement as a whole. "I stand for the profit system," Meany emphasized when he became the AFL-CIO's first president. "I believe in the free enterprise system completely. I believe in the return on capital investment. I believe in management's right to manage." Almost two decades later he was proudly explaining: "Our members are basically Americans. They basically believe in the American system, and maybe they have a greater stake in the system now than they had fifteen or twenty years ago, because under the system and under our trade union policy, they have become 'middle class.' They have a greater stake."[62]

Commitments on the part of key Freedom Budget partisans to the George Meany wing of the labor movement, and to the George Meany current in the Democratic Party, would pull them further away from the kind of activist proposals advanced by such partisans as Martin Luther King Jr. and members of SNCC, which had been consistent with what Bayard Rustin was saying up through the spring of 1964.

Socialists Debate Freedom Budget

Such developments as these helped generate a debate in the Socialist Party itself, which splashed onto the pages of *New America*, regarding the value of the Freedom Budget. The debate reflected festering political differences and a series of debilitating fissures that had been afflicting the Socialist Party at least since 1963 and would undermine the ability of the organization to play a significant role in Freedom Budget efforts.

Rick Congress, Secretary of the Chicago Local of the Socialist Party, argued that the Freedom Budget was "a hodge-podge of Keynesian palliatives that has been transformed into a revolutionary radical program" by "our realignment comrades." Terming it "the extension of welfare state capitalism à la Keyserling and Keynes," Congress pointed out that the Freedom Budget admitted in its own text that "this is no socialist document, there will be no infringement on property ownership, no hard times for the corporate rich, no tampering with the arms budget or the war in Vietnam." Adding that "the Budget won't be adopted and won't even get a hearing of any length in . . . [the U.S.] Congress," he agreed that "it can facilitate propagandizing and forging an alliance" of labor, civil rights, progressive, religious, and socialist forces, concluding that "the fight for the Freedom Budget is the only good part of the budget from the radical point of view."[63]

New America editor Paul Feldman challenged Congress's point that the Freedom Budget was bad except as a device to forge alliances and make propaganda in the fight for it: "If one believes that, how can one urge others to support it? I couldn't." He went on to insist: "If the Freedom Budget is implemented, and of course that won't happen without major social struggle, and certainly not without significant changes in the power structure, it will raise the living standards and improve the social conditions of millions of Americans at the bottom of the economic ladder." But it went beyond this, he insisted:

> Just as important for socialists, the Freedom Budget can bring these exploited millions into the struggle for their social and economic freedom. It is the continuation of the "unfinished revolution" sparked by the March on Washington for Jobs and Freedom which first tentatively brought into existence the coalition of labor, Negroes, liberals and other progressive middle-class elements, passed two major civil rights bills, and first raised the issue of poverty. The Freedom Budget is attempting to reunite these forces and bring into the coalition the large majority of black and white poor who have not yet been organized behind a more fundamental economic program. This will be another major step toward building a majority movement of the democratic left that could take power in its own name. Only these forces can provide the social base for socialism.

Admitting that the Freedom Budget "is not a battle-cry for a frontal assault on the Military-Industrial Complex," he argued that "the dynamics of the movement that will grow around this program will be in that direction," asking: "Can anyone believe that this will not lead to a major political struggle between those who call for 'Guns over Butter, higher corporate profits,' and those who demand that 'the poor not pay for the war' and that programs for their benefit be sharply increased?" Regarding the charge of "Keynesian palliatives," he asserted that "Keynesian economic theory is neutral and only means government intervention in the economy." This poses the key question of politics: "How the government intervenes and to whose benefit is determined not by economic theory but by the nature, relative strength, and consciousness of political forces."

Feldman added that building an action-oriented mass movement "should take priority over and is in fact a precondition for any effective electoral strategy. (In this regard, A. Philip Randolph opposes working within the major parties, while Norman Thomas and Bayard Rustin favor a realignment strategy.)" He urged unity among Socialist Party comrades and others, "subordinating our differences over the question of electoral action to this larger and more meaningful task." He insisted that "a strong movement built around the Freedom Budget can throw down a serious challenge to both major parties, which is what we all want to do."

It is especially instructive to consider Feldman's view on how such radical mass struggle was important to the Socialist Party and how, in turn, the Socialist Party was important to the struggle (suggesting the importance of *cadre* discussed in chapter 3):

> It is only through such work that the Socialist Party can "reassert its lost position as the center of progressive democratic opposition to the power structure"—a position it deserves.[64] But we cannot do this merely by holding aloft a banner inscribed by our uniqueness; a transitional program is required, as masses cannot be organized around rhetorical flourishes against "the establishment." No socialists who have been active in mass movements, which are at times confused programmatically and disoriented, can fail to recognize the importance of the Socialist Party and just how precious it is to every democratic socialist activist. The tragedy, and our dilemma, has been that the Socialist Party has been so small. But we need a concrete perspective for growth in membership and influence.[65]

Congress was not won over. Quoting from Marx that the state is "the executive committee of the ruling class" and adding that "the power of the ruling class [is] anchored in the huge corporation," he insisted that "given a chance, the Government will always favor the corporate rich." Related to this, he argued that Keynesianism is not neutral but is "a device designed to stabilize a capitalist economy," and pointedly commented:

> The argument between those who favor government intervention which aids the rich and the military-industrial complex and those who wish to bend it toward social welfare spending, is really a dispute between two types of capitalist politicians—the corporate conservative and the corporate liberal, with some civil rights and labor leaders scrapping about the heels of the corporate liberal imagining that they are in there with "the movers and shakers."

He also insisted that "the Budget fails to attack the roots of poverty and tacitly supports the war in Vietnam." The Vietnam War was obviously a more central issue for him than it seemed to be for Feldman. (Saying that "the poor should not pay for the war," and referring to the war as "tragic" and as something that "should end" is not the same as calling for *U.S. withdrawal from Vietnam*, which Feldman and those sharing his perspective did not do.) Congress elaborated:

> The question of the war in Vietnam is important. I need not recount the horrors of the war for the Vietnamese people, or embark on a discourse on how the war pollutes the politics of the U.S. But for the sake of the Freedom Budget supporters, a certain point must be made. The Budget is supposed to be financed by the yearly growth rate dividend of the Gross National Product. Where is that dividend going at present? It is being used to pay for the war in Vietnam. If the Budget is to be implemented, its supporters have to attack the war head-on. Its very life depends upon rechanneling the growth rate dividend being used for the war. Dr. Martin Luther King recognized this when he declared at the March 24 rally to end the war in Vietnam, in Chicago, that the war must be stopped in order that domestic welfare programs may be expanded.[66]

It is intriguing to note that there are convergent elements in both Congress's and Feldman's arguments suggesting how the Freedom Budget could have been advanced as a radical campaign consistent with the way the Martin Luther King and SNCC's Courtland Cox were urging, and consistent as well with some of the more radical rhetoric employed by Rustin and Randolph, suggesting a revolutionary variant of the Freedom Budget. At the same time, the critical edge of Congress's remarks, and certain aspects of Feldman's (on the "neutral" quality of Keynesianism and the avoidance of a clear position on Vietnam), suggested what the reformist variant might be. The question of Vietnam was certainly a strong point in Congress's critique and merits greater attention.[67]

Guns and Butter—and Vietnam

"In the past two or three weeks, the euphoria which had been evoked by the passage of so many 'Great Society' programs has begun to dissipate," wrote Michael Harrington in the December 18, 1965, issue of *New America.* "The escalation of the war in Vietnam has led reactionaries and even some moderates to argue that there is now a choice between guns or butter." Commenting on the imminent presentation of the Freedom Budget by A. Philip Randolph and others (actually it would not appear for another ten months), he continued: "There are two aspects to the guns or butter question. Can the United States fight a hot war in Vietnam and a social war on the home front with its present resources? That is an economic issue. But then, even if such a two-front strategy were possible in an economic sense, is it politically feasible?"

Harington's answer went like this: "It seems clear to me that the American economy could provide the funds for the tragic war in Vietnam and for the stepped-up war on poverty. . . . Financing both wars . . . would require the reimposition of some taxes on the rich, i.e., the breakup of the Johnson consensus. But this neither the President nor the men of wealth are currently willing to do." The Freedom Budget would therefore require a massive political struggle on the part of civil rights, labor, religious, liberal, and radical activist forces. Harrington's lament over the next two years can be summarized in the headlines of two reviews of President Johnson's 1966 and 1967 proposed Federal Budget: "LBJ Budget: Not Enough Butter" and "LBJ Budget: Guns Over Butter."[68]

In her 1997 survey of policies and proposals regarding the urban poor, Helene Slessarov has mistakenly tagged the Freedom Budget as having "a strong pro-war stance," and utilizing a 1987 interview she conducted with liberal lawyer Joseph Rauh, quotes him as saying that the Freedom Budget "was a fake. . . . It was an effort to make the Vietnam War look good. . . . All this period, Bayard was fighting against King talking against the Vietnam War. . . . As an agent of the labor movement, they [apparently Rustin and his co-thinkers] were trying to stop King."[69] Among the difficulties with this interpretation are: (1) twenty years earlier, Rauh and the organization he headed, Americans for Democratic Action, were endorsers and active supporters of the Freedom Budget; (2) as we have seen, King himself was a very strong supporter of the Freedom Budget; (3) as we will note, the Freedom Budget studiously avoided taking a position on the Vietnam War, one way or the other; (4) Rustin did not oppose King taking a position against the Vietnam War.[70]

Ossie Davis and Ruby Dee, early opponents of the U.S. war in Vietnam, were among the endorsers of the Freedom Budget. Davis later summed up how he viewed the situation:

> A. Phillip Randolph drew up a Freedom Budget. It called for government to make a modest investment: $10 billion a year for a period of ten years for a jobs program—all in the spirit of the President's War on Poverty. Randolph showed him how to have his war against the Vietcong in Asia and the one against poverty here at home. But Lyndon never responded to the proposal.
>
> The black leaders felt that Lyndon, though a man with good intentions, had become hooked on the war in Vietnam, and that the victory he so eagerly sought was getting further away every day. Still, they had no jobs to carry back to their burning cities, so all they could do was wait.
>
> Martin [Luther King] waited, too, as long as he could, but he couldn't wait forever. Finally in 1967, he attacked the President's war policy. When Martin declared his own war against Johnson's war in Vietnam in a speech at Riverside Church in New York, the time of his own death was exactly one year away.[71]

In his introduction to the Freedom Budget, Randolph explained the matter in this way: "The Freedom Budget is not predicated on cutbacks in national defense nor on one or another position regarding the Vietnam conflict, which is basically a thorny question to be viewed in its own terms. The fundamental proposition is that the broad approaches of the 'Freedom Budget' can and should be implemented, whether or not an early termination of the Vietnam conflict is achieved, or even were there to be substantial increase in its economic and financial burdens."[72]

As we have seen, some critics see all of this as indicating that the initiators of the Freedom Budget, and the budget itself, were in support of the U.S. military budget and the war in Vietnam. This is a serious misperception, but it touches on certain realities that lend credence to the accusation. "You don't understand power, you don't understand power," Rustin said to a close friend in the War Resisters League, explaining his failure to take the lead in opposing the war. "You guys can't deliver a single pint of milk to the kids in Harlem, and Lyndon Johnson can." The FBI, which had been monitoring Rustin's phone calls for some time, reported that in talking with an "unidentified female," Rustin explained that he was "for peace, but he [did] not want to make any enemies over Vietnam and cloud the issue."[73]

Seymour Melman, a radical economist who had done much to critique the manner in which the military-industrial complex distorts the U.S. economy, was openly critical of the Freedom Budget's factoring military spending into its calculations, in his opinion making it "a war budget."[74] In response, Rustin explained:

One thing people say about the Freedom Budget is: "Well, Mr. Rustin, you've got a section in there in which you actually talk about Defense figures. How could you talk about Defense figures? Aren't you against the war in Vietnam?" *I most certainly am.* But my friends, if you're going to make a chart as to how money can be spent, and if that money is coming from the GNP, then you have to chart that on the basis of *all* the money the government gets and *all* the things they have to spend money for, to prove that they can take three-and-a-half percent of it for the Freedom Budget, which is precisely the figure we took in order to have the Marshall Plan to lift Europe. Well now if you're going to have the Marshall Plan, you can't say, well I'm going to [turn] my back to the fact that we're spending money on the military. We *had* to put those figures in to prove how all the money would be going to be spent. Therefore we had to estimate how much the Federal government was going to spend on military things. It wasn't that we *wanted* them to do it, but we had to make a sensible estimate.[75]

We have already noted that the Freedom Budget was developed under the leadership of people in and around the Socialist Party, particularly those influenced by Max Shachtman. The two most influential people in that organization were Shachtman and Norman Thomas. Both were vehemently anti-Communist and not sympathetic to the possibility of the two halves of Vietnam (the anti-Communist South and the Communist North) being united under a Communist regime. Both had even been inclined to support some aspects of U.S. foreign policy to nurture the artificial government of South Vietnam, which turned out to be an unpopular dictatorship incapable of surviving without U.S. support.[76]

By 1965 Thomas had become an outspoken critic of U.S. policy in Vietnam and called for an end to the U.S. war there. While disagreeing with Melman's attack on the Freedom Budget, he raised his own questions. "Long experience makes me pretty sure that we have small chance of persuading the American people in terms of their political psychology to finance the Freedom Budget and the war," he wrote to Keyserling in December of 1966. "This is no reason for you to stop, or for me to withhold support of the Freedom Budget. But it is a reason in my judgment for the kind of attack on the war and the military budget which I have been making for a long time." Interestingly, Keyserling indicated agreement with the substance of Thomas's points (adding somewhat vaguely: "I certainly do not agree with some aspects of our international policies"), but indicated that for tactical reasons he was inclined "to confine myself to domestic issues which are being so egregiously neglected."[77]

For Max Shachtman, however, the decision to keep the question of the Vietnam War separate from the Freedom Budget was not purely tactical. He favored a continuation of U.S. military involvement until independent, democratic forces in South Vietnam became strong enough to endure. He explained, in 1965, that the regime in South Vietnam, though corrupt and repressive, did "permit the possibility of people fighting for their rights. . . . In South Vietnam, you can organize a demonstration and get beat on the head. You can't do that much in North Vietnam." [78]

Thomas, on the other hand, was a major speaker at a mass antiwar rally in Washington on November 27, 1965, calling forthrightly for an end to the war and saying "I would rather see America save her soul than her face." Michael Harrington leaned toward Thomas's position, in 1965 writing that the war represented a "tragic, immoral, impossible American commitment to a land war in Asia," but he and some of his comrades straddled the issue until the early 1970s, in part to avoid coming into conflict with their mentor, Shachtman. It was difficult for some of his comrades to pull away from this "spellbinding luminary of backroom New York dialectics" (as historian Taylor Branch has put it) or to break from the charmed circle of his followers, protégés, and political kin. Branch tells us that "*Dissent* magazine founder Irving Howe made notes on Rustin's misery under group pressure not only to compromise his lifelong pacifist stance but speak favorably of the American war cause."[79]

Yet there are clear indications that Rustin, while never prepared to break from Shachtman, did not fully succumb to the pressure. He was among the earliest critics of the war, and never seems to have moved away from personal opposition to it. He avoided taking the position, however, of his earlier pacifist mentor, A. J. Muste, for immediate and unconditional U.S. withdrawal from Vietnam, but the thinking he shared in a 1967 interview was complex:

> I believe that the great majority of the American people may well want to get out of Vietnam. The question, therefore, is: How do we get out? And it's not enough to just keep saying, "Get out." I think that many groups in the peace movement fail to provide a step-by-step method by which the U.S. can get out and still have any national pride. Now it may be that they are right and I am wrong, and that there is no way to gradually educate people for a way out. I happen to believe, however, that there is, and therefore I call for negotiations. I call for sitting down with everyone involved. I call for the United States taking unilateral steps, to stop bombing in the North. Now if the nation does all that and the other side rejects it, my next step may be to take the Muste position.
>
> Now many people argue that you can have both guns and butter, and economically this is possible. Psychologically it is quite *im*possible. And therefore *perhaps* the greatest danger of the war in Vietnam—over and above that it lays waste to Vietnam—is that it is destroying us inwardly. It is destroying our spirit, it is destroying our imagination, it is destroying our ability to deal with domestic problems, and it is leading to riots in our streets by frustrated poor people . . . War has its own logic. It makes important everything that is ugly and destroys everything that is beautiful.[80]

Within the Socialist Party, regarding formal positions on Vietnam and other matters, Rustin appeared to be aligned with Shachtman and his followers. It seems likely, however, that his thinking was in harmony with that of his civil rights and labor mentor, A. Philip Randolph, who commented:

I have always been opposed to wars in principle—though as in the case of World War II, I am able to support those that are vital to the survival of our democratic institutions. Vietnam does not seem to me to be such a war. It represents, as far as I can see, no defense of our vital national interests. The moral commitment of the American government went beyond the reaches of liberal concern for our own problems in the sense that it committed an enormous and costly amount of the nation's resources to Vietnam—in terms of both money and human life. This, as I see it, is a great moral loss and a weakening of the country's moral fiber. As for Dr. King's decision to oppose the war, I cannot say I regard it as any great contradiction. He was, after all, one of the moral leaders of the country. Opposing wars and fighting for civil rights have natural and complementary motivations.[81]

We can see, then, that the Freedom Budget avoided taking any position, one way or the other, on the U.S. war in Vietnam and also on the matter of military spending. It assumed, in its calculations, a continuation of the Vietnam War as well as a rising level of military spending —although it didn't advocate either—in order to accommodate a broad Freedom Budget coalition that could accommodate both pro-war and antiwar forces. We have also noted that Rustin, who was, along with Randolph, personally opposed to the war, suggested that continuing the war while implementing the Freedom Budget was possible economically but not politically, and this insight highlights what turned out to be the Achilles' heel of the way that he proposed to build the struggle for the Freedom Budget.

5. THE POLITICAL ECONOMY
OF THE FREEDOM BUDGET

IN THIS BOOK we consider the Freedom Budget not simply historically, but as something that has relevance for our own time. In this chapter, we consider specifics of the Freedom Budget advanced in 1966, with reference to certain limitations and to its contemporary relevance. In chapter 9, we suggest ways in which it might be enhanced to become relevant to the specific circumstances we face in the early decades of the twenty-first century.

Conception and Construction of the Freedom Budget

The Freedom Budget was conceived and constructed in a straightforward manner. It operated on the principle that for the political freedoms demanded by the civil rights movement to be realized fully, there must also be freedom from economic want and insecurity. Those who suffer poverty, for example, cannot be free, even if they have the right to vote or if employers cannot discriminate against them because of their race. What the Freedom Budget does, therefore, is provide a way for the society to eliminate economic want and insecurity and thus make real the political freedoms that were the initial goals of the struggle for civil rights.

A budget consists of two parts: expenditures and revenues. Let's look at each one in turn. Obviously, the United States would have to spend money to eliminate poverty. Given that we have a capitalist economy, it would be foolish to imagine that private businesses might take it upon themselves to make a budget to eliminate poverty. There are economists who believe that the interactions of self-interested business owners, customers, and workers will generate an optimal social outcome. However, most do not, and very few did in the early 1960s. Leon Keyserling and the other talented economists who constructed the Freedom Budget understood that the market fails when it comes to inadequate incomes, unemployment, good schools, and a host of related social problems. Only governments can tackle such issues, and though state and local governments can lend a hand, only the federal government is equipped, through its powers to levy taxes, issue bonds, and print money, to solve them. Therefore, the Freedom Budget put the responsibility for ensuring that no one suffered from want and economic insecurity on the federal government. The budget envisioned was that of the national government.

The first step in solving a problem is to delineate its nature. The Freedom Budget states that the problem is poverty, and it specifies that its main goal is the elimination of poverty within ten years from the time the budget is implemented (for example, 1966 through 1975). It is poverty that denies economic freedom, without which political freedoms are meaningless. Two caveats were included in the overall charge to end poverty. First, the budget would pay special attention to the exceptionally poor economic conditions of black Americans. The legacy of slavery and nearly one hundred years of Jim Crow in the South had left black people in dire economic straits, with rates of poverty and every other measure of economic well-being much inferior to those of the white majority. Black men, women, and children were waging a valiant and heroic war to win political equality with whites, and so if the Freedom budget was to help all Americans be economically secure, it would have to devote extra resources to the black community. However, we should note that the Budget was aimed at all Americans. But if the nation committed itself to ending poverty, black people would benefit the most, since they were the poorest.

Second, the budget construed poverty broadly, to include not just those who lived below the meager "official" poverty income but also those living in a state of "deprivation," unable to achieve what was then called a "moderate but adequate" standard of living. The poverty level of income was first constructed by the federal government as part of the "war on poverty." The formula devised began with the Department of Agriculture's minimum food budget, one that embraced restrictive assumptions, such as people always shopping for the lowest price, that they could buy in bulk, and that they were efficient cooks.

As the Department of Agriculture admitted, this food budget was inadequate for maintaining good health. With the food budget established, and assuming that the poor spent one-third of their incomes on food, as was true in empirical studies of middle-income families in the 1950s, the poverty level of income was simply three times the minimum food budget. As observers noted at the time, the poverty income, like the minimum food budget, was wholly inadequate for an individual or a family to live decently. There were millions of persons whose incomes placed them above the poverty level of income but who still suffered deprivation. So these would have to be included in any budget aimed at eliminating poverty.[1]

What Factors Cause Poverty?

Those who constructed the budget next examined the factors that might cause poverty.[2] These would have to be dealt with directly through the budget, and each of them contained goals worthy of attainment, in and of themselves. Let us briefly review each one.

1. UNEMPLOYMENT. Poverty is directly linked to the lack of job opportunities. The drafters of the Freedom Budget linked the situation of at least 40 percent of the poor directly to unemployment. They also pointed out that the official unemployment rate excluded millions of men and women who were underemployed, most notably those part-time workers who wanted but could not find full-time employment and those who had become too discouraged to look for work. To be unemployed, we must actively try to find a job; if we do not, we are not counted as unemployed, even if we would gladly work if jobs were available.

Again, the budget placed the duty for achieving full employment on the federal government. First, the Employment Act of 1946[3] committed the government to promote full employment. And second, the federal government had the means at its disposal to drive the economy toward full employment. It could directly use its budget—its taxing, spending, and bond selling—to increase its own spending and stimulate that of the private sector of the economy. This spending would raise the demand for goods and services, which, in turn, would elicit a greater supply of output and more employment. The federal government could also hire workers directly, through any number of public works projects, as it did with the New Deal during the Great Depression.[4] The government could also increase total spending and employment in the economy through its monetary policy. The monetary authority (the Federal Reserve) has a variety of techniques it can employ to put downward pressure on interest rates, making it easier for businesses and consumers to borrow money. As borrowed funds are spent, total demand and employment would increase.

The Freedom Budget noted that programs aimed at reducing unemployment would be, in part, self-financing, because the greater number of people employed, the higher society's output and income and the greater the tax revenues of the federal government. Furthermore, full employment raises the sense of well-being of everyone; those newly employed have a heavy burden lifted and a better sense of self-worth, and those who fear unemployment feel more secure because they know that there is now a smaller chance they will become unemployed. These could raise productivity in the economy, also raising output, incomes, tax revenues, and employment. Another "self-financing" aspect of job creation, one not mentioned in the Budget, is the reduction in government spending for transfer payments necessitated by unemployment, such as unemployment compensation and welfare payments.

The increase in output caused by a reduction in unemployment was tied directly to what the Freedom budget called the "growth dividend." The more employment there is, the higher the growth rate of the economy, with growth augmented as well by the technological advances spurred on by prosperity. High growth rates would then provide the incomes needed to finance the war on poverty, and would also mean that those with higher incomes would not have to suffer a loss of income to pay for this war. This presumably would make the Freedom Budget palatable to most Americans.

2. LOW WAGES/INADEQUATE INCOMES. Even if the economy achieved full employment, there would be no guarantee that wages would be high enough to ensure freedom from want. If there was substantial unemployment, the situation would be all the worse, since at least when unemployment is low, labor markets are relatively "tight," with labor shortages beginning to appear in at least some markets, putting upward pressure on wages. However, wages might still not be high enough to eliminate want.

Those whose wages do not support a family at the official poverty level of income are called the working poor. Thus, to eliminate poverty, it would not be sufficient to have full employment. It would also be necessary for wages to be sufficiently high to guarantee that workers were free from want. How high this wage needed to be depends on how we define "want."

The Freedom Budget recommended two major ways to increase wages. First, it said that the federal government had to raise the minimum wage, and by implication, as many workers as possible had to be covered by it. Congress has the power, under the Fair Labor Standards Act, to increase the minimum wage, and it could index it to inflation or even to some measure of productivity. If the minimum wage is to reduce poverty, it should be high enough to allow a person earning it to support a family at above the poverty level of income. Second, the budget mentioned, but only in passing, that unions help workers achieve a living wage. It is surprising that more attention wasn't given to unions, given that thirty-five prominent labor leaders endorsed it and that economists had already done good empirical work showing a considerable impact of unions on wages, with this effect spilling over to those workers who were not in unions. Non-union employers often increased wages and provided benefits just to remain union-free. Unions also were strong supporters of minimum wage legislation and most of the other measures the budget proposed to end poverty. In connection with its remarks on unions, the budget demanded that right-to-work laws be struck down. These laws, then prevalent mainly in the South, make it illegal for an employer and a union to negotiate a union security clause in a collective bargaining agreement. Such a clause made it mandatory that every member of a bargaining unit join the union, thereby preventing workers from benefiting—"free riding"— from what the union won in negotiations without paying union dues. There is considerable evidence showing that states with right-to-work laws have higher incidences of poverty, as well as everything that goes along with poverty, from infant mortality to poorly performing schools and prison admissions.

The Freedom Budget recognized that decent wages alone cannot eradicate poverty. Millions of people either cannot or should not be wage laborers. In the mid-1960s, poverty was widespread among the elderly; about 30 percent of all those sixty-five and older had incomes below the poverty level. The budget recommended substantial increases in the funding of Social Security, so that older men and women could live without deprivation. Poverty also disproportionately afflicted households headed by women. The budget stated that many of these women did or would prefer to work for wages. These would be helped by a full-employment program, higher wages, more union-friendly laws, and readily available and subsidized daycare facilities. However, some women who head households should not work; they have young children, compounded in some cases by other household and labor market problems, such as lack of transportation or inadequate training. Such women must receive income, the budget argued, in the form of transfer payments from the federal government. This would necessitate expansion of the public assistance programs and the addition of new ones. Finally, those disabled, physically or mentally, must also be guaranteed income, so that they, too, can survive without deprivation.

In connection with adequate income, the Freedom Budget made a case for a guaranteed income. It isn't clear if the authors meant this to be applied only to those unable to work or to the unemployed. They made a point of stressing that if the federal government implemented a full-employment policy, with jobs available in public employment to guarantee adequate job openings, then the guaranteed income would apply to those who could not or should not work for wages. However, a more radical policy might be implied in the budget; that is, every adult, working or not, should receive a basic income. The level of security from want that this would provide would be a truly revolutionary act.

3. INSUFFICIENT AND SUBSTANDARD HOUSING. The Freedom Budget considered decent housing as both an end in itself and a means to eliminating poverty:

> The removal of the slum ghettoes which now infect our cities, and of substandard housing in other areas as well, is the top specialized priority in the "Freedom Budget," as distinguished from the broader objectives of getting rid of excess unemployment and poverty. It is an "end" priority because slum-living is an ultimate evil in itself, both a cause and by-product of poverty, and perhaps the main factor in what has been called the "self-perpetuating" nature of poverty. And it is a "means" priority, because rapid expansion of home construction, with the other outlays it would spark, can perhaps contribute about half of the 22–27 million new jobs we need by 1975.[5]

Needless to say, substandard housing plagues the poor more than any other income group. One reason why poor people are stuck in such housing is because it is unprofitable for private businesses to make better housing available to them. No private production occurs if no profit can be made, a fact amply shown during the Great Depression, when there was an obvious need for thousands of goods and services, and yet these did not get produced. Developers will not build apartments and houses unless they can sell them for a profit. Since poor people cannot pay a rent or price that generates a profit sufficient to satisfy the builders, landlords, and realtors, they will not get adequate housing. So, if everyone was to have decent housing, the federal government would have to provide it, through its own building projects, through rental and mortgage subsidies, or some combination of the two. State and local governments could participate in this, but as with every aspect of the Freedom Budget, the federal government, the government of all the people and the one directly responsible for the people's welfare, had to take the lead and provide most of the monies.

As with reducing unemployment, the provision of housing would be partly self-financing. Tens of thousands of workers would be employed to perform the many tasks required to plan, construct, landscape, furnish, lease, and sell housing units. These workers would spend their paychecks, and this spending would multiply through the economy, raising aggregate national income and returning some of the money laid out by the government, as tax revenues. In the sections of the budget on unemployment, the authors contended that funds would be needed to educate and train those who lacked various job skills. In the case of housing, a strong case can be made that unemployed and underemployed people could be taught to perform some of the labor needed to provide housing for the poor. The nation would gain productive citizens, who could continue to do various kinds of work that utilized the skills learned when federally funded housing projects were undertaken. During the Great Depression, the unemployed were put to work doing thousands of useful tasks. At Mount Hood in Oregon, the beautiful Timberline Lodge was built under the auspices of the Works Progress Administration and the Civilian Conservation Corps. Many unemployed workers lived and labored at Mount Hood, learning new skills from those who had them. Wood carving, furniture making, ironwork, sewing draperies and upholstery, weaving, and much more were done by workers trained to do such labor. The Freedom Budget noted that inferior housing does damage to the psyches of inhabitants. Similarly, long-term unemployment leaves its victims depressed and feeling inadequate. However, WPA officials saw that when unemployed men and women did skilled work, and moreover, produced something that they thought socially worthwhile, their spirits were uplifted. If those ill-housed helped build the places in which they would soon live, they would be doubly blessed, gaining marketable skills and making something of great social value.[6]

An interesting feature of the Freedom Budget was its grasp that poverty wasn't just a matter of the inner cities. Widespread rural poverty marked the United States as well. Housing woes afflicted the rural poor, and these had to be addressed. The same held true for poverty itself. Those who earned a living as small farmers or as laborers and shopkeepers in rural towns were often among our poorest citizens. When President Lyndon Johnson declared a "war on poverty" in his 1964 State of the Union Message, he no doubt was motivated in part by his own poor childhood in the Hill Country of West Texas.[7] Rural poverty is no less debilitating than that in what the Freedom Budget calls our "slum ghettoes." The Budget forcefully states:

> The extraordinary concentration of poverty in rural America, the economic disenfranchisement of a majority of our farm people, and the lag in public services in rural areas, even relative to the gross deficiencies in urban areas, call for both generalized and specialized approaches. Most of these point ultimately to Federal responsibility, both in the form of a drastically reconstructed farm policy and Federal equalization policies designed to help the poorer areas of the nation serve public needs. Underemployment is rife in agriculture. Hired farm workers, especially migratory, are among the most neglected and exploited in America.[8]

4. DEFICIENCIES IN HEALTH CARE, EDUCATION, AND TRAINING. Medicare was enacted just before the Freedom Budget was published. Given the utter inadequacy of health care for tens of millions of Americans in the mid-1960s, the passage of Medicare represented a radical change. It established a federally funded program by which those at least sixty-five years old have medical insurance. However, the Budget made the obvious point that only the elderly are covered by Medicare. What about everyone else? The budget said that national health insurance should be our goal. President Truman wanted universal national health care, as did many other political, labor, and civil rights leaders. The fight for this was abandoned, but it presumably was to be renewed through the Freedom budget. Unfortunately, no detail is provided as to how this would work; nor is any plan described to bring it into being.[9]

What the Budget did provide for was the building of hospitals and other health care facilities, the training of thousands of new doctors, dentists, and other health personnel, and a much stronger commitment to health research.

Like all of the other factors that contribute to poverty, poor health is not just a consequence of being poor. Once a person succumbs to illness or becomes disabled, that person is much less likely to leave the ranks of the poor. What is more, we know that unemployment directly affects health, both physical and mental. The poor are more likely to be unemployed, and lack of work will make a poor person more likely to be ill. The Freedom Budget attacked the widespread belief, fostered not just by certain politicians but scholars as well, that people are poor because they possess character defects. Instead the budget looked to structural factors. Whatever problems poor people face, they are best attacked by society making sure that everyone has decent employment, adequate income when not working or unable to work, good health care, superior housing, and the like. Then all the factors that combine and reinforce one another to create an institutional structure that makes poverty inevitable will be made irrelevant. Every person will be able to develop his or her capacities, without the fear and insecurity that haunt those without money.

Education looms large in poverty discourse in the United States. There are two forces at work here. First, the poor themselves have demanded access to education; one of the first things those who had been slaves did once free was build schools for their children. Working people were strong advocates of public schools. But second, economic and political elites maintained that proper education is necessary for economic growth and international competitiveness. A tension inevitably exists between these two forces, one that often reflects different notions of the nature of a democracy and what it means for people to be able to fully develop their capacities. However, the Freedom Budget did not deal with this issue. Instead it insisted that more schools be built, more teachers be trained, more aid given to college-age students, and more vocational and technical training and retraining be made available. Once again, a full-employment program would make educational investments effective. What point is there to educating youth if no jobs are available for them when they graduate?

5. REGRESSIVE FISCAL AND MONETARY POLICIES. In terms of overall economic policy, the federal government employs two basic tools—fiscal and monetary policy. Fiscal policy uses the government's budget—taxes, discretionary spending, and debt—to influence the level of the country's economic activity. For example, if the economy slumps, which could happen for any number of reasons, the federal government could increase its expenditures on goods and services and transfer payments. Some spending increases more or

less automatically, such as unemployment compensation payments, and these serve to stabilize consumer incomes and spending, preventing the economy from contracting by more than it otherwise would. Or the government could ask Congress to authorize more spending for infrastructure such as highways, bridges, and airports. If monies for this cannot be raised easily by new taxes, the government could simply sell bonds to pay for new spending. This is called deficit financing, and it will stimulate the economy because those who buy the bonds would most likely have saved the money anyway. As the spending generates output, employment, and income, tax revenues will rise automatically, providing funds to pay interest and principal on the bonds.

Another potential way to influence the macro economy is for the federal government to simply cut taxes. Personal and corporate income taxes are the most likely candidates for tax relief. As individuals face a lower tax burden, they may spend more money on consumer goods, which should cause increases in production and employment. When corporations pay less to the government, they may spend more on capital goods, similarly increasing production, incomes, and employment. The difficulty with tax cuts is twofold. First, if the economy contracts, consumers and businesses may become more pessimistic about the future, and simply giving them more spendable income will do nothing to ensure that that income will, in fact, be spent. If they are not, the expected expansion of the economy will not occur. This is not a problem when the government raises its own spending. A new or repaired highway represents an increase in total national output (an increase in the Gross Domestic Product or GDP), and the funds paid to contractors and employees will be spent, at least in part, on other goods and services, multiplying the initial rise in government spending. Even if the new spending is financed by taxation, the GDP will still increase, as long as the taxes are paid out of savings, that is, monies that were not going to be used to purchase newly produced goods and services in the first place.

A second problem with relying on tax reductions for economic growth relates to the question of who benefits from tax relief. President Kennedy put a broad tax reduction plan before Congress, and President Johnson secured its passage after Kennedy's assassination. The corporate tax rate was lowered considerably, as was the top marginal income tax rate, which affected the highest incomes. Given that most economists have concluded that the corporate income tax is ultimately borne mainly by the stockholders of the businesses, this meant that both tax cuts benefited most those who had the largest incomes. In other words, the tax cuts were regressive, as opposed to progressive, which would have been the case had the tax decreases been aimed at those with lower incomes. The result was that incomes became more unequal after the tax reductions than they were before. So, the tax cuts did little to reduce poverty.

The Freedom Budget noted the income inequality existing in the 1960s, with the richest 20 percent of income recipients allocated a share of the total economic pie several times larger than that received by the poorest 20 percent. Unless a direct attack on poverty and deprivation was mounted, most of the income generated by economic growth would accrue to the already well-to-do, leaving those at the bottom continuously worse off relative to those at the top.

The focus of the Freedom Budget, then, was unequivocally Keynesian in its macroeconomics. The key to eliminating economic want and to the realization of economic freedom was government spending, aimed directly at those most in need. If the spending was to be financed by taxation, the taxes had to be progressive. But if not enough money could be raised through taxation, the spending should be financed by debt—by bond sales. As the economy reached full employment, the government's budget would come naturally into balance as tax revenues grew.

The second economic weapon available to the federal government is monetary policy. The Federal Reserve, managed by a board of governors appointed by the president, dictates this policy, the aim of which is to make credit more or less available to businesses and consumers as conditions warrant. Historically, the Board of Governors has been closely allied with the nation's banking community. Financial institutions make great sums of money by issuing loans. As creditors, they fear rising prices, because inflation means that the money the borrowers pay back to them contains less purchasing than the money they loaned out. Given the fact that numerous members of the Board of Governors came directly from the financial sector of the economy or were allied with it, the Federal Reserve has often exhibited, as have central banks everywhere, a strong anti-inflation bias. When the economy "heats up" as a result of rapidly growing demand for goods and services, prices invariably rise. As long as production begins to catch up with demand, this is not a particularly serious problem. However, the Board of Governors has frequently tried to stop the inflation before the GDP reached its full employment level. It did this by using its various tools to put upward pressure on interest rates, which had the effect of making it more difficult for buyers of homes, cars, and capital goods to get credit. This then caused a diminution of spending, production, and employment. The Freedom Budget faulted the Federal Reserve for too often pursuing a high interest rate policy that stifled employment growth. If those stricken by poverty got employment as a consequence of ant-poverty efforts by the government, and then the monetary authorities forced credit to tighten, the resulting GDP contraction would have as its first casualties the very people these efforts were supposed to help. The Freedom Budget chastised the Federal Reserve for its high interest rate bias, and by implication argued that monetary policy should accommodate the expansionary fiscal policy necessary to do away with poverty. And in the end, poverty was such a crucial problem that it could not be sacrificed to an attack against inflation.

6. PROBLEMS IN LAND AND RESOURCE USE. The Freedom Budget criticized the ways in which the country was utilizing its farmland and the poverty of so many farmers. Land was being removed from agriculture, while people went without proper nutrition. Both the reduction in farmland and malnutrition were addressed in the budget, which demanded a better emergency food distribution system (extending food stamps, for example) and policies that would allow small farmers to keep their land and earn a decent living from it. The policy of paying farmers not to produce was to be abolished. Better social services needed to be available in rural communities, and farmers had to have easier access to bank credit.

With respect to natural resources, the budget noted shortages of water and power, as well as the maldistribution of these resources. At the same time, it noted that air and water were polluted, and recreation facilities were unavailable to those who needed them most. Resource conservation and allocation would generate jobs and income and provide for essential public needs. Unfortunately, the budget recommended the development of nuclear power to meet the country's energy needs.

Black Americans

The civil rights movement was led by black Americans, with the goal of righting the civil and criminal wrongs that had been done to them for so many years. The Freedom Budget, while aimed at all poor people—black, white, brown, red, and yellow—made note of the fact that black people would benefit most from the Freedom Budget, but only because they were economically at "the bottom of the barrel." They had the highest unemployment rates, the greatest incidence of poverty, the most substandard housing, the lowest incomes, the poorest health, the least access to social services, the most inferior education. Yet the role of black Americans in the Freedom Budget would not be as the main beneficiaries of the government expenditures if it were enacted. It would be as protagonists in the struggle to compel the society to make the budget a reality.

> There is an absolute analogy between the crusade for civil rights and liberties and the crusade which the "Freedom Budget" represents. This is because the "Freedom Budget" would achieve the freedom from economic want and oppression that is the necessary complement to freedom from political and civil oppression. And just as the progress thus far made on the front of civil rights and liberties has immeasurably strengthened the entire American political democracy, so will the "Freedom Budget" strengthen immeasurably our entire economic and social fabric.
>
> The Negro's greatest role on both of these fronts is not as a beneficiary, but rather as a galvanizing force. Out of his unique suffering, he has gone a long way toward awakening the American conscience with respect to civil rights and liberties. The debt which the whole nation owes him will be increased many times, as he helps to win the battle against unemployment and poverty and deprivation.[10]

During the strike of Memphis sanitation workers in 1967, which Martin Luther King Jr. was so eloquently supporting just before he was murdered, the picketers carried signs that read, "I Am a Man." The power of this phrase spoke to the demand by these black laborers, whom white America saw as the least of men, that they and all black men and women be treated as full human beings, equal to everyone else and as deserving of a good life as the rest of us. The subtext of the words spoke to the brutal hypocrisy of U.S. society. How could it claim to be free, a model for the world no less, when so many of its people were denied the most fundamental human rights? But by struggling so valiantly and with immense courage, black America compelled white America to make it part of the nation, with equal political rights. By doing so, our black brothers and sisters remade the country, made it more what the propaganda said it was, a land of free and equal people. The United States was made a better place because this exploited and oppressed minority made Americans look in the mirror and ask themselves who they really were. Similarly, the authors of the Freedom Budget said that black Americans should and would be in the forefront of the war to be fought for the right to be free from deprivation. And if they succeeded in achieving the goals set out in the Freedom Budget, they would have taken another step toward making the United States a model for the world.

The Growth Dividend

The Freedom Budget went to great lengths to say to those who were not poor that the programs envisioned in the budget would not reduce their standard of living. That is, the budget was based on the premise that its provisions would raise up those at the bottom without dragging down those at the top. No doubt this was meant to allay the fears of those with some wealth: this did not imply class warfare, it would not be a confiscatory plan, one aiming to expropriate the property of some ruling class. Instead the budget looked at the productive potential of the U.S. economy, what it could produce, if freed from unemployment, inefficient use of resources, and the harmful consequences of poverty. It contended that if the nation's GDP grew at a rate consistent with the elimination of these factors, the higher incomes deriving from such growth would more than pay for the Freedom Budget. This the budget termed the "growth dividend." Economic growth, in other words, would allow the country to eliminate poverty and deprivation without costing those who were not poor or deprived anything.

The assumptions made by the budget concerning the GDP growth rate were in two parts. The budget's time frame was ten years—1966 to 1975. Between 1965 and 1968, growth rates were assumed to be higher than the years between 1968 and 1975. This is because in the first years of the plan, unemployment would be falling, so that output would rise as formerly unproductive (in the sense of not producing goods and services) men and women were put to work. Once full employment was achieved and thereafter maintained, output would grow as a result of new (net) entrants into the labor force and increases in productivity. Allowing for some reduction in the length of the workweek, consistent with then current trends, the budget assumed an annual GDP growth rate of between 4.5 and 5.0 percent for the last six years and an unspecified higher rate for the first four years. These numbers assumed, therefore, that the economy would double in size in about fourteen to sixteen years.

These assumed growth rates reflected the economic conditions then prevalent in the United States. The Great Depression had ended around 1942, just twenty-three years before the Freedom Budget was completed. The Second World War showed what the U.S. economy could produce in a very short period of time and how rapidly mass unemployment could disappear. The war also demonstrated how the poorest people benefit the most when the economy prospers, as well as how groups previously discriminated against in employment, such as persons of color and women, could be absorbed into the labor force, performing jobs once denied them. Although the postwar years were marked by periodic recessions, the overall growth rates remained high. The mid-1960s were prosperous economic times for many white working-class Americans, and a general sense of optimism prevailed in what some economists termed the Golden Age of the American economy. We believe that most economists would say that the growth rates assumed in the Freedom Budget were not unrealistic and that the growth dividend would indeed have allowed for both its implementation and the achievement of its goals.

The War in Vietnam

Previous chapters have discussed the various viewpoints on the war in Vietnam among those whose work culminated in the Freedom Budget. In 1965, President Johnson greatly escalated the war, sending hundreds of thousands of troops in an attempt to defeat the Vietnamese liberation struggle. The war reduced unemployment in the United States, both because it absorbed some men who would have otherwise been unemployed and the federal government could spend billions of dollars for war materials, money that wound its way through the civilian economy, further stimulating spending. However, as the economy grew, inflationary pressures built, not least because the government printed money to finance a good deal of war-induced spending. Global financial imbalances grew as well. War spending began to glut the world with dollars, putting downward pressure on the dollar's exchange value. Given the existence of fixed international exchange rates, this pressure was hidden, but those who held the dollars were free to convert them into gold at the set price of $35 per ounce. However, this gave rise to the possibility of a run on U.S. gold reserves and the unraveling of the international monetary agreements made after the Second World War that had benefited the United States enormously.

As the direct and indirect economic consequences of the war made themselves felt, conservatives could argue with some plausibility that a war on poverty could not be waged while the war in Vietnam escalated and showed no signs of ending. Though not directly confronting the war, the Freedom Budget's assumptions about GDP growth rates allowed its authors to argue that after the ten years during which poverty was being eliminated, federal government spending on defense and defense-related areas would not have been cut so social welfare spending could increase. The budget, in effect, demonstrated that an economy as rich as that of the United States could afford to allocate sufficient funds for defense, including a war, and still end poverty.

In his Introduction to the Freedom Budget, A. Philip Randolph directly challenged conservative opponents. He reminded readers that they were hostile to President Johnson's Great Society programs before the escalation of the war. He might have added that they were opposed to the civil rights movement as well. Randolph also confronted other political forces, presumably on the left, who said that the war must be ended before the war on poverty could be effectively fought and won. He somewhat disingenuously said that poverty must be ended irrespective of what happens in Vietnam. He hoped the war would end "on safe and honorable terms."[11] This seems weak and somewhat lacking in courage. The brutality of the war, the criminal destruction of a peasant nation, the interminable war crimes, all reflected a side of America in conflict with the human liberation the Freedom Budget aimed to win. Whereas eradicating poverty and want should never be halted or slowed down, the war needed to be attacked with the same vehemence with which Randolph assailed the conservatives. Martin Luther King was doing this in the last year of his life.

The war in Vietnam did more than give conservatives a way to slow down the war on poverty. The U.S. government slaughtered people of color, just as it had destroyed the lives of so many of its own people of color. What is more, given who was sent to Vietnam, the war there was, in truth, a war against the U.S. poor. These facts should have been hammered home by all of those who supported the war on poverty. This would have brought new strength to those who vigorously opposed the war, and it could have helped to form a coalition of civil rights and antiwar activists that might have begun to transform U.S. politics. In addition, the war gave us tens of thousands of drug- and alcohol-addicted veterans, suffering physical and mental illnesses, greatly increasing the number of people who would need all the Great Society help they could get. Lyndon Johnson accomplished a great deal in his War on Poverty, more than any other president. It is not difficult to see the bind that civil rights leaders were in when it came to challenging the war. They needed Johnson's support. The Freedom Budget argued that ending poverty was a moral issue, and this was true. But the war was a moral issue as well. Randolph's and Bayard Rustin's failure to directly and consistently address the war was a moral failure. In the end, a country willing to do what the United States did in Vietnam was unlikely ever to fully embrace political and economic freedoms. Certainly not without a political movement with the same fervor and militancy of that waged on behalf of civil rights.

Taxation, the Construction of the Freedom Budget, and Preliminary Assessment

The growth dividend provided a way for the Freedom Budget to indicate that paying for it would not require any appreciable increase in taxes. In fact, tax revenues would rise so significantly that tax rates could be reduced and there would still be enough money to pay for all government spending, including every part of the Freedom Budget.

The budget made careful and sophisticated estimates of the scope of each problem it had to address, and then showed year by year how much money had to be allocated to fulfill the goal of eliminating poverty and deprivation. There is no reason to believe that the numbers in the budget were not reasonably accurate, nor that the nation did not have the means to do what the budget demanded.

The Freedom Budget received many endorsements, and it had friends in Congress. However, it was never made part of any bill before Congress, and so was never implemented. Still, those who constructed it, and those who fought for it, were part of a great movement in the United States for civil rights and economic freedom. President Kennedy favored civil rights, as did Johnson. Johnson forced important civil and economic rights bills through Congress. Yet neither would likely have done anything significant had not our brave freedom fighters been in the streets demanding action, insisting that the nation live up to what it claimed were its core values. The Freedom Budget must be seen in light of the deep and bitter struggles taking place before, during, and after it was conceived and written. Its framers were among those to whom we owe an enormous debt of gratitude. Because of what they did, changes were made and millions of people did enjoy better, more secure lives.

Evidence for this is not hard to find. Overall poverty rates fell dramatically between 1966 and 1975, as did those for black families and, most dramatically, for those sixty-five and older. More public housing was constructed, and public assistance transfers increased. It became more difficult for employers to discriminate on the basis of race. Social Security payments were more generous. These were substantial achievements, for which those who created the Freedom Budget share some of the credit. The Freedom Budget is barely remembered today. This is a pity; it deserved a better fate. Perhaps the time has come to resurrect it, for a new day, to see if it is relevant to the myriad economic problems we face now.

6. DEFEAT OF THE FREEDOM BUDGET

IF THE FREEDOM BUDGET had been successfully adopted and successfully implemented, the history of the United States and of the world would have been qualitatively different from the way things have turned out from the 1980s until now. Of course, conservative partisans of laissez-faire capitalism would argue that only bad things would have resulted, and they can certainly write reviews, articles, even books to explain why. But in our opinion, such people would have seemed at least as strange and marginal in our post–Freedom Budget world as they seemed to most Americans in the wake of Franklin Roosevelt's New Deal.

An additional question could be raised from the left: Is it possible for the Freedom Budget actually to be implemented successfully under capitalism? It seems clear that some of its advocates—certainly the veteran New Dealer Leon Keyserling—believed the answer was *yes*. If the answer is *no*, then either it is a fraud or it approximates what some revolutionary Marxists would call a *transitional demand*. This is a proposal for social-economic improvement that makes sense to a majority of people, which could consequently mobilize massive and militant support in the here-and-now, but which the capitalist system of the here-and-now cannot provide—a situation that could result in the revolutionary challenge to, and under the right conditions, the overturn of capitalism.[1] Aspects of this question will be touched on in this chapter and the next. Let us first consider, however, what the successful implementation of the Freedom Budget, whether under capitalism or socialism, would mean.

If the Freedom Budget had become a reality, most obviously poverty in the United States would have been abolished. Everyone who wanted a job would have had a job. Instead of economic inequality dramatically increasing over the past several decades, all people would be better off as the wealth gap narrowed and human needs were not sacrificed to amass super-profits for the top one percent. The very young, the elderly, and everyone in between would enjoy greater care, greater security, greater dignity.

There would be universal health care as a matter of right. Quality education and educational opportunities would have been available to all people as a matter of right, without students amassing exorbitant debt in the process. There would be decent housing for all, as a matter of right, and there would be no slums. Our social and economic infrastructure—roads, bridges, public transportation, parks, libraries, hospitals, etc.—would have been improved and expanded as never before. It is likely that growing environmental and ecological concerns and knowledge would have been incorporated into the rebuilding of our economy and society. Cultural opportunities, individual creativity, and personal development would be encouraged and greatly enhanced.

Crime would have significantly diminished with the elimination of so many of the things that cause crime. More than that, the criminal profiteering that has guided so much of U.S. foreign policy, amounting all too often to policies involving deceit and theft and killing, would have been powerfully challenged and dramatically diminished. Violence would be pushed back in many areas of life.

The immense power of big business corporations over our economic, political, social, and cultural life would be diminished, while the power of the great majority of the people (the 99 percent) over these things would be greatly enhanced (that is, there would be greater democracy), and the tremendous expansion of well-being and opportunities for all would mean an expansion and deepening of personal freedom.

Institutional racism would be gone—not just the Jim Crow system but also de facto racism, including the racial differentials historically and currently existing among the different racial groups in our society. Related to this, personal racism would be greatly diminished—attitudes and prejudices and practices caused by fear and want among ethnically and racially diverse peoples, and by different groups competing for scarce resources.

Despite differences, many of the more radical and the less radical partisans of the Freedom Budget were in agreement that the adoption and implementation of the budget would come about only through mass struggle, challenging and pushing back existing power structures and self-interested but influential defenders of an unjust and oppressive status quo. They agreed that such a struggle could be won only through a mass movement reaching out to win the support of, and effectively mobilize, the great majority of people—the working-class majority, trade unions, civil rights groups, those who oppose war and militarism, liberal-minded professionals, progressive religious constituencies, and the interracial poor—in a mighty coalition capable of bringing power to the people.

Martin Luther King Jr. once explained that "power at its best is love implementing the demands of justice, and justice at its best is power correcting everything that stands against love." He elaborated:

> Power properly understood is nothing but the ability to achieve purpose. It is the strength required to bring about political and economic change. Walter Reuther defined power one day. He said, "Power is the ability of a labor union like the UAW to make the most powerful corporation in the world, General Motors, say 'Yes' when it wants to say 'No.' That's power."[2]

Winning the Freedom Budget would have involved a dramatic power shift whose implications and dynamics would have gone far beyond the specific confines of the Freedom Budget itself. It would have represented a dramatic expansion of freedom, equality, and democracy, moving powerfully in the direction of socialist transformation, which is nothing but the realization of all that has been said here.

This did not happen. The Freedom Budget failed to gain traction. It was defeated, and the hopes it encompassed were destined to evaporate. History proceeded not as it might have, but as it actually did. In this chapter we will explore that defeat and its aftermath.

We first need to give attention to the two variants of the Freedom Budget conception already suggested—the reformist and the revolutionary. Then we need to consider a weakness contained in "The Strategy" of which the Freedom Budget was a component. We turn our attention as well to what strikes us as mistakes made by key players among the Freedom Budget's central advocates. These contributed to the diminishing cadres and the fragmenting of the coalition, which ensured that the Freedom Budget would go nowhere.

Reformist and Revolutionary Variants of the Freedom Budget

In chapter 4 we saw that neither A. Philip Randolph nor Bayard Rustin followed Martin Luther King's path of open, public, vigorous opposition to Lyndon B. Johnson's war policies in Vietnam. To do so would have cut them off from the close working relationship they had cultivated with such Democratic Party allies as President Johnson and Vice President Hubert Humphrey. It would have cut them off also from the staunchly pro-war president of the AFL-CIO, George Meany, whose organization was funding the A. Philip Randolph Institute and who they now saw as key to a labor–civil rights alliance. This alliance was at the heart of the broad coalition that they believed could make the Freedom Budget a reality.

There was, indeed, an organic bond that had developed with the AFL-CIO, reflected in the financial realities. Of the Randolph Institute's $85,000 estimated income from September 1966 through August 1967, $25,000 was to come from the AFL-CIO, another $25,000 came from the AFL-CIO's Industrial Union Department, and a significant amount of the rest came from "international and local unions." It is said that Meany, now feeling guilty about not supporting the March on Washington, wished to make up for that. "As you well know," Rustin acknowledged to Meany in the spring of 1967, "the growth and development of the Randolph Institute was made possible by the cooperation and financial support of the AFL-CIO." For his part, Meany believed this was "one of the best investments" the AFL-CIO ever made. His close aide Don Slaiman explained that the institute brought "the overwhelming majority of trade unions into contact with civil rights leaders." This was hardly a question of Randolph and Rustin being "bought off." Both men had consistently, over the years, shown themselves to be incapable of such a crass abandonment of their principles. As militant SNNC veteran Michael Thelwell explained it in regard to Rustin: "As a socialist, he always had a sense that the labor movement was a logical ally of the black movement. In intellectual terms, that was true. In terms of reality, that wasn't necessarily correct. But that was Rustin's consistent position, and there was nothing false about it."[3]

The "reality that wasn't necessarily correct" involved the institutional growing together of the elements of the civil rights movement gathered around Randolph and Rustin with the AFL-CIO as represented by George Meany. There was a logic to it, but also a de-radicalizing dynamic, a deepening difficulty in maintaining any meaningful political independence from the deeply pro-capitalist labor reformism that was essential to Meany's fundamental orientation.

King, on the other hand, articulated a perspective that had become far more radical than what his two erstwhile co-thinkers were now prepared to risk. As *New York Times* columnist and author Russell Baker commented, by 1967 King "had lost faith in the existing political system," and, in a new and meaningful sense, "had become a revolutionary."[4] We have noted that King's socialist inclinations had been there all along, but new developments gave these a sharper edge. In his 1967 statement on Vietnam, for example, he did more than review the details and history of U.S. involvement in Vietnam and delineate the values of nonviolence. His address also contained elements of a radical economic analysis suggesting that the dynamics of *capitalism* were inseparable from an essentially *imperialist* foreign policy:

> I say we must enter the struggle [against the Vietnam War], but I wish to go on now to say something even more disturbing. The war in Vietnam is but a symptom of a far deeper malady within the American spirit. . . .
>
> In 1957 a sensitive American official said that it seemed to him that our nation was on the wrong side of world revolution. . . . Increasingly, by choice or by accident, this is the role our nation has taken—the role of those who make peaceful revolution impossible by refusing to give up the privileges and the pleasures that come from the immense profits of overseas investment.
>
> I am convinced that if we are to get on the right side of the world revolution, we as a nation must undergo a radical revolution of values. We must rapidly begin the shift from a "thing-oriented" society to a "person-oriented" society. When machines and computers, profit motives and property rights are considered more important than people, the giant triplets of racism, materialism, and militarism are incapable of being conquered.
>
> . . . A true revolution of values will soon look uneasily on the glaring contrast of poverty and wealth. With righteous indignation it will look across the seas and see individual capitalists of the West investing huge sums of money in Asia, Africa and South America, only to take the profits with no concern for the social betterment of the countries, and say: "This is not just." It will look at our alliance with the landed gentry of Latin America and say: "This is not just." The Western arrogance of feeling that it has everything to teach others and nothing to learn from them is not just. A true

revolution of values will lay hands on the world order and say of war: "This way of settling differences is not just." . . . A nation that continues year after year to spend more money on military defense than on programs of social uplift is approaching spiritual death. . . .

These are revolutionary times. All over the globe men are revolting against old systems of exploitation and oppression and out of the wombs of a frail world new systems of justice and equality are being born. . . . Our only hope today lies in our ability to recapture the revolutionary spirit and go out into a sometimes hostile world declaring eternal hostility to poverty, racism, and militarism.[5]

What King lays out here is a conceptualization of the U.S. economic system consistent (making allowances for a somewhat different terminology) with such revolutionary socialist theorists as Karl Marx, Rosa Luxemburg, and Vladimir Ilyich Lenin—the latter two being especially significant given their analyses of imperialism.[6] This suggests a different political pathway from that followed by certain supporters of the Freedom Budget, including some with whom King shared a socialist outlook. As they were tending to move toward pragmatic compromises inconsistent with their radical rhetoric, King's analysis was less compromising. (It is intriguing to note a comment of Rustin's that seems to correspond to King's analysis, that a reordering of society would be required to change the policies that had brought on the war: "I believe it is absolutely imperative to go very deep. I do not accept the theory that a few people have dragged us into the war. I believe that our whole way of life has dragged us into the war.")[7]

It is by no means the case that the people whose ideas we have been discussing were aligning themselves in a self-conscious "revolutionary versus reformist" confrontation. Max Shachtman saw himself as "a lifelong revolutionary Marxist,"[8] and those who were "Shachtmanites" in the Socialist Party in that period were inclined to see him and themselves in a similar manner. Nor did King see himself as a revolutionary follower of Marx, Lenin, or Luxemburg. The revolutionary he followed, he insisted, was Jesus of Nazareth.[9] But Shachtman's late 1960s orientation inclines toward the *reformist* definition laid out in the first chapter of this book, while King's (inconsistently to be sure) corresponds more closely to the *revolutionary* definition.

As King was writing the words we examined here, Shachtman-follower Michael Harrington, one of the theoretically most sophisticated representatives of the Socialist Party, and one of those who helped develop the Freedom Budget, was laboring to complete a new book, *Toward a Democratic Left: A Radical Program for a New Majority*. He integrated into it a rich array of ideas, in this case blending discussion of the problems of capitalism and a socialist future, with perspectives about how to get there, which included campaigning for and implementing the Freedom Budget, and also advancing the realignment orientation that would make the Democratic Party a truly progressive instrument "of working people and the poor," merging "with the values of the college-educated and religiously inspired." He brightly informed his readers that "it is highly significant that the support of the Freedom Budget came from precisely those movements and institutions which form an incipient new domestic political majority in the United States."[10] The kind of perspective then being voiced by King, however, was being articulated by others in the growing U.S. left of that time, and it raised troubling questions Harrington felt a need to address (without referring to King).

"In one way or another, these people argue that America's very social structure impels it toward world-wide reaction," he observed. "It is said that there are domestic contradictions that must be exported or super-profits that have to be made." Making reference to the work *Imperialism: The Highest Stage of Capitalism*, Harrington added: "V. I. Lenin believed that capitalism's ability to resolve its own internal contradictions drove it to seek imperium over the entire world. This is one of the most influential ideas of the twentieth century."

But Harrington argued that though there was an element of truth to this view, things really didn't need to be that way. He concluded that "the United States is an almost-imperialism," that in fact "it has palpable, material reasons for shoring up the injustices of the international economy, but it is not inevitably forced to do so." This meant that civil rights, labor, and socialist activists could work through the Democratic Party (with its more or less progressive capitalist and non-capitalist forces), and through it work on gradually reforming away negative aspects of the domestic oppression and global injustice. One could do so without being hopelessly naïve and without betraying one's democratic or humanist or socialist ideals.

He wrote: "In summary, if America's imperialist heritage of economic interest, ideology and feelings of superiority were rooted in economic necessity, there would be no hope of overcoming it. Since it is not, there is some hope." By *hope*, it would seem that Harrington was actually referring to hope for the prospects of his reformist perspective, not simply hope for the future as such.

(Similarly, we can see that Martin Luther King Jr. seemed hopeful about the prospects of his own more revolutionary perspective.)[11]

In an effort to advance this "almost-imperialism" perspective, sociologist S. M. Miller, a contributor to *New America* and *Dissent*, wrote an essay with two colleagues, published in 1970, titled "Is Imperialism Necessary for the U.S. Economy?"—concluding, with Harrington, that it was not. They were challenging well-known Marxist economist Harry Magdoff, who had articulated and documented an updated variant of Lenin's theory.

"In sum, the Critics' analytical method is to separate out the various parts of the U.S. and world economy and to sever economics from politics," wrote Magdoff in response. "They arrive at the conclusion that by tinkering with some of the parts through political pressure, capitalism can be reformed so that it can live and grow without imperialism." He concluded:

> Our point of view is that the separate parts must be understood in the context of their interrelations with the social organism of world monopoly capitalism. Further, it is important to recognize the essential unity of the economics, politics, militarism, and culture of this social organism. We reach the conclusion that imperialism is the way of life of capitalism. Therefore the elimination of imperialism requires the overthrow of capitalism.[12]

This question is similar to another we raised in chapter 4 regarding poverty, and now we are left with a dual question: Are poverty and imperialism necessary and organic aspects of capitalism? If not, a truly reformist conception of the Freedom Budget, as outlined by Harrington, for example, is eminently reasonable. If they cannot actually be eliminated within a capitalist framework, however, then King's more revolutionary approach (shared with SNCC activists) makes more sense. Local organizing, mass actions, and other struggles outside of the electoral-party context, building toward popular mobilizations in favor of the Freedom Budget, would be an approach having profoundly revolutionary implications.

A Weak Point in "The Strategy"

The overarching civil rights strategy that guided King, Randolph, Rustin, and others posited a number of new factors coming together by the mid-twentieth century that would make the civil rights breakthrough possible. This was reviewed as "The Strategy" in chapter 2.

One of these factors involved the new political situation existing in the United States and in the Cold War world that (as we have noted) caused the powerful elites defending the global interests of U.S. capitalism to see racist segregation and the denial of voting rights to African Americans as practices the United States could ill afford. Such Republicans as Nelson Rockefeller and Earl Warren and Democrats such as the Kennedy brothers and Lyndon Johnson agreed that "Jim Crow must go" sooner or later, and perhaps the sooner the better.

It was not the case, however, that the more "liberal" element within the ruling circles would be prepared to lead the struggle for civil rights; they were definitely not revolutionaries. That would have to be the work of those who more or less were (Socialists, Communists, independent radicals, followers of a revolutionary Jesus, etc.), who would organize and help mobilize mass struggles to win more and more people to the civil rights cause and put increasing pressure on "the powers-that-be." This is what set the stage for what SNCC leader Bob Moses referred to as the "coalition of the bottom with the top."

The concern to get the balance right in relating to these allies at the top divided the civil rights movement, the more moderate elements being concerned to make friends and influence people in the upper circles, and to avoid ruffling feathers. But the more radical activist wing of the movement was more concerned with organizing an independent power base among those below (masses of urban and rural blacks, allies in the labor movement, progressive religious forces, idealistic students) for the purpose of applying the pressure necessary to make the political deals that could push through meaningful civil rights legislation. And as we have seen, within the activist wing differences developed about how to get the balance right.

But the actual civil rights victories that were won, which "didn't go far enough"—that is, didn't achieve the entire set of goals associated with "The Strategy"—but did end the Jim Crow system and helped to change consciousness and reality within the United States, were brought about by this dialectical dance, this interplay or "coalition of the bottom with the top."

According to "The Strategy," the gains in consciousness, support, and momentum in the struggle against Jim Crow would set the stage for the earnest implementation of the next stage of the "Strategy": the struggle for economic justice that would be necessary to complete the triumph over racism. The Freedom Budget and the projected mass campaign to win it were key elements of this second stage.

Although there was significant openness and support within the "ruling class" for the elimination of the Jim Crow system, this did not include an embrace of the movement's economic justice program. The second stage did not involve replacing capitalism with socialism. But these powerful economic and political figures were absolutely *not* inclined to be supportive of things that would challenge and diminish the power and prerogatives of big business corporations. They would not be sympathetic in any way to mass mobilizations involving an alliance of the labor and civil rights movements and assorted left-liberals, radicals, and socialists aimed at giving greater power to the diverse working-class majority (blue collar, white collar and professional, working poor and unemployed, etc.) at their expense.

The adoption of the Freedom Budget was a far more radical proposition than the adoption of the Civil Rights Act of 1964, and the Voting Rights Act of 1965, or the relatively limited adoption of policies to help overcome de facto segregation in workplaces and schools in the North, or President Johnson's "Great Society" Poverty Program. The partisans of the Freedom Budget, both the more radical and those who were less radical, were in open agreement that what they were pushing for went beyond any of this. One of A. Philip Randolph's biographers, Paula Pfeffer, has perceptively elaborated on the matter. "Neither Congress nor the administration was interested in the wholesale social changes the Freedom Budget would have entailed," she writes, noting that "Johnson never considered a restructuring of American society; rather, his anti-poverty measures were planned on the minimum scale his advisors thought necessary to defuse black protest."[13]

Therefore, while some friendly liberal politicians may have been prepared to give lip service to the virtues of the Freedom Budget's goals, the powerful forces that had entered into a symbiotic relationship with activists fighting against Jim Crow were not inclined to do so with those wanting to eliminate poverty in the United States in a ten-year period, or probably ever. From this standpoint, the Freedom Budget was doomed from the start, as some of the more pragmatic political friends of its partisans did not hesitate to point out. For that matter, one of Martin Luther King Jr.'s closest aides, Stanley Levison, seems to have been of the same opinion. This is especially interesting, since the FBI had tagged him as a Communist who, presumably, was manipulating

King in a subversive direction. Here is how one of King's biographers, David Garrow, summarizes Levison's views (as of 1965):

> Rustin's belief that a March on Washington-style coalition would support "a radical program" to "alter the social structure of America" was hopelessly naïve, Levison told King. "America today is not ready for a radical restructuring of its economy and social order. Not even the appeal of equality will weld all into one fighting unit around a program that disturbs their essentially moderate tendencies." Civil rights forces had to appreciate those clear limits on the achievable goals, for "the movement can head into a cul-de-sac if it can see no real progress without radical alteration of the nation."[14]

Levison was insistent that the civil rights movement might have a revolutionary quality in the South, but that in the North it was not revolutionary. "It is a reform movement not unlike the essentially reform movement of the trade union movement in the thirties," according to Levison. Garrow adds that "King pondered Levison's message." It would seem from all that followed that his own perspective was closer to that which Levison was warning against, although he seems to have remained truer to it, in the end, than Rustin himself.

We have seen that the orientation of the Freedom Budget partisans posited mass struggle and mass mobilization, incorporating the power of the labor movement in very substantial ways that had not been accomplished in the struggle against Jim Crow, and building an even broader interracial coalition to achieve its purposes. But for some this was more rhetorical than practical. The immense power of the owners, managers, publicists, and allies of the big business corporations encompassed the mass media and, one way or another, the bulk of the politicians in both major political parties, much of the governmental apparatus, and even influenced the leaderships and apparatuses of various institutions and organizations in civil society, certainly within the AFL-CIO and the moderate civil rights organizations. A number of people and groups from these milieus might be prepared to endorse the Freedom Budget, but to what extent would they be prepared to struggle, take risks, make sacrifices, and burn bridges with powerful elements in the ruling circles in order—perhaps—to force them to say *yes* when they were very powerfully determined to say *no*?

To win the Freedom Budget simply through reformist channels would not be possible. To build a movement capable of forcing through the Freedom

Budget suggested a revolutionary approach. This revolutionary understanding was reflected in the rhetoric that Randolph, King, Rustin, and their varied
co-thinkers utilized. But to translate such rhetoric into reality would be an
immense challenge. If they underestimated this (and it could be argued that
they did, based on what actually happened), that constitutes a serious weakness in "The Strategy."

Dilemmas, Mistakes, Twists of Fate

It is always possible to conclude that because things happened in a particular
way, they *had* to happen in that particular way. It was Destiny or God's Plan or
the Iron Laws of History. Similarly, if activists and organizers come up against
a problem or a set of problems, and they are defeated in the face of these, they
may be tempted to insist that those problems are the explanation for the failure,
pure and simple. But reality is rarely so pure and simple; it is open-ended, with
multiple sets of possibilities, some more positive than others. The possibilities
that are realized depends on what activists do or fail to do. Mistakes are inevitable, and we can learn from them, but sometimes an accumulation of mistakes
can close off possibilities. And sometimes an accumulation of unanticipated
factors can combine to open up new possibilities. If we hope to learn "lessons"
from the past that may be useful for the future, it makes sense to sift through
dilemmas, mistakes, and twists of fate with critical minds not overly weighed
down with a sense of "inevitabilities."

Aside from dilemmas arising from underestimating the difficulties of transitioning from the first phase (anti–Jim Crow) of "The Strategy" to the second
(economic justice), the central dilemma for the Freedom Budget organizers
was the U.S. war in Vietnam.

For all their insistence that the Freedom Budget could be implemented
despite huge military expenditures and a continuation of the Vietnam War,
Rustin himself noted in 1967 that "economically this is possible," but that
"psychologically it is quite *im*possible," and that "the greatest danger of the
war in Vietnam, over and above that it lays waste to Vietnam," was that perhaps "it is destroying us inwardly," including undermining chances for the
Freedom Budget. "Was it politically possible simultaneously to give a top priority to the tragedy in Indochina and the fight for a decent America?" asked
Michael Harrington in 1973. "I thought not and feel that history has proved

my case. When the war took over in Washington in 1965, the talent, the passion, the political power that had been mobilized for the fight against poverty were diverted to Vietnam."[15] Rachelle Horowitz has described the situation this way:

> The Freedom Budget met resistance from unexpected quarters. The war in Vietnam was escalating. Harrington and Kahn had hoped that hawks and doves could unite on domestic programs. But the doves in the peace movement and the hawks in the Johnson administration did not see it that way. The administration did not have to do much to kill the Freedom Budget; the left opposition did it for them. The conservatives argued that you couldn't have "guns and butter," and many doves said the call for butter had to wait until the guns had stopped.[16]

This echoes the polemics of some of Horowitz's Socialist Party comrades against antiwar protestors from 1966 through 1968 and beyond, but it is misleading. It is not clear that many opponents of the U.S. war in Vietnam were actually saying the struggle for economic justice would have to "wait" until the war was over. Most opponents actually shared the perspective expressed by Martin Luther King—that in order to struggle effectively and realistically for economic justice, one would also have to struggle against the U.S. war in Vietnam as well. This was the line articulated, for example, in the call of the Mobilization Committee to End the War in Vietnam, which organized the April 15, 1967, mass demonstration in which King participated:

> As the war cruelly destroys in Vietnam, so it denies hope to millions in the United States. The need for decent homes, quality education, jobs and fair employment are brushed aside. Our cities smother in smoke and grime, strangle in traffic. Our slums continue to rot. Streams and rivers are polluted and the very air we breathe is fouled. Our vast wealth could in a short time eliminate these ills. It goes instead to murder and destroy. . . . This national mobilization will affirm the will of the American people for peace in Vietnam and a new life for America and for all mankind.[17]

The Freedom Budget could easily have been integrated into, and made a centerpiece of, such antiwar mobilizations. But this would have created a serious problem for the variant of "The Strategy" pursued by Rustin, Kahn,

Harrington, Shachtman, and others. "In our socialist cadre we all agreed that we wanted hawks and doves to unite on domestic programs," Harrington later recounted. "The position of George Meany and the AFL-CIO Executive Council on the war was, I thought, wrong [that is, they were thoroughly in favor of it]. But that did not change the fact that Meany and the Federation were the most politically powerful and committed forces fighting for . . . social investments crucial to the Freedom Budget."[18] It is not clear, however, that if Harrington and his Socialist Party comrades integrated the Freedom Budget with an uncompromising antiwar struggle that Meany and the AFL-CIO would have stopped fighting for social programs crucial to the Freedom Budget. (This leaves aside the fact that Shachtman and at least some of his followers were, like Meany, absolutely opposed to an uncompromising struggle for a U.S. withdrawal from Vietnam.)

Of course, if the Freedom Budget and its partisans became too closely identified with opposition to the U.S. war in Vietnam, Meany would very likely have broken with them and the Freedom Budget. On the other hand, Meany himself hadn't actually endorsed the Freedom Budget, nor did he and the AFL-CIO actually fight for it or attempt to mobilize the actual labor movement, with its millions of members, in any struggle whatsoever for the Freedom Budget.[19] Harrington later noted that Shachtman and his co-thinkers believed "they were being utterly Marxist in lining up more and more uncritically with George Meany. After all, they were proving their loyalty to the existing working class (for they confused the working class with the AFL-CIO and the AFL-CIO with Meany)."[20]

Interviewed years later, Rustin aide Norman Hill suggested that Meany was genuinely representative of the actual labor movement, but he also emphasized a dilemma arising from a lack of commitment by Meany's AFL-CIO:

> The labor movement had an ambivalent attitude toward the Freedom Budget. The unions didn't incorporate it into their legislative program. [AFL-CIO lobbyist Andrew] Biemiller said it was too broad. Bayard responded we can mobilize public support and PR if you make it a central part of your program. We hoped to get the AFL-CIO to make it part of its primary legislative thrust. When that didn't happen, the whole movement kind of stalled.[21]

As Harrington went on to note, however, the AFL-CIO and its affiliates tended to be "rather monolithic," not vibrantly democratic expressions of an organized working class. He quoted a leader of the International Ladies Garment Workers Union, Gus Tyler, who was describing realities in his own union and in most of the labor movement: "Unions, by their very nature, are easily affected by the virus of bureaucratic rule. Unions tend to be monosocial (like a parish church); to be combative (like an army); to be administrative (like a government agency); to be market-oriented (like a business). Taken together, these traits form a strong natural bent in established unions toward the 'one-party' system."[22]

There were, however, unions and prominent union activists not conforming to this undemocratic model that were sympathetic to the ideas and ideals in the Freedom Budget, and also opposed to the U.S. war in Vietnam. Beyond this, there were a growing number AFL-CIO unions that were formally critical of the U.S. war in Vietnam, and a growing number of union members as well as unorganized workers who felt the same way. Helping to win more and more to an antiwar position could have been linked to helping win more and more support for the Freedom Budget. But this would have put Freedom Budget organizers at loggerheads with Meany and the AFL-CIO leadership. For those centrally involved in overseeing Freedom Budget efforts, this was not something they were prepared to do. Indeed, if the A. Philip Randolph Institute hoped to continue to receive AFL-CIO funding, it was an impossibility. Yet Meany's AFL-CIO could not deliver the goods when it came to the "mass struggle" that Freedom Budget partisans seemed to agree would be necessary for success. This was a highly bureaucratized organization that had become adept at high-level consultations with employers and powerful political figures, but was much more inclined toward lobbying and incremental deal making, and less inclined to attempt the serious organization, activation, and mobilization of workers for any kind of radical crusade.[23]

Masses of people were mobilized, however, in an increasingly huge antiwar movement. In addition to old-line pacifists and assorted left-wing organizations, there was the radical-activist wing of the civil rights movement, some of the more liberal and radical forces in the labor movement, progressive forces in the religious community, academics and students, passionate and idealistic young activists, many veterans and some active-duty government personnel, even some elected officials—year after year mobilizing tens of thousands, hundreds of thousands, ultimately millions. This approximated the kind of coalition that the organizers of the Freedom Budget had envisioned. Ultimately, in all the years of antiwar campaigning, a majority of the American people came to oppose the war. A number of issues were openly and aggressively linked to the central issue of opposing U.S. military involvement in Vietnam, including opposition to racism and demands for economic justice. But not the Freedom Budget.

This was a lost opportunity that cut both ways. With the ending of the war—if education and agitation around the goals of the Freedom Budget had been part of the antiwar effort—it is possible that the struggle for it would have been a live issue through the 1970s, giving focus to efforts of at least some of the diverse forces that had been part of the antiwar movement. "At some point the Vietnam War will be over," Rustin argued, "and unless the concepts expressed in the Freedom Budget are accepted, then the funds which will become available will be diverted to . . . sending rockets to Venus rather than to alleviate the social condition of the poor."[24]

Evaporating Cadres

Bayard Rustin, as perceptively and eloquently as anyone, addressed the issue of the youth radicalization and the rise of the "New Left" that swept the country in the second half of the1960s:

I think that the real phenomenon is that great numbers of young people are alienated. They do not really believe that a society which engages in the kind of war [waged] in Vietnam, a society which leaves so many millions of people poor, a society which will not give true equality to Negroes and other minorities, a society which will not make it possible for all people who want work to have it, they cannot *believe* in that society, and they cannot engage in wars which that society carries on. Now in their effort to reject the society, they must put something in its place, and they reject democracy as we know it and are making experiments in democracy, participatory democracy—meaning get people involved, get people talking, get people trying to make their own decisions. Now I think this is a good move.

"I don't necessarily come out where they come out because I think in large groups you cannot really make decisions in this manner," he added, explaining: "I don't know how you can get a thousand people in a room and have them talk until a decision is reached." But he concluded, "That's not the important thing. The important thing is that these young people are probing. I welcome this probing."[25]

Rustin hoped to make the Freedom Budget a rallying point that could some-how help channel the radicalizing energies he described. Masses of radicalizing young activists, if they were aware of the Freedom Budget at all, however, saw it as something being promoted by political elements that were distant from their own concerns and struggles, associated with pro-war liberals and hostile labor bureaucrats.

The cadres of SNCC became uninterested in what seemed to them to be tepid or at best irrelevant efforts of sectarian ex-comrades, onetime heroes and former mentors. Dissatisfaction with what some saw as the dilution of the 1963 March on Washington deepened into a sense of betrayal around the treatment of the Mississippi Freedom Democratic Party at the 1964 Democratic Party Convention, and disillusionment around the failure of people like Rustin to lead the way in opposing the Vietnam War. "He seems to have sold his soul completely to the Democratic Party," mused Julian Bond. The black nationalism associated with the ideas of Malcolm X, and the radicalism of various third world revolutionaries, became increasingly influential as they sought alternatives to an orientation that seemed to them to have become discredited. The key ideas Malcolm X advanced in his final year (in the words of editor-biographer George Breitman) "were black leadership of black people, summarized in the slogan 'black power'; self-defense; black pride and solidarity; identification with Africa and the colonial liberation struggles; intransigent opposition to the white capitalist power structure and its twin parties; opposition to all imperialist interventions against colored peoples; collaboration after their own unification with those militant whites who, following the example of John Brown, are ready to do more than talk about fighting racial injustice and social inequality." Most of this was unac-ceptable to Rustin and his co-thinkers.[26]

A similar decline of engagement with the Freedom Budget and "The Strategy" took place among activists in CORE. Norman Hill, who was close to Rustin, had been for some time a prominent staff member of CORE, serving as its Program Director. Yet throughout 1964 he found himself on a collision course with some of the others in the organization's leadership and member-ship. As with so much else, the situation was complex. Although CORE's longtime National Director, James Farmer, himself had come from a socialist background, he suspected that Hill and his wife, Velma, might be engaged in a Socialist Party maneuver to engineer the comeback of Bayard Rustin. Serving with Farmer in the Fellowship of Reconciliation, and joining with him and others to form CORE in 1942, Rustin had served as the organization's first Field Organizer under Farmer, and in 1947 helped to organize the Journey of Reconciliation, the very first of the "Freedom Rides." It was suspected that a plan was afoot to have Rustin replace Farmer. Hill denied the accusation. But at least as important in generating tensions within CORE were deeper differences regarding political direction.[27]

Hill had been arguing for an approach involving outreach to the black working class, especially the unemployed and the urban poor in the nation's ghettoes, with a less generalized, more judicious use of protest demonstrations and civil disobedience, and systematic focus on community organizing. He linked this to a call for moving away from CORE's traditional stand of remaining independent from partisan politics, arguing that it should be a CORE priority to organize and mobilize for the defeat of the conservative political wave represented by the presidential candidacy of Barry Goldwater. He outlined his orientation (which obviously reflected the variant of "The Strategy" that he, Rustin, and others had been guided by for some time) with a clarity that won him considerable support in the organization:[28]

First, the passage of the Civil Rights Act and, even earlier, the internal evolution of the movement have presaged a reallocation of energies away from "civil rights" as narrowly defined and toward the fundamental social and economic problems confronting the Negro—jobs, housing and schools.

As the movement's focus has shifted to these deeply rooted de facto forms of racism, three lessons have clearly emerged:

1. Fair employment which means full employment, decent housing, and quality integrated education are not merely racial goals but social goals. Their achievement requires a major overhaul of our social and economic institutions.
2. Such an overhaul cannot be carried out by private citizens acting voluntarily but requires the massive intervention of government. That is, it requires the exercise of political power.
3. As a numerical and racial minority, Negroes cannot hope to exercise such power alone but can only do so as part of a coalition of progressive forces whose objective interests overlap or parallel ours. Among these forces I would list the progressive sections of the labor movement and of the churches, liberals, democratic radicals, and intellectuals. I do not see how

the broad goals of the Negro community can ultimately be achieved except in a political alliance with these elements, however much we may criticize the inadequacy of their performance and commitment in given instances.[29]

The fact that this orientation was put forward in Hill's letter of resignation from CORE suggests that another important base of support for the Freedom Budget would be eroded. But Hill's own base of support inside CORE had been falling away. At first this was not clear. The organization's national steering committee, "by no means Socialist-oriented, was impressed by Hill's coherent strategy" (according to historians Meier and Rudwick), and he "had a substantial influence on chapter leaders like Ruth Turner and Tony Perot in Cleveland, and George Wiley in Syracuse, who were enormously impressed by his plea that CORE shift its priorities and address itself to the concerns of slum dwellers." Even Hill's more controversial argument that the organization should shift from street protests to electoral politics linked to the Democratic Party gained significant support as CORE joined with SNCC and other forces to help build the Mississippi Freedom Democratic Party efforts and Atlantic City challenge of 1964. But it all unraveled. Most left-wing CORE militants supporting the Mississippi effort, such as George Wiley, were strongly aligned with SNCC (and against the compromise urged by Rustin and Hill).

According to Meier and Rudwick, "The ghetto-orientation and community-organization thrust" ironically dovetailed "with [black] nationalist tendencies" that Hill (and Rustin) opposed, particularly with the developing "realization that lower-class black subculture had many positive attributes, a view that quite naturally converged with the message of race pride preached by men like Malcolm X." Ruth Turner commented that "the melting pot has had a pretty homogeneous and uninteresting flavor to me," and concluded that even if racial barriers were lifted, African Americans would and probably should choose to live together. Blyden Jackson had been another of Hill's allies in CORE, starting a community-focused East River CORE chapter, along with such Socialist Party members as Velma Hill, Paul Feldman, Sandra Feldman, Penn Kemble, and a number of energetic black youths. By 1964, however, Jackson was accusing Hill, Rustin, and their "white Socialist friends" of "trying to take over the show." Despite his substantial contributions to the organization, the erosion of Hill's base caused him to shift his energies first to the AFL-CIO, then later to the A. Philip Randolph Institute. Within two years of his departure, CORE chose to take the kind of outright antiwar stand that Rustin, Hill, and other realignment advocates believed civil rights organizations should avoid. "We [in CORE] cannot accept the current premise of the [Johnson] administration that we can afford guns and butter," proclaimed the organization's new National Director, Floyd McKissick, "particularly in light of the massive requirements for social reconstruction outlined in the Freedom Budget." While CORE gave critical support to the Freedom Budget, it could not be counted on to partici-pate in the kind of campaign that Rustin was attempting to coordinate.[30]

Serious problems were cropping up in other quarters as well. Charlotte Roe, the YPSL-oriented president of the U.S. Youth Council, reported to Rustin that a suspiciousness and even hostility toward the Freedom Budget were grow-ing among youth organizations that had been inclined, or might be expected, to support it. The president of the NAACP Youth Council, for example, was asserting that "you couldn't call for guns and butter." The student-run *Harvard Crimson* tartly commented: "It would seem almost impossible to bring a major coalition [together] which does not take the war into account." Even sharper was the attack from a staff member at the National Council of Churches, who denounced the Freedom Budget as a device "to provide 'responsible' positions from which to attack 'militants' and 'radicals' who link foreign and domestic policy," and as a way to draw young activists into "a consensus coalition that will 'get them off the streets.' " In a debate with Rustin on the concept of Black Power and notions of strategy and tactics for black liberation, SNCC leader Stokely Carmichael argued (according to an FBI report dated December 19, 1966) against Rustin's argument to support Lyndon Johnson as "the lesser of two evils," that "it is about time for this country to say we do not vote for evil men." Concluding that the Freedom Budget was not a step forward because "it automatically supports the war in Vietnam," he asked that his name be removed as an endorser of the Freedom Budget. Such a break from a onetime protégé (whom he still viewed as "so essentially a humanist, terribly bright, and always willing to put his body on the line") was difficult for Rustin, but its meaning for the future of the Freedom Budget was even more serious.[31]

The break from the League for Industrial Democracy (LID) by Students for a Democratic Society (SDS) was marked by similar dynamics and also consti-tuted a serious loss. This was an organization with several thousand members including a number of bright and capable activists who were initially inclined to work positively with LID leaders Kahn and Harrington. The relationship had become tense and antagonistic by 1964 as Kahn, Harrington, and others unsuc-cessfully sought to maintain ideological and political control over an increasingly radicalizing organization. Prominent SDS figure Tom Hayden later spoke of "the YPSL cabal" that sought to control SDS "while recruiting future YPSL cadres one by one." Another SDS leader, Steve Max (who was in full agreement with the Harrington-Kahn realignment perspective and ended up working closely with them), later recalled: "Harrington's plan had always been that the YPSLs would take over SDS. They had a very concrete plan which they told me about." But the fundamental problem involved political differences: SDS's bent toward an ideological diversity characteristic of the early New Left, an inclination to be more critical toward liberals and of the AFL-CIO than the LID felt comfortable with, and going "too far" in its rejection of Cold War anti-Communism. And, again, a key issue involved deep differences on the Vietnam War.[32]

Whereas the October 1965 separation of the two organizations was amicable, the two quickly became distant from each other and mutually antagonistic. Based on an accumulation of negative dynamics with some of its leading proponents, SDS activists were increasingly inclined to shrug off the Freedom Budget. Harvard SDS activist Michael Kazin, for example, denounced it as "welfarism at home and imperialism abroad. . . . They're willing to keep all the defense money intact just so they can get George Meany on their side."[33] Another SDS activist, Paul Le Blanc (nineteen years old at the time), was powerfully moved in a similarly hostile direction after sitting in on a private discussion, during a December 1965 SDS conference, which he vividly remembered years later:

> Jeremy [Brecher] and a friend of his, Doug Ireland, who were somewhat inclined toward the coalitionist wing [within SDS] and felt that relations with the LID were important, invited me to an informal "bull session" taking place in a room shared by Tom Kahn and Paul Feldman, editor of the Socialist Party paper *New America*. Also present was a young member of the party's Young People's Socialist League but more importantly a seasoned activist from SNCC, Ivanhoe Donaldson. I simply sat, watched, listened. In fact, Kahn and Donaldson did most of the talking, with Feldman chiming in occasionally to agree with one or another thing Kahn said.
>
> It was a fascinating verbal dance. Donaldson and Kahn obviously knew each other well, comparing notes and sharing thoughts, as old friends, on recent and current specifics of the civil rights movement in the South. But the pattern of discussion shifted, with Kahn questioning, then needling, then pulling into a positive mode to explain what he meant. After some positive give-and-take, his considerable humor and sharp criticism would

merge into a harder jab, from which he then backed off with a friendly word only to create a balance for a yet harder push to drive his point home. Much of the time, it began to seem, he listened to Donaldson only for the purpose of advancing his own agenda.

Kahn was challenging what did seem like a nebulous idealism of what he termed "mystical militants" whom he saw as all too prevalent in SNCC and SDS. ("We need to deal with the real world, real world!" he would admonish.) Against a naively emotional militancy, he emphasized the necessity of analysis, program, strategy, tactics. One must, he emphasized (employing what was clearly a Marxist perspective, well argued), understand the necessary interplay between the struggles for racial and economic justice, and the fact that it is the working class (with all of its diversity and contradictions) that is central to this combined struggle. This made essential the development of closer and broader ties between the civil rights movement and the labor movement. This, in turn, meant that SNCC and others working for civil rights in the South must be connecting seriously with AFL-CIO unions there. (This sounded right to me.)

Yeah, Donaldson responded, but those unions are all-white and racist, if they're there at all. Where are these representatives of "progressive" unionism you're talking about? Kahn ticked off the names of AFL-CIO officials in one or another Southern city. Donaldson pointed out the limitations of each—but Kahn would not concede the point.

The discussion then took a more disturbing turn—Kahn's angry, sneering attack on "Stalinist influence" and "Stalinoid" operatives in the civil rights movement. (Inwardly I bristled—it reminded me of J. Edgar Hoover's hateful book [*Masters of Deceit*] that had attacked my own roots.) "What are you talking about?" Donaldson challenged. Kahn named names—this and that "movement lawyer," this and that advisor and financial donor, this and that staff member, and when he refused to consider the SNCC activist's responses and kept on the attack, Donaldson finally walked out.

Then Kahn turned his attention to my SDS comrades. "Was I too hard?" he mused—but this turned out to be the prelude to a repetition of a similar dance, with substantially the same themes adapted to SDS specifics, and ultimately building up to the same end-result.

When we three SDSers were once more by ourselves, Doug furiously employed curses I had never heard before, Jeremy voiced a despairing commentary over how rigid and destructive Kahn could be, and I passionately concluded that I much preferred the openness of the new left to the smug and dogmatic certainties of the old.[34]

Paralleling these developments was a fragmentation within the Socialist Party and decline of the Young People's Socialist League (YPSL). Socialist Party members who were committed to helping organize for U.S. withdrawal from Vietnam tended to be marginalized in the organization throughout the 1960s. YPSL became a factional battleground on the issue, with opposition to the war being combined with opposition to the realignment perspective of coalition inside the Democratic Party. The organization was dissolved, in order to ensure its recomposition with a politics in line with the majority position of the Socialist Party-Social Democratic Federation, but its membership shrank from 1,100 in 1962 to about 300 in 1967. Paul Jacobs and Saul Landau, in *The New Radicals* (1966) viewed it as a relatively stagnant group, commenting that "its politics and style lack energy and spirit," and the new YPSL combined promoting the Freedom Budget with working for Democrats while criticizing the antiwar movement, the New Left, and other radical forces. A significant segment of the youth and a few elders (identifying with the pre-1960 positions of Shachtman) broke away to form the Independent Socialist Clubs, later transformed into International Socialists. Some, such as the pacifist leader of the War Resisters League, David McReynolds, left by the end of the decade. Disagreement over Vietnam—and also over how to relate to the rest of the left—continued to plague the organization into the 1970s.[35]

Several years later, Michael Harrington, attempting to make sense of the development of some of his comrades' extreme impatience toward others in the larger movement (and toward oppositionists in the Socialist Party), suggested that many of them were "full-time functionaries for social democratic, liberal or trade union organizations. These include the SP itself, the LID, the Randolph Institute, Frontlash, the Thomas Fund, the Middle East Committee, the AFT [American Federation of Teachers] and the AFL-CIO in Washington." While asserting that all of these organizations had positive value, as did the presence of socialists on their staffs, he added, "There being a relationship between social existence and consciousness, a faction of functionaries can . . . have a tendency to look at politics in purely organizational terms, to stress disciplined immediate activity to the exclusion of considering larger questions and to orient too exclusively toward those forces which provide financial support for the organizations in question."[36] Ironically, this grouping—acting like a relatively airtight, self-assured, mutually reinforcing coterie of "cadre"—advanced a political orientation and utilized a political-organizational mode of functioning destined to push many potential cadres away from the Freedom Budget campaign.

It had been precisely the kind of cadres and activists discussed above, especially those in YPSL, SNCC, CORE, and SDS, who had played an essential role in the success of the March on Washington for Jobs and Freedom, and in the civil rights crusade leading up to it.[37] These were the kinds of cadres, organizers, and activists whose energies, skills, and moral passion would have been essential for building the campaigns and mobilizing the forces essential to making the Freedom Budget politically relevant. Without that, there would be no way to respond to liberal Democrats such as Pennsylvania Senator Joseph Clark when he explained that his constituents were not ready for anything as far-reaching as the Freedom Budget. It would be impossible to give substance to the challenge that the Vietnam War should not be paid for on the backs of the poor. Without these activists helping to organize and mobilize, it would remain nothing more than a rhetorical flourish to assert, as Paul Feldman did, that implementation of the Freedom Budget "won't happen without major social struggle, and certainly not without significant changes in the power structure." Early on, Leon Keyserling, while very positive about Rustin's efforts, was concerned that "the army of supporters" who had initially gathered around the Freedom Budget "seems to be vanishing in thin air."[38]

All of this was to have devastating consequences for the Freedom Budget. Untroubled by major social struggles on behalf of the Freedom Budget, the lobbyists and politicians and bureaucrats in whose hands its fate now rested were content to set it aside. Quite simply, as Rustin put it later, the Freedom Budget "didn't sell" among the Democrats around Lyndon B. Johnson. And during his victorious campaign for the presidency in 1968, Republican Richard Nixon argued: "The demand for a Freedom Budget, amounting to billions of dollars for the poor, is not the road to bring people out of poverty into the sunshine of self-respect and human dignity."[39]

Coalition in the Streets: Civil Rights, Labor, and the Poor

It was in the midst of Martin Luther King Jr.'s Poor People's Campaign, and of his and Rustin's involvement in the strike of Memphis sanitation workers, that the Freedom Budget made its last substantial, and tantalizing, appearance.

By 1967 King was wrestling with the ramifications of a weakness built into "The Strategy"—the absence of serious interest among substantial elements within the ruling circles in dealing with the matter of economic justice in the way that some of them had been prepared to deal with Jim Crow. Coming out against the Vietnam War, King had cut himself off from powerful allies, although it is unlikely that they would actually have been prepared to respond positively to his struggle to bring about major economic change.[40]

A dramatic radicalization in this period challenged and threatened to outflank King, but he struggled to keep pace with it, without compromising his own principles. Radicalization can find different expressions, sometimes going in a practical revolutionary direction, sometimes instead going in the direction of militant posturing and impractical, no-win, even suicidal perspectives. King hoped to channel the radicalization, at least partly, toward a more revolutionary, and effective, variant of "The Strategy." But the widespread leftward lurch of the late 1960s was incredibly diffuse, a great burst of radicalizing steam going in all directions without benefit of a piston box that might have made it a force to be reckoned with. Some of King's closest allies (Randolph, Rustin, Kahn, and their co-thinkers) were now veering in less radical directions than he was. Others in SNCC were veering toward what seemed to him a hyper-revolutionary stance infused with a black nationalism and rhetorical violence that he saw as a dead end.

In the book King wrote shortly before his death, *Where Do We Go From Here?*, King had made a point of promoting the Freedom Budget, asserting that "the ultimate answer to the Negro's dilemma will be found in a massive federal aid program for all the poor along the lines of A. Philip Randolph's Freedom Budget, a kind of Marshall Plan for the disadvantaged." These were the themes underlying the entire Poor People's Campaign. Yet King—dynamically and boldly trying to find a way to move "The Strategy" forward, and becoming increasingly radical as he sought to do this—had still not found his footing.

King envisioned a massive, interracial convergence and occupation of the poor in Washington in June 1968, in many ways similar to Bayard Rustin's initial radical vision of what eventually became the much-moderated 1963 March on Washington. Rustin himself (with his eye on the 1968 presidential elections) believed that the effort would backfire and therefore opposed it.[41]

But then King got involved in the strike of black sanitation workers in Memphis, Tennessee, seeing this tough fight as a natural and necessary prelude to the Washington convergence. It was, in itself, also a vibrant realization of "The Strategy," the fight for racial justice flowing into that for economic justice, with the convergence of the labor and civil rights movements. As the struggle was unfolding, Rustin had been invited to address a southern regional conference of predominantly AFL-CIO trade unionists, held in Memphis. It is worth pondering the account by historian Michael Honey:

> Not "love or affection" but mutual interests dictated alliance between blacks and the labor movement, Rustin told delegates. Reiterating themes raised in King's 1961 AFL-CIO speech, he told them, "You can't win without us [blacks], and we can't get a damn thing without you." Rustin promoted moving "from protest to politics," based on an expanded black franchise in the wake of the Voting Rights Act, and he listed reforms that would benefit both blacks and labor, including a "freedom budget" funding full employment, improved education and wages, and other antipoverty measures. Rustin, like King, wanted to shift the freedom movement from "phase one" to "phase two."[42]

Ironically, the dynamics of the Memphis struggle forced Rustin to join forces with King and others in a non-electoral struggle to advance "The Strategy" more meaningfully in the 1968 elections. There had been long-standing interest on the part of the FBI to exploit the "considerable potential" for developing "certain animosities" between Rustin and King (particularly those around King), but that too was pushed to the margins in this brief moment. Rustin now labored to help mobilize nationwide support in labor and civil rights circles for the strike, to help raise money, and to help mobilize on-the-ground forces and enthusiasm in Memphis itself. His contribution was essentially supplementary to the efforts of Memphis workers and civil rights activists, and to the dramatic involvement of King himself, but it was an important element in the chemistry of the situation.[43]

And then King was killed by an assassin's bullet.

In the aftermath, Rev. James Lawson, one of the central leaders of the Memphis struggle, was able to persuade Rustin to help organize a powerful march and rally of more than 40,000 people to honor King and advance the struggle in which he had given his life. "In a very real way, he was my executive director for the march," Lawson said of Rustin. The rally was a key element in helping to push the strike forward to a resounding victory for the workers.[44]

A struggle and victory in Memphis was for King a prelude to the radical Poor People's encampment and confrontation in Washington, D.C. But organizing efforts for the Poor People's Campaign had been difficult, and, two months out from when it was supposed to take place, King and others still had not worked through what they needed to do for it to have any hopes for success. There was a last-minute effort at assistance from Rustin, who had agreed to head the campaign, but his political differences with many others involved quickly resulted in his dismissal. The basically leaderless effort, neither fully thought out nor fully prepared, ended in failure. What was to be a mass rally on the scale of the 1963 March on Washington was able to draw only 50,000 people, and the Poor People's encampment, mired in mud and confusion, was easily dispersed.[45]

What King hoped would be a key element in moving to the second phase of "The Strategy" turned out to be nothing of the sort. The possibility for somehow crafting a radical-activist campaign for economic justice, in which the Freedom Budget would have had relevance, blinked out of existence, relevant only to speculations on "what might have been." Nor did the electoralist hopes of Rustin and his co-thinkers open up any other possibilities, as a pro-war liberal Democrat (with a potential base deeply divided by the war) proved unable to defeat a pro-war center-right Republican (with a party unified and militant) in the 1968 elections.

Defeat

A. Philip Randolph saw the failure of the Freedom Budget as being rooted in the fact that "this system is a market economy in which investment and production are determined more by the anticipation of profits than by the desire to achieve social justice." It turned out that the forces necessary to challenge this effectively could not be mobilized, and the Freedom Budget campaign ground to a halt. By 1971, an utterly frustrated Leon Keyserling (who had earlier praised Rustin: "I marvel that you do as much as you do") was complaining that the Freedom Budget "faded from the landscape, not because it was rejected but because it was abandoned," adding curtly: "I am not interested in the strategic or tactical reasons why this was done." Rustin's own summary explanation: "Unfortunately, the election of a conservative President and Congress, and the division which took place around the war in Vietnam, made it very difficult to continue to push for the Budget legislatively."[46]

The defeat and evaporation of the Freedom Budget campaign also constituted the dead end "The Strategy" had run into. Since 1965, many had argued that the civil rights movement was in crisis. James Bevel, a seasoned veteran of SCLC, had commented: "There is no civil rights movement. President Johnson signed it out of existence when he signed the voting rights bill."[47] This obituary may have been slightly premature, but certainly by the end of 1968 the civil rights movement of Randolph, Rustin, and King had passed out of existence, the tasks it had set itself only partially finished. Soon SNCC and then CORE fell apart. Part of this was from internal contradictions and political confusion, although in the case of SNCC, state repression also played a role.[48] Some of the organizations continued, including SCLC and most impressively the moderate but durable NAACP. There were also new groups and new projects, some enjoying a certain amount of success, others ending in disappointment or disaster. None had proved able to complete "The Strategy's" remaining tasks by the dawn of the new century. Nor did Rustin or Randolph end up having more to show for their efforts.

Historian C. Vann Woodward inadvertently highlighted the tragedy in his glowing tribute to Rustin, which appeared in the 1971 collection of the lifelong activist's writings, *On the Line*:

> Throughout the years of tumult and shouting, pseudo-revolutionaries, miraculously appearing and disappearing "black leaders," and overnight reversals of strategy and goals, Bayard Rustin has hewed to the line he has pursued all along. This is the line of civil rights, equality, and integration, and the strategy of the ballot, the union card, and coalition politics. While the demand for equality itself is not revolutionary, he insists that "the response that must be made in order to satisfy the demand very much is. By this I mean that justice cannot be done to blacks in the absence of a total restructuring of the political, economic, and social institutions of this country." Never willing to settle for a "symbolic victory" or a pseudo-revolution, he holds out for "nothing less than the radical refashioning of our political economy."[49]

By the following year, a defeated Rustin basically withdrew from the civil rights efforts to which he had devoted his life. One of his biographers, Jervis Anderson, tells us he was "wearying of civil rights work in America," which seems unlikely for this lifelong fighter, although there may have been a sense of demoralization linked to definitive defeat.[50] Writing about his mentor, A. Philip Randolph, in 1986, he demonstrated how this defeat added up to far more than simply a personal tragedy:

In Randolph's view, perhaps the most important contribution he attempted was a failure. That was his introduction of the Freedom Budget for all Americans. While he got the signatures of many, many liberals in all walks of life and civil rights leaders to endorse the Freedom Budget, they never considered it a priority. Randolph foresaw the further decline of the black family—and all the consequent pathology, including drugs, crime, illegitimacy, etc.—and the creation of economic "untouchables" in the black, Hispanic, and white communities, and general decline of the working class should the Freedom Budget not be accepted.[51]

King died a martyr's death in 1968. Some were inclined to argue that the other two lived too long, agreeing with noted African American scholar Manning Marable's judgment about "Rustin's and Randolph's accommodation to racism and betrayal of the black working class." Others would insist that this was too harsh, that the two made imperishable contributions, and that their apostasy was neither as clear-cut nor as complete as all that. "I watched him adopt more conservative positions in the late '60s and '70s with dismay," former SNCC activist Julian Bond wrote of Rustin, adding, nonetheless, that our society is "richer for having had him for a while." Randolph lingered as "the grand old man" of civil rights and labor, but passed away in 1979. Rustin's fate was seen by many of his erstwhile comrades as particularly tragic, given what he had been and might have been. Yet he was fated to enjoy something of a rebirth, certainly as a gay rights advocate before his 1995 death, but in ways even more afterward, as growing numbers of younger people sought to connect with inspiring aspects of his story and his ideas.[52]

Reformist Tragedy

In 1967, David McReynolds—who several years later would identify Rustin as one of his central pacifist and socialist mentors "who was, more than any single person, the hero of my life"—wrote a critique of Rustin and Michael Harrington (addressed to Harrington) in which he tried to explain what had happened:

Both Mike and I and many others on the democratic Left voted for Johnson. Our support was critical and limited, but it was real. We broke our backs to get as heavy a vote as possible for Johnson because Goldwater was the front man for the radical right: the military, the racists. We believed that a broad coalition of civil rights, peace, trade union, and liberal groups could compel Johnson to embark on a serious program for social reform at home, while restraining the military from adventures abroad.

God help us, Mike, we won. We fought our good and rational political fight and defeated Goldwater's war policy. We got Santo Domingo, Stanleyville and Saigon.[53] We defeated the reactionary domestic policy of the GOP and have seen the poverty fight cut to shreds. There are now 500,000 dead Vietnamese and 15,000 dead Americans—most of them killed since we won our striking victory at the polls. A victory that "clearly proved" that democratic political processes can defeat reaction. Let us pray God we never endure another such victory.

Here is truly the existential tragedy. Bayard Rustin, like some hero in a Greek tragedy, broke off personal and political ties of decades to make a courageous effort, through direct cooperation with the power structure, to get some real action on the ghetto problem. That action never came, and Bayard, whom I admire because he was willing to walk through the deepest shit of politics because he genuinely cared more about the slum kids than about his reputation as a radical purist, now must surely rage in the silence of the night, knowing what he has lost and at how great a cost, and how little, how terribly little, he has won. And you, Mike, who knows poverty as few other intellectuals, and who, like Bayard, truly cared about poor people, seeing them as human beings trapped in futility and not as statistics or as an excuse for slogans, you saw a chance, after a life spent in socialist sloganizing, to actually *do* something about poverty. Like Bayard, you "went into the camp of the enemy"—as the sectarians might say—hoping to find there enough decency and common sense to make some kind of program possible. And now the war on poverty is over, its forces demoralized and in retreat, for the energy of the nation is involved in Vietnam.

McReynolds concluded: "We may, all of us, have learned from 1964 that, at the core of radical politics (and not incidental to it), is a sense of morality." He suggested that "we cannot really predict the results of our acts, and that, for the radical, it is essential to judge the value of the act itself." It should be added that Rustin apparently saw things differently. His later companion, Walter Naegle, notes: "Some of Rustin's colleagues in the pacifist movement, he felt, were not opposing the war from pacifist positions but from more generalized 'end the war now' and anti-imperialist positions, and some in the antiwar movement favored a victory of Communist forces in Vietnam. They wanted to see a U.S. defeat. He disagreed."[54]

McReynolds's comments bring to mind passages from the prison letters of another of his heroes, Rosa Luxemburg, who commented that "for every person, for every creature, one's own life is the only single possession one really has," and also: "To be kind and good is the main thing! Plainly and simply, to be good—that resolves and unites everything and is better than all cleverness and insistence on 'being right.' " Being true to one's self, with one's actions being consistent with humanistic ideals and beliefs, is better than being "practical" or "effective"—for what one "wins" may be superficial if one loses the best of one's self. But the atheist Luxemburg might have felt less comfortable with the added formulation that McReynolds (himself an atheist) chose: "Means are in the hands of men—the ends are in the hands of God." She would more likely have made reference to what one can expect from compromising with the inherently imperialist, militaristic, exploitative, and anti-democratic political order that capitalism generates. She insisted, after all, that there was no middle way for humanity; there would be "either transition to socialism or regression into barbarism." And there is no question that if she felt that the leaders of her country, whether Germany or Poland or Russia, were conducting an imperialist war, she would certainly have wished for their defeat.[55]

If Rustin and his comrades had shared McReynolds's or Luxemburg's position, it is unlikely that the Freedom Budget campaign could have moved forward to victory. But as it turned out, it could not move forward even with their compromises. Perhaps its only hope was to be associated with the kind of radical and radicalizing struggle that King was waging at the end of his life. In such a context, its defeat might have provided, as did King's defeat, inspiration for future struggles around an undefiled vision.

Aftermath

The political landscape in the United States shifted sharply to the left in the 1960s and 1970s, but with no strategic focus or ideological coherence. Consequently, a number of youthful radical forces, veering in ultra-left directions, ran into dead ends, and self-destructed. Some drifted back into the

Democratic Party, a few shifted far to the right, others focused on other projects—including labor struggles, anti-racism, opposition to U.S. interventions in Central America, environmental efforts, anti-poverty work, women's rights issues, the gay rights movement, and more. But this diverse mass of projects and activists were unable to mount anything like the transformative dynamic that had been suggested by the more radical campaign perspectives of the Freedom Budget.[56]

"In 1964 and 1965 it seemed to us socialists that our dream of a political realignment in America was about to come true," remembered Michael Harrington in his 1973 memoir *Fragments of the Century*, a scant eight years after all those dreams had utterly fallen apart. The year before, the Socialist Party had split into two pieces. Disappointed with their efforts in the Democratic Party, some were inclined to support the presidential candidacy of Richard Nixon (running against the despised "dove" George McGovern). Max Shachtman, before his 1972 death, asserted admiringly that George Meany "has guts" for refusing to back the Democrats in that election. Michael Harrington and others—deciding to come out in full and active opposition to the Vietnam War, and to relate openly and positively to others on the left previously scorned and spurned (by Shachtman, Kahn, Feldman, and Harrington himself)—broke away to become the Democratic Socialist Organizing Committee, which transitioned into the larger and more influential Democratic Socialists of America (DSA). Harrington could be said to represent "political realignment with a human face" with great charisma, popularity, and influence. He was taken by cancer in 1989, but even before that the organization had "failed to invent a meaningful political role for local members to play as *socialists*," as Maurice Isserman has put it, and the bulk of its 5,000 or so members did little more, as DSAers, than pay dues and attend an occasional meeting or event.[57]

The fragment not following Harrington retained such significant figures as Rustin, Randolph, Shachtman, and Kahn. It renamed itself Social Democrats USA, or SDUSA, tagged "seduce-ahh" by some left-wing unfriendlies, and actually was able to "seduce" few new members. By the late 1980s it had fewer than a thousand members, with no renewal in sight. This declining cohort—harboring grudges against most of the left, although intimate with the George Meany and Lane Kirkland leadership of the AFL-CIO, and serving as a bastion of Cold War anti-Communism, had little appeal for young activists. Tom Kahn became a top aide and speechwriter for Meany and Kirkland, then was chosen as the labor federation's Director of International Affairs in 1986. His work, and that of other SDUSA veterans, involved close ties with the U.S. State Department and Central Intelligence Agency, particularly under Ronald Reagan. One commentator hailed Kahn (upon his death from AIDS at age fifty-three) as "a hero of the Cold War," and another (more critically) noted that he "exercised a profound influence in the export of anti-communist ideology and U.S. influence under the guise of promoting democracy." Reagan, who seemed more reliably anti-Communist than Democrat Jimmy Carter, won much support from SDUSA members. Yet some stalwarts, such as well-known anti-Communist labor scholar Robert J. Alexander, quit "in disillusionment," according to his biographer, "over its increasingly conservative direction."[58]

More than some, Rustin seemed to retain considerable humor and buoyancy, which he channeled into human rights projects and ultimately into the gay rights movement. Accepting a figurehead position as national chairman of SDUSA, Rustin remained only peripherally involved. Critics chastised him for uncritical support of Israel against the Palestinians, and for invariably expressing support for SDUSA Cold War positions. He never renounced his socialist ideals, however. When discussing his father-figure mentor, A. Philip Randolph, he emphasized that "Randolph's socialist background and philosophy was the cornerstone that formed the core of his thinking regarding civil rights matters." Rustin himself, writing in the late 1980s, continued to insist on the relevance of "the basic position of the socialist analysis."[59]

There were others in SDUSA who saw no point in maintaining any pretense of socialism, transitioning into neo conservative partisans of capitalism, connecting with conservative journals, right-wing think tanks, and government service in Republican administrations. For some, however, there was a continued commitment to the AFL-CIO and the Democratic Party, and even to some variant of the socialist idea. But unable to renew itself, the organization simply aged and shrank. One of its last big events was a 2003 panel discussion of members and former members (including prominent neo conservatives) about whether socialism still has any relevance, with a significant number arguing *absolutely not*. With the premature death of an incredibly loyal and patient Penn Kemble, who had kept the organization going up to 2005, it disintegrated.[60]

The rest of the left-wing organizations of the 1960s also declined dramatically as the twentieth century wore on. By the end of the 1960s, Robert Allen noted that the most substantial revolutionary currents in the black liberation movement, SNCC and the Black Panther Party, proved unable to meet the challenges facing them: "Both SNCC and the Panthers tried to provide an analysis, but because of the uncertainties and ambivalences of their own leaders, the basic content varied from month to month, sometimes contradicting previous formulations." Neither group proved able to endure for very long, with relentless government repression (taking advantage of violent rhetoric) finishing the job.[61]

With the conclusion of the Vietnam War in 1975, the left in general seemed unable to cohere around any central focus. By the end of the Cold War, the collapse of Communism entailed considerable confusion and disillusionment in some sectors of the left, as did the defeats and degeneration of third world revolutionary efforts. Others were thrown into crisis by the failure of a fighting U.S. working class to "move to center stage" as many had expected. Though radicalized attitudes had permeated popular consciousness and culture, and there were some leftward-thinking young people who were ready to join socialist organizations, the fact remains that this was not a period of social struggle and insurgency capable of putting wind in the sails of such groups.[62]

Contributing to the de-radicalization and de-mobilization of social movements was the absorption of many radical activists into bureaucratic and electoral organizational structures. Though they may have perceived this shift as providing further relevance for their radical perspectives, it actually integrated them into institutions that help sustain the status quo. Such a process was evident in the Socialist Party and SDUSA, but participant observers with a scholarly bent were able to perceive a similar development within the civil rights movement as a whole. Frances Fox Piven and Richard A. Cloward noted in the 1970s that "the socioeconomic programs of the Kennedy-Johnson years . . . helped to absorb and divert the civil rights movement," and more generally the major institutions of society "overtook the movement, depleting its strength by incorporating its cadres and by organizing blacks for bureaucratic and electoral politics." Surveying the scene more broadly two decades later, Adolph Reed Jr. commented:

> Passage of the Voting Rights Act, along with its subsequent enforcement, was the signal event marking that struggle's success; it also initiated a substantial reorientation of the character and practical objectives of black politics. In the decade after 1965 black political activity came increasingly to revolve around gaining, enhancing, or maintaining official representation in public institutions and the distribution of associated material and symbolic benefits.[63]

But this did not result in genuine "black power" for African Americans, nor did it bring about the realization of the magnificent goals, the liberating social transformation and economic justice for all, that had been projected by King or Rustin or Randolph. At the close of the twentieth century, Adolph Reed commented on the "commonplace" observation regarding "the apparent irony that exponential increases in black public officeholding since the early 1970s have been accompanied by a steady deterioration in the material circumstances of large segments of the inner-city black citizenry." Those on the left making this observation were making a point about "the insufficiency of capturing public office," while those on the right were inclined to make the observation "either [to] disparage the pursuit of public action on behalf of blacks and poor people in general or [to] push more or less oblique claims about black incompetence."[64]

Given the general decline of living standards for the white sectors of the U.S. working class, one could presumably make similar claims about white incompetence. But trends hitting the African American sectors of the U.S. working class in the 1950s and 1960s, and deepening in the final decades of the twentieth century, were hitting and dragging down more and more of the working class as a whole, regardless of race, from the 1980s onward, in the United States and globally.[65]

Such economic injustice will undoubtedly be with us until it is overcome by conscious mass action, as Randolph and King insisted when they called for the Freedom Budget.

7. THE U.S. POLITICAL ECONOMY FROM THE FREEDOM BUDGET TO THE PRESENT

THE FREEDOM BUDGET BEGINS to do something that all serious activists and revolutionaries have a responsibility to do—envision, in specific terms, how oppressive problems of the capitalist here-and-now can be overcome. Read nearly fifty years after its completion, the Freedom Budget remains a powerful document, chastising a nation for denying economic justice to its poorest citizens and demonstrating with the cold, hard facts of the matter that there was no reason for this to be so. It is worth building on what those who developed the Freedom Budget did as we seek to address such things in our own time. This can help provide a strategic pathway for a better future.

While the problems addressed by the Freedom Budget continue to exist, the world of the twenty-first century is not the same as that of the 1960s and 1970s. In developing a Freedom Budget for our own time, it will be necessary to factor in the changes that have taken place over the past five decades, which we will review later in this chapter. But there is also the need for a critique of certain aspects of the Freedom Budget. After all, the effort to win the battle to implement it decisively failed, and in our opinion aspects of this failure can be traced to serious limitations embedded in the Freedom Budget itself, which involved the sidestepping of important issues.

A Critique of the Freedom Budget

We have already focused on one of these issues—the Vietnam War. As Martin Luther King Jr. eloquently emphasized, this war was such a gross violation of human rights and social justice that it could not be separated from the struggle for the same things in the United States. One could hardly expect masses of people to fight for freedom and dignity in the United States while turning a blind eye to their being violated by our own government elsewhere.[1] Why, then, treat it as gingerly as A. Philip Randolph does in his Introduction, where he appears to lump together the conservatives who both supported the war and opposed the War on Poverty and those presumably, left-leaning supporters of the civil rights movement, who argued that opposition to the war was no less a political priority than overcoming poverty?

The authors of the Freedom Budget state that it is not socialistic but socially minded:

The "Freedom Budget" does not contemplate that this "growth dividend" be achieved by revolutionary nor even drastic changes in the division of responsibility between private enterprise and government under our free institutions. To illustrate, in 1965, 63.7 percent of our total national production was in the form of private consumer outlays, 16.5 percent in the form of private investment, and 19.8 percent in the form of public outlays at all levels for goods and services. Under the "higher" goals in the "Freedom Budget," these relationships in 1975 would be 63.5 percent, 16.9 percent, and 19.6 percent.[2]

This seems overly conciliatory. The private economy had failed miserably to end poverty, raise incomes, provide housing, take care of the aged and disabled, and in many other ways. If ever there was a time to be bold, to take a more radical economic position, the 1960s was it. It may be the case that it would not have been politically possible, given what the authors of the Freedom Budget were hoping to accomplish in the context of 1966, for the document to provide discussion of exactly what a capitalist economy and social system is. No doubt the Cold War and the McCarthyite attacks on radicals meant that care had to be taken to present the budget in terms that would win maximum support. But this silence on the inherent instabilities of capitalism, and on the destructive desire of those who run its commanding heights to be free to make as much money as they could, did not prepare its potential supporters—masses of working people and others—to reach an understanding of the powerful barriers to the Freedom Budget's actualization. Speaking in a frank and informed way about such realities might have resonated with a substantial number of people.[3]

In connection with the obeisance made in the budget to "our free institutions," there is no obvious awareness present in it of the nature of government in capitalist economies. The furies of private interest place pressures upon the state to ensure that the government acts in the interest of private capital. Most politicians are tightly allied to powerful business entities, whose owners contribute to their political campaigns and employ an army of lobbyists to get government to do their bidding.[4] To win popular victories, those that benefit the poor, for example, requires tactical alliances, but those who seek such victories must maintain a radical posture, always demanding much more than can be won at any particular time. And one of the jobs of a bold plan, like the Freedom Budget, is to educate the public about the merits of the plan and the nature of the society in which it is being proposed.

This brings us to perhaps the most critical flaw in the Freedom Budget. It lacks specificity in terms of how its proponents go about getting it enacted. The budget exudes an air of expertise, complete with a long list of prominent endorsers. The civil rights struggle, of course, had many great leaders, and many outstanding politicians, scholars, labor leaders, and clergy were integral parts of it. However, it was the courage of "common" men and women whose mass resistance forced action. Such mass resistance would be needed to compel acceptance of something those with economic power did not want to grant. Yet a plan of attack is missing from the budget.

A great strength of the Freedom Budget's architects was the notion of the centrality of the organized working class to the budget's implementation, as well as the notion of a labor-civil rights alliance, supplemented by an even broader coalition. To build effective support for the budget would have required tactical alliances, mass education, and widespread militant actions. It might well have required struggles on many fronts.

At the same time, there were complications. For example, the first signature on the "Signatories of 'Freedom Budget'" page is that of I. W. Abel, president of the United Steelworkers of America. However, the USW had in place in its collective bargaining agreements seniority clauses that gave preference to the seniority a worker had in a particular department. Black steelworkers were confined to the coke plants and foundries, the harshest, dirtiest areas of the plants.

If they used their seniority to transfer to a better job, their department seniority went to zero, and if there were layoffs in their new department they would be first to go, even though they might have the highest overall plant seniority of anyone in that department.[5] Similarly, C. L. Haggerty, president of the Building and Construction Trades Department of the AFL-CIO, oversaw a group of unions notorious for their racism, and support for the war in Vietnam as well. In other words, union support for the Freedom Budget was probably thin in these and other cases, so that a good deal of work would have had to be done to make the appropriate alliances with labor, and to take issue right away with the absence of civil rights in many labor unions.

There was truth in Bayard Rustin's initial notion—expressed at the Socialist Party's conference on "The Civil Rights Revolution" after the 1963 March on Washington—that "the executive council of the AFL-CIO is not representative of the elements which make up the labor movement," and that "the alliance between Negroes and white workers . . . will come from the streets and from that movement which emerges from the streets." For this, the more radical and militant elements in the labor movement were far more important allies than an Abel, a Haggerty, or a George Meany. To rely on bureaucratized union official-dom was to build on sand.

Similar arguments can be made with respect to politicians and the war in Vietnam. The civil rights leaders invited to the White House by Lyndon Johnson when he decided to push hard for civil rights legislation were impressed, and rightly so, with his sincerity. When Martin Luther King heard Johnson, in his 1964 State of the Union message, say "We shall overcome," aides said it was the only time they had seen him cry. Robert Caro, in his masterful multivolume biography of Johnson, says that the months after Kennedy's assassination brought out the best in LBJ. His sympathy for the poor and downtrodden came to the fore, and his mastery of power politics, combined with the nation's distress over the death of a popular president, allowed Johnson to win legislative victories, remarkable in their scope, on behalf of black Americans. However, by the time the Freedom Budget was completed, Johnson had won reelection, and he no longer had to cater to convenient allies. The baser aspects of his character returned with a vengeance and the secret escalation of the war in Vietnam moved into the open.[6]

Not many civil rights stalwarts joined King in his deep and permanent opposition to the war, tying what was happening in Vietnam to life in the United States. The moderation ingrained in the Urban League's Whitney Young and the NAACP's Roy Wilkins made it unlikely that they would ever take such a step. Randolph and Rustin, on the other hand, had risen to great stature in earlier years by making precisely such links. The moderation of their own radical principles for the purpose of connecting with more moderate allies in the civil rights movement, the labor movement, and the political mainstream did not, ultimately, advance the cause of the Freedom Budget, a cause in which the moderates turned out to be, perhaps predictably, lukewarm allies. To build the kind of movement necessary for the enactment of the Freedom Budget would most likely have required a full embrace of the antiwar movement. The loss of halfhearted allies would have resulted as well in a complete break with the Johnson administration, which was, in any event, doomed, given its pursuit of an increasingly unpopular, immoral, and unwinnable war. If the push for the budget had been coupled with an all-out fight to end the war, there is certainly no guarantee that the Freedom Budget would have triumphed. But the antiwar movement did triumph, and it seems to us that the struggle for the Freedom Budget too might have gotten much further had it been connected with that victorious effort.

The U. S. Economy at the Time of the Freedom Budget

Both of the authors of this book came of age during the "Golden Age" of U.S. capitalism, a period marked by strong GDP growth rates, rising wages and benefits for a significant segment of the working class, high union density, and stable if still considerable income inequality. Unfortunately, things began to change dramatically toward the end of the ten-year time frame (1966–1975) envisioned by the Freedom Budget. Today it is difficult to remember the hopefulness of those days. We live in a radically different time. To lay the groundwork for consideration of a "New Freedom Budget," let us look at what has transpired over the past forty years, using 1973 as the beginning of the end of the Golden Age.

The United States came out of the Second World War the dominant world economic power, its productive capacity intact and its main economic rivals utterly devastated by the war. During the war, political and economic elites began to plan for a postwar ruled by the United States.

Several factors contributed to the postwar economic prosperity. First, the inability of consumers to purchase a wide range of goods during the war, despite good wartime wages, gave rise to tremendous pent-up demand. Accelerating demand stimulated production and employment. An important component of consumer demand was what Paul Baran and Paul Sweezy, in their influential book *Monopoly Capital*, termed the second wave of automobilization in the United States. Fueled by the extension of credit for car purchases, people bought automobiles in record numbers. The car was the most important of what Baran and Sweezy called "epoch-making innovations," ones that brought in their wake enormous capital spending and helped push the entire economy into a period of long-term expansion. Automobiles required not just gigantic, integrated plants for their production, but also steel, glass, rubber, oil, and roads on which to travel, each calling forth large amounts of capital spending. The roads and the cars, in turn, made truck transport possible, travel quicker, suburbs possible, and opened up markets for motels, service stations, and all of the accoutrements of modern, mobile life.[7]

Second, spending by the federal government exceeded its prewar proportion of the Gross Domestic Product. Rising government spending on military, highway, and social welfare projects helped the economy to sustain high growth rates. It also created a floor for the macro-economy, meaning that its permanence prevented a return to the circumstances of the Great Depression. And as we saw in chapter 5, another benefit of government spending was that some of it—especially unemployment benefits, welfare payments, and Social Security—helped to make downturns in the economy, which economists began to call recessions, less severe. As the economy contracted, government transfer payments rose automatically, buttressing incomes, spending, and employment. The tax system also helped. Federal taxes were progressive overall, meaning that as incomes rose, a larger fraction of income was collected in taxes. But when incomes fell, tax rates fell, giving individuals more money to spend than they would otherwise have had, again stabilizing spending and employment.

Third, for the destroyed economies of Europe and Japan to rebuild, they needed enormous amounts of capital goods and raw materials, which they obviously could not produce. The one country that could provide these was the United States. Its factories were soon converted back to civilian production, and steel, machine tools, coal, and thousands of other needed products produced by the global economic juggernaut that was U.S. capitalism soon found their way overseas, fueling the rapid recovery of Japan and Germany, along with many other countries. As output, incomes, and employment rose in these places, more money was spent on U.S. consumer goods, and all in all, a virtuous circle of U.S. production, income, and employment sped the U.S. economy forward. It was a remarkable chain of events, with one country producing most of the world's capital goods and reaping the benefits of doing so.

Fourth, the preeminent economic position of the United States was deepened by the international monetary arrangements the United States was able to dictate after the war. While gold was the international medium of exchange, the dollar was tied directly to a fixed gold price of $35. In other words, for all practical purposes, the dollar became the medium of exchange for international trade. This gave the United States a tremendous advantage compared to all other countries. There was no need to worry that dollars in the rest of the world, from its own imports, would be converted to gold, because other countries would want to hold dollars, the global exchange medium. It was as if people never cashed your checks because they wanted your autograph.

Fifth, the United States dealt effectively, from an economic growth point of view, with conflict between workers and employers, which can throw a monkey wrench into the process of capital accumulation and slow down the pace of profit making. A tremendous strike wave after the Second World War is a case in point. These strikes had the potential to both disrupt production and deepen the radicalism that had been a significant part of the renewal of the U.S. labor movement in the 1930s. Employers and the government were quick to address any expansion of working-class upheaval, and they did so in two ways. First, Congress enacted the Taft-Hartley Act in 1947, which not only restricted solidarity actions by workers, but also demanded that all union officers, at every level of a union, sign an oath declaring that they were not members of the Communist Party. Refusal to do so denied workers and their unions protection under the National Labor Relations Act. Most officers signed the oath. Ambitious labor leaders like Walter Reuther of the United Auto Workers (UAW) union used the refusal of UAW radicals to sign as an excuse to red-bait and gain control of the union. In an act of complete capitulation to the Cold War mentality promoted by the federal government, business leaders, and reactionary politicians, several left-led unions were thrown out of the CIO. This isolated the most socially conscious leaders of the working class, those most committed to civil rights and opposed to U.S. war making and imperialism, as well as those who had helped to negotiate the strongest collective bargaining agreements.[8] These were also the men and women who would have been the strongest advocates of the Freedom Budget inside the labor movement. They almost certainly would have given more than lip service to it, and they could have been instrumental in forging the civil rights–labor coalition envisioned in "The Strategy." They would also have provided a strong union base for opposition to the war in Vietnam.

Once the radicals were neutralized, employers in unionized businesses, in alliance with liberal but not radical union leaders, worked out an accord with labor. The unions agreed to cede control of the shop floor to management, and to discipline members when they engaged in wildcat strikes and other forms of direct confrontation. In return, employers agreed in collective bargaining to regular wage increases, cost-of-living adjustments, and benefits such as health care and pensions. With fewer unexpected disruptions in production, employers could take full advantage of the multiple possibilities for high profits arising from the special conditions facing U.S. companies after the war. The relationship between labor and capital began to take on the form of a ritual, with unions occasionally calling strikes, but by and large these were no longer the no-holds-barred class struggles of the past. The CIO abandoned a short-lived effort to organize black workers in the South, which meant that most unions were not actively involved in the burgeoning civil rights movement. Not that they did not support it or refuse to sign on to something like the Freedom Budget. But certainly the civil rights movement might have been joined with the kind of rights spelled out in the budget from the beginning, with results that can only be imagined. At the same time, unions became rigidly bureaucratic and increasingly undemocratic, more and more removed from the rank and file.[9]

The Golden Age Ends

Long periods of prosperity often hide underlying weaknesses in the economy. Economists and politicians, and even ordinarily savvy business executives, come to believe that the good times will never end and that the recessions and depressions of the past were special cases, never to be repeated. However, the nature of capitalist economies is one of inherent instability, for any number of reasons. For example, mainstream economists base their analyses on the assumption that all markets are competitive, in the sense that there are so many firms in each market that no one business can influence the price at which any good or service sells. However, the reality of capitalism is that corporations never tolerate an absence of control, and they will try with whatever means at hand to eliminate competition. They do this by developing lower-cost production methods and using the resulting above-average profits to undersell their rivals and to expand into other markets. Mergers and acquisitions are also used to achieve market control. Thus the tendency of capitalist economies favors the growing monopolization of markets, their domination by a few large firms. With the control over prices that this gives them, along with large and sophisticated marketing departments, and research capabilities that contain costs, monopoly firms make very large profits. But in mature capitalist economies, there are typically not enough capital expenditure outlets to absorb these profits. As investment slows down as a result of this, overall economic growth slows down. Profits, however, always seek a profitable outlet, and owners will want to shift profits to outlets in other countries, or use them to purchase already existing assets, like real estate, stocks, bonds, and the like, in the hope of making a capital gain by selling an asset at a price higher than that at which it was bought.

Employers are also cognizant of any factors that raise the power of their workers and might threaten their long-term ability to make money. These could be high rates of union density, or, as is usually the case when unions are strong, more generous government social welfare expenditures, such as unemployment benefits and social insurance. Both factors increase the security of workers and make them less vulnerable to employer exploitation and sometimes more likely to engage in class-conscious actions that threaten profits.

Along with growing monopolization, relatively strong unions, and liberal public social welfare spending, U.S. businesses began to face more intense global competition, especially from capitalist enterprises in Germany and Japan, which with the aid of U.S. funds had rebuilt themselves, using the most advanced and lowest-cost production techniques. The growth-inducing impact of the second wave of automobilization began to wane as well. All of these things resulted in lower profit margins, which forced capital to find ways to restore them.

Beginning in the mid-1970s, capital, in alliance with major elements within the state apparatus, succeeded in routing progressive forces, including the civil rights and labor movements, ultimately imposing upon them what has come to be known as neoliberalism. There are many elements in this strategy, a full examination of which is beyond the scope of this book. However, several of its most important aspects must be stressed before we can see if a modern-day Freedom Budget is conceivable, much less likely to be put into effect.

The heart of neoliberalism is the freeing of capital from whatever social bonds were placed upon it by popular movements. The key to its success in the United States was the attack on the labor movement. Ironically, capital was helped in this by labor leaders themselves. A rash of rank-and-file movements erupted in the 1970s, as workers fought to regain control of their unions and resist the burden of tightening managerial control in the workplace. The now bureaucratic and autocratic unions waged their own war against members, isolating and defeating them and lessening the likelihood that labor would resist the neoliberal onslaught. Labor unions then embraced a strategy of cooperation with employers, agreeing to all manner of concessions, with the promise that corporations would share some of the cost saving with those workers who remained employed. Both the defeat of the rank-and file movements and the espousing of cooperation set the stage for labor's capitulation to neoliberalism.[10]

Employers financed a number of think tanks to provide ideological cover for their efforts to restore and raise profit margins. Organizations such as the Heritage Foundation and the American Enterprise Institute, along with lobbying groups such as the Business Roundtable, promoted the idea that the Keynesian economics that served as the foundation for social welfare spending and direct government intervention in the economy (and, we should add, the Freedom Budget) was flawed and was in fact responsible for lower corporate profits and the slowdown in growth. Research reports, "fact" sheets, and press releases brought an endless stream of anti-labor and pro-corporate propaganda to the media and the public. Markets were to be left unfettered, so that they could do their job of providing maximum production and societal welfare. Government intervention was castigated as evil, doomed to failure, and counterproductive even to its alleged goals, such as reducing poverty.

Once the groundwork was set, capital assaulted labor directly. Scabs were more frequently hired during strikes; employers began to lock workers out in preemptive strikes when collective bargaining agreements expired; and employers routinely violated labor laws, especially during union organizing campaigns and in negotiations (by refusing to bargain in good faith). The federal government accommodated the war on labor, beginning with President Reagan, who appointed anti-labor persons to the National Labor Relations Board, which oversees and enforces the most important labor laws, and then, in the most important, and symbolic act, smashed the strike of the relatively conservative air traffic controllers union. He did this by jailing its leaders and firing its 11,500 members, replacing them with non-union workers, thereby encouraging similar union-busting efforts throughout the country.

Inside workplaces, employers introduced a variety of new and more insidious control mechanisms, which have been summed up with the phrase "lean production." Production has been decentralized, with peripheral supplies tightly connected to core firms, as in the automobile industry, where much work has been contracted out to companies that produce, for example, car seats, which are then supplied to the automobile manufacturers as they are needed. The car companies save wage and inventory costs with this system. Workers faced speedups and constant pressure to do more work in less time, with fewer people.[11]

Although the labor movement was the major enemy of the corporate offensive, civil rights were also targeted. The power of the civil rights laws was weakened by court decisions, which narrowed their scope and placed a greater burden on individual plaintiffs to demonstrate that defendants had an intent to discriminate, something difficult to prove. In addition, courts made it harder for large groups of aggrieved victims of discrimination to file class action suits. This, along with the wording of the civil rights laws themselves, which appeared to privilege individual plaintiffs, limited the effectiveness of these statutes to benefit working-class minorities as a whole. Unlike the National Labor Relations Act, which privileges and protects the collective actions of the working class, the civil rights laws aim to protect individuals. This worked to the advantage of middle-class blacks, who soon began to move from black neighborhoods, separating an important part of this community from the rest of it.

At the conclusion of chapter 6, we noted that much of the civil rights movement after 1968 was subjected to a process of what has been called "co-optation"—facilitating the rise of a layer of African Americans, many of whom had been energetic activists, into relative affluence and status, in some cases through increasing involvement in the Democratic Party. Of course, there were some who were not inclined to take this path. From the start of the civil rights movement, there were radical elements, often attuned to a philosophy of black nationalism and separation from white allies. These groups ranged from the Black Panthers and various black liberation organizations to the Nation of Islam, whose most famous minister was Malcolm X. Most of these groups eschewed the nonviolent ethic of Martin Luther King, and they also advocated various self-help and black-controlled institutions, from lunch programs to schools and farms. The FBI carried out a campaign of vilification, infiltration, and assassinations to weaken and split these groups.[12]

While all of this was taking place, capital began to push for a restructuring of the global economic architecture, using the political power that their money gave them to bend the government to their will. From the 1980s until the present, capital has demanded and gotten an end to public regulation of their businesses and the use of their money. Banking was deregulated, so that financial institutions could make loans, underwrite corporate expansion and mergers, create scores of new, often risky financial instruments, and hold minimal reserves as protections against financial turbulence. Of great importance, governments began to allow the free flow of money and investment across international borders. Trade agreements took from governments the power to regulate foreign investment and finance. The financial sector of the economy grew to become the commanding height of capitalism, accounting for a continuously larger share of total corporate profits.

To further weaken the working class, capital pressured governments at all levels to privatize public services. As governments did this, public workers lost employment and the public suffered a marked decline in what they had come to expect from government. Perhaps the most radical privatization has occurred in public education, which has also become a center for the indoctrination of children into the wonders of "free" markets.

The new freedom won by capital revolutionized the U.S. economy. Manufacturing was devastated as businesses moved operations to lower-wage countries and utilized electronic technology to employ workers in India and elsewhere to do the kinds of work once done in the United States. The state no longer pretended to be neutral in the struggle between capital and labor, but openly sided with employers and suppressed labor. Financial institutions gained the power to dictate how non-financial businesses operated and where. Employment growth slowed, even during economic expansions, as lean production allowed employers to maintain output with ever fewer workers. The ability of capital to move freely around the world stopped employment growth almost altogether in goods and services that are tradable on global markets and confined it to the public sector, health care (which is heavily dependent on government spending), food service and entertainment, and retail. The only one of these sectors that is heavily unionized is government, and neoliberalism has targeted public sector union members for elimination in recent years.[13]

Some Consequences of Neoliberalism

The consequences of neoliberalism vary greatly, depending on whether we are talking about the rich or the not so rich. Corporations and their owners have reaped tremendous profits from lower labor costs and globalized production. Working men and women, on the other hand, have suffered declining or stagnating wages and benefits since the 1970s.

Working-class households tried to maintain their living standards by a combination of more hours of work and additional family members entering the workforce. These stratagems helped some, but each added new stresses to daily life, and they had limits, which appear to have been reached in many households. To compensate, worker households used debt, with credit cards and second mortgages on their homes, to finance all manner of expenditures.

The new contours of global capitalism brought the financial sector of the economy to the fore. The movement of money and capital goods across borders required a host of new financial instruments to protect it. Once President Nixon took the United States off the international gold standard, exchange rates were left to fluctuate according to the demand for and supply of particular currencies. When currency speculators believe that a country is doing things that will cause the demand for its currency to rise or fall, they can make bets that one or the other will happen, and what they do can make the exchange value of a currency rise or fall rapidly by large amounts. Those moving money and capital across borders need protection against these fluctuations, and new financial instruments were created to try to provide this. Similarly, insurance against political changes that might jeopardize foreign investments (nationalization, for example) is needed, and financial instruments were created for this as well. The sale of these instruments brought large profits to financial firms and strengthened their economic and political power.

As workers tried to borrow their way out of lower real wages, banks created various loan instruments to provide the money. These were then repackaged and sold, as were insurance policies presumably aimed at protecting the holders of the newly created financial instruments.

Once finance got rolling, those whose job it was to sell the new instruments created still newer ones and engaged in a massive marketing campaign to get gullible buyers around the world to purchase them. The big financial corporations, as well as Federal Reserve chairman Alan Greenspan, assured everyone that modern statistical techniques, pioneered by mathematical wizards on Wall

Street, guaranteed that little risk inhered in buying and even speculating in the new instruments, and what risk there was could be hedged against by buying other financial instruments.

A long boom in the stock and other financial markets commenced in the 1980s, and as always happens, market participants began to develop an irrational euphoria that prices would continue to rise. In the 1990s, new electronic technology helped fuel an explosion of high-tech stock offerings and rapid increases in the stock prices of tech companies, many of which never made a profit. When savvy investors began to sell such stocks in the early 2000s, the bubble in prices collapsed. As those who lost money cut their spending, the economy slumped. To get it going again, the Federal Reserve cut interest rates. However, we began to see a new phenomenon when the economy recovered. Unemployment remained high well after the end of the downturn, in what economists call a jobless recovery. The low interest rates then fueled a new bubble, this time in the housing market. The bursting of this bubble in 2007 led to the worst economic collapse since the Great Depression, with results familiar to all of us. We will revisit these shortly. For now it is sufficient to note that we have experienced another jobless recovery. The spread of capital around the world, ever in search of lower costs and higher profits, along with lean production, have meant that production can now rise anywhere in the world without being accompanied by rapidly rising employment.[14]

Before we examine the prospects for a New Freedom Budget, let us briefly summarize the changed political terrain that has resulted from the radically new economy that has been constructed by capital in the United States since the mid-1970s:

1. The primary agents of working-class power, the unions, have been decimated, with union density in the private economy at less than 8 percent, a number lower than at any time in the past nearly hundred years. In the public sector, density is much higher, but everywhere public sector unions are under attack. The downward spiral in which the labor movement finds itself shows no signs of abating.

2. The state-imposed fetters on capital enacted during and after the Great Depression have been eliminated. Capital now has a freedom of movement not seen in eighty years. This has further weakened the power of workers. Employers can and do threaten their employees with capital flight if they

make demands for better wages, benefits, and working conditions. Capital is now awash in money.

3. Labor now has little political power; the state is firmly controlled by capital. Social welfare programs, such as those put in place during the era of the Freedom Budget, have been gutted or put on the political chopping block. The civil rights laws have become shells of their former selves, as have the labor laws. Today austerity is the watchword for all but war making and bailing out businesses "too big to fail."

4. There is no civil rights movement to speak of in the United States today. It has become as much a casualty of the neoliberal juggernaut as the labor movement. And even though, as we will see, the United States continues to wage wars nearly as destructive as the war in Vietnam, there is nothing comparable to the antiwar movement that rocked the country in the 1960s and 1970s.

5. As capital has spread its wings to fully encompass the entire world, including the former Soviet Union and its satellites in Europe as well as China, capital has become much more able to resist social controls that governments might seek to place upon it. Should one nation seek to alleviate serious social problems, such as poverty and unemployment, capitalists can and do shift their operations elsewhere to avoid bearing the costs of public intervention and to send a signal to governments that they proceed at their own peril. At the very least, we can no longer assume that the multiplier impact of government spending will remain in any particular nation. Increases in consumer incomes might be spent on imports, and higher corporate profits might not result in domestic investments.

8. POVERTY AND ITS ATTENDANT
EVILS TODAY

ALTHOUGH THE FREEDOM BUDGET was never implemented, some of what it proposed came to pass. As we noted in previous chapters, health care, housing, and public assistance for the poor were improved. Racial minorities won better access to schooling. Unemployment compensation and Social Security were made more generous. Environmental protection laws were enacted. However, the problems spelled out in it are still very much with us, and some new ones have appeared since the budget was proposed. In this chapter, we show the contemporary scope of poverty and its attendant evils and set the stage for the development of a New Freedom Budget.

Poverty Today

The official poverty rate fell sharply from 1959—the first year for which data are available—until 1973—roughly when the post–Second World War long wave of prosperity and growth ended.[1] The national incidence of poverty then rose gradually, from a low of 11.1 percent in 1973 to more than 15 percent today, only broken by a short period of decline during the second half of the 1990s, when it fell back to what it had been in 1973. The Great Recession brought sharp increases in the incidence of poverty, and rates continued to rise through 2011. Poverty now afflicts more than 46,000,000 people. Worse yet, the share of the poor in deep poverty—defined as one-half of the official poverty level of income—has risen steadily since the mid-1970s. In 1975, about 30 percent of the poor were in deep poverty; in 2010, 44.3 percent were. In 2010, the official poverty income for a family of four was $22,314 (this is a pre-tax number). So, those in deep poverty must survive, in a family of four, on $11,157. More than 20,000,000 persons live in what can only be described as destitution.

Child poverty is a special curse, and the U.S. rates are unconscionably high. Using the U.S. government's official definition of poverty, 22.0 percent of children under eighteen and 25.8 percent under six live in poverty in the richest country on earth. In fact, the United States has far and away the highest incidence of child poverty of any of the world's wealthy, developed nations. To compare poverty in different countries, we must use the same definition of poverty everywhere. A common cut-off point for the poverty level of income, different than the U.S. official definition, is one-half of a nation's median income (the median income is that at which half the population is equal to or above it, and half is equal to or below it). Using this measure for 2009, the U.S. child poverty rate was 23.1 percent. By comparison, Finland's was 5.3 percent, Germany's was 8.5 percent, and Japan's was 14.9 percent.

The Freedom Budget used an old government budget concept called "moderate but adequate" to expand the definition of poverty—that is, to argue that many more people were in fact "in want" but not classified as officially poor. Today, there are several alternative definitions of poverty. We have already seen that the global standard for poverty is one-half the median level of income. By this standard, the United States has the highest overall incidence of poverty, 17.3 percent in the late 2000s compared to 6.1 percent in Denmark and 7.2 percent in France. Recently, the Bureau of Labor Statistics in conjunction with the U.S. Census Bureau developed a Supplemental Poverty Measure, which was released in 2011. This measure recognizes that people's consumption patterns have changed dramatically, in response both to changing relative prices (families now spend a much smaller percentage of income on food than the one-third assumed in the official measure) and an entirely new basket of goods and services now available. In addition, before we can spend our income, we have to pay taxes; and we also might receive government transfer payments, either in the form of money or as money equivalents, such as food stamps. The Supplemental Measure, therefore, bases the poverty threshold on a complete set of goods and services, not just food, and it deducts taxes and includes government transfer payments to get the actual income that will be compared to the poverty threshold to determine who is poor. Using this measure, we see that the incidence of poverty is somewhat higher than that of the official measure. In 2010, the official incidence of poverty was 15.2 percent, while it was 16 percent using the Supplemental Measure. An interesting difference between the two definitions shows up for those sixty-five and older, the group for whom poverty has risen most dramatically since the time of the Freedom Budget. In 2010, poverty for the elderly was 9 percent officially but 15.9 percent with the new definition. The increase is due primarily to the much higher medical costs borne by older men and women.

Factors Connected to Poverty: The Old Ones Are Still with Us, and New Ones Have Arisen

Unemployment

Central to the Freedom Budget was full employment. There had to be jobs available for all who sought them. Given the centrality of work to human existence, a good society must be structured in such a way that we can engage in meaningful work. At a minimum, then, there has to be enough work to go around. How has the U.S. economy performed in this area?[2]

The Freedom Budget was proposed at a time when unemployment rates were falling. President Johnson's Great Society spending programs and the war in Vietnam, along with sharp tax cuts, helped drive unemployment down from 5.2 percent in 1964 to 3.5 percent in 1969. However, after this, as the impact of these factors stabilized or fell and as the special features of the post–Second World War recovery in the United States petered out, unemployment rates rose and stayed relatively high for many years. Between 1970 and 1997, the unemployment rate fell below 5 percent only once, in 1973. A severe recession in the early 1980s drove the rate up to 9.7 and 9.6 percent in 1982 and 1983, respectively. This period marked the beginning of a severe contraction in manufacturing and the hollowing out of once prosperous working-class towns and cities across the country, especially in the Midwest. One of the authors was working at the time in Johnstown, Pennsylvania, a major steel-producing town, and the local unemployment rate during some months in 1982 was close to 30 percent.

There were other recessions after the one at the beginning of the 1980s, but until those that struck in the twenty-first century, unemployment fell sharply once the downturn ended. Since 2000, this has not been the case, and economists now speak of "jobless recoveries." Something seems to have broken the connection between GDP growth and employment gains. Nowhere is this more clearly seen than in the Great Recession. Although this officially ended in June 2009, job growth has remained sluggish and unemployment stubbornly high. Unemployment actually rose in 2010, to 9.6 from 9.3 percent in 2009, and it was still 8.1 percent in 2012.

The only period since the mid-1970s when unemployment dropped below 5 percent was during the second half of the 1990s, when the technology boom and relatively low interest rates boosted demand enough to reverse for a short time the tendency toward high unemployment rates. Between 1995 and 1999, the rate fell from 5.6 to 4.2 percent. Such a decline has not occurred since.

The Bureau of Labor Statistics, which calculates the unemployment rate, also estimates and publishes several other measures of labor market distress, found on the BLS website under the category "Alternative Measures of Labor Underutilization." The Freedom Budget discussed these when it looked at underemployment. The two main types of underemployment are involuntary part-time work and marginal attachment to the labor force. The first is composed of all those surveyed each month who say they are working part-time but want full-time work. The second includes all those who want a job, have not looked for one in the past four weeks (this would count them as officially unemployed), but have sought work during the past year. Total labor underutilization then equals the officially unemployed, involuntary part-timers, and those marginally attached to the labor force. This number divided by the labor force (which for the official unemployment rate includes all who are employed or unemployed, but for the expanded measure includes also those marginally attached) gives an expanded unemployment rate. In the BLS data, this is called "U6" (the official rate is "U3"). U6 is, of course, much higher than U3. During and after the Great Recession, U6 rose, from 8.3 percent in 2008 to 16.7 percent in 2010. It fell back only to 14.7 percent in 2012. In 2008, this meant that at least 26.2 million persons suffered serious labor market distresses, one in every six workers. Millions more family and household members must have suffered deprivation as well.

A special problem surfaced during the Great Recession—the extent and depth of long-term unemployment. Older workers especially found it difficult to find employment when they lost their jobs. The lean production techniques and the electronic technology discussed above have allowed employers to get more and more production from fewer and fewer workers. Or they have discovered that they can substitute part-time for full-time labor, saving wages and benefits by doing so. The Great Recession added a tremendous shortfall of aggregate demand to the mix. Long-term unemployment is typically defined as six months or longer; six months is the maximum time a laid-off worker can collect unemployment benefits (unless the federal government extends them). The share of the officially unemployed out of work six months or longer rose from 17.5 percent in 2007 to an astonishing 45.5 percent in March of 2011. In February 2013, long-term unemployment still accounted for 40.2 percent of the total.

When people are unemployed for an extended period of time, both their skills and their confidence erode. And in a society built upon an ideology of individualism, we tend to blame ourselves for our economic woes. Not surprisingly, research has found a strong correlation between unemployment and a host of individual and societal problems. Harvey Brenner at Johns Hopkins University pioneered research in this area.[3] Using a methodology similar to that used to uncover the links between cigarette smoking and disease, he found that a rising unemployment rate was associated with increases in suicide, homicide, arrests, prison admissions, admissions to mental hospitals, hypertension, and cirrhosis of the liver. Unemployment tears families apart, fostering the conditions that can lead to divorce and spousal and child abuse. Needless to say, society must bear many of the costs of these developments.

There is a direct and strong connection between falling unemployment rates and the incidence of poverty. Falling rates improve wages at the bottom of the wage scale more than at the top. The Economic Policy Institute, in its *State of Working America,* found, for example, that "Wage gains from lower unemployment are roughly twice as high for the lowest-wage male workers as they are for middle- and high-wage workers."[4] Thus, the lower unemployment rates of the late 1990s produced lower poverty rates as well.

Low Wages/Inadequate Incomes

As we noted in chapter 5, full employment is a necessary but not sufficient condition for eradicating poverty. Also needed are good wages and benefits. The catastrophic decline in union density, especially in the private sector, has removed one of the major determinants of wages and benefits—the collective power of the working class. As a consequence, for private sector production and non-supervisory workers, real hourly wage rates (these are adjusted for inflation and thus measure purchasing power) are barely higher today than in 1973. Twenty-eight percent of all jobs pay a wage that would not, with full-time, year-round labor, support a family of four at the official poverty level of income. This is a wage rate of $11.06 per hour in 2011. If we consider these persons as the "working poor," we are talking about millions of jobs that confine their holders to poverty. What is more, $11.06 is the upper limit for poverty wages. The average wage for these jobs was $8.66 an hour, compared to an average wage rate of $25.85 per hour for everyone earning above the poverty-level wage. They are much less likely to have health insurance than non-poverty workers (19.9 percent versus 61.3 percent), and the same is true for pensions (14.3 percent versus 53.7 percent). They seldom have paid sick days or vacations.[5]

The Freedom Budget said that an increase in the minimum wage was a necessity for a reduction in poverty. Unfortunately, the minimum wage has not even kept pace with inflation since the Freedom Budget was published. The purchasing power of an hour's labor at minimum wage is about 12 percent lower today than it was in 1967. Minimum wage workers are, therefore, much worse off compared to average workers, whose real wages have risen, than they were nearly fifty years ago. As the *State of Working America* puts it:

In 2011, the minimum wage was worth only about 37 percent of what an average worker earned per hour, not far above its lowest point, reached in 2006, in 47 years. In contrast, the minimum wage's share of the average wage was about 50 percent in the late 1960s, about 45 percent in the mid-1970s, and about 40 percent in the early 1990s.[6]

Some states do have higher minimum wages than the federal law mandates, and this has helped our poorest workers earn higher yearly incomes, but overall, the failure of the minimum wage to keep pace with inflation is a national disgrace.

In a careful empirical study of what the impact would be on income, employment, and GDP growth of an increase in the minimum wage to $10.10, economists David Cooper and Doug Hall reached these conclusions:

Increasing the federal minimum wage to $10.10 by July 1, 2015, would raise the wages of about 30 million workers, who would receive over $51 billion in additional wages over the phase-in period.

Across the phase-in period of the minimum-wage increase, GDP would increase by roughly $32.6 billion, resulting in the creation of approximately 140,000 net new jobs (and 284,000 job years) over that period. [7]

As all research shows, unions force employers to raise wages and benefits. However, as we have seen, union strength has diminished markedly since the Freedom Budget went to press. One of the authors of this book summed up both the union impact on wages and benefits and how this impact has diminished as union density has fallen:

> For all workers in the United States, the union wage premium in 2011 was 13.6%. That is, on average, union members earn this much more than their non-union counterparts. The comparison is made especially significant since it holds the following wage-determining factors constant: experience, education, region, industry, occupation, race/ethnicity, and marital status. This means that if we compare those with the same education, race, occupation, etc., union workers still make more money. We get similar results if we look at benefits. Union employees are more likely to have employer-financed health insurance (28.2%), pensions (53.9%), and time off (14.3%). Union benefits are also better. For example, union workers have lower deductibles and co-payments in their health care plans and are much more likely to be covered when they retire. They are more likely to have defined benefits pensions (in which they are guaranteed certain pension payments, as opposed to defined contribution plans in which employees pay fixed amounts into an individual retirement account but are guaranteed nothing in terms of pension pay-outs).
>
> The collapse of union membership, especially in the private sector of the economy, has reduced the union advantage considerably. . . . The decline in union membership among blue collar and less formally educated workers has been precipitous. . . . [and this is] associated with a weakening of the union impact on wages between these two years from 11.5% to 3.5% for blue-collar unionists and from 8.2% to 2.6% for union members with a high school education.
>
> The weakening of the union impact on the wages and benefits of blue-collar and less formally educated workers doesn't just lower their standards of living. It also leads to greater inequality in wages; the gaps between college-educated and high school graduates and between white collar

and blue-collar workers have been growing at the same time that union densities have been falling. According to *The State of Working America*, "deunionization can explain about a fifth of the growth in the college/high school wage gap among men between 1978 and 2011." And the "lessened effect of unionism can account for 76.1 percent" of the growth of wage inequality between white- and blue-collar employees. What is more, the growing disparity between those at the top of the income and wealth distributions—the infamous 1% justifiably vilified by the Occupy movement—and the rest of us has its roots in the rapidly growing power of the rich and the dwindling power of workers.[8]

The Freedom Budget argued in favor of a guaranteed annual income, at least for those who cannot or should not work. This would include those disabled and incapable of wage labor and those heads of households who are single and with young children. As we saw in chapter 5, it is not clear whether the budget envisioned such an income for everyone, which would mean that each person would receive an income irrespective of wage or other income. This would be akin to Social Security, for which nearly everyone is eligible but for which there is no means test. Rich and poor alike receive the payments.

The chief argument made by economists against a guaranteed income is that people would reduce their work effort or stop working altogether if they were guaranteed a money payment no matter what they did. However, in the one major experiment with a guaranteed income, performed during the administration of President Richard Nixon, such reductions in work effort did not occur. The program was aimed at poor, two-parent families in several cities. A monthly stipend went to each family irrespective of labor market activity. Records were kept of hours of work and whether the husband and wife were in the labor force or not (working or looking for work). The recipients' race was also noted. The results startled the economists. For men, there was either little change in work effort (true for white men) or an *increase* in hours of work and labor force participation. For women, who were not likely to be employed to start with, there was a decline in labor market activity. However, the extra time was used to attend school or devote more attention to children, both of which must be considered socially productive. Unfortunately, the Nixon-era experiment was not replicated.[9]

We have come a long way from this. Under President Clinton, cash public assistance to the poor, mainly single women with children, was sharply curtailed, and those who had received such monies were punitively forced to seek

POVERTY AND ITS ATTENDANT EVILS TODAY / 203

work. Thus we now have the irony of poor women doing low-wage labor, such as taking care of the children of those much richer than they, while relatives and neighbors watch their children. The notion that women who stayed at home to care for young children were serving any useful function, either as mothers or as the watchdogs of their neighborhoods, has been thoroughly rejected, and the stereotype of lazy young women with dubious mores has been reinforced. The Nixon experiment showed that when people gain the security of a guaranteed income, the hope this engenders has effects opposite of what mainstream economists, with their narrow and jaundiced view of "human nature," tell us will happen when we give people "something for nothing."

Insufficient and Substandard Housing

Inadequate and substandard housing still plague the United States, and are no closer to remediation than they were in 1966. Three public health experts with the Centers for Disease Control and Prevention put the benefits of decent housing succinctly in a 2011 report:

> Healthy homes are essential to a healthy community and population. They contribute to meeting physical needs (e.g., air, water, food, and shelter) and to the occupants' psychological and social health. Housing is typically the greatest single expenditure for a family. Safe housing protects family members from exposure to environmental hazards, such as chemicals and allergens, and helps prevent unintentional injuries. Healthy housing can support occupants throughout their life stages, promote health and safety, and support mental and emotional health. In contrast, inadequate housing contributes to infectious and chronic diseases and injuries and can affect child development adversely.[10]

One of the offshoots of the civil rights struggle was the building of a number of poor people's movements, which fought for and often won improvements in the lives of those whose circumstances were often desperate. More public housing and more generous public assistance benefits were directly tied to the direct and militant actions of the poor. There are organizations based upon the grassroots efforts of this era that have formed in more recent times, but the hopes of the past, for the most part, have been dashed.

Housing difficulties today take several forms. There are more than 630,000 homeless persons in the United States, many of whom suffer serious mental and substance abuse problems. The housing market meltdown that triggered the Great Recession has put more families on the streets as well. For low-income households, there is a severe shortage of affordable housing. Using data from the 2010 American Community Survey (ACS), the National Low-Income Housing Coalition (NLIHC) looked at the "disparity between the current supply of homes for rent and the number of low income households who need rental homes they can afford." For the two poorest groups, the findings are disheartening.

Extremely Low Income (household income = 0–30 percent of the median family income in a metropolitan area): In 2010 there were 9.8 million renter households in this category. But there were only 5.5 million affordable rental units available for these people, affordable defined as rent that would absorb no more than 30 percent of household income on rent and utilities. Put another way, for every 100 extremely low-income households, there were only 56 affordable units available. Just one year earlier, in 2009, this number was 59. However, the situation is much worse than these numbers indicate, because many affordable units are already occupied by households with higher incomes. For every 100 households in this category, there were only 30 affordable and available units.

Very Low Income (income = 31–50 percent of median family income in a metropolitan area): In 2010, for every 100 very low income households, there were 87 affordable units for every 100 households, down from 94 in 2009. However, there were just 58 units per 100 very low income households that were both affordable and available.

The NLIHC sums up the consequences of such severe housing deficits in stark language:

What are the consequences of this severe deficit of housing units that are both affordable and available to the lowest-income renters? Some families must live in substandard housing, at the mercy of landlords who know their tenants have no other choice. Many must live long distances from their jobs, reducing family time. Others "double up" with other households, often resulting in crowded and stressful conditions.

But the most common result is that the vast majority of ELI households must spend excessive portions of their limited income on rent and utility costs. Some owner and renter households at all income levels face some level of housing cost burden, but it is ELI renters who experience the most severe cost burdens. If the standard for housing affordability is 30% or less of household income, anyone who pays more than that is said to have a housing-cost burden. Paying more than half of one's income for housing and utility costs is considered a severe housing-cost burden.

In 2010, half (50%) of all renters had some level of housing-cost burden and of those, 27% had a severe housing-cost burden, compared to 29% of all homeowners living with a housing-cost burden, and just 12% of those owners facing a severe housing-cost burden. Of those renters paying more than half of their income on housing costs, 68.1% of them were ELI, 23.8% were VLI, 6.6% were LI, and just 1.4% earned 80% or more of AMI. . . . Three-quarters (76%) of ELI renter households spent the majority of their income on rent and utilities, leaving them with little money left for other necessities such as food, medicine, transportation, and childcare. These are the households that are most vulnerable to becoming homeless if their incomes go down or they have unexpected expenses.[11]

This quote mentions "substandard" housing. One of the authors of this book has been traveling around the United States for the past twelve years, and he has seen numerous examples of substandard housing. Throughout the western United States, where he has spent most of these years, hundreds of thousands of immigrant workers—those who labor in our restaurants, hotels, motels, grocery stores, resorts, farms, and ranches, and do every kind of construction labor—live in flimsy trailers, shoddy houses, cramped apartments, dormitories, even tents. The Census Bureau does a regular census of housing and notes how many units are substandard. In the Centers for Disease Control and Prevention report cited above, substandard (and unhealthy) housing is defined as follows:

The definition of inadequate housing is related to the basic structure and systems of a housing unit, whereas the definition of unhealthy housing is related to exposure to toxins and other environmental factors. Inadequate housing is defined as an occupied housing unit that has moderate or severe physical problems (e.g., deficiencies in plumbing, heating, electricity, hallways, and upkeep). Examples of moderate physical problems in a unit include two or more breakdowns of the toilets that lasted >6 months, unvented primary heating equipment, or lack of a complete kitchen facility in the unit. Severe physical problems include lack of running hot or cold water, lack of a working toilet, and exposed wiring. (The specific algorithm used to categorize a unit as inadequate has been published elsewhere.) For the purposes of this report, CDC has defined unhealthy housing as the presence of any additional characteristics that might negatively affect the health of its occupants, including evidence of rodents, water leaks, peeling paint in homes built before 1978, and absence of a working smoke detector.[12]

The report tells us that "among the approximately 110 million housing units in the United States, approximately 5.8 million are classified as inadequate and 23.4 million are considered unhealthy. Inadequate and unhealthy housing disproportionately affects the populations that have the fewest resources (e.g., persons with lower income and limited education)."[13] The incidence of inadequate and unhealthy housing is much higher among women, blacks, Hispanics, and Native Americans.

The housing situation was made worse by the Great Recession, which saw home prices plummet and household finances, which had been propped up by the housing bubble, devastated. Home equity comprises almost two-thirds of the median wealth holder's assets. The bursting of the bubble forced foreclosure on millions of households, wiping out the main asset of those who were foreclosed and greatly raising the level of household insecurity. At the same time, evictions put much pressure on rental markets, driving up rents and hurting the poorest households the most.

Construction of public housing slowed in the 1980s and has nearly stopped altogether today. Expensive rent subsidies to private landlords replaced construction, but these have been cut dramatically. The Center on Budget and Policy Priorities reports: "From 2010 to 2012, funding for housing assistance fell by $2.5 billion, or 5.9 percent just in 'nominal terms'—i.e., not counting the additional losses due to the effects of inflation—while funds for community development programs fell by $1.5 billion, or 24 percent. Policymakers cut funds for public housing and housing and community development block grant programs most sharply."[14]

Deficiencies in Health Care, Education, and Social Security

HEALTH CARE

The multiple gains made by poor and working-class Americans during the "Golden Age" of U.S. capitalism in health care, education, and Social Security are well documented. However, the federal government's commitment to these has been waning for at least three decades. The number of persons in the United States without health insurance has been rising steadily; in 2011, 47.9 million were uninsured, up 11.7 million from 2000. One study predicted that this number of uninsured would result in about 48,000 needless deaths.[15]

Most Americans under sixty-five have health insurance through their employers, but the fraction of workers covered has been declining because companies seek to cut labor costs, a trend exacerbated by the Great Recession. Economic Policy Institute economist Elise Gould found that "In 2011, the share of non-elderly Americans with employer-sponsored health insurance declined for the 11th year in a row, falling from 58.6 percent in 2010 to 58.3 percent. Since the ESI coverage rate in 2000 was 69.2 percent, the total decline from 2000 to 2011 was 10.9 percentage points. In 2011, 14.2 million fewer non-elderly Americans had ESI than in 2000."[16] Only federal legislation that allowed parents to keep their children covered on parental plans prevented a still larger decline. Meanwhile, the price of health care has far outstripped overall inflation. In February 2013, the consumer price index for all urban consumers (CPI-U) was 232, with 1982–84 as the base period. This means that for all of the goods and services used to construct the index, prices rose by 2.32 times since the base period. But for medical care services, the index was 452, meaning that these services rose in price, on average, 4.52 times over this same number of years. Since the demand for such services is relatively inelastic, this tells us that consumers must now spend more money even if they consume less medical care. It is not surprising, then. that the United States devotes a larger share of its GDP to health care than other rich countries, but at the same time people get less benefit from the health care system. A PBS report sums up the depressing facts of U.S. health care:

How much is good health care worth to you? $8,233 per year? That's how much the U.S. spends per person.
Worth it?

That figure is more than two-and-a-half times more than most developed nations in the world, including relatively rich European countries like France, Sweden and the United Kingdom. On a more global scale, it means U.S. health care costs now eat up 17.6 percent of GDP.

A sizable slice of Americans—including some top-ranking politicians— say the cost may be unfortunate but the U.S. has "the best health care in the world."

But let's consider what 17 cents of every U.S. dollar is purchasing. According to the most recent report from the Organization for Economic Cooperation and Development (OECD)— an international economic group comprised of 34 member nations—it's not as much as many Americans expect.

In the United States:

- There are fewer physicians per person than in most other OECD countries. In 2010, for instance, the U.S. had 2.4 practicing physicians per 1,000 people—well below the OECD average of 3.1.
- The number of hospital beds in the U.S. was 2.6 per 1,000 population in 2009, lower than the OECD average of 3.4 beds.
- Life expectancy at birth increased by almost 0 years between 1960 and 2010, but that's less than the increase of over 15 years in Japan and over 11 years on average in OECD countries. The average American now lives 78.7 years in 2010, more than one year below the average of 79.8 years.[17]

The two major programs of federally financed health care—Medicare and Medicaid—are more efficiently administered than private health care, but both have been subjected to savage budget cuts, which are likely to continue. Liberals have lavishly praised President Obama's health care plan, but good research shows that it will be extremely expensive, will put billions of dollars into the pockets of insurance companies, and will not greatly improve health outcomes.

EDUCATION

The Freedom Budget made a strong plea for more public schools, more teachers, more and better vocational training, and more funding for colleges and the deprived young persons who could not afford to attend them. In those days, public education was marked by enormous disparities, stemming from the fact that schooling is funded by grossly unequal local property taxes and from brutal racial discrimination.[18] Since the years of the Freedom Budget, discrimination has weakened, and many more students attend college today, including minorities, whose access to higher education was limited fifty years ago. Public school teachers formed labor unions, building formidable and wealthy national organizations, making teachers much better paid and no longer subject to draconian restrictions on their personal lives, such as the prohibition against female teachers getting married.

Yet today, crisis still stalks public education. Cities strapped for revenues are closing schools. The teachers' unions are under attack, blamed for the poor performance of students. Privatization has swept the nation, with the move toward charter schools. Dropout rates are phenomenally high, especially where people are poor. However, the answer of our leading politicians and business moguls is to force public school teachers to devote most of their school time to preparing for tests that are supposed to indicate their preparedness for life. This strategy has improved neither the basic reading and mathematical skills of students nor even their test scores. Rampant cheating by school administrators to inflate scores and thereby receive government money has been uncovered. An unbiased observer would not be wrong to believe that some hidden motive must be behind such lunatic policies. No doubt, it is money. Billions of dollars are being made and billions more will be made as the vast testing industries make schools centers of capital accumulation. And in higher education, the situation is just as dire. Like health care, tuition increases have far exceeded the overall rate of inflation. But courses are more and more taught by super-exploited part-time teachers with low pay and no benefits. Private colleges operating solely online reap large profits selling their third-rate educations to gullible and insecure working people duped into believing that a college degree from one of these "digital diploma mills"[19] will win them good jobs.[20]

Journalists and education activists Doug Henwood and Liza Featherstone paint a gloomy picture of what the United States gets for all the money it spends on the "testing model" of public education:

> It's remarkable how similar the U.S. educational system is to our health care system: by world standards, we spend gobs of money on both, in return for underwhelming outcomes. On education, we spend a third more than the OECD average, the second-highest of any country, to produce merely mediocre scores on internationally comparable tests.

Let's examine the dimensions of spending, and the enrollment and attainment numbers.

In 2007, the U.S. spent 7.6 percent of GDP on education, 1.9 points above the OECD average, and exceeded only by Iceland. But before this is turned into a right-wing, "See, you just can't throw money at this problem" homily, several factors lurking below this fat headline number must be discussed.

First, 41% of that spending is on tertiary education (college and beyond), 15 points above the average. Spending on primary and secondary education, is 4.0% of GDP, matched or exceeded by six countries, and just 0.5 point above the average. So we stint on mass education in favor of elite.

And despite all that spending, a surprisingly small share of our population is in school—at all levels. The OECD presents data on the number of years for which 90% or more of the population is enrolled. The average is 13 years; in most Western European countries, it's 14 or more. But in the U.S., it's just 11 years, tied with Mexico, behind Slovenia and just two years ahead of Brazil. Enrollment rates for those aged 5–19 are slightly below the OECD average—and somewhat further below the EU average. Enrollment rates drop the further up the age ladder you go: less than a quarter (23%) of Americans in their 20s are enrolled in some sort of school, 2 points below the OECD average. (That despite spending a bundle on tertiary education.) And the U.S. isn't lagging because college is delayed until later in life; we're also below average for people over 30.

Underperformance is even more extreme at the other end of the age spectrum: just 47% of 3–4-year-olds are in preschool, 24 points below the OECD average, and 3 points behind Brazil. In most Western European countries and Japan, preschool is nearly universal. Many studies have shown that kids who go to preschool do better in school, make more money, get along with other people better, and are less likely to end up in jail than those who don't.

Breaking down expenditures by category is no more flattering to the U.S. than the enrollment numbers. Almost 12% of U.S. spending on primary and secondary schools is devoted to capital expenditures, 4 points above the average and one of the highest shares in the world (or at least the subset for which the OECD reports data).

Current—as opposed to capital—spending in the U.S. shows an unusually large share devoted to administrative and support staff, and a small share devoted to teachers' salaries. But what do our education reformers want to do? Spend more on computers and other gadgetry, and break teachers' unions and cut their salaries.[21]

SOCIAL SECURITY

The Freedom Budget insisted on large increases in Social Security funding and benefit payments. This happened, and as we have seen, the reduction in poverty among the elderly has been remarkable. Social security especially benefits women and minorities, and it protects participants against disability and children against the loss of a parent. The Social Security system is extraordinarily well administered, with administrative costs of 0.8 percent of total expenditures.[22] Benefits are funded by a regressive tax on payrolls, but the payments themselves are progressive, helping the poor relatively more than the rich.

Despite impressive results and sound administration, the Social Security system has been under the gun since the Reagan era. Attacks escalated sharply during and after the Great Recession, with opponents trying to capitalize on fear of rising deficit spending and the large increase in the total debt of the federal government. The supposition that, under current conditions, the system might not be able to pay full benefits decades from now has been used by politicians, financiers (who want to get their hands on the billions of dollars in the Social Security trust funds), think tanks, and the mainstream media to scare us into accepting an austerity agenda. These foes of Social Security say we should raise the retirement age, cut benefits, and allow individuals to contribute less to the Social Security funds and use the extra money to make their own financial investments.

Contrary to what its enemies say, the Social Security system will be financially sound for the foreseeable future, and any shortfalls in revenues can be easily corrected. The government could raise the payroll tax rate; it could increase the amount of individual wage income that is taxed (there is now a cap on taxable income); it could make all income subject to the tax; it could use its general tax revenues to fund the system; it could even sell bonds to the federal reserve banks, which would pay for these with newly printed money, as they did to bail out the financial institutions responsible for the financial meltdown of the Great Recession.[23]

Regressive Fiscal and Monetary Policies

One of the results of capital's offensive against workers and the poor that commenced in the 1970s has been the near-complete subservience of the state—at all levels: federal, state, and local—to business interests, whose goal is to compel the government to make sharp cuts in social welfare spending. The main role of government, these interests argue, must be to secure private property and profit opportunities against organized protests, from workers, the poor, or Occupy-type movements. The Freedom Budget's economics were Keynesian; it was the duty of the government to maintain progressive tax and spending programs to aid those whose economic insecurity was the greatest. Debt-financed spending to accomplish this was perfectly acceptable, even desirable.

During the 1970s, the growing monopolization of production generated both higher unemployment and rising prices, and this new phenomenon gave ammunition to capital's champions, who argued that Keynesian deficit spending was responsible. These forces preached fiscal austerity, combined with tax cuts for business and high-income individuals. The tax cuts would lead to a flurry of business activity that would ultimately greatly increase tax revenues, and cuts in social welfare spending would make people more willing to work, once government handouts were taken away. The resulting economic growth would lift all boats and do more for the poor than the Great Society anti-poverty programs. As conservative think tanks and their media outlets propagandized this agenda and as corporate money helped get elected politicians sympathetic to it, regressive fiscal (and monetary) policies became the order of the day.

The new public economic regime did not yield the outcomes its proponents said it would. Economic growth did not rise; tax revenues did not increase; business investment did not boom; and poverty did not decrease. As we have seen, just the opposite happened. Yet this neoliberal political doctrine has become the common sense of political discourse; every president since Jimmy Carter has been beholden to it. Nowhere has this been better illustrated than in the administration of Barack Obama. The devastation wrought by the Great Recession cries out for a massive Keynesian spending stimulus. However, after bailing out the banks and forcing draconian concessions on automobile workers in return for the bailouts of General Motors and Chrysler, Obama has called for austerity, willing to cut Social Security, Medicare, and every other social welfare measure to appease his business friends.

Monetary policy has proved somewhat more flexible than its fiscal counterpart. At the end of the 1970s and during the 1980s, it followed a draconian regime of high interest rates, to choke off spending and bring inflation under control. This led to the collapse of the steel industry, among others, and a sharp rise in unemployment. However, during and after the Great Recession, the

Federal Reserve kept interest rates at near-record lows, trying, in vain, to get the economy growing again. The low rates did push stock priors markedly higher and gave banks an enormous windfall; they could borrow money from Federal Reserve banks at close to zero interest rates and lend the money out at much higher ones. Those dependent on interest from savings to support themselves have suffered great losses due to low interest payments.

Inequality of Income and Wealth

While the Freedom Budget briefly addressed income inequality, we doubt that the framers of the budget could have imagined the tremendous increase in inequality that commenced in the mid-1970s and accelerated thereafter. No longer are the gains in productivity that allow the economy to produce more output shared roughly equally by each quintile of the income distribution, leaving relative income disparities unchanged.

It is worth spelling out the degree to which inequality has worsened, especially since this has much deeper implications for a New Freedom Budget than inequality did for the original budget. Unlike the authors of the Freedom Budget, we look at both income and wealth inequality.[24]

Incomes are ordinarily flows of money that go to persons over some period of time, such as a wage per hour or a yearly dividend. In 2010, according to U.S. Census data, the richest 20 percent of all households received 50.2 percent of total household income and the poorest 20 percent got 3.3 percent, representing a gain of 13.8 percent for the most affluent households and a loss of 21.4 percent for the least affluent since 1980. The census breaks out the richest 5 percent of households from the top quintile. The income share of the richest 5 percent rose from 16.5 percent in 1980 to 21.3 percent in 2010, a gain of 29.1 percent. In 2010, the share of the top 5 percent was greater than that of the bottom 50 percent of households.[25]

An article on *The Atlantic* website presents U.S. inequality starkly: "Income inequality is more severe in the United States than it is in nearly all of West Africa, North Africa, Europe, and Asia. We're on par with some of the world's most troubled countries, and not far from the perpetual conflict zones of Latin America and Sub-Saharan Africa."[26]

Economists William Piketty and Emanuel Saiz have used federal income tax data, with their broader definition of income and truer reporting, to provide a more detailed and refined picture of the U.S. income distribution. Their find-ings show that the income share of the richest 1 percent of individuals (note that individual and household incomes are not necessarily the same) is now at its highest level since just before the Great Depression, standing at 23.5 percent in 2007. This share fell some during the Great Recession, but it is reasonably certain that this decline has since been reversed. What is more, it has been rising sharply since 1980, when it was about 10 percent. If we take the total gain in household income between 1979 and 2007, 60 percent of it went to the richest 1 percent of individuals, while just 8.6 percent accrued to the poorest 90 percent. An incredible 36 percent found its way into the pockets of the richest 0.1 percent (one one-thousandth of all individuals).

Amazingly, there is stark income inequality even at the top of the income distribution. In the United States in 2007, it is estimated that the five best-paid hedge-fund managers "earned" more than all of the CEOs of the Fortune 500 corporations combined. The income of the top three hedge-fund managers (James Simon, John Paulson, and George Soros) taken together was $9 billion in 2007.[27]

If incomes are unequal and becoming more so, the same can also be said for a more important, though related, statistic—wealth. Simply put, wealth is the money value of what we own at a given point in time. It includes houses, cars, computers, cash, stocks, bonds—anything convertible into cash. If we subtract what we owe from what we own, we get net worth. Wealth is important for many reasons. Some types of wealth, such as stocks and bonds, generate income, such as dividends, interest, and capital gains. If incomes are unevenly divided, and if rich households save a bigger fraction of their income than do poor ones, wealth will get steadily more unevenly divided, even if the income distribution remains stable. Wealthy individuals can live, and live well, without ever working, simply by spending some of the income that derives from their wealth. Some wealth represents possession of the means of production, such as factories, land, banks, and the like, and such ownership is obviously important in terms of economic power. Even more mundane forms of wealth such as automobiles and houses can provide secu-rity and aid us in earning our incomes. Wealth can be used as collateral for loans; the more of it we have, the more we can borrow and the more favorable the terms of the loans. Wealth can be inherited and thus passed down, with its advantages intact, to future generations. Our capacities to work and earn wages, on the other hand, die with us.

Sylvia Allegretto of the Economic Policy Institute has done an extended analysis of the current U.S. wealth distribution. She found that in 2009, the top 1 percent of households owned 35.6 percent of net wealth (net worth) and a whopping 42.4 percent of net financial assets (all financial instruments such as stocks, bonds, bank accounts, and all the exotic instruments that helped trigger the Great Recession, minus non-mortgage debt). The bottom 90 percent owned 25 percent of net wealth and 17.3 percent of net financial wealth. The richest 1 percent had 33.1 percent of net worth in 1983, an increase of 7.5 percent; if we extend our view to the wealthiest 5 percent, we see a rise in share from 58.1 to 63.5 percent, an increase of 9.3 percent. The bottom four-fifths of households suffered a decline in their share of net worth, from 18.7 to 12.8 percent, a loss of nearly 32 percent. Allegretto shows the share of the poorest 20 percent of households; it is negative and declining, meaning that, on average, these households owe more than they own, and the gap between what they own and owe is getting larger. To put these numbers in proper perspective, she notes that the wealth of the "1 percent" is now 225 times larger than the median wealth of all households, the highest ratio on record. It was 131 in 1983.

Allegretto provides two particularly striking facts about wealth. First, as with income at the very top, there is inequality, too. For the super wealthy in the Forbes 400, a list compiled by *Forbes* magazine of the richest persons in the United States, average net worth was $3.2 billion in 2009. However the top wealth holder of the "400" had wealth fourteen times greater than the average for all 400. In 1982, this ratio was 8.6. Second, the share of households with zero or negative net worth increased by 60 percent between 1983 and 2009; we now have about a quarter of all households in this wealth-less state.[28]

Rapidly growing inequality has a wide variety of harmful social consequences. The growing riches of those at the top fuel lavish, energy-wasting, and environmentally damaging consumption. They polarize everything from residential neighborhoods to access to wilderness areas to political influence. The very wealthy get the best of everything, and the rest of us get what is left. The vast savings of the super rich generate price bubbles in many types of markets. And in addition, inequality has directly deleterious effects upon those at the bottom of the income distribution. Just as unemployment, in and of itself, is correlated with suicides, prison admissions, heart attacks, and the like, so too is inequality, independent of other variables, correlated with a host of undesirable individual and social outcomes.

One researcher studied the states in the United States and found:

States with greater inequality in the distribution of income also had higher rates of unemployment, higher rates of incarceration, a higher percentage of people receiving income assistance and food stamps, and a greater percentage of people without medical insurance. Again, the gap between rich and poor was the best predictor, not the average income in the state.

Interestingly, states with greater inequality of income distribution also spent less per person on education, had fewer books per person in the schools, and had poorer educational performance, including worse reading skills, worse math skills, and lower rates of completion of high school.

States with greater inequality of income also had a greater proportion of babies born with low birth weight; higher rates of homicide; higher rates of violent crime; a greater proportion of the population unable to work because of disabilities; a higher proportion of the population using tobacco; and a higher proportion of the population being sedentary (inactive).

Lastly, states with greater inequality of income had higher costs per person for medical care, and higher costs per person for police protection.[29]

Problems in Land and Resource Use

A modern reader will not find all of the Freedom Budget's proscriptions for land and resource use very useful, especially its espousal of nuclear power, which, in the wake of the 2011 Fukushima disaster in Japan, cannot possibly be part of a New Freedom Budget. The main difficulty with what it says in this area is that the situation has changed so dramatically today. The trend toward mass-produced food in factory farms and the demise of smaller family farms has continued. Farm laborers are still poor and overworked. Children are still hungry. However, we now face what can only be called catastrophic environmental problems, much worse than those that existed when the Freedom Budget was introduced. Noted environmental sociologist John Bellamy Foster has recently written:

Scientists, led by the Stockholm Resilience Centre, have recently indicated that we have crossed, or are near to crossing, nine "planetary boundaries" (defined in terms of sustaining the environmental conditions of the Holocene epoch in which civilization developed over the last 12,000 years): climate change, species extinction, the disruption of the nitrogen-phosphorus cycles, ocean acidification, ozone depletion, freshwater usage, land cover change, (less certainly) aerosol loading, and chemical use.[30]

An examination of such monumental problems is beyond the scope of this book, but they do have implications for a New Freedom Budget, as we will see in the next chapter.

Black Americans

The Freedom Budget explicitly highlighted the special role that black Americans could play in winning its passage, a role based on their centrality in the civil rights movement and on their horrendous economic circumstances. Since then, black people have seen many improvements in their lives, gaining access to both better job opportunities and political offices. It could never have been imagined in 1966 that the United States would someday have a black president, but in 2008 Barack Obama was elected.

Yet despite undeniable progress, seemingly intractable racial disparities remain, nearly fifty years after landmark civil rights legislation was enacted. Consider the following summary of the economic condition of black America, using many of the categories enumerated in the Freedom Budget.[31]

1. Income: In 1947, the ratio of median black family income to white family income was 51.1 percent. In 2010, it was 61.0 percent. After the heroic struggles of the civil rights movement and the enactment of numerous civil rights laws, this seems a small gain, smaller even than the ratio of 61.3 percent of 1967.[32]
2. Wealth: In 2010, the median net worth (all assets, including homes, minus all debts) of black households (a household is not necessarily a family) was $4,900, 5 percent of that for whites, for whom it was $97,000. If we confine our data to median net financial wealth (assets include mutual funds, trusts, retirement and pension funds, etc.), in 2009 black households had $200, whereas whites had $36,100, for a ratio of black to white of .0056. In 2009, nearly twice as many black households as white had zero or negative net worth (39.2 versus 20.3 percent).[33]

3. Wages and Jobs: Black workers earn less than their white counterparts; black men, for example, earn less than three-quarters the wages of white men. The black-white earnings ratio is less than one for every level of schooling. Part of this is due to the fact that blacks, no matter their level of schooling, are overrepresented in jobs with relatively low wages and underrepresented in higher-paying jobs. A report from the Economic Policy Institute tells us that "the average of the annual wages of occupations in which black men are overrepresented is $37,005, compared with $50,333 in occupations in which they are underrepresented." Further, "A $10,000 increase in the average annual wage of an occupation is associated with a seven percentage point decrease in the proportion of black men in that occupation."[34] Another part of the reason for the relatively low wages of blacks is that they earn less money within the same occupations. A summary of data collected by the Bureau of Labor Statistics shows that "in 2010, median usual weekly earnings of . . . white men ($1,273) working full-time in management, professional, and related occupations (the highest paying major occupation group) were well above the earnings of black men ($957) in the same occupation group." For women, the numbers were $932 for whites and $812 for blacks. Racial wage discrepancies exist in every occupational category. If instead of specific occupations, we look just at low-wage work, we find racial disparities. About one-quarter of all jobs in the United States pay a wage that, for full-time, year-round work, would put a family of four below the poverty level of income. But for jobs held by black workers, this figure is nearly 35 percent.[35]

4. Poverty: In 2010, the incidence of poverty for non-Hispanic whites was 9.9 percent; for blacks it was 27.4 percent. 13.5 percent of blacks lived at less than one-half of the poverty level of income. For black children (less than six years old), the incidence of poverty was 45.8 percent; the rate for white children was 14.5 percent.[36]

5. Unemployment: The official unemployment rate has almost always been about twice as high for blacks as for whites. In March 2013, these rates were 13.3 and 6.7 percent, respectively. Double-digit unemployment rates are more common than not for black workers, a condition that would be unacceptable if it were true for white workers. In 2011, the underemployment rate was 13 percent for whites and nearly 25 percent for blacks.[37]

6. Housing: Homes are the most important form of wealth for most households. Not unexpectedly, there is a racial gap here, too. Whites are 25 percent

more likely to own homes than blacks. In addition, the current meltdown in housing prices has disproportionately hurt black homeowners. In connection with housing, it is useful to mention the 2012 study by the Manhattan Institute, which received a great deal of media attention, that housing segregation has dramatically declined. The study's authors use a "dissimilarity index" as a measure of segregation and show that this has fallen. An Economic Policy Institute (EPI) evaluation of the study explains: "They find a national dissimilarity (or segregation) rate of about 55 percent for African Americans—in other words, 'only' 55 percent of African Americans would now have to move to neighborhoods with more non-blacks in order to evenly distribute the black population throughout all neighborhoods in their metropolitan areas. This is a substantial decline from the segregation level of about 80 percent in 1970." Against the optimistic gloss that has been put on the Manhattan Institute analysis, the EPI authors make several salient points. First, a 55 percent segregation rate is nothing to brag about, and it will rise now that black homeowners in white neighborhoods have been experiencing so many foreclosures. Second, the dissimilarity index is a somewhat indirect measure of black and white interaction. By another measure, the typical black person lived in a neighborhood that was 40 percent white in 1940; today this has fallen to 35 percent. And even for the dissimilarity index, some of the decline is due to an influx of Asians and Hispanics into black localities, while another part of it is the consequence of the greater economic mobility of the black middle class. Poor blacks have been left behind, stuck in almost totally segregated areas, without jobs as manufacturing left town, and unable to follow jobs to the suburbs. The "high poverty" neighborhoods are home to 40 percent of all poor blacks (only 15 percent of poor whites live in such neighborhoods).[38]

7. Life Expectancies and Infant Mortality: There is no reason to expect that, other things equal, one group of people in a country should exhibit different life expectancies and infant mortality rates than another. In 2010, blacks could expect to live four years fewer than whites. Infant mortality rates are more than double for black than for white women.[39]

8. Prisons and the Criminal Justice System: Here the racial divide is startling. In 2010, 2,226,800 persons were incarcerated in the United States, and another 4,887,900 were either on probation or parole. So, the United States has a criminal justice system population of over seven million people. Nearly 40 percent of this population is black; more than triple the black

share of the U.S. population. At every step in the criminal justice system—arrest, arraignment, legal representation, plea bargaining, jury selection, verdict, sentencing, chance for parole, prospects after imprisonment—blacks fare worse than whites.[40]

The Growth Dividend

Much of the economics and politics of the Freedom Budget was based upon a "growth dividend." During the mid-1960s, the economy grew at a brisk pace. And for the 1950s and 1960s, the GDP rose at a rate of more than 4 percent per year. The Budget assumed, correctly, that as poverty and unemployment fell, production would grow even more rapidly, providing the tax revenues that would allow the federal government to continue its efforts to end poverty.

Today the economic picture has darkened considerably, and there are now at least three reasons why we can no longer depend on a growth dividend. First, since the 1960s, growth rates have slowed and growth has become less labor using. GDP growth rates fell in the 1970s and 1980s to about 3 percent, and over the last ten years, the average growth rate has been below 2 percent. If we look at a chart of the trend in growth rates since 1960, it is unmistakably downward sloping.[41] Liberal economist J. Bradford DeLong warns that the Great Recession bodes poorly for a recovery of growth rates to their past heights, noting that this downturn may well cost the economy about 1.6 years' worth of output when all is said and done. Slow growth may well be the order of the day going forward, barring massive federal government spending.[42] The private economy is unlikely to overcome slow growth.

Second, we have seen above that there has been a tremendous increase in income and wealth inequality. Since the late 1970s, nearly two-thirds of the growth in aggregate income has gone to the richest 1 percent of individuals, and more than one-third went to the richest .1 percent. So, even if we suppose that the economy grows at a decent pace, what good will this do for the poor if the gains from growth accrue to a tiny minority of wealthy people?

Third, whatever growth the economy sustains, the nature of capitalism will mean that the environment will continue to be abused in the name of profits. For example, we are in the midst of a frenzy of water and air polluting drilling for natural gas and oil. These commodities are being produced to be used, to fuel growth and further despoliation of the natural world. The world simply will not be able to tolerate rapid capitalist growth. It might not even be able to sustain itself if the growth is generated by a socialist economy.

The U.S. economy, despite its enormous production capabilities and great natural wealth, has not been able, over the past fifty years, to end poverty and its attendant evils. They are still with us, and they show no signs of disappearing. If we put our minds outside the propaganda machine that keeps telling us we live in the best of all possible worlds, this fact is shocking. Unfortunately, most of us have been unable to do this. Instead of getting angry and demanding that something be done about the human misery our economic system generates, many of us simply have lowered our expectations.[43] There are those who have protested, and we hope their numbers grow. We offer our thoughts on a New Freedom Budget, one we think will provide ammunition and food for thought for everyone whose expectations for freedom have not diminished and all those who can be convinced to raise their voices for a different kind of world.

9. TOWARD A NEW FREEDOM BUDGET

OUR SOCIETY TODAY needs a Freedom Budget on the scale of what was proposed by A. Philip Randolph, Rev. Martin Luther King, Jr., and their cothinkers almost half a century ago. However, it will now need to incorporate lessons learned from previous defeats, and at the same time adjust to new realities.

The development of such a New Freedom Budget will need to embrace more than what we can achieve with this book. A broader consultation and consideration, reflecting the political and social forces that would be capable of making the New Freedom Budget a living reality, will need to take place. In the hope that such a process can be generated, we are offering here some thoughts on aspects of the principles, the objectives, the policies and the strategic perspectives that might be embodied in such a New Freedom Budget. We are convinced that, at this point in history, only a more radical variant of what had been proposed can bring about the goals that Randolph and King were reaching for.

The hopeful days of the earlier Freedom Budget are gone. Barring radical changes, the masses of poor and working-class men and women will be condemned to lives of disappearing hope. Austerity is everywhere the watchword of our economic and political rulers. For us, this means that it is long past time to put forward the kinds of demands that the mainstream political parties are unlikely to embrace (just as neither the Democratic nor the Republican Party was inclined to accept labor rights or racial justice before the labor movement and civil rights movement were able to mobilize massive and militant activity in years gone by). But unless we are prepared to struggle for the kinds of principles and objectives offered here, our freedom will never be achieved.

Basic Principles of a New Freedom Budget

Our conception of the New Freedom Budget is grounded in five fundamental principles:

1. *Liberty and justice for all: equal rights, equal opportunities—no exceptions.* These are among the highest ideals articulated by the overwhelming majority of people in our society. The New Freedom Budget must allow for and help to nourish the free development of each and every individual, with no exceptions in relation to race, ethnicity, national origin, religion, gender, age, sexual preference, political orientation, physical characteristics, and the like.

2. *Deepening democracy—politically, socially, economically.* Democracy, rule by the people, must be the keystone of the New Freedom Budget. There is a growing conviction throughout the world that the political, social, and economic institutions of society must not be subordinated to tyrants or privileged minorities. The resources on which all of us are dependent, the resources that make our society possible, should be overseen democratically for the benefit of all. The notion that our country's economy should develop as an integral part of a democratic commonwealth is sometimes labeled *socialism*, which is why the authors of this book consider themselves to be socialists. Regardless of such labels, we are convinced that a thoroughgoing democracy must be a defining principle of the New Freedom Budget.

3. *Commitment to future generations.* We do not conceive of the New Freedom Budget as some kind of a "quick fix." Its principles and objectives are meant to be durable, providing for the freedom and well-being of people in the here-and-now, but also their children and their children's children, and beyond. This has obvious implications for the manner in which our resources must be utilized as we seek to provide for the needs of all.

4. *Comprehensive solution—reject tokenism and fragmented "remedies."* We are persuaded by the insight of A. Philip Randolph, who said that in efforts for racial and economic justice, "we encounter the pessimists and the

tokenists, those who counsel 'gradualism' and those who urge piecemeal and haphazard remedies for deep-rooted and persistent evils." Randolph's response to this holds true for the New Freedom Budget. Such a limited approach "becomes an excuse for not beginning or for beginning on a base too small to support the task, and for not setting goals; and the scattered, fragmented remedies, lacking priorities and coordination, often work at cross purposes."

5. *Harmony with global neighbors.* This principle addresses what we see as one of the most serious limitations of the earlier Freedom Budget, highlighted by its "neutrality" in regard to the U.S. war in Vietnam. The United States cannot resolve its own problems if it is guided by a foreign policy designed to establish or maintain something like "the American Century," which meant domination of the global political economy by the United States. The well-being of the people of the United States cannot be secured at the expense of other peoples. There must be harmony between U.S. foreign policy and the domestic policies associated with the New Freedom Budget. As Martin Luther King Jr. insisted, policies of violence and exploitation must be replaced with those of mutual respect, cooperation, and economic justice.

Basic Objectives of a New Freedom Budget

We have expanded the list of objectives in the Freedom Budget to reflect the economic and social changes that have occurred over the past fifty years. These have created new difficulties for the masses of people, and they must be addressed now if freedom is to be achieved. We believe that to make freedom a reality, we must struggle to win:

1. Full employment
2. Adequate income for all who are employed
3. A guaranteed minimum adequacy level of income for those who cannot or should not work
4. Adequate and safe housing for all
5. Health care for all
6. Educational opportunity for all
7. Secure and expanded transportation infrastructure

8. Secure and expanded Social Security
9. Food security for all
10. A sustainable environment
11. Cultural freedom and enrichment for all (arts, parks, sports, recreation)
12. Reduction in the inequality of income and wealth to ensure realization of objectives

We have seen in previous chapters the extent to which these objectives have not been realized since the Freedom Budget was proposed. Many have gotten worse. We have also examined in some detail the specific harm to individuals, families, groups, and the society as a whole that this failure to realize these objectives has caused. Here we discuss briefly the social and personal benefits of winning these objectives, list some concrete ways in which they can be won, and the economic feasibility of putting them in place.

1. FULL EMPLOYMENT

Work is central to human existence; it is how we transform the natural world to meet our needs and how we interact with other people to, in effect, produce ourselves as we create the output we must have to survive. The intimate connection between unemployment and poverty and between unemployment and a host of social and personal pathologies tells us that we need to work. Capitalism, especially in its neoliberal version, inevitably wastes people, unconcerned when millions lose jobs, have to settle for part-time work, or simply drop out of the labor force when finding work proves impossible.

There is no compelling reason why government cannot aggressively pursue a full-employment policy. It can create meaningful jobs in many areas: day care, housing, public transit, schools, health care, our public parks and lands, and so forth. Jobs and training could go hand-in-hand, producing not just useful goods and services, but productive human beings. Or subsidies could be given to groups of people so they could form cooperatives or purchase existing businesses. Such projects would, to a large extent, be self-financing, as some of the incomes generated return as tax revenues, as unemployment compensation payments go down, and as the costs borne because of the social and individual damages done by unemployment diminish.

The jobs created by governments or with public funds must be good jobs, especially in the sense that they allow workers to develop the human capacity to both conceptualize and execute work. We must be able to participate fully in the planning of our labor and not be subjected to the mindless detailed division of labor that condemns us to repetitively perform routine and boring work. We must have the right to determine the kinds of outputs we make, with an eye toward producing socially useful goods and services. If public and publicly financed employment had these characteristics, then jobs provided by private employers would be pressured to follow suit.

If, as is inevitably the case under capitalism, the economy faces a recession, the government should have in place policies that allow workers to labor fewer hours, with the government paying part of the loss of pay. Germany does this, as economist Dean Baker tells us. Despite roughly similar GDP growth rates during and after the Great Recession, Germany kept its unemployment rate much lower than in the United States.

The secret to Germany's better outcomes is that the country has an explicit policy of pushing employers toward shortening work hours rather than laying off workers. A key part of this picture is the short work program, which is an alternative to unemployment insurance. With traditional unemployment insurance, when a worker gets laid off the government pays roughly half of the worker's wages.

Under work sharing, if firms cut back a worker's hours by 20 percent, the government makes up roughly half of the lost wages (10 percent of the total wage in this case). That leaves the worker putting in 20 percent fewer hours and getting 10 percent less pay. This is likely a much better alternative to being unemployed.[1]

Workers in the United States have the longest average work year of any rich nation, while at the same time suffering massive underemployment. It is time for the enactment of statutes that guarantee everyone several weeks of paid vacations and a number of paid holidays, as is the case in every rich country.[2] A law placing a maximum on weekly hours, as well as sharper penalties for overtime work, is long overdue. Not only would this result in more employment, but it would also surely improve the mental and physical well-being of the mass of working men and women.

2. Adequate income for all who are employed

Simply having a job does not mean that a person is not poor or deprived. All jobs must pay a wage that ensures an adequate income. Full employment and the elimination of poverty are obviously connected to such decent income levels, which provide purchasing power capable of sustaining consumer demand for goods and services produced by our labor force. Several simple steps would insure such income levels. First, the minimum wage must be increased at least to a level that would, with full-time, year-round work, allow support for a family of four at the official poverty level of income. The minimum wage must rise each year to reflect the increase in the Consumer Price Index and the national increase in labor productivity. As many economists have shown, raising the minimum wage, even significantly, does not reduce employment.[3] Raising the minimum wage would increase employment and significantly reduce the incidence of poverty.

Second, the best way for those employed to improve their wages, hours, and conditions of employment is to form a labor union. Today, the labor laws are stacked against workers, and they must be changed. Harsh penalties should be imposed on employers who violate the right of workers to form unions. All those who labor for wages must be protected by our labor laws, including farm workers and domestic employees, both of whom are currently excluded. Section 14b of the National Labor Relations Act, which allows states to enact right-to-work laws, must be repealed. Such laws lower both wages and benefits.[4] Workers should be free to form unions. In contrast to what typically happens today, union elections should be conducted with no employer interference or intimidation. It can be argued that employers should be compelled to recognize the democratic will if a majority of employees in a bargaining unit sign a petition stating that they want the union to be their collective representative at the workplace, or if they sign cards authorizing the union to represent them.

There should be no question about workers having the right to strike for a union, without fear of being fired or replaced. Unionized workers should also be free to solicit the active support of other workers and consumers in their struggles, something severely restricted by U.S. labor laws. Finally, all workers, including public employees, should be free to strike whenever they deem it necessary to do so. Restrictions on the right to strike smack too much of involuntary servitude to withstand close scrutiny. As Abraham Lincoln put it in contrasting the free labor system to the slave labor system: "I am glad to know that there is a system of labor where the laborer can strike if he wants to! I would to God that such a system prevailed all over the world."[5]

3. A GUARANTEED MINIMUM ADEQUACY LEVEL OF INCOME
FOR THOSE WHO CANNOT OR SHOULD NOT WORK

Those who cannot or should not labor for wages need income just the same. Single poor parents should be provided an income, so that they can care for their children and themselves. Raising children is difficult and demanding work, critical to the functioning of any society. All of the punitive federal, state, and local laws limiting access to income by poor parents must be abolished, replaced with laws guaranteeing incomes. All persons physically or mentally incapable of work must be guaranteed adequate incomes.

4. ADEQUATE AND SAFE HOUSING FOR ALL

As is true for inequality, unemployment, lack of income, and the like, inadequate housing forces society to bear costs that would be absent if everyone had comfortable and safe places to live. Chester Hartman, Research Director of the Poverty & Race Research Action Council, provides some details on these costs:

> The health problems of poor people caused and exacerbated by poor housing conditions require massive subsidies through Medicaid and other public sources. Emergency fire and police costs, paid for largely via local taxes, are disproportionately high for slum neighborhoods. The human and financial costs of crime affect everyone, directly or indirectly, as victims and potential victims. Homelessness is accompanied by disproportionate violence of various types. The productivity lost as a result of the multiple impacts of poor housing conditions negatively affects the standard of living for others. Educational deficits attributable to inadequate housing harm the entire society. The dominant way we now deal with those suffering the most extreme housing problem, homelessness—overnight shelter and emergency services—requires public expenditures that far exceed the costs of a more rational and humane housing approach, a conundrum explainable only in complex sociological and political terms.[6]

Inadequate housing, like many of the difficulties associated with poverty, is both a consequence and cause of poverty. Yet, as with every poverty-related problem, there are obvious solutions. Inexpensive, comfortable, safe, and energy-efficient homes can be built for everyone who needs it, either new housing or rehabilitated existing structures.

5. Health care for all

The best way to ensure good health care for all is a single-payer nationally financed system of health care. Nearly every rich nation in the world has such a system, and the health outcomes in them are better than those in the United States. The evidence in favor of such a system is overwhelming. Nearly every rich nation in the world has such a system, and the health outcomes in them are better than those in the United States.[7]

6. Educational opportunity for all

Our public schools must be adequately and equitably financed, and all students must be guaranteed a quality education, one that helps them fully to develop their capacities. Schools at all levels should educate the whole person and not neglect literature, the arts, and physical training. The current mania to test, to close public schools in poor neighborhoods, to form quasi-private charter schools needs to end. None of these can make our schools better; in fact, they make them worse. What we need are more and modern schools, comfortably furnished, safe, with libraries, art and music supplies, gymnasiums, and athletic fields. Schools should be full and equitably funded; teachers should be well paid and well trained; and administrative staff should be kept to a minimum. Public college education should be available free of charge to all who want to attend. No one should be saddled with student debt, and all current student debt should be abolished.

7. Secure and expanded transportation infrastructure

People in all major communities rely on transportation to travel from their homes to work, school, hospitals, shopping areas, recreational facilities, places of worship, the homes of family and friends, and more. Public mass transit is part of the infrastructure of any healthy metropolitan area, as well as roads and highways, bridges, streetlights, and other essentials of urban life. Safe, reliable, environmentally sustainable, convenient and affordable mass transit systems—railways, busways, etc.—should be accessible to all, with no communities left out.[8]

8. Secure and expanded Social Security

Social Security benefits should be made more, not less, generous. They must not be subject to any austerity measures, which will increase the incidence of poverty among the elderly. The federal government's effort to change the method by which benefits are indexed to inflation—the chained index—must be rejected. As we have seen, the contention that the system is close to bankruptcy is false, and a good example of how propaganda so often trumps facts in public discourse.

9. Food security for all

Not only can governments increase monies for food purchase to those in need, but they can also encourage the production of nutritious food. They could subsidize organic farming by small farmers and cooperatives; they could promote urban agriculture, using the exceptional example set by Cuba.[9] Governments must, at the same time, end subsidies to agribusinesses, either to generate more harmful outputs such as ethanol or to discourage the productive use of the soil. Pesticide use should be prohibited or heavily taxed. Food inspection must be radically expanded.

10. A sustainable environment

If poverty is ended, and every one of its attendant evils is eliminated as well, nothing can be sustained if we do not deal with our growing environmental crisis. With respect to the overall environment, subsidies to energy companies that provide incentives for the production of oil and natural gas by whatever means should be ended. Oil from tar sands and natural gas by hydraulic fracturing must be prohibited, as should nuclear power. Everything we do should be done with an eye toward its environmental impact. Most generally, we must tamp down the growth mania that is the hallmark of capitalism and instead plan collectively at all levels of government to address the looming environmental catastrophe. Concretely, we must think about and act upon our conceptualizations to alter the very way we live and conduct our system of production and distribution. This would include everything from the kind of energy we use, the size and energy efficiency of the homes we live in, the types of roads, schools, factories, offices, and the like that we build, and more.

11. Cultural freedom and enrichment for all
(arts, parks, sports, recreation)

Arts, parks, sports, and recreation are all important aspects of daily life, and when people do not have access to them, they cannot be fully human. There is a tremendous mismatch in the United States between arts, parks, sports, and recreation and income and wealth. Those without material means do not have easy access to open spaces, woods, parks, sports facilities, and the arts. Poor people, for example, typically do not have the money to travel to the national parks or attend cultural events. Therefore, public efforts must be made to ensure that these are freely available to everyone. Our national parks and recreation areas must be expanded and ways must be found to make them accessible to all. Possibilities should also be provided to encourage all people who wish to explore and develop their abilities for participation in sports activities and various forms of artistic expression.

Public spaces should not be areas dominated by commercial activities, especially those that damage the environment. Logging, cattle grazing, and other profit-making activities on public lands must be prohibited.

12. Reduction in the inequality of income and wealth,
to ensure realization of objectives

Our society's ability to achieve the previous objectives of the New Freedom Budget will be dependent on the realization of a reduction in inequality of income and wealth. The dramatic growth of inequality has been central to the damage done to the quality of life in the United States over recent decades. If it is true that most of the nation's income growth now goes to those at the very top of the income and wealth distributions, and if this alone gives rise to serious individual and social problems, then it is essential for a New Freedom Budget to address inequality head on.

The growth of economic inequality is now every bit as much both a cause and consequence of poverty as is unemployment and substandard housing. Inequality of income and wealth means inequality of economic and political power. Those at the top have the power to make the rest of us do their bidding, and as they exert their power, it deepens, allowing them to garner still more wealth and income. This vicious cycle will never be broken unless a great deal more equality prevails. The benefits of equality are numerous: better physical and mental health, less crime, less fear and stress, healthier children, more demand and production of basic necessities and less demand and production of luxury goods and services, less environmental damage, and, most important, more democracy.[10] None of the other problems we have examined in this book can be dealt with unless we have much more economic equality than we now do. A two-tier society, like the two-tier wage agreements for which so many labor unions have bargained, cannot form the basis for human solidarity and cooperation.

Many policies would diminish inequality, and most of these would also directly attack the other problems laid out in the objectives of a New Freedom Budget.[11] These include more progressive income taxes; taxes on wealth, such as those on estates, net assets (including houses above a minimum purchase price, stock holdings, and the like); taxes on financial transactions, including the massive trade in derivatives; a cap on executive salaries; and progressive government spending. Many of the policies aimed at achieving the other objectives of the New Freedom Budget will also reduce inequality.

The Feasibility of a New Freedom Budget

The wars in Iraq and Afghanistan and the Great Recession showed clearly that the richest country in the world never lacks the money for whatever its leaders think necessary to further its global interests or to cope with a domestic crisis. Economists Linda Bilmes and Joseph Stiglitz estimate the past, present, and future costs of the two wars at three trillion dollars.[12] The federal government spent hundreds of billions of dollars in fiscal stimulus to combat the worst downtown since the Great Depression, and the Federal Reserve pumped much more than this into the financial sector of the economy to prevent credit from seizing up completely. The federal government and the Federal Reserve have vast powers to spend money and increase the availability of credit. The government can raise taxes to finance its spending, and it can issue bonds as well. It can even sell bonds to the Federal Reserve banks, and these banks can pay for the bonds with newly printed money. That is, the government can finance its spending by printing money, which it has done many times in the past.

What this means is that if the federal government were intent on eliminating poverty and its attendant evils, it could do so. It could employ expansionary fiscal and monetary policies to do this, and if it wanted, it could eradicate all of the problems described in the Freedom Budget with considerable speed.

Of course, the fact that the means exist for achieving all of the objectives listed and discussed above does not mean it will be done. This is because what really matters is power. Governments react to power. Those who wield it tend to get what they want; those who lack power do not. We leave the issue of power to the last part of this chapter. Here, we look at some obvious ways in which money could be made available for the achievement of the objectives of the New Freedom Budget.

The original Freedom Budget made detailed estimates of the expenditures that the federal government would have to make over ten years to eliminate poverty and deprivation. It made projections for the Gross Domestic Product (GDP) for each year, based upon its growth estimates, and it then proposed increases, based on its analysis, in the various budget areas needed to attack each problem (housing and community development, health services and research, public welfare, labor and manpower, contribution to Social Security, economic opportunity, education and research, agriculture, and natural resources).

The projections of economic growth for the U.S. economy, expected to provide for the old Freedom Budget's realization, were made almost five decades ago. We have seen that these cannot be the basis for achieving the objectives of the New Freedom Budget; growth will not be that high, nor can it be from an environmental perspective. Therefore, it will be more fruitful to provide examples of what could be done with monies that amount to a small fraction of the nation's current GDP.

We just noted that the wars in Iraq and Afghanistan have an extraordinarily large price tag. The money already spent cannot be gotten back, and spending in the future will have to be done if only to take care of those injured in these conflicts. However, there is no good reason why such wars have to happen again. The U.S. government spends enormous sums of money planning and fighting wars, developing and using new weapons, operating military bases in every part of the world, and engaging in covert actions at home and abroad. Direct government spending on defense in 2012 was $809 billion. Even a 10 percent reduction would provide more than $8 billion for other uses in the first year alone.

Let us look at two other government expenditures: health and education. The United States spends about 17.6 percent of its GDP on health care. The thirty-four rich nations that comprise the Organization for Economic Cooperation and Development (OECD) spend, on average, only 9.5 percent of their GDPs on health care.[13] The difference is 8.1 percent. Yet, as we saw in chapter 8, health outcomes in the United States are among the worst in OECD countries. Suppose, then, that the United States put in place a national health care system, employing all of the cost-containing techniques used by France, Japan, Canada, and other countries, and spent, say, 10 percent of GDP on health care. In 2012, GDP in the United States was $13.6 trillion. If we take 7.6 (17.6 minus 10) percent of this, we get a little over $1 trillion. This is a great deal of money that could be deployed in other areas. Of course, the government would have to ensure employment for workers displaced from private insurance companies, but it would, if the New Freedom Budget's objectives were fulfilled, already have employment programs in place. And the new national health care plan itself would require workers. Also, healthier men, women, and children would produce a healthier, more robust economy.

In education, the United States spent, in 2009, 7.3 percent of GDP on education, about one percentage point higher than the OECD average.[14] Assuming that these figures held true for 2012, this means that the United States spent about $136 billion more than it would have spent had it met the OECD average (1 percent of $13.6 trillion). And in education, as in health, the United States exhibits inferior education outcomes compared to most other rich countries. If we revamped our system of schooling to be more like those in other rich countries, we could achieve better results at a lower cost.

If we look at taxation, governments at all levels, but especially the federal government, could have at their disposal large sums of money to meet the objectives of a New Freedom Budget. Income tax rates have become less progressive since 1960. Since 1979, the federal income tax as a share of income has fallen for the top 20 percent of income recipients and for each subgroup (top 10, 5, and 1 percent) within this richest quintile. We have seen that tax rates on corporate net income have dropped dramatically since the years of the original Freedom Budget, and because this tax ultimately bears most heavily on those with the smallest incomes, the overall income tax system has become still less progressive. Capital gains tax rates have also gone down precipitously, and since these gains accrue overwhelmingly to the rich, tax rates once again become less progressive. Hundreds of billions of dollars of revenue could be raised by governments if the tax structure became more progressive. If we look at the highly regressive payroll tax that funds the Social Security system, simply phasing out the income ceiling on taxable income would eliminate any funding problems the system might face in future decades. Doing this would increase the funds in the Social Security trust fund by more than one trillion dollars over the next ten years.[15]

While most of the focus of budget reformers is on income tax changes, we believe that a fruitful approach would be to tax wealth as well. The distribution of wealth is far more unequal than that of income, and it has become much more so over the past few decades. Today, total household wealth in the United States is approximately $60 trillion. The richest 1 percent of households own about one-third of this wealth, some $20 trillion.[16] The richest 400 individuals in the United States alone own more than $120 billion.[17] Why not tax this super wealth? The worst that could happen is that some wealthy households would have to sell assets to pay their taxes, and the government would have to keep a wary eye out for efforts to escape payment. The government could hire thousands of special tax agents to monitor the rich and see to it that they paid their taxes and weren't hiding assets. Now that would be real public service work! A 2 percent tax on just the wealth of the top 1 percent would raise 400 billion dollars per year.

Another way to get public revenue from those who have the most wealth is to levy a tax on financial transactions. Such a tax is levied on trades in financial instruments such as stocks, bonds, derivatives, and foreign exchange. The levy proposed by those favoring such a tax is usually very small. One estimate for a .03 percent tax (3 cents on every $100 in trades) suggests that the federal government could raise $352 billion over ten years.[18]

We could give other examples of how money could be saved on various potentially socially useful programs and how revenue could be raised with changes in the tax code and the introduction of new types of taxes. However, the result would be clear: there is no shortage of funds to make the objectives of a New Freedom Budget a reality.

Perhaps a concrete example of what we could do concerns housing. Suppose we had available just the money from twenty years' worth of a financial transactions tax, that is, $704 billion. Assume that a housing unit, an apartment newly constructed or one rehabbed in an old building, has a cost of $50,000. The construction is done under the auspices of some combination of federal, state, and local governments. No profit is built into the work done by what would be public employees, and the governments use their large-scale buying power to obtain materials at the lowest possible cost. Let us suppose finally that $10 billion per year is devoted to training workers to perform the necessary work and to develop community organizations to help plan and then to manage the new housing. How many housing units could be built with this money? With $504 billion available, ten million housing units could be built over twenty years. If we assume three persons per unit, thirty million persons could be housed. In addition, workers would be trained, and local control could be put into place, enhancing democracy.

It is important to understand that as we win the objectives of the New Freedom Budget, there will be interaction effects among them. They will reinforce and strengthen one another, lowering the overall costs of the Budget and increasing tax revenues at the same time. For example, building adequate housing for all who need it meshes with efforts to reduce unemployment, improves individual health and lowers the costs of health care, increases incomes and tax revenues, reduces inequality—which, in turn, makes people healthier, reduces crime, improves school outcomes, and so forth. This is what economists call a virtuous circle, in which an improved outcome becomes the basis for a positive change in another outcome, which, in turn, becomes the basis for a further improvement in the first outcome, and so on.

What It Would Take to Achieve a New Freedom Budget

We do not have a blueprint for winning the objectives of a New Freedom Budget. People learn from struggle, and each of the objectives has been, and will continue to be, fought for by various groups operating at local, state, and national levels. The hope here is that the budget will help us think about achieving a broad and interconnected set of goals and organize to get all of them. Although there is little to be gained from making a detailed proposal of the strategy and tactics that should be employed to achieve the New Freedom Budget, several general points are worth considering.

First, something lacking in most contemporary struggles is an overarching ideology or mindset, which can offer guidance for what needs to be done and how to go about doing it. Many of us see that our futures are constrained by the dire circumstances in which we find ourselves. But some do not know why this is so. With nothing coherent to anchor our thinking, one can be susceptible to ideas that support actions not in our best interests. Someone who is otherwise a decent person might nonetheless be drawn into blaming immigrants, or minorities, or unions, or "big government" for the problems afflicting us. Those who see the need for radical change must engage in ideological education, reaching out not just to those who are in basic agreement with them, but to broader layers of the population.

The five basic principles set forth at the beginning of this chapter might serve as entry points for such education. For example, government leaders and the media constantly promote the United States as a democratic and egalitarian society. Large numbers of its citizens believe that they live in the best, most free nation on earth. Yet at the same time many people have the uneasy feeling that these things are not true, that the country is ruled by the rich and the chances for success are narrowing. These contradictory ideas can provide openings for presenting radical arguments—with neighbors, workmates, and community members—suggesting that it is our duty to make our society what it says it already is. This could also be used to point out the glaring contradiction between the formal democracy we enjoy politically and the dictatorship most of us face at work. Similar education could occur with respect to rights and obligations. We are obliged in a system such as ours to spend most of our lives laboring for others, so should we not have the right to decent health care, quality education, and income security in old age?

Especially difficult to deal with effectively is the often blind nationalism so prevalent in the United States. This takes the form of disdain for other countries and immediate support for wars. Antiwar sentiment exists, but it has seldom been sufficient to stop the mayhem the U.S. government visits upon its enemies. The "war on terror" has taken an awful toll on lives around the world, and it has greatly compromised civil liberties in the United States. To counter this, we must make connections between democracy and opposition to the imperial ambitions of our own government and between both of these and the global scope of capital accumulation, which offers little in the way of democracy and freedom to peoples anywhere on earth.

Ideological education needs to go hand-in-hand with actions, as emphasized by the old Freedom Budget's partisans. Bayard Rustin referred to the necessity of "getting into the streets."

SNCC's Courtland Cox emphasized that the outlook must be "not, 'Please give us a handout,' but make it impossible for the country to function if it does not put the Freedom Budget into action." As Paul Feldman put it, a change as important as the Freedom Budget "won't happen without major social struggle, and certainly not without significant changes in the power structure." At the same time, we were struck by Rachelle Horowitz's comment that "something wonderful happens to people when they are somehow determining their own destiny and beginning to control and change their own conditions."

Such comments from those who went before suggest two forms of action: mass economic and political protests and organizations, but also collective self-help efforts. These are not mutually exclusive tactics for making radical change, and each might include the other. Collective self-help measures are ways to build cooperative entities inside the shell of capitalism, yet they have had greatest impact when part of social movements engaged in struggle.

For example, in the 1930s, both the Minneapolis general strike and the Flint sit-down strike included mass kitchens to provide food for working-class families, child care, medical services, and cultural activities that were an integral part of the struggle and enhanced the feeling of power, community and self-confidence among participants. In the 1960s, SNCC's Mississippi Freedom Summer Project involved a similar combination of self-help and political action efforts. Among black liberation efforts embracing a more separatist path for struggle the same kind of dynamics emerged. The Black Panther Party established a number of "survival programs," such as the Free Breakfast for Children Program and a large number of free services, such as "clothing distribution, classes on politics and economics, free medical clinics, lessons on self-defense and first aid, transportation to upstate prisons for family members of inmates, an emergency-response ambulance program, drug and alcohol rehabilitation, and testing for sickle-cell disease." The Nation of Islam ran schools and day care services, operated a food distribution network, and established farms. More recently, those who occupied Zuccotti Park in Manhattan during the Occupy Wall Street uprising organized sleeping, food supplies, cooking, sanitation, demonstration logistics, open-air classrooms, public relations, and media production. Through this they developed a sense of social cohesion, an appreciation for the necessity and difficulty of democratic decision making, and confidence in their capacities to do things that they might not have done otherwise. [19]

Mass economic and political protests and social organizations take a wide variety of forms. The most important of these has been the labor movement, which has operated on both economic and political planes. Given the nature of capitalism, as a mode of production in which society's surplus is extracted by the exploitation of wage laborers, it is difficult to imagine that the objectives of the New Freedom Budget can be made real without the full participation of the working class. The architects of the original Freedom Budget saw it being realized through the joint efforts and power of labor and civil rights forces. We have suggested earlier in this book some of the reasons why this was not successful. However, if we look toward the future, the same combination of movements will still be needed to eliminate poverty and to meet the needs of all of our people. Now, however, it is much clearer than it was in the 1960s that labor unions themselves will have to be radically altered, and unions will have to be embedded in and make common cause with the communities of the poor, especially those of the black and other minority working class.

A good example of the trajectory that labor unions will likely have to follow if labor is to be a force for radical social change is the Chicago Teachers Union (CTU). Faced with a vicious neoliberal campaign to close schools in poor communities, demonize teachers and the parents of minority children for the poor performance of their children, gut the CTU's collective bargaining agreement, and impose draconian policies on the schools left open, a reform group, the Caucus of Rank-and-File Educators (CORE), challenged the union leadership's failure to resist these attacks. Through a campaign of building solidarity with poor communities (and later middle-class ones as well), CORE mobilized teachers to go on the offensive. Within a year of democratically winning leadership of the union, CORE conducted and won a strike, the first in more than twenty years in the city. What makes the new CTU so exciting is that workers who provide an important service to those whom a New Freedom Budget would benefit most are allying themselves in a mutually beneficial alliance to ensure that quality education for all becomes a right. The CTU has begun to break with the business union model that sees a union as a provider of benefits to the members, exclusive of a concern for social justice.[20] Similar concerns for those who utilize essential public services have been shown by health care and transit unions.

Numerous other organizations have formed to struggle for radical change. These have operated mainly on a local level, though the issues often have a national scope. Good examples are environmental groups opposed to tar sands oil, natural gas hydrofracking, nuclear power plants, mountaintop removal for coal strip mining, and coastal oil drilling. Other organizations have focused on preventing home foreclosures, stopping wars and preventing the use of drones, ending the testing frenzy in public schools, debt relief for school loans, stopping cuts in Social Security and Medicare, promoting single-payer health care, demanding public transportation improvements, and a host of others. Modern electronic media allow these groups and organizations to communicate rapidly and to make their causes known to millions of people. Hopefully, this will eventually promote more cooperation and joint projects among the various entities, so that a broad-based mass movement can be built.

Out of such efforts, struggles, and movements, the political consciousness and broad social forces may develop that can actually put a New Freedom Budget on the agenda. This naturally brings us face-to-face with an engagement or confrontation with the government. The state is a complex set of institutions, some of which are fundamentally repressive, some of which are susceptible to democratic influences that can be pressured to do things that benefit the working-class majority, those who are poor, paid low wages, unemployed, with inadequate health care, and so forth. The federal government all too often has carried out destructive and morally indefensible wars, but it also, for example, administers the Social Security system and hundreds of other programs that help protect those without the means to privately secure themselves and their families. In all of this, it functions basically to maintain "social order," which in a capitalist system generally adds up to policies designed to preserve the power of big business, at the expense of the rest of us whenever deemed necessary.

Both mainstream political parties in the United States have been an integral part of this system. The history of the previous effort to achieve the Freedom Budget—and a considerable amount of history since then—has shown that both parties are committed to maintaining a system of economic inequality and injustice and that neither is an adequate vehicle for achieving the objectives of the Freedom Budget. It can be argued that one or another represents a "lesser evil," but choosing the "lesser evil" has inevitably involved making compromises that only lead to more compromises.

Forces of progressive social change must move forward outside of and independently of the state, but ultimately the New Freedom Budget's objectives cannot be achieved unless the government is confronted and compelled to take action by the democratic power of social movements representing society's majority. History has shown time and again that powerful forces in our society, and within the government itself, will inevitably press against this realization of economic justice. Because the government is a battleground in which contending social forces try to get the state to do what they want, it seems clear to us that achieving the new Freedom Budget's goals must involve a fundamental power shift, socially and politically, which will democratize the government and make it represent the will of the people much better than it now does.

Final Thoughts

We hope that this book not only gives readers an interesting and inspiring history of the original Freedom Budget but gives them the desire to put a New Freedom Budget into practice. The principles, objectives, and analysis of this chapter should be seen as catalysts for further development by everyone who wants a different, more egalitarian and humane society than the one in which we now live. This book could be the basis for study groups, and it could provide ammunition for any organization fighting to meet any or all of the objectives of the New Freedom Budget. We are certain of one thing. Unless radical change occurs, unless the power of the 1 percent is broken and the power of the 99 percent is asserted, the people of the United States—and nearly every other country—are soon going to inhabit a world in which most of us will experience declining economic and political security, rising workplace exploitation, and a rapidly deteriorating environment. The time to think, to act, to make the world we want, is now.

A FREEDOM BUDGET FOR ALL AMERICANS

A Summary

INTRODUCTION

I believe, and profoundly hope, that from this day forth the opponents of social progress can take comfort no longer, for not since the March on Washington has there been such broad sponsorship and enthusiastic support for any undertaking as has been mobilized on behalf of The Freedom Budget for All Americans.

These forces have not come together to demand help for the Negro. Rather, we meet on a common ground of determination that in this, the richest and most productive society ever known to man, the scourge of poverty can and must be abolished—not in some distant future, not in this generation, but within the next ten years!

The tragedy is that the workings of our economy so often pit the white poor and the black poor against each other at the bottom of society. The tragedy is that groups only one generation removed from poverty themselves, haunted by the memory of scarcity and fearful of slipping back, step on the fingers of those struggling up the ladder.

And the tragedy is that not only the poor, the nearly poor, and the once poor, but all Americans, are the victims of our failure as a nation to distribute democratically the fruits of our abundance. For, directly or indirectly, not one of us is untouched by the steady spread of slums, the decay of our cities, the segregation and overcrowding of our public schools, the shocking deterioration of our hospitals, the violence and chaos in our streets, the idleness of able-bodied men deprived of work, and the anguished demoralization of our youth.

For better or worse, we are one nation and one people. We shall solve our problems together or together we shall enter a new era of social disorder and disintegration.

What we need is an overall plan of attack.

This is what the "Freedom Budget" is. It is not visionary or utopian. It is feasible. It is concrete. It is specific. It is quantitative. It talks dollars and cents. It sets goals and priorities. It tells how these can be achieved. And it places the responsibility for leadership with the Federal Government, which alone has the resources equal to the task.

The "Freedom Budget" is not a call for a handout. It is a challenge to the best traditions and possibilities of America. It is a call to those who have grown weary of slogans and gestures to rededicate themselves to the cause of social reconstruction. It is a plea to men of good will to give tangible substance to long-proclaimed ideals.

—A. PHILIP RANDOLPH
October 26, 1966

FOREWORD

After many years of intense struggle in the courts, in legislative halls, and on the streets, we have achieved a number of important victories. We have come far in our quest for respect and dignity. But we have far to go.

The long journey ahead requires that we emphasize the needs of all America's poor, for there is no way merely to find work, or adequate housing, or quality integrated schools for Negroes alone. We shall eliminate slums for Negroes when we destroy ghettos and build new cities for all. We shall eliminate unemployment for Negroes when we demand full and fair employment for all. We shall produce an educated and skilled Negro mass when we achieve a twentieth century educational system for all.

This human rights emphasis is an integral part of the Freedom Budget and sets, I believe, a new and creative tone for the great challenge we yet face.

The Southern Christian Leadership Conference fully endorses the Freedom Budget and plans to expend great energy and time in working for its implementation.

It is not enough to project the Freedom Budget. We must dedicate ourselves to the legislative task to see that it is immediately and fully achieved. I pledge myself to this task and will urge all others to do likewise. The Freedom Budget is essential if the Negro people are to make further progress. It is essential if we are to maintain social peace. It is a political necessity. It is a moral commitment to the fundamental principles on which this nation was founded.

—MARTIN LUTHER KING, JR.
October 26, 1966

A "FREEDOM BUDGET" FOR ALL AMERICANS

The Freedom Budget is a practical, step-by-step plan for wiping out poverty in America during the next 10 years.

It will mean more money in your pocket. It will mean better schools for your children. It will mean better homes for you and your neighbors. It will mean clean air to breathe and comfortable cities to live in. It will mean adequate medical care when you are sick.

So where does the "Freedom" come in?

For the first time, everyone in America who is fit and able to work will have a job. For the first time, everyone who can't work, or shouldn't be working, will have an income adequate to live in comfort and dignity. And that is freedom. For freedom from want is the basic freedom from which all others flow.

This nation has learned that it must provide freedom for all if any of us is to be free. We have learned that half measures are not enough. We know that continued unfair treatment of part of our people breeds misery and waste that are both morally indefensible and a threat to all who are better off.

As A. Philip Randolph put it: "Here in these United States, where there can be no economic or technical excuse for it, poverty is not only a private tragedy but, in a sense, a public crime. It is above all a challenge to our morality."

The Freedom Budget would make that challenge the lever we can grasp to wipe out poverty in a decade.

Pie in the sky?

Not on your life. Just simple recognition of the fact that we as a nation never had it so good. That we have the ability and the means to provide adequately for everyone.

That simple justice requires us to see that everyone—white or black; in the city or on the farm; fisherman or mountaineer—may have his share in our national wealth.

The moral case for the Freedom Budget is compelling.

In a time of unparalleled prosperity, there are 34 million Americans living in poverty. Another 28 million live just on the edge, with income so low that any unexpected expense or loss of income could thrust them into poverty.

Almost one-third of our nation lives in poverty or want. They are not getting their just share of our national wealth.

Just as compelling, this massive lump of despair stands as a threat to our future prosperity. Poverty and want breed crime, disease and social unrest. We need the potential purchasing and productive power the poor would achieve, if we are to continue to grow and prosper.

In short, for good times to continue—and get better—we must embark immediately on a program that will fairly and indiscriminately provide a decent living for all Americans.

The Freedom Budget provides seven basic objectives, which taken together will achieve this great goal within 10 years. They are:

1. To provide full employment for all who are willing and able to work, including those who need education or training to make them willing and able.
2. To assure decent and adequate wages to all who work.
3. To assure a decent living standard to those who cannot or should not work.
4. To wipe out slum ghettos and provide decent homes for all Americans.

5. To provide decent medical care and adequate educational opportunities to all Americans, at a cost they can afford.

6. To purify our air and water and develop our transportation and natural resources on a scale suitable to our growing needs.

7. To unite sustained full employment with sustained full production and high economic growth.

The Freedom Budget shows how to do all this without a raise in taxes and without a single make-work job—by planning prudently NOW to use the economic growth of the future, and with adequate attention to our international commitments.

The key is jobs.

We can all recognize that the major cause of poverty could be eliminated, if enough decently paying jobs were available for everyone willing and able to work. And we can also recognize that, with enough jobs for all, a basic cause of discrimination among job-seekers would automatically disappear.

What we must also recognize is that we now have the means of achieving complete employment—at no increased cost, with no radical change in our economic system, and at no cost to our present national goals—if we are willing to commit ourselves totally to this achievement.

That is what the Freedom Budget is all about.

It asks that we unite in insisting that the nation plan now to use part of its expected economic growth to eliminate poverty.

Where will the jobs come from? What will we use for money?

If all our nation's wealth were divided equally among all us Americans, each share would be worth roughly $3,500. Of this, we grant to the Federal government a slice equal to roughly $500 in the form of taxes, leaving us an average of about $3,000 to spend on our other needs.

If our nation's productivity continues growing at the same rate as in recent years—and it will if the Freedom Budget is adopted—each share will grow to about $5,000. Thus, the Federal government's slice will grow to $700, with the present Federal tax structure, and we will still have $4,300 left for our other needs.

What the Freedom Budget proposes is this: Budget a fraction of the $200 million increase in Federal tax revenues to provide jobs for all who can work and adequate income of other types for those who cannot.

No doles. No skimping on national defense. No tampering with private supply and demand.

Just an enlightened self-interest, using what we have in the best possible way.

By giving the poor a chance to become dignified wage earners, we will be generating the money to finance the improvements we all need—rich and poor alike.

And we would be doing it by making new jobs with new money, so that no one who is now earning his own living would suffer.

The Freedom Budget recognizes that the Federal government must take the lead in attaining the eradication of, poverty. The Federal government alone represents all 200 million American individuals. It alone has the resources for a comprehensive job. And it has the responsibility for fulfilling the needs which are the basis for the Freedom Budget plan.

First, here's where the jobs would be coming from:

- Right now, the nation should begin budgeting to replace the 9.3 million "seriously deficient" housing units that make living in them a misery and form slums that are a blight upon our land.

  The housing program contained in the Freedom Budget would have practically all Americans decently housed by 1975—while providing a wide range of jobs for the unemployed in housing construction and urban redevelopment.

- Critical shortages of water and power persist in many highly populated areas. Air and waters remain polluted. Recreation facilities are unavailable for those who need them most.

  The Freedom Budget proposes the creation of millions of jobs in a program that will correct these pressing problems.

- We need, at a conservative estimate, 100,000 new public classrooms a year for the next six years, as well as considerable expansion of our institutions of higher learning.

  Only the Federal government can meet the largest share of these needs, as well as providing for the hundreds of thousands of new teachers who also will be needed.

- We must double our rate of hospital construction if we are to keep up with our minimum requirements in this field, and we must expand rehabilitation and outpatient facilities.

As these and other programs swell the number of productive workers, cut down unemployment and increase consumption, the private sector of our national economy will inevitably grow also.

The Freedom Budget recognizes that full employment by itself is not enough to eradicate poverty. Therefore, it also proposes—and budgets for— a $2-an-hour Federal minimum wage covering everyone within Federal jurisdiction; a new farm program to provide adequate income to the 43 per cent of farm families who now live in poverty; and immediate improvements in Social Security, welfare, unemployment compensation, workmen's compensation and other programs designed to support those who cannot or should not work.

Where will the money come from?

The Freedom Budget recognizes that we cannot spend what we do not produce. It also recognizes that we must spend wisely what we do produce.

It proposes that a portion of our future growth—one thirteenth of what can reasonably be expected to be available—be earmarked for the eradication of poverty. The Freedom Budget proposed outlay of $185 billion in 10 years sounds like a great deal of money, and it is a great deal of money.

But it will come from the expansion of our economy that will in part be the result of wise use of that very $185 billion. It will build homes and schools, provide recreation areas and hospitals. It will train teachers and nurses.

It will provide adequate incomes to millions who now do not have them. And those millions will in turn buy goods they cannot now buy.

So the wage earner of today will benefit as well. His earnings will go up and his enjoyment of life will be increased. The opportunities for private enterprise will increase.

The breeding grounds of crime and discontent will be diminished in the same way that draining a swamp cuts down the breeding of mosquitoes, and the causes of discrimination will be considerably reduced.

But the Freedom Budget cannot become reality without a national effort. It requires a concentrated commitment by all the people of America, expressed in concrete goals and programs of the Federal Government. These goals and programs must encourage to the utmost the efforts of state and local governments and private enterprise.

It is not lack of good-will that has prevented the achievement of these great goals in the past. All of us, 200 million strong, are united in our willingness to share the abundance of America in equal impartiality with our fellows, and to grant equal opportunities to all.

What we must do—and what the Freedom Budget provides—is to express that will in the most direct, quickest and fairest way.

The Freedom Budget, then, is a new call to arms for a final assault on injustice. It is a rallying cry we cannot fail to heed.

The "Freedom Budget": Questions and Answers

1. Aren't We Making Progress in Eliminating Poverty through the Kind of Sharp Economic Growth We've Had in the Past Two Years? What New Dimensions Does the "Freedom Budget" Add?

There is no evidence that the economic growth of the last two years has significantly dented poverty. Economic growth is a precondition for abolishing poverty, but it is not sufficient by itself. To it must be added programs that reach toward a more equitable distribution of our abundance. This is the dimension added by the "Freedom Budget."

2. Will Programs to Help the Poor Really Enable Them to Break the Cycle of Poverty?

Of course. The overwhelming majority of the poor don't want to be poor. They have been kept in poverty, in some cases for two or more generations. They are the victims of technological changes, of wrong-headed economic policies, of political powerlessness, of discrimination, of the environment of poverty itself. Their despair and demoralization can be dispelled only by the opening of genuine economic opportunity. When such opportunity is provided, along the lines suggested in the "Freedom Budget," the cycle of poverty can and will be broken.

3. How Many of the People in Poverty Are Capable of Handling Jobs and How Many Would Take Jobs if They Were Offered?

First of all, 20% of those in poverty are in families whose breadwinners already work full-time but at wages below the poverty level. Another 40% are victims of unemployment or underemployment; their problem is not unwillingness to work but the absence of Jobs. Thus, fully 60% of the poverty problem could be eliminated if we achieved full employment at decent wages.

The remaining 40% of those in poverty either cannot or should not be working. Included are the physically disabled, the elderly, women with young children, etc. For them the "Freedom Budget" demands improved public assistance, Social Security and other payments, culminating in a guaranteed annual income.

Our past experience shows that federal programs such as the progressive income tax, social security, protection of collective bargaining and others have raised the income level of millions of people.

4. Won't the Spending of So Much Money Mean the Creation of More Government Agencies and Just Expand Bureaucracy?

The expansion of bureaucracy results from the effort to solve problems in a haphazard, piecemeal way. A coordinated national plan, such as the "Freedom Budget," does not call for new agencies; it calls for new levels of economic performance. People who are fully employed at decent wages do not need bureaucracies; the poor and disadvantaged do.

5. Will Taxes Have to Be Raised to Provide the Money to Implement the Freedom Budget Programs?

Our current tax structure is very responsive to economic growth. If total output expands—and it will if "Freedom Budget" proposals are enacted—revenues to the federal government will rise by $10 billion each year. For the ten years, the cumulative effect will be to add in excess of $400 billion to our present tax revenue.

6. Where Will All the Money Come From?

From what the "Freedom Budget" calls the "economic growth dividend." If we put all of our resources to work, the country's total production will jump from $663 billion in 1965 to roughly $1.2 trillion in 1975. To reach this figure, the gross national product would rise each year by an average of $244 billion. Thus, over a ten-year period, the aggregate increase in the gross national product would be $2.4 trillion higher than if the economy remained at its present level.

This is what is meant by "economic growth dividend." At present tax rates, such a dividend would result in an additional $400 billion or more in Federal revenues over the next decade. It is from these additional revenues that the "Freedom Budget" proposes the allocation of $185 billion to meet our critical social needs.

7. Aren't We Asking the American Public to Devote a Tremendous Amount of Money to Help Just a Small Group within Our Society?

While it is true that poverty afflicts only a minority of Americans, it reflects a malfunctioning of our national economy which affects all Americans. The persistence of unemployment and underuse of resources detract from our total wealth. Had there been maximum employment and production between 1953–65, as would have been achieved under programs such as those proposed in the "Freedom Budget," our gross national product would have been $550 billion higher, total private consumption would have been $364 billion higher, and public revenues would have been $135 billion higher. All Americans would have shared in this greater abundance.

Thus, we have all been deprived of the contribution the poor can make, as producers and consumers, to our economy. Moreover, nobody is untouched by the spread of slums, the decay of social services, and the human waste that lead to violence, crime and chaos. Every American suffers from outmoded urban transit, air and water pollution, inadequate schools and hospitals.

This is a "Freedom Budget" for all Americans.

8. Would Not a $2.00 Minimum Wage, Particularly in Agriculture, Reduce the Number of Jobs?

This is a standard argument against higher minimum wages, but it has no basis in fact. There was no increase in unemployment when minimum wages were raised in 1961 and again in 1963. On the contrary, because a $2.00 minimum wage would boost consumer purchasing power, total employment would probably rise.

Government programs should be established to help small enterprises achieve greater efficiency and to tide them over while they are adjusting to payment of a living wage.

9. Won't $185 Billion More in Spending Create Such High Demand for Goods and Services that Sharp Inflation Will Be Inevitable?

There is no evidence of serious shortages in goods at present. Should such shortages develop, however, or if tendencies toward inflation threaten, the "Freedom Budget" contends that the Federal Government has sufficient fiscal and monetary tools to deal with the problem, without scuttling our commitment to abolish poverty.

10. Does the "Freedom Budget" Assume that National Defense Expenditures Would Not Rise?

No. For national defense, space technology and all international outlays, the federal budget in 1967 was $64.6 billion. The "Freedom Budget" assumes this figure would rise to $87.5 billion in 1975.

In making this estimate, the Freedom Budget neither endorses nor condemns present military spending policies. It relies on the judgment of informed experts. Obviously, if the international situation improves and a reduction in military spending is in order, so much more money will be available for social needs. But even if military spending increases faster than now envisioned, the Freedom Budget proves that we can afford to carry out the necessary programs. But the abolition of poverty is too precious a goal to be made contingent on such a reduction.

SELECT BIBLIOGRAPHY

Listed here are key sources consulted in the writing of this study. Not all sources utilized in writing this book are included, but all are accounted for in the endnotes of each chapter.

MANUSCRIPT COLLECTIONS

Michael Harrington Papers, Tamiment Library
Tom Kahn Papers, Library of Congress
A. Philip Randolph Papers, Library of Congress
Bayard Rustin Papers, Library of Congress
Max Shachtman Papers, Tamiment Library

INTERVIEWS AND CORRESPONDENCE

Rick Congress (correspondence: 6/21/12; 8/1/12)
Joel Geier (interview, June 30, 2012)
Norman and Velma Hill (interview, September 15, 2012)
Rachelle Horowitz (correspondence: 9/24/12; 9/25/12; 9/30/12)
David McReynolds (interview, June 23, 2012; correspondence: 6/28/12; 1/20/13;1/21/13)
Walter Naegle (interview, November 11, 2012; correspondence: 9/27/12)

BOOKS AND PAMPHLETS

A. Philip Randolph Institute. *A "Freedom Budget" for All Americans: Budgeting Our Resources, 1966–1975 to Achieve "Freedom from Want."* Revised. New York: A. Philip Randolph Institute, (October) 1966.

Ad Hoc Committee. "The Triple Revolution: Cybernation—Weaponry—Human Rights." In *Seed of Liberation.* ed. Paul Goodman (New York: George Braziller, 1964); http://www.marxists.org/history/etol/newspape/isr/vol25/no03/adhoc.html.

Alexander, Robert J. *International Trotskyism, 1929–1985: A Documented Analysis of the Movement.* Durham, NC: Duke University Press, 1991.

Allen, Robert L. *Black Awakening in Capitalist America: An Analytic History.* Trenton, NJ: Africa World Press, 1990.

Anderson, Jervis. *A. Philip Randolph, A Biographical Portrait.* Berkeley: University of California Press, 1986.

_____. *Bayard Rustin: Troubles I've Seen, A Biography.* New York: HarperCollins, 1997.

Aptheker, Herbert, ed. *A Documentary History of the Negro People in the United States,* 7 vols. New York: Citadel Press, 1993.

Braden, Anne. *The Southern Freedom Movement in Perspective,* special issue *Monthly Review,* July-August 1965.

Branch, Taylor. *At Canaan's Edge: America in the King Years 1965–68.* New York: Simon and Schuster, 2006.

_____. *Parting the Waters: America in the King Years 1954–63.* New York: Simon and Schuster, 1988.

_____. *Pillar of Fire: America in the King Years 1963–65.* New York: Simon and Schuster, 1998.

Buhle, Mari Jo, and Paul Buhle, Dan Georgakis, eds. *Encyclopedia of the American Left*, 2nd ed.. New York: Oxford University Press, 1998.

Carmichael, Stokely, with Ekwueme Michael Thelwell. *Ready for Revolution: The Life and Struggles of Stokely Carmichael (Kwame Ture)*. New York: Scribner, 2003.

Card, David, and Alan B. Krueger. *Myth and Measurement: The New Economics of the Minimum Wage*. Princeton: Princeton University Press, 1997.

Caro, Robert. *The Years of Lyndon Johnson: Master of the Senate*. New York: Alfred A. Knopf, 2003.

_____. *The Years of Lyndon Johnson: Means of Ascent*. New York: Alfred A. Knopf, 1991.

_____. *The Years of Lyndon Johnson: The Path to Power*. New York: Alfred A. Knopf, 1990.

_____. *The Years of Lyndon Johnson: The Passage of Power*. New York: Alfred A. Knopf, 2012.

Carson, Clayborne. *In Struggle: SNCC and the Black Awakening of the 1960s*. Cambridge, MA: Harvard University Press, 1981.

Davis, Ossie, and Ruby Dee. *With Ossie and Ruby: In This Life Together*. New York: William Morrow, 1998.

D'Emelio, John. *Lost Prophet: The Life and Times of Bayard Rustin*. Chicago: University of Chicago Press, 2003.

Drucker, Peter. *Max Shachtman and His Left: A Socialist's Odyssey through the "American Century."* Atlantic Highlands, NJ: Humanities Press, 1994.

Duberman, Martin. *A Saving Remnant: The Radical Lives of Barbara Deming and David McReynolds*. New York: New Press, 2011.

Euchner, Charles. *Nobody Turn Me Around: A People's History of the 1963 March on Washington*. Boston: Beacon Press, 2010.

Finn, James. *Protest: Pacifism and Politics*. New York: Vintage Books, 1968.

Foster, John Bellamy, and Robert W. McChesney. *The Endless Crisis: How Monopoly-Finance Capital Produces Stagnation and Upheaval from the USA to China*. New York: Monthly Review Press, 2012.

Garrow, David J. *Bearing the Cross: Martin Luther King and the Southern Christian Leadership Conference*. New York: Vintage Books, 1988.

Gettleman, Marvin, and David Mermelstein, eds. *The Great Society Reader: The Failure of American Liberalism*. New York: Vintage Books, 1967.

Goldfield, Michael. *The Color of Politics: Race and the Mainsprings of American Politics*. New York: New Press, 1997.

Hall, Jacquelyn Dowd. "The Long Civil Rights Movement and the Political Uses of the Past." *Journal of American History*, March 2005.

Halstead, Fred. *Out Now! A Participant's Account of the American Movement against the Vietnam War*. New York: Monad/Pathfinder Press, 1979.

Hamilton, Dona Cooper, and Charles V. Hamilton. *The Dual Agenda: The African-American Struggle for Civil and Economic Equality*. New York: Columbia University Press, 1997.

Harrington, Michael. *Fragments of the Century, A Social Autobiography*. New York: E. P. Dutton, 1973.

_____. *The Long-Distance Runner, An Autobiography*. New York: Henry Holt, 1988.

_____. *The Other America: Poverty in the United States*. New York: Scribner, 1997 (originally published 1962).

_____. *Toward a Democratic Left: A Radical Program for a New Majority*. Baltimore: Penguin Books, 1969.

Hart-Landsberg, Martin. *Capitalist Globalization: Consequences, Resistance, and Alternatives*. New York: Monthly Review Press, 2013.

Hill, Norman. "Crisis in the Movement." *New America*, November 15, 1963.

Hill, Velma. "Bayard Rustin: The Whole Story." *New York Sun*, March 3, 2003; reproduced on old website of Social Democrats USA, http://www.socialdemocratsusa.org/oldsite/VelmaHill.html#top.

Hodgson, Godfrey. *America in Our Time: From World War II to Nixon—What Happened and Why*. Princeton: Princeton University Press, 2005.

_____. *The World Turned Right Side Up: A History of the Conservative Ascendancy in America*. Boston: Houghton Mifflin, 1996.

Honey, Michael K. *Going Down Jericho Road: The Memphis Strike, Martin Luther King's Last Campaign*. New York: W. W. Norton, 2007.

Horowitz, Rachelle. "Tom Kahn and the Fight for Democracy: A Political Portrait and Personal Recollection." *Democratiya* 11 (Winter 2007): 204–51.

Isserman, Maurice. *If I Had a Hammer: The Death of the Old Left and the Birth of the New Left*. New York: Basic Books, 1987.

_____. *The Other American: The Life of Michael Harrington*. New York: Public Affairs, 2000.

Jackson, Thomas F. *From Civil Rights to Human Rights: Martin Luther King, Jr. and the Struggle for Economic Justice*. Philadelphia: University of Pennsylvania Press, 2007.

Jacobs, Paul, and Saul Landau. *The New Radicals: A Report with Documents*. New York: Vintage, 1966.

Jacobson, Julius. "Coalitionism: From Protest to Politicking," in Hall, Burton, ed. *Autocracy and Insurgency in Organized Labor*. New York: Transaction Books, 1972, 324–345.

James, C. L. R. *C. L. R. James and Revolutionary Marxism, Selected Writings of C. L. R. James*. Edited by Scott McLemee and Paul Le Blanc. Atlantic Highlands, NJ: Humanities Press, 1995.

_____. *C. L. R. James on the "Negro Question."* Edited by Scott McLemee. Jackson: University of Mississippi Press, 1996.

_____. *Modern Politics*. Detroit: Bewick, 1973.

Jones, William P. "The Unknown Origins of the March on Washington: Civil Rights Politics and the Black Working Class." *Labor Studies in Working-Class History of the Americas* 7/3 (Fall 2010): 33–52.

Kahn, Tom. *Civil Rights: The True Frontier*. New York: Donald Press, 1963.

_____. *The Economics of Equality*. New York: League for Industrial Democracy, 1964.

_____. "Max Shachtman: His Ideas and His Movement." *Democratiya* 11 (Winter 2007): 252–259.

_____. "Preferential Treatment for Negro Masses, Full Employment Essential," *New America*, 1964.

_____. "Radical in America." *The Social Democrat*, Spring 1980.

_____. *The Unfinished Revolution*. New York: Socialist Party-Social-Democratic Federation, 1960.

Kahn, Tom, and Rachelle Horowitz. *Civil Rights and American Society*. New York: Young People's Socialist League, 1961.

Kahn, Tom, and August Meier. "Recent Trends in the Civil Rights Movement." *New Politics*3/2 (Spring 1964): 34–53.

King, Martin Luther Jr. *A Testament of Hope: The Essential Writings and Speeches of Martin Luther King, Jr.*, ed. James M. Washington. San Francisco: HarperCollins, 1986,

_____. *"All Labor Has Dignity,"* ed. Michael K. Honey. Boston: Beacon Press, 2012.

_____. *Where Do We Go from Here: Chaos or Community?* Boston: Beacon Press, 2010.

Le Blanc, Paul. "Martin Luther King, Jr.: Christian Core, Socialist Bedrock." *Against the Current*, January/February 2002, http://www.solidarity-us.org/node/1030.

_____. *Marx, Lenin and the Revolutionary Experience: Studies of Communism and Radicalism in the Age of Globalization*. New York: Routledge, 2006.

_____. *Work and Struggle: Voices from U.S. Labor Radicalism*. New York: Routledge, 2011.

Levine, Daniel. *Bayard Rustin and the Civil Rights Movement*. New Brunswick, NJ: Rutgers University Press, 1999.

Luxemburg, Rosa. *Socialism or Barbarism: The Selected Writings of Rosa Luxemburg*. Edited by Paul Le Blanc and Helen C. Scott. London: Pluto Press, 2011.

Malcolm X. *Malcolm X Speaks: Selected Speeches and Statements*. Edited by George Breitman. New York: Grove Weidenfeld, 1990.

Marable, Manning. *Black American Politics, from the Washington Marches to Jesse Jackson*. London: Verso, 1985.

_____. *From the Grassroots: Social and Political Essays Towards Afro-American Liberation*. Boston: South End Press, 1980.

_____. *Race, Reform and Rebellion: The Second Reconstruction and Beyond in Black America, 1945–2006*, 3rd ed. Jackson: University Press of Mississippi, 2007.

Mason, Paul. *Live Working or Die Fighting: How the Working Class Went Global*. Chicago: Haymarket, 2010.

_____. *Why It's Still Kicking Off Everywhere, The New Global Revolutions*. London: Verso, 2012.

Martínez, Elizabeth, Matt Meyer, and Mandy Carter, eds. *We Have Not Been Moved: Resisting Racism and Militarism in 21st Century America*. Oakland, CA: PM Press, 2012.

McReynolds, David. "Militant Protest, then Politics." *New America*, June 18, 1965.

_____. *We Have Been Invaded by the Twenty-First Century*. New York: Grove Press, 1971.

Meier, August, and Elliott Rudwick. *CORE: A Study in the Civil Rights Movement 1942–1968*. New York: Oxford University Press, 1972.

_____. *From Plantation to Ghetto*, 3rd ed. New York: Hill and Wang, 1994.

Miller, James. *"Democracy Is in the Streets": From Port Huron to the Siege of Chicago*. New York: Simon and Schuster, 1987.

Mishel, Lawrence, Josh Bivens, Elise Gould, and Heidi Shierholz. *The State of Working America*. Ithaca, NY: Cornell University Press, 2012.

Moody, Kim. *Labor in a Lean World: Unions in the International Economy*. New York: Verso, 1997.

_____. *U.S. Labor in Trouble and Transition*. London: Verso, 2007.

Muste, A. J. *The Essays of A. J. Muste*, ed. by Nat Hentoff. New York: Simon and Schuster, 1970

_____. *Nonviolence in an Aggressive World*. New York: Harper and Brothers, 1940.

O'Dell, Jack. *Climbin' Jacob's Ladder: The Black Freedom Movement Writings of Jack O'Dell*. Edited by Nikhil Pal Singh. Berkeley: University of California Press, 2010.

Pfeffer, Paula F. *A. Philip Randolph, Pioneer of the Civil Rights Movement*. Baton Rouge: Louisiana State University Press, 1990.

Phillips-Fein, Kim. *Invisible Hands: The Making of the Conservative Movement from the New Deal to Reagan*. New York: W. W. Norton, 2009.

Pickett, Kate, and Richard Wilkinson. *The Spirit Level: Why Greater Equality Makes Societies Stronger*. London: Bloomsbury Press, 2011.

Piven, Frances Fox, and Richard A. Cloward. *Poor People's Movements, Why They Succeed, How They Fail*. New York: Vintage Books, 1979.

Randolph, A. Philip. "For a Political and Economic Revolution against Racism." *New America*, September 24, 1963.

Rawick, George. *Listening to Revolt: Selected Writings*. Edited by David Roediger, with Martin Smith. Chicago: Charles H. Kerr, 2010.

Reed, Adolph, Jr. *Stirrings in the Jug: Black Politics in the Post-Segregation Era*. Minneapolis: University of Minneapolis Press, 1999.

Robinson, Cleveland. "New Directions for the Unfinished Revolution." *New America*, October 21, 1963, 6–7.

Robinson, Jo Ann Ooiman. *Abraham Went Out, A Biography of A. J. Muste*. Philadelphia: Temple University Press, 1981.

Roediger, David R. *How Race Survived U.S. History: From Settlement and Slavery to the Obama Phenomenon*. London: Verso, 2010.

Rose, Nancy E. *Put to Work: The WPA and Public Employment in the Great Depression*, 2nd ed. New York: Monthly Review Press, 2009.

Rustin, Bayard. *Down the Line: The Collected Writings of Bayard Rustin*. Chicago: Quadrangle Books, 1971.

_____. *I Must Resist: Bayard Rustin's Life in Letters*. Edited by Michael G. Long. San Francisco: City Light Books, 2012.

_____. *Time on Two Crosses: The Collected Writings of Bayard Rustin*. Edited by Devon W. Carbado and Donald Weise. San Francisco: Cleius Press, 2003.

Rustin, Bayard, and Eleanor Holmes. "Politics and Protest" (debate). *New America*, September 1964.

Rustin, Bayard, Tom Kahn et al. "The Negro Movement: Where Shall It Go Now?" In Irving Howe, ed., *The Radical Imagination*. New York: New American Library, 1967.

Sale, Kirkpatrick. *SDS*. New York: Alfred A. Knopf, 1973.

Schitz, Eric A. *Inequality and Power: The Economics of Class*. London: Routledge, 2011.

Sellers, Cleveland, with Robert Terrell. *The River of No Return: The Autobiography of a Black Militant and the Life and Death of SNCC*. Jackson: University of Mississippi Press, 1990.

Shachtman, Max. "Drive Out the Dixiecrats for Jobs and Freedom." *New America*, September 24, 1963.

Singh, Nikhil Pal. "'Learn Your Horn': Jack O'Dell and the Long Civil Rights Movement." Introduction to Jack O'Dell, *Climbin' Jacob's Ladder*, see above.

Slessarev, Helene. *The Betrayal of the Urban Poor*. Philadelphia: Temple University Press, 1997.

_____. "The Collapse of the Employment Policy Agenda: 1964–1981." In *Dream and Reality: The Modern Black Struggle for Freedom and Equality*, ed. Jeannine Swift. Westport, CT: Greenwood Press, 1991, 107–124.

Stone, I. F. *The Best of I. F. Stone*. Edited by Karl Weber. New York: Public Affairs, 2006.

Sugrue, Thomas J. *Sweet Land of Liberty: The Forgotten Struggle for Civil Rights in the North*. New York: Random House, 2008.

Sweezy, Paul M., and Paul A. Baran. *Monopoly Capital: An Essay on the American Economic and Social Order*. New York: Monthly Review Press, 1966.

Swift, Jeannine, ed. *Dream and Reality: The Modern Black Struggle for Freedom and Equality*. Westport, CT: Greenwood Press, 1991.

Troxell, Richard R. *Looking Up at the Bottom Line: The Struggle for the Living Wage*. Austin, TX: Plain View Press, 2010.

Woodward, C. Vann. *The Strange Career of Jim Crow*, 3rd rev. ed. New York: Oxford University Press, 1974.

Yates, Michael D. *Naming the System: Inequality and Work in the Global Economy*. New York: Monthly Review Press, 2002.

_____. *Power on the Job: The Legal Rights of Working People*. Boston: South End Press, 1994.

_____. *Why Unions Matter*, 2nd ed. New York: Monthly Review Press, 2009.

Zaroulis, Nancy, and Gerald Sullivan. *Who Spoke Up? American Protest against the War in Vietnam 1963–1975*. New York: Holt, Rinehart and Winston, 1985.

ONLINE SOURCES

Antolini, Tini, "Mr. Rustin and the Freedom Budget," http://stateofthereunion.com/mr-rustin-and-the-freedom-budget.

Bayard Rustin speech on Freedom Budget, 1967, http://dev.forum-network.org/lecture/bayard-rustin-live-speech-freedom-budget.

Columbia University Wiki on Social Justice, Freedom Budget, http://socialjustice.ccnmtl.columbia.edu/index.php/Freedom_Budget.

March on Washington (1963) radio coverage :

A. Philip Randolph and Bayard Rustin at March on Washington: http://dev.forum-network.org/lecture/1963-march-washington-medgar-evers-ballad.

Bayard Rustin at March on Washington leading pledge: http://dev.forum-network.org/lecture/1963-march-washington-freedom-demands-pledge-prayer.

Social Democrats USA panel discussion, "Socialism: What Happened? What Now?," May 1, 2002 (Penn Kemble, Joshua Muravchik, Rick Hertzberg, Marshall Wittman, Paul Berman, Jeane Kirkpatrick, Sandra Feldman), http://www.socialdemocrat-susa.org/oldsite/MayDayTranscript.html#kirkpatrick.

State of the Re-Union Radio, "Bayard Rustin—Who Is This Man?," http://stateofthere-union.com/home/season-2/bayard-rustin.

WGBH Interview with Bayard Rustin, 1982, http://openvault.wgbh.org/catalog/vietnam-a3b1e1-interview-with-bayard-rustin-1982.

NOTES

1. INTRODUCTION

1. Godfrey Hodgson captures much of the general context in his well-informed survey offered in the late 1970s, *America in Our Time, from World War II to Nixon— What Happened and Why* (Princeton: Princeton University Press, 2005). Although Hodgson focuses significant attention on the civil rights movement's rise and fall, and leaders of its activist wing , he misses the steady and mounting counterattack of conservative forces.

2. Sean Wilentz, *The Age of Reagan, A History 1974-2008* (New York: HarperCollins, 2008), 124. On the right-wing triumph, see Godfrey Hodgson, *The World Turned Right Side Up: A History of the Conservative Ascendancy in America* (Boston: Houghton Mifflin, 1996); Patricia Cayo Sexton, *The War on Labor and the Left: Understanding America's Unique Conservatism* (Boulder, CO: Westview Press, 1991); and Kim Phillips-Fein, *Invisible Hands: The Making of the Conservative Movement from the New Deal to Reagan* (New York: W. W. Norton, 2009).

3. Among the many sources that document this are Kevin Phillips, *Wealth and Democracy, A Political History of the American Rich* (New York: Broadway Books, 2002); and Robert Scheer, *The Great American Stickup: How Reagan Republicans and Clinton Democrats Enriched Wall Street While Mugging Main Street* (New York: Nation Books, 2010). Also see David Fireside, Amy Gluckman, Snriti Rao, Alejandro Reuss, and the Dollars & Sense Collective, eds., *The Wealth Inequality Reader* (Boston: Dollars & Sense—Economic Affairs Bureau, 2009).

4. See Roger D. Hodge, *The Mendacity of Hope: Barack Obama and the Betrayal of American Liberalism* (New York: HarperCollins, 2010); and John Nichols, *The "S" Word: A Short History of an American Tradition . . . Socialism* (London: Verso, 2011).

5. C. L. R. James, *Modern Politics* (Detroit: Bewick, 1973), 65. Eric Foner's useful and detailed discussion of Roosevelt's administrations from 1933 to 1945 can be found in *Give Me Liberty! An American History* (New York: W. W. Norton, 2006), 696-775. Worth considering are comments of Leo Huberman, *We The People*, rev. ed. (New York: Harper and Brothers, 1947): "The President made it clear, again and again, that he was a reformer, not a revolutionist. He strove to save the capitalist system by eliminating

its evils, ignoring the fact that those evils were an inevitable product of that system. . . . The New Deal philosophy was derived from the pressure of economic forces on the working class and the middle class and, to a smaller extent, on a few comparatively enlightened capitalists." Huberman concluded: "The New Deal was a reshuffle of the old deck of cards. It was not a revolution in economics" (345, 346). Substantial recent biographies are provided by Jean Edward Smith, *FDR* (New York: Random House, 2007); and H. W. Brands, *Traitor to His Class: The Privileged Life and Radical Presidency of Franklin Delano Roosevelt* (New York: Anchor Books, 2009).

6. See http://en.wikipedia.org/wiki/Four_Freedoms.

7. See http://en.wikipedia.org/wiki/Second_Bill_of_Rights#.E2.80.9CThe_Economic_Bill_of_Rights.E2.80.9D. The phrase quoted by Roosevelt—"necessitous men are not free men"—comes from the legal judgment of England's Lord Chancellor, Robert Henley, in *Vernon v. Bethell* (1762).

8. "Communism" under the regime of Joseph Stalin and his successors in what was then the Union of Soviet Socialist Republics (USSR or Soviet Union), and in other countries adopting its model of a collectivized and planned economy, projected itself—in many cases effectively—to large numbers of workers, peasants, and others in the world as a positive economic alternative to capitalism, although it also was seen (and in many cases was experienced) by millions the world over as an extremely oppressive dictatorship. Both dimensions come through in David Priestland, *The Red Flag: A History of Communism* (New York: Grove Press, 2009) and Geoff Eley, *Forging Democracy: The History of the Left in Europe 1850–2000* (New York: Oxford University Press, 2002).

9. In addition to sources in notes 2 and 3 above, see Thomas Frank, *The Wrecking Crew: How Conservatives Ruined Government, Enriched Themselves, and Beggared the Nation* (New York: Henry Holt, 2009); Michael Meeropol, *Surrender: How the Clinton Administration Completed the Reagan Revolution* (Ann Arbor: University of Michigan Press, 2000); and Naomi Klein, *The Shock Doctrine: The Rise of Disaster Capitalism* (New York: Picador/Holt, 2007).

10. See, for example, Thomas Frank, *Pity the Billionaire: The Hard Times Swindle and the Unlikely Comeback of the Right* (New York: Metropolitan Books, 2012).

11. The definition of socialism used here was articulated in 1918 by Socialist Party of America leader Eugene Victor Debs: "I believe . . . in common with all Socialists, that this nation ought to own and control its own industries . . . that all things that are jointly needed and used ought to be jointly owned—that industry, the basis of our social life, instead of being the private property of the few and operated for their enrichment, ought to be the common property of all, democratically administered in the interest of all." *Writings and Speeches of Eugene V. Debs*, ed. Joseph Bernstein (New York: Hermitage Press, 1948), 438. Three brief introductions to socialism, having somewhat different approaches, can be found in Leo Huberman and Paul M. Sweezy, with an essay by Albert Einstein, *Introduction to Socialism* (New York: Monthly Review Press, 1968); Michael Newman, *Socialism, A Very Short Introduction* (London: Oxford University Press, 2005); and Alan Maass, with an afterword by Howard Zinn, *The Case for Socialism*, 3rd ed. (Chicago: Haymarket Books, 2010).

12. Jacquelyn Dowd Hall, "The Long Civil Rights Movement and the Political Uses of the Past," *Journal of American History* (March 2005): 1234, 1263. Also see a

challenging response, which shares much of the spirit of Hall's essay, in Sundiata Keita Cha-Jua and Clarence Lang, "The 'Long Movement' as Vampire: Temporal and Spatial Fallacies in Recent Black Freedom Studies," *Journal of African American History* (April 2007): 265–88.

13. The two different approaches are summarized in Michael Heinrich's remarkably succinct *An Introduction to the Three Volumes of Marx's 'Capital'* (New York: Monthly Review Press, 2012); and Manfred B. Steger and Ravi K. Roy, *Neoliberalism, A Very Short Introduction* (Oxford: Oxford University Press, 2010).

14. Frances Fox Piven and Richard A. Cloward, *Poor People's Movements: Why They Succeed, How They Fail* (New York: Vintage Books, 1979), 33.

15. Two fine biographies presenting the lives, the contexts, and the ideas of Bernstein and Luxemburg, and highlighting their debate, are Peter Gay, *The Dilemma of Democratic Socialism: Eduard Bernstein's Challenge to Marx* (New York: Collier Books, 1962); and Paul Frölich, *Rosa Luxemburg, A Life* (Chicago: Haymarket Books, 2011).

16. Eduard Bernstein, *Evolutionary Socialism* (New York: Schocken Books, 1961), 197. It is important not to read back into the 1890s later meanings of the term *social democrat*, which at the time was synonymous with the term *socialist*. In later decades of the twentieth century, social democrats were those favoring a reformist approach, although some went further. The sophisticated social-democratic historian George Lichtheim explained in his *A Short History of Socialism* (New York: Praeger Publishers, 1970), 269, that among European social democrats there were "differences between wholesale nationalizers and advocates of a mixed economy with a large private sector," the latter being "content with reformist labor and welfare policies," whereas those to their left *within* the social democracy were "authentic Socialists who aimed at something qualitatively different from capitalism," a mild variant of the latter approach being embraced by Bernstein himself. "Nationalization or communalization of private enterprises are the classical formulas of socialization," he commented, and urged that "it could be allowed to develop gradually through laws and regulations that curtail private control." He continued to look forward to a socialist future, but felt "the potential for complete takeover lies only in the far distant future." See Eduard Bernstein, "Revisionism in Social Democracy," and "What Is Socialism?" in *Selected Writings of Eduard Bernstein, 1900–1921*, ed. Manfred Steger (Atlantic Highlands, NJ: Humanities Press, 1996), 75, 154, 155.

17. Rosa Luxemburg, "Reform or Revolution," in *Socialism or Barbarism: The Selected Writings of Rosa Luxemburg*, ed. Paul Le Blanc and Helen C. Scott (London: Pluto Press, 2010), 48.

18. Rosa Luxemburg, "The Mass Strike, Political Party, and Trade Unions," in ibid., 109, 110, 111, 119, 149.

19. Eduard Bernstein, "Political Mass Strike and Romanticizing Revolution," in *Selected Writings*, 139; Luxemburg, "Theory and Practice," in *Socialism or Barbarism*, 150. Among the civil rights activists in the mid-twentieth-century United States, some, such as King and Rustin, would insist that mass action and violence did not need to go together, drawing from such Gandhi-influenced sources as Richard B. Gregg, *The Power of Non-Violence* (Philadelphia: J. B. Lippincott, 1934). It was, of course, the

perspective of Gandhi rather than Luxemburg (combined in varying degrees with that of Marx) that was the dominant influence for both Rustin and King.

20.   Manning Marable, *Black American Politics, From the Washington Marches to Jesse Jackson* (London: Verso, 1985), 91; Paul Le Blanc, "Martin Luther King, Jr.: Christian Core, Socialist Bedrock," *Against the Current* (January/February 2002), http://www.solidarity-us.org/node/1030.

2. THE BATTLE FOR CIVIL RIGHTS

1.   This challenges an aspect of the analysis offered in the stimulating survey of Michael Goldfield, *The Color of Politics: Race and the Mainsprings of American Politics* (New York: New Press, 1997), 295. In discussing the civil rights movement of the 1950s and 1960s, he comments: "The exclusive focus on [civil] rights led the movement largely to gloss over those class issues that were at the root of problems faced by poor and working-class African Americans."

Ahmed Shawki, in his thoughtful study *Black Liberation and Socialism* (Chicago: Haymarket Books, 2006), expresses a concern that is similar to Goldfield's when he writes: "Movements of the oppressed have no social power to fundamentally transform the system unless they become transformed into a movement of the exploited and the oppressed, that is, unless they are allied or become part of the workers' movement and can champion the demands of all workers" (252). But unlike Goldfield, in his survey of the actual history Shawki presents a reality marked by greater complexity and radicalism.

Seeming to go a step further conceptually, in his seminal "The National Question and the Black Liberation Struggle," George Breitman argues that the very reality of the African American experience combines (1) "an oppressed racial minority bent on self-determination, freedom, and human rights," and (2) "super-exploited workers crowded into city slums who are the victims of intolerable conditions of life and labor in the richest and most advanced capitalism." This results in an explosive "combined character of their struggle, which is both national-democratic in its demands and proletarian-socialist in tendency." In Anthony Marcus, ed., *Malcolm X and the Third American Revolution: The Writings of George Breitman* (Amherst, NY: Humanity Books, 2005), 138.

The reality that Breitman identifies resulted in a combined and yet contradictory dynamic in the civil rights movement of the 1950s–60s that is not adequately accounted for in what is presented by Goldfield or even by Breitman himself, and which is at best vague in Shawki's account. The lack of clarity is related to some of the most articulate elements in the radical-activist wing of the civil rights movement as they were evolving away from an earlier revolutionary standpoint to one that was increasingly reformist. This shift substantially contributed to an unintended failure, yielding the result (significant change on civil rights issues, failure to change on class-based issues) that Goldfield highlights.

The fact remains that over three decades ago knowledgeable analysts observed that "the black struggle was waged for two main goals. One was to secure formal political rights in the South, especially the political franchise; the other was to secure economic advances." While "the winning of democratic political rights" was secured in the South, "by contrast, economic gains were limited." See Frances Fox Piven and Richard A. Cloward, *Poor People's Movements: Why They Succeed, How They Fail* (New York: Vintage Books, 1979), 181, 182. However, these authors partially misstate the reality when they also assert that "the cadres of the civil rights movement were simply brave reformers committed not to the total transformation of American society but to reforms consistent with American doctrines" (xx).

"American doctrines" could be interpreted as being (1) that all of us "are created equal, endowed by our Creator with certain unalienable rights" that include "life, liberty and the pursuit of happiness"; (2) that there should be "liberty and justice for all"; (3) that we should have "government of the people, by the people, and for the people." Martin Luther King Jr. was the quintessential civil rights spokesman framing goals according to the precepts of these doctrines. But he also believed, as we shall see, that the realization of these goals would involve a "total transformation" of U.S. society along the lines of deepening democracy politically and economically: socialism. Nor was King unique among the cadres of the activist wing of the civil rights movement. Though there is no question that many activists *were* more or less "simply brave reformers," many of them were powerfully influenced by and largely following the lead of cadres envisioning "total transformation."

2. For a useful general history, see August Meier and Elliott Rudwick, *from Plantation to Ghetto*, 3rd ed. (New York: Hill and Wang, 1976). A remarkable synthesis can be found in David R. Roediger, *How Race Survived U.S. History, From Settlement and Slavery to the Obama Phenomenon* (London: Verso, 2010). Critical focus is offered in Manning Marable, *Race, Reform, and Rebellion: The Second Reconstruction and Beyond in Black America, 1945–2006*, 3rd ed. (Jackson: University of Mississippi Press, 2007); as well as Jack M. Bloom, *Class, Race and the Civil Rights Movement* (Bloomington: Indiana University Press, 1987). An invaluable documentary collection is provided in Herbert Aptheker, ed, *A Documentary History of the Negro People in the United States*, 7 vols. (New York: Citadel Press, 1994). A useful synthesis of U.S. history as a whole, embracing and integrating the African American experience, is offered in Eric Foner, *Give Me Liberty! An American History* (New York: W. W. Norton, 2006).

3. See Bruce Levine, *Half Slave and Half Free: The Roots of the Civil War*, rev. ed. (New York: Hill and Wang, 2005); James M. McPherson, *Abraham Lincoln and the Second American Revolution* (New York: Oxford University Press, 1991); and Robin Blackburn, *An Unfinished Revolution: Karl Marx and Abraham Lincoln* (London: Verso, 2011).

4. Tom Kahn, *The Economics of Equality* (New York: League for Industrial Democracy, 1964), 13. This basically follows the analytical trajectory to be found in W. E. B. Du Bois, *Black Reconstruction in America, 1860–1880* (1935: repr., New York: Free Press, 1998), and developed in later scholarship by Eric Foner, *Reconstruction: America's Unfinished Revolution 1863–1877* (New York: HarperCollins, 1988). James had been more or less part of the same political tradition as Kahn, but in an earlier period, see Scott McLemee and Paul LeBlanc, eds., *C. L. R. James and Revolutionary Marxism, Selected Writings of C. L. R. James* (Atlantic Highlands, NJ: Humanities Press, 1995); and Scott McLemee, ed., *C. L. R. James on the "Negro Question"* (Jackson: University of Mississippi Press, 1996). The younger Rawick,

also in the same general political milieu as both Kahn and James, did pioneering work on the history of slavery and racism; see George Rawick, *Listening to Revolt: Selected Writings*, ed. David Roediger, with Martin Smith (Chicago: Charles H. Kerr, 2010).

5. We are grateful to Russell Pryor for helping think through and formulate this point. Considerable information and documentation are provided in Bloom, *Class, Race, and the Civil Rights Movement*, 18–73. Also see Pete R. Daniel, *Breaking the Land: The Transformation of Cotton, Tobacco and Rice Cultures since 1880* (Urbana: University of Illinois Press, 1986); and the study of a decade earlier by Piven and Cloward, *Poor People's Movements*, 184–211.

6. Thomas J. Sugrue, *Sweet Land of Liberty: The Forgotten Struggle for Civil Rights in the North* (New York: Random House, 2008), xiii, xviii.

7. O'Dell is quoted in Nikhil Pal Singh, "'Learn Your Horn': Jack O'Dell and the Long Civil Rights Movement," in Jack O'Dell, *Climbin' Jacob's Ladder: The Black Freedom Movement Writings of Jack O'Dell*, ed. Nikhil Pal Singh (Berkeley: University of California Press, 2010), 14. For an illuminating contemporary account of the early 1940s, animated by the spirit from the late 1930s to which O'Dell refers, see Roi Ottley, *New World A-Coming: Inside Black America*, rev. ed. (New York: World Publishing, 1945).

8. Sources on most of the historical sweep summarized here can be found in nn. 2 through 5 above. Also see Goldfield, *The Color of Politics*, esp, 176–295; and Adolph Reed Jr., *Stirrings in the Jug: Black Politics in the Post-Segregation Era* (Minneapolis: University of Minnesota Press, 1999), 59–65. On the Cold War influence, see Mary L. Dudziak, *Cold War Civil Rights: Race and the Image of American Democracy* (Princeton: Princeton University Press, 2000); and Thomas Borstelmann, *The Cold War and the Color Line: American Race Relations in the Global Arena* (Cambridge, MA: Harvard University Press, 2001).

9. Marable, *Race, Reform, and Rebellion*, 17; Singh, "'Learn Your Horn'," 25–26.

10. The group In Friendship is discussed in Barbara Ransby, *Ella Baker and the Black Freedom Movement: A Radical Democratic Vision* (Chapel Hill: University of North Carolina Press, 2003), 161–69. On Highlander, see John M. Glen, *Highlander, No Ordinary School*, 2nd ed. (Knoxville: University of Tennessee Press, 1996). An outstanding brief survey of the early civil rights movement and its background is provided in a special pamphlet-length issue of an independent socialist magazine: Anne Braden, "The Southern Freedom Movement in Perspective," *Monthly Review* 17/8 (July–August 1965): 1–93. Covering much of the same ground in considerably more detail is Taylor Branch, *Parting the Waters: America in the King Years 1954–63* (New York: Simon and Schuster, 1989); and in *Pillar of Fire: America in the King Years 1963–65* (New York: Simon and Schuster, 1999). On Braden and SCEF, see Catherine Fosl, *Subversive Southerner: Anne Braden and the Struggle for Racial Justice in the Cold War South* (Lexington: University Press of Kentucky, 2006).

11. Ella Baker, "Organization without Dictatorship," interview, December 27, 1966, in *To Redeem a Nation: A History and Anthology of the Civil Rights Movement*, ed. Thomas R. West and James W. Mooney (St. James, NY: Brandywine, 1993), 198. Also see Joanne Grant, *Ella Baker: Freedom Bound* (John Wiley & Sons, 1998); and Ransby, *Ella Baker and the Black Freedom Movement*.

12. An exhaustive early account from the 1940s is provided in Gunnar Myrdal, *An American Dilemma: The Negro Problem and Modern Democracy*, 2 vols. (New York: Harper and Row, 1962). More recent and more succinct are C. Vann Woodward, *The Strange Career of Jim Crow*, 3rd rev. ed. (New York: Oxford University Press, 1974); and Roediger, *How Race Survived U.S. History*.

13. Municipal segregation ordinances were declared unconstitutional in 1917, but "improvement associations" generated racially restrictive covenants (agreements among white property owners not to sell or rent to blacks) that were upheld by courts until 1948; such de jure support for de facto racism was buttressed by New Deal housing policies during the Great Depression . See August Meier and Elliott Rudwick, *From Plantation to Ghetto*, 3rd ed. (New York: Hill and Wang, 1994), 234–37, 261. Systematic "informal" perpetuation of these patterns was continued long after.

14. Michael Harrington, *The Other America, Poverty in the United States*, 50th anniversary ed. (New York: Scribner, 2012), 71.

15. Kahn's primary point was that the majority of African Americans were part of an economic class that had been able to make important gains through employment in an industrial economy but that "the position of this class is deteriorating because of technological developments which are revolutionizing the structure of the labor force." (Within two decades, "globalization" would exacerbate the problem by shifting many industrial jobs overseas.) What was seen as a "black problem" in the 1960s became a dramatic problem for a growing number of white workers by the 1980s. Of course, something like the Freedom Budget would have counteracted this. Kahn, *The Economics of Equality*, 15, 16, 17–18, 21, 26, 29. Kahn's views relate to a manifesto, "The Triple Revolution: Cybernation—Weaponry—Human Rights," that Harrington and Rustin had just signed as part of the Ad Hoc Committee (composed of various left-liberal figures) meeting at the Center for the Study of Democratic Institutions, an offshoot of the Fund for the Republic. The document posited a revolution of "cybernation" (combining computers and automated self-regulated machines), creating "a system of almost unlimited productive capacity which requires progressively less human labor," guaranteeing rising unemployment. Second was a weapons revolution, which raised questions about the future viability of war, given the development of new weaponry of horrific destructiveness. The third was a global human rights revolution, represented in the United States by the civil rights movement. This further reinforced the notion that the merger of struggles for economic justice and civil rights—given the changes in the economy—would have revolutionary implications. Some anticipated that the consequent massive unemployment would cause a working-class radicalization by the 1970s, which would combine with the "human rights" revolution to create the possibility for fundamental social and economic change. See Ad Hoc Committee, "The Triple Revolution: Cybernation—Weaponry—Human Rights," *Seeds of Liberation*, ed. Paul Goodman (New York: George Braziller, 1964), 396–413. See also Thomas F. Jackson, *From Civil Rights to Human Rights: Martin Luther King, Jr. and the Struggle for Economic Justice* (Philadelphia: University of Pennsylvania Press, 2007), 196–98, on the document's impact on "democratic socialist" and New Left activists. Further on the left, some in the Socialist Workers Party also took

this seriously, reprinting it (see http://www.marxists.org/history/etol/newspape/isr/vol25/no03/adhoc.html) and in the person of James P. Cannon positively discussing it (see http://marxists.architexturez.net/history/etol/audio/cannon/29.mp3). Others, however, were inclined to be dismissive; see, for example, Leslie Evans, *Outsider's Reverie, A Memoir* (Los Angeles: Boryana Books, 2009), 155, 157–58.

16. See Jo Ann Oiiman Robinson, *Abraham Went Out: A Biography of A. J. Muste* (Philadelphia: Temple University Press, 1981). Also relevant to some of the more general points being made here is what Aldon Morris has termed "movement halfway houses," existing in "a relative isolation from the larger society" and "developing a battery of social change resources such as skilled activists, tactical knowledge, media contacts, workshops, knowledge of past movements, and a vision of a future society." Morris sees Highlander Folk School, the Southern Conference Educational Fund, and the Fellowship of Reconciliation as fitting this profile. See Aldon D. Morris, *Origins of the Civil Rights Movement: Black Communities Organizing for Change* (New York: Free Press, 1986), 136, 140, 157–66. Obviously, other left-wing groups also fit the profile.

17. Harry Fleischman, *Norman Thomas, A Biography, 1884–1969* (New York: W. W. Norton, 1969); W. A. Swanberg, *Norman Thomas, The Last Idealist* (New York: Scribner, 1976); H. Wayne Morgan, ed., *American Socialism 1900–1960* (Englewood Cliffs, NJ: Prentice-Hall, 1964); and David A. Shannon, *The Socialist Party of America: A History* (Chicago: Quadrangle Books, 1967).

18. An outstanding source on various aspects of the U.S. left is Mary Jo Buhle, Paul Buhle, and Dan Georgakas, eds., *The Encyclopedia of the American Left*, 2nd ed. (New York: Oxford University Press, 1998). Also worth consulting is the critical-minded account of "Socialists, Communists, and Self-Determination," in Robert L. Allen with Pamela P. Allen, *Reluctant Reformers: The Impact of Racism on American Social Movements* (Washington, D.C.: Howard University Press, 1974), 207–45.

19. Henry Winston, "Unity and Militancy for Freedom and Equality," in *A Documentary History of the Negro People in the United States*, ed. Herbert Aptheker, 7:529. See also Mark Solomon, *The Cry Was Unity: Communists and African Americans, 1917–1936* (Jackson: University of Mississippi Press, 1998); and Albert Fried, *Communism in America: A History in Documents* (New York: Columbia University Press, 1997).

20. Braden, "The Southern Freedom Movement in Perspective," 11–12.

21. On the Civil Rights Congress, see Sugrue, *Sweet Land of Liberty*, 102–4,107–9; Murali Balaji, *The Professor and the Pupil: The Politics and Friendship of W. E. B. Du Bois and Paul Robeson* (New York: Nation Books, 2007), 201–8, 366–67; and lengthy discussions in the memoirs of two of its leading activists: William L. Patterson, *The Man Who Cried Genocide: An Autobiography* (New York: International Publishers, 1991); and Jessica Mitford, *A Fine Old Conflict* (New York: Vintage Books, 1978).

On anti-Communist repression in the United States, see David Caute, *The Great Fear: The Anti-Communist Purge under Truman and Eisenhower* (New York: Touchstone, 1979); and Albert Fried, *McCarthysim, The Great American Red Scare: A Documentary History* (New York: Oxford University Press, 1996).

On Stalin's crimes, see Russian Institute of Columbia University, *The Anti-Stalin Campaign and International Communism: A Collection of Documents* (New

York: Columbia University Press, 1966); Robert Conquest, *The Great Terror, A Reassessment*, 40th anniversary ed. (New York: Oxford University Press, 2007); and Roy Medvedev, *Let History Judge: The Origins and Consequences of Stalinism* (New York: Columbia University Press, 1989). The impact on U.S. Communists is indicated in reminiscences of a number of former Communists: for example, Howard Fast, *Being Red, A Memoir* (New York: Houghton Mifflin, 1990); Steve Nelson, with James Barrett and Rob Ruck, *Steve Nelson, American Radical* (Pittsburgh: University of Pittsburgh Press, 1992); Junius Scales, with Richard Nickson, *Cause at Heart: A Former Communist Remembers* (Athens: University of Georgia Press, 2005).

22.   Irving Howe, "New Styles in 'Leftism,'" in Irving Howe, *Selected Writings 1950–1990* (New York: Harcourt Brace Jovanovich, 1992), 198. On the *National Guardian*, which contains information on the milieu Howe refers to, see Cedric Belfrage and James Aronson, *Something to Guard: The Stormy Life of the National Guardian 1948–1967* (New York: Columbia University Press, 1978).

23.   On the Lovestoneites, see Robert J. Alexander, *The Right Opposition: The Lovestoneites and the International Communist Opposition of the 1930s* (Westport, CT: Greenwood Press, 1981), and Paul Le Blanc and Tim Davenport, eds., *'American Exceptionalists': The Rise and Fall of the Lovestone Group, 1929–40, A Documentary History* (Leiden, The Netherlands: Brill Academic Publishers, 2013, forthcoming). Also see Ransby, *Ella Baker and the Black Freedom Movement*; and Yvette Richards, *Maida Springer: Pan-Africanist and International Labor Leader* (Pittsburgh: University of Pittsburgh Press, 2004).

24.   Jervis Anderson, *A. Philip Randolph, A Biographical Portrait* (Berkeley: University of California Press, 1986), 62.

25.   Abner Berry, "Thunder in the South," in Aptheker, *A Documentary History of the Negro People in the United States*, 6:345, 346.

26.   Braden, "The Southern Freedom Movement in Perspective," 24–25; Tom Kahn, *The Unfinished Revolution* (New York: Socialist Party–Social-Democratic Federation, 1960), 9.

27.   Tom Kahn and Rachelle Horowitz, *Civil Rights and American Society* (New York: Young People's Socialist League), 1961, 1–2.

28.   Ibid., 3–5. This point was made in a section titled "The Rising Tide of Nationalism," in which special attention was given to a critical analysis of the Nation of Islam (though no mention was made of Malcolm X) and a negative assessment of black nationalism in general, to which A. Philip Randolph's perspective was positively contrasted.

29.   Ibid., 7, 9–10 .

30.   Kahn, *The Unfinished Revolution*, 15, 30, 38, 39.

31.   Quoted in Paula F. Pfeffer, *A. Philip Randolph, Pioneer of the Civil Rights Movement* (Baton Rouge: Louisiana State University Press, 1990), 10.

32.   Anderson, *A. Philip Randolph*, 110–19. Also see Sondra Kathryn Wilson, ed., *The Messenger Reader: Stories, Poetry and Essays from* The Messenger *Magazine* (New York: Modern Library/Random House, 2000); and Theodore G. Vincent, ed., *Voices of a Black Nation: Political Journalism in the Harlem Renaissance* (Trenton, NJ: Africa World Press, n.d., pub. 1974).

33.   Quoted in Anderson, *A. Philip Randolph*, 231–32.

34. Bayard Rustin, "The Total Vision of A. Philip Randolph," in *Time on Two Crosses: The Collected Writings of Bayard Rustin*, ed. Devon W. Carbado and Donald Weise (San Francisco: Cleius Press, 2003), 196–97. A far more critical assessment was offered in Manning Marable, "A. Philip Randolph and the Foundations of Black American Socialism," in *From the Grassroots: Social and Political Essays towards Afro-American Liberation* (Boston: South End Press, 1980), 59–85.

35. Anderson, *A. Philip Randolph*, 229–82; Pfeffer, *A. Philip Randolph*, 32–168; Manning Marable, *Black American Politics, from the Washington Marches to Jesse Jackson* (London: Verso, 1985), 81; Paul Le Blanc, *Work and Struggle: Voices from U.S. Labor Radicalism* (New York: Routledge, 2011), 215–28, on Second World War see 222–25.

36. A. Philip Randolph, "Race, Class, and a Strong Labor Movement" [originally titled "What They Say"], in LeBlanc, *Work and Struggle*, 225.

37. David J. Garrow, *Bearing the Cross: Martin Luther King and the Southern Christian Leadership Conference* (New York: Vintage Books, 1988), 537. Many of the themes associated with King's presumed latter-day radicalization can be found as well in what he was saying in the 1950s and early 1960s. See Martin Luther King Jr., *"All Labor Has Dignity,"* ed. Michael K. Honey (Boston: Beacon Press, 2012).

38. Garrow, *Bearing the Cross*, 716–17. James's perspectives were powerfully influenced by the ideas of Marx and Lenin, but he was also a longtime anti-Stalinist.

39. Coretta Scott King, "Thoughts and Reflections," in *We Shall Overcome: Martin Luther King, Jr. and the Black Freedom Struggle*, ed. Peter J. Albert and Ronald Hoffman (New York: Pantheon Books/United States Capitol Historical Society, 1990), 253, 254, 255. See also Paul Le Blanc, "Martin Luther King, Jr.: Christian Core, Socialist Bedrock," *Against the Current* (January/February 2002), http://www.solidarity-us.org/node/1030; much of which is corroborated in Thomas F. Jackson, *From Civil Rights to Human Rights*, particularly 25–50, 82, 103, 115, 121, 133, 174, 250–51, 270–71, 276–77, 320, 331–32, 362, 364. A similar interpretation has been offered by Clayborne Carson, who noted that as early as the 1950s "the works of Karl Marx had reinforced his long-held concern 'about the gulf between superfluous wealth and abject poverty,'" and "King charged that capitalist materialism was 'always in danger of inspiring men to be more concerned about making a living than making a life.' His version of social gospel Christianity also incorporated socialist ideas as well as anti-colonial sentiments spurred by the African independence movements." See Clayborne Carson, "Rethinking African American Political Thought in the Post-Revolutionary Era," in *The Making of Martin Luther King and the Civil Rights Movement*, ed. Brian Ward and Tony Badger (New York: New York University Press, 1996), 117. Also see Douglas Sturm, "Martin Luther King, Jr. as Democratic Socialist," *Journal of Religious Ethics* 18/2 (Fall 1990): 79–105.

40. Garrow, *Bearing the Cross*, 43.

41. Walter Rauschenbusch, *Christianity and the Social Crisis* (New York: Macmillan, 1907), 327, 408, 409, 413; Reinhold Niebuhr, *Moral Man and Immoral Society* (New York: Charles Scribner's Sons, 1932), xv, 149, 179, 180, 194; A. J. Muste, *Nonviolence in an Aggressive World* (New York: Harper and Brothers, 1940), 54, 98; V. I. Lenin, "The Revolutionary Proletariat and the Right of Nations to Self-Determination," in *Revolution, Democracy, Socialism*, 233–34.

42.   Randolph and Rustin are dealt with at length in this chapter and the next. On Baker, see Ransby, *Ella Baker and the Black Freedom Movement,* and Grant, *Ella Baker: Freedom Bound.* A considerable amount of information on Levison and O'Dell is offered in Branch, *Parting the Waters*; and Garrow, *Bearing the Cross.* Also see Jack O'Dell, *Climbin' Jacob's Ladder: The Black Freedom Movement Writings of Jack O'Dell,* ed. Nikhil Pal Singh (Berkeley: University of California Press, 2010).

43.   Martin Luther King Jr., *Stride toward Freedom,* excerpted in A *Testament of Hope: The Essential Writings and Speeches of Martin Luther King, Jr.*, ed. James M. Washington (San Francisco: HarperCollins, 1986), 746–47.

44.   While controversies rage over the outlook (and for some, the very existence) of Jesus, scholarly studies—not in full agreement with each other on various points—presenting him as a revolutionary include Marcus Borg, *Jesus: Uncovering the Life, Teachings and Relevance of a Religious Revolutionary* (New York: HarperCollins, 2008); John Dominic Crossan, *Jesus: A Revolutionary Biography* (San Francisco: HarperCollins, 1994); Bart D. Ehrman, *Jesus: Apocalyptic Prophet of the New Millennium* (New York: Oxford University Press, 2001); Ben Witherington III, *The Jesus Quest: The Third Search for the Jew of Nazareth* (Downes Grove, IL: InterVarsity Press, 1997).

45.   Martin Luther King Jr., "Where Do We Go From Here?" in King, *A Testament of Hope,* 250–51.

APPENDIX. THE BATTLE FOR CIVIL RIGHTS

1.   Biographical information on Marx and Engels, with useful examination of their historical context, can be found in David Riazanov, *Karl Marx and Frederick Engels, An Introduction ot Their Lives and Work* (New York: Monthly Review Press, 1973), available online at http://www.marxists.org/archive/riazanov/works/1927-ma/index. htm; and Mary Gabriel, *Love and Capital: Karl and Jenny Marx and the Birth of a Revolution* (New York: Little, Brown, 2011). Both are classics, one from 1927, the other a much more recent and incredibly rich contribution.

2.   For discussions of Marxism consistent with what is presented here, see Phil Gasper, *Karl Marx and Frederick Engels, The Communist Manifesto: A Roadmap to History's Most Important Political Document* (Chicago: Haymarket Books, 2005); Paul Le Blanc, *From Marx to Gramsci* (Amherst, NY: Humanity Books, 1996); August Nimtz, *Marx and Engels: Their Contribution to the Democratic Breakthrough* (Albany: State University of New York Press, 2000); and Terry Eagleton, *Why Marx Was Right* (New Haven: Yale University Press, 2011).

3.   As Marx noted in chapter 10 on "The Working Day" in the first volume of *Capital*: "In the United States of America, every independent workers' movement was paralyzed as long as slavery disfigured a part of the republic. Labor in the white skin cannot emancipate itself where it is branded in a black skin." See Karl Marx, *Capital* (New York: Vintage Books, 1977), 1:414.

4.   Paul Le Blanc, "The Absence of Socialism in the United States: Contextualizing Kautsky's 'American Worker,'" *Historical Materialism* 11/4 (2003): 136–37, 140; Karl Marx and Frederick Engels, *Marx and Engels on the United States,* ed. Nelly Rumyantseva (Moscow: Progress Publishers, 1979), 272; August H. Nimtz Jr., *Marx, Tocqueville, and Race in America: The "Absolute Democracy" or "Defiled*

Republic" (Lanham, MD: Lexington Books, 2003), 198. Also see Robin Blackburn, *An Unfinished Revolution: Karl Marx and Abraham Lincoln* (London: Verso, 2011); and Kevin B. Anderson, *Marx at the Margins: On Nationalism, Ethnicity, and Non-Western Societies* (Chicago: University of Chicago Press, 2010).

5. A considerable amount of information incorporating new scholarship on democratic aspects of Lenin's thought can be found in Lars Lih, *Lenin* (London: Reaktion Books, 2011); and V. I. Lenin, *Revolution, Democracy, Socialism: Selected Writings*, ed. Paul Le Blanc (London: Pluto Press, 2008). On the Russian Revolution as a democratic upsurge, see John Reed's eyewitness account, *Ten Days that Shook the World* (New York: International Publishers, 1926); and Rex Wade's scholarly synthesis, *The Russian Revolution 1917*, 2nd ed. (New York: Cambridge University Press, 2005). On the divergence of Stalinism from Leninism, see Victor Serge, *From Lenin to Stalin*, 2nd ed. (New York: Pathfinder Press, 2000); E. H. Carr, *The Russian Revolution: From Lenin to Stalin 1917-1929* (New York: Palgrave Macmillan, 2004); and Moshe Lewin, *The Soviet Century* (London: Verso, 2005).

6. One can find this defense of a democratic Leninist-Trotskyist conception in Shachtman's writings from the 1930s through the 1960s in Sean Matagama, ed., *The Fate of the Russian Revolution* (London: Phoenix Press, 1998); and Max Shachtman, *The Bureaucratic Revolution: The Rise of the Stalinist State* (New York: Donald Press, 1962), available online at http://babel.hathitrust.org/cgi/pt?id=mdp.39015074199814, as well as his introductions to Trotsky's *Terrorism and Communism* (Ann Arbor: University of Michigan Press, 1961), v–xvii; and *The New Course* (Ann Arbor: University of Michigan Press, 1965), 1–6. Also relevant are his comments of 1958, as the International Socialist League prepared to merge with the Socialist Party, at http://www.chicagodsa.org/audarch2.html.

7. Tom Kahn, "Archive: To Max Shachtman," *Democratiya* 11 (Winter 2007): 210. This outlook was not unique to Shachtman. C. L. R. James and his co-thinkers similarly insisted: "The struggle for socialism is the struggle for proletarian democracy. Proletarian democracy is not the crown of socialism. Socialism is the result of proletarian democracy. To the degree that the proletariat mobilizes itself and the great masses of the people, the socialist revolution is advanced. The proletariat mobilizes itself as a self-acting force through its own committees, unions, parties, and other organizations." See C. L. R. James, with Raya Dunayevskaya and Grace Lee Boggs, "The Invading Socialist Society," in *A New Notion: Two Works by C. L. R. James*, ed. Noel Ignatiev (Oakland, CA: PM Press, 2010), 28. James P. Cannon, a founder of both the U.S. Communist Party and U.S. Trotskyism, spoke in similar terms: "Socialists should not argue with the American worker when he says he wants democracy and doesn't want to be ruled by a dictatorship," he said in the wake of the 1956 Hungarian workers' and students' uprising against Stalinist bureaucratic tyranny. "Rather, we should recognize [the worker's] demand for human rights and democratic guarantees, now and in the future, is in itself progressive. The socialist task is to not to deny democracy, but to expand it and make it more complete." See James P. Cannon, "Socialism and Democracy," in *Speeches for Socialism* (New York: Pathfinder Press, 1971), 356, 361.

8. See, for example, Herbert Aptheker, *The Nature of Democracy, Freedom and Revolution* (New York: International Press, 1969); and much of the material

gathered in Philip Bart, Theodore Bassett, William W. Weinstone, Arthur Zipser, eds., *Highlights of a Fighting History: 60 Years of the Communist Party USA* (New York: International Publishers, 1979). For example, "We called for the fullest possible use of the 1936 elections to defeat the reactionaries and build the united front of the people for democracy and peace" (Earl Browder, 1938); "The central goal of this [proposed progressive southern] movement is to eliminate anti-democratic, feudal and autocratic political and economic relations, laws, institutions, and practices from the South" (Southern Regional Committee of the Communist Party USA, 1953); "The aim of the . . . program . . . advocated by the Communist Party is to bring about a strategic breakthrough to a deeper and wider degree of democracy" (Henry Winston, 1973): and "We have to explain that we are a force for democracy, that we are for the rule of the majority, that we would retain and adopt many features of this system [such as the Bill of Rights]" (Gus Hall, 1976), 175, 307, 426–27, 482.

9. See the rich proliferation of other leftist groups discussed in Angela D. Dillard, *Faith in the City: Preaching Radical Social Change in Detroit* (Ann Arbor: University of Michigan Press, 2007); Dan Georgakis and Marvin Surkin, *Detroit: I Do Mind Dying, A Study in Urban Revolution* (Chicago: Haymarket Books, 2012); and Michael Staudenmaier, *Truth and Revolution: A History of the Sojourner Truth Organization 1969–1986* (Oakland, CA: AK Press, 2012). Radical pacifism, socialism, and anarchism can also be found in the remarkable blend reflected in *Liberation* magazine, many of whose articles are gathered in Paul Goodman, ed., *Seeds of Liberation* (New York: George Braziller, 1964). The complex experience and collapse of U.S. Maoist groups is detailed in Max Elbaum, *Revolution in the Air: Sixties Radicals Turn to Lenin, Mao and Che* (London: Verso, 2002).

10. This generalization finds corroboration in a number of works, including Joe Allen, *People Wasn't Made to Burn: A True Story of Race, Murder, and Justice in Chicago* (Chicago: Haymarket Books, 2011); Fred Stanton, ed., *Fighting Racism in World War II* (New York: Pathfinder Press, 1980); Anthony Marcus, ed., *Malcolm X and the Third American Revolution: The Writings of George Breitman* (Amherst, NY: Humanity Books, 2005); Angela D. Dillard, *Faith in the City*, 10–11, 23, 209, 218, 220, 230–31, 263, 264–65, 275–76, 299; Barry Sheppard, *The Party: The Socialist Workers Party, 1960–1988*, vol. 1 (Chippendale, Australia: Resistance Books, 2005), 35–40, 54–57, 76–79, 93–95, 110–19, 175–67, and *The Party: The Socialist Workers Party, 1960–1988*, vol. 2 (London: Resistance Books, n.d. [2012]), 73–91.

11. O'Dell quoted in Nikhil Pal Singh, "'Learn Your Horn': Jack O'Dell and the Long Civil Rights Movement," in Jack O'Dell, *Climbin' Jacob's Ladder: The Black Freedom Movement Writings of Jack O'Dell*, ed. Nikhil Pal Singh (Berkeley: University of California Press, 2010), 25.

3. FOR JOBS AND FREEDOM

1. Jervis Anderson, *Bayard Rustin: Troubles I've Seen, A Biography* (New York: HarperCollins, 1997), 238.

2. Stokely Carmichael, with Ekwueme Michael Thelwell, *Ready for Revolution: The Life and Struggles of Stokley Carmichael (Kwame Turé)* (New York: Scribner, 2003), 95.

3. Anderson, *Bayard Rustin*, 55, 56.

4. Shirley Le Blanc (mother of one of the authors of this book) was a graduate student at the University of Pittsburgh's School of Social Work at this time and, as part of an assignment, conducted a telephone interview with Rustin, who made the comment on the *Communist Manifesto* during what she remembered as a fascinating discourse on society's problems.

5. John D'Emilio, *Lost Prophet: The Life and Times of Bayard Rustin* (Chicago: University of Chicago Press, 2003), 276.

6. Ibid., 297–300; David J. Garrow, *The FBI and Martin Luther King, Jr.* (New York: Penguin Books, 1983), 49–51.

7. Garrow, *The FBI and Martin Luther King, Jr.*, 60–70; Nikhil Pal Singh, "'Learn Your Horn': Jack O'Dell and the Long Civil Rights Movement," in Jack O'Dell, *Climbin' Jacob's Ladder: The Black Freedom Movement Writings of Jack O'Dell*, ed. Nikhil Pal Singh (Berkeley: University of California Press, 2010), 16, 23, 25, 30; D'Emilio, 371–73, 394–96, 405–6, 453–60.

8. It would seem that Rustin did not actually become a formal member of the Socialist Party until the late 1960s. Similarly, Harrington's biographer, Maurice Isserman asserts that "either Harrington or Bogdan Denitch," who became Shachtmanites together in the 1950s, told him "that the two of them were never members of the ISL proper—just of the YSL. It seemed an important distinction to them at the time." Isserman speculates that "as YSL members they had a degree of autonomy they would not have had in the ISL—for instance, establishing friendly ties with Irving Howe's *Dissent* crowd [made up largely of ex–ISL members], which Shachtman, in the mid-50s, had a vendetta against." Isserman, correspondence with Paul LeBlanc, September 21–22, 2012. This desire for relative autonomy may account for Rustin's late membership in the Socialist Party, and for his much earlier decision in the 1930s, while a leader of the Young Communist League, not to join the Communist Party.

9. D'Emilio, *Lost Prophet,* 278.

10. Peter Drucker, *Max Shachtman and His Left: A Socialist's Odyssey through the "American Century"* (Atlantic Highlands, NJ: Humanities Press, 1994), 268. This "approach to African–American rights" that Shachtman "had advocated since the 1930s" had basically four components: 1) blacks had great revolutionary potential because of "the proletarian and semi-proletarian character of the Negro race, his role and place in capitalist society, his continuous expression of resentment against his oppression"; 2) overcoming the oppression of blacks "can only be realized in connection with the struggles of the white workers . . . with the black and white proletarians fused in the heat of the class struggle"; 3) "the militant proletariat inscribes upon its banner in this country the uncompromising demand for full and equal rights for the oppressed Negro"; and 4) the joint struggle of black and white workers "for the proletarian revolution . . . will sweep away the abominable structure . . . under which the millions of American Negroes suffer today." This can be found in a document drafted in 1933 in Max Shachtman, *Race and Revolution* (London: Verso, 2003), 102; and in the 1945 Workers Party majority resolution he supported, drafted by Ernest Rice McKinney and titled "Negroes and the Revolution," available at http://www.marxists.org/history/etol/newspape/ni/vol11/no01/coolidge.htm.

11. Bryan Palmer, *James P. Cannon and the Origins of the American Revolutionary Left 1890–1928* (Urbana: University of Illinois Press, 2007), esp. 252–84.
12. Julius Jacobson, "The Two Deaths of Max Shachtman," *New Politics* 10/2 (Winter 1973); 96, 97; quoted in George Breitman, Paul Le Blanc, Alan Wald, *Trotskyism in the United States, Historical Essays and Reconsiderations* (Atlantic Highlands, NJ: Humanities Press, 1996), 10; see also Robert J. Alexander, *International Trotskyism, 1929–1985: A Documented Analysis of the Movement* (Durham, NC: Duke University Press, 1991), 761–813, 899–910.
13. For an exhaustive survey of theories regarding the nature of the USSR, see Marcel van der Linden, *Western Marxism and the Soviet Union, A Survey of Critical Theories and Debates since 1917* (Chicago: Haymarket Books, 2009), esp. 69–96. On the general perspectives Shachtman shared and then broke from, see Leon Trotsky, *Writings from Exile*, ed. Kunal Chattopadhyay and Paul Le Blanc (London: Pluto Press, 2011).
14. Tom Kahn, "Max Shachtman: His Ideas and His Movement," *Democratiya* 11 (Winter 2007): 252; Jacobson, "The Two Deaths of Max Shachtman," 96; Breitman, Le Blanc, Wald, *Trotskyism in the United States*, 11.
15. Alexander, *International Trotskyism*, 810–13, 899; Tim Wohlforth, *The Prophet's Children: Travels on the American Left* (Atlantic Highlands, NJ: Humanities Press, 1994), 24–75; Barry Sheppard, *The Party, A Political Memoir: The Socialist Workers Party 1960–1988*, vol. 1: *The Sixties* (Chippendale, Aus.: Resistance Books, 2005), 25–27, 33–40; Milton Fisk, *Socialism from Below in the United States: The Origins of the International Socialist Organization* (Cleveland: Hera Press, 1977), 27–36.
16. Martin Smith, "Joel Geier: A Life in the Revolution," in *Vive La Révolution*, ed. Candace Cohen (Chicago: Privately Printed, May 2008), 7, 8.
17. Maurice Isserman, *If I Had a Hammer: The Death of the Old Left and the Birth of the New Left* (New York: Basic Books, 1987), 189, 190; Smith, "Joel Geier: A Life in the Revolution," 8, 10, 11, 12; Michael Harrington, *Fragments of the Century, A Social Autobiography* (New York: E. P. Dutton, 1973), 117.
18. Isserman, *If I Had a Hammer*, 61–62; Maurice Isserman, *The Other American: The Life of Michael Harrington* (New York: Public Affairs, 2000), 146; Paul Feldman, "The Making of a Social Democrat" (unpublished ms., n.d., 1980s?), 4, available at http://www.socialdemocratsusa.org/oldsite/feldman1.pdf.
19. Michael Harrington, *The Other America: Poverty in the United States* (1962; repr., New York: Scribner, 1997), 1–2.
20. Ibid., 171, 176, 177.
21. Philip M. Crane, *The Democrat's Dilemma* (Chicago: Henry Regnery, 1964), 347–48. In addition to discussing Harrington and the revitalized LID, the Birch Society's Stang included information about SDS and especially about Bayard Rustin, noting his and Harrington's desire for an alliance of black and white workers (and the civil rights and labor movements), with their talk about "revolutionary restructuring" and socialism, all of which Stang presented as part of a grimly subversive Communist plot. See Alan Stang, *It's Very Simple: The True Story of Civil Rights* (Boston: Western Islands Press, 1965), 105–7, 112, 116, 121, 127, 131–33, 135, 136–38, 143–44, 145, 163, 165, 171, 178, 189, 190, 191.

22. Rachelle Horowitz, "Tom Kahn and the Fight for Democracy: A Political Portrait and Personal Recollection," *Democratiya* 11 (Winter 2007): 215 (also available at http://www.socialdemocratsusa.org/oldsite/Kahn.html).
23. Tom Kahn, *The Unfinished Revolution* (New York: Socialist Party–Social Democratic Federation, 1960), 59, 45.
24. Ibid., 6.
25. Horowitz, "Tom Kahn and the Fight for Democracy," 206; D'Emilio, *Lost Prophet*, 372; Carmichael, *Ready for Revolution*, 158.
26. Quoted in Anderson, *Bayard Rustin*, 237. Thelwell goes on to note that Kahn "spoke glowingly of Bayard Rustin's political history and his Gandhian-pacifist-socialist approach to the black struggle," adding: "Rustin became our intellectual and political mentor. We adopted his view that the integration of American society required a radical coalition of social and interracial forces. We admired Bayard's intellectuality. He sometimes came to speak on campus, and he seemed far more creative, articulate, and analytical than others in the established civil rights leadership. He was an activist in direct action, a theoretician and a practitioner, a dramatic and romantic figure who had traveled throughout the world for peace and freedom. We became Bayard Rustin people."
27. Horowitz, "Tom Kahn and the Fight for Democracy," 225.
28. Ibid., 216; Peter Drucker, *Max Shachtman and His Left: A Socialist's Odyssey through the "American Century"* (Atlantic Highlands, NJ: Humanities Press, 1994), 269, 273–78; Isserman, *If I Had a Hammer*, 191–194.
29. Handwritten notes by Kahn, 1962, in YPSL and SDUSA folder, Tom Kahn Papers.
30. Ibid.; Tom Kahn, *Civil Rights: The True Frontier* (New York: Donald Press, 1963), 3.
31. Ibid., 4, 9, 13, 14.
32. Ibid., 24.
33. Tom Kahn, "Radical in America," *The Social Democrat*, Spring 1980, 3, 4.
34. Charles Euchner, *Nobody Turn Me Around: A People's History of the 1963 March on Washington* (Boston: Beacon Press, 2010), 17, 18–19, 35; William P. Jones, "The Unknown Origins of the March on Washington: Civil Rights Politics and the Black Working Class," *Labor: Studies in Working-Class History of the Americas* 7/3, 2010, 41; Stanley Aronowitz, http://www.stanleyaronowitz.org/new/biography; D'Emilio, *Lost Prophet*, 327–28; Jervis Anderson, *A. Philip Randolph, A Biographical Portrait* (Berkeley: University of California Press, 1986), 324; Anderson, *Bayard Rustin*, 239–40; David J. Garrow, *Bearing the Cross: Martin Luther King and the Southern Christian Leadership Conference* (New York: Vintage Books, 1988), 266; Peter B. Levy, *The New Left and Labor in the 1960s* (Urbana: University of Illinois Press, 1994), 7–8.
35. "Preamble to the March on Washington," in Bayard Rustin, *Time on Two Crosses: The Collected Writings of Bayard Rustin*, ed. Devon W. Carbado and Donald Weise (San Francisco: Cleis Press, 2003), 112–15; D'Emilio, *Lost Prophet*, 327–28.
36. Anderson, *A. Philip Randolph*, 299, 300, 310; Daniel Levine, *Bayard Rustin and the Civil Rights Movement* (New Brunswick, NJ: Rutgers University Press, 2000), 272 n17; Garrow, *Bearing the Cross*, 280.
37. Anne Braden, "The Southern Freedom Movement in Perspective," *Monthly Review* 17/8 (July–August 1965): 46, 47; Martin Luther King Jr., "Letter From a

Birmingham Jail," in A *Testament of Hope: The Essential Writings and Speeches of Martin Luther King, Jr.*, ed. James M. Washington (San Francisco: HarperCollins, 1986), 289–302.

38. Braden, "The Southern Freedom Movement in Perspective," 47–48; Taylor Branch, *Parting the Waters: America in the King Years 1954–63* (New York: Simon and Schuster, 1988), 673–845; Horowitz, "Tom Kahn and the Fight for Democracy," 221.

39. Cleveland Sellers, with Robert Terrell, *The River of No Return: The Autobiography of a Black Militant and the Life and Death of SNCC* (Jackson: University of Mississippi Press, 1990), 62.

40. Euchner, *Nobody Turn Me Around*, 77; Anderson, *Bayard Rustin*, 241; D'Emilio, *Lost Prophet*, 344.

41. Branch, *Parting the Waters*, 846–48; Anderson, *Bayard Rustin*, 247–48; D'Emilio, *Lost Prophet*, 338–39, 347.

42. Anderson, *Bayard Rustin*, 249, D'Emilio, *Lost Prophet*, 340; author's interview with Joel Geier, June 30, 2012.

43. Correspondence between Harrington and Shachtman, Max Shachtman Papers, Tamiment Library.

44. Michael Harrington, "Socialists and Civil Rights," *New America*, August 31, 1963, 3.

45. "Socialist Party Testifies Before Congress: Rights Bill Needs to Be Expanded and Strengthened," and "Randolph Commends S.P. Rights Program," *New American*, special supplement, August 10, 1963, 2S– 3S.

46. For example, see Branch, *Parting the Waters*, 846–48; Euchner, *Nobody Turn Me Around*, 21–23; D'Emilio, *Lost Prophet*, 337–39.

47. Anderson, *Bayard Rustin*, 242, 245–56; Euchner , *Nobody Turn Me Around*, 78.

48. Branch, *Parting the Waters*, 873–74; Garrow, *Bearing the Cross*, 281–83; Euchner, *Nobody Turn Me Around*, 45–49, 150–53, 164–66. Texts of the speech that Lewis actually gave along with the precensored speech can be found in Herbert Aptheker, ed., *A Documentary History of the Negro People in the United States* (New York: Citadel Press, 1994), 7:245–49.

49. John Lewis, "A Serious Revolution," in Aptheker, *A Documentary History of the Negro People in the United States*, vol. 7, 246, 247.

50. Quoted in Anderson, *Bayard Rustin*, 250. Also see Manning Marable, *Black American Politics, from the Washington Marches to Jesse Jackson* (London: Verso, 1985), 92–93.

51. Euchner, *Nobody Turn Me Around*, xv, 57–58; Russell Baker, *Looking Back* (New York: New York Review of Books, 2002), 80; D'Emilio, *Lost Prophet*, 345, 369; Branch, *Parting the Waters*,182, 256–57, 836, 861–62; David J. Garrow, *The FBI and Martin Luther King, Jr.* (New York: Penguin Books, 1983), 153–56. For massive documentation, see Michael Friedly and David Gallen, *Martin Luther King, Jr., The FBI File* (New York: Carroll and Graf Publishers, 1993).

52. Branch, *Parting the Waters*, 836–38, 861–62, 902–3; Euchner, *Nobody Turn Me Around*, 58; D'Emilio, *Lost Prophet*, 344, 346–50.

53. Jones, "The Unknown Origins of the March on Washington," 46.

54. Malcolm X, "Message to the Grassroots," in *Malcolm X Speaks*, ed. George Breitman (New York: Grove Press, 1990), 16. Malcolm X, particularly in his final years, advanced a sharp and often telling critique of "The Strategy," especially in its

realignment version. As time went on, this critique resonated powerfully with radical-ized activists, and it deserves greater attention than can be offered here. See George Breitman, *The Last Year of Malcolm X: The Evolution of a Revolutionary* (New York: Schocken Books, 1968); Peter Goldman, *The Death and Life of Malcolm X*, rev. ed. (Urbana: University of Illinois Press, 1979); and Manning Marable, *Malcolm X, A Life of Reinvention* (New York: Penguin Books, 2011). Rustin's account of his interac-tions with Malcolm X in Washington at the time of the March, which included some joking back and forth as well as agreement between the two that "this dream of King's is probably going to be a nightmare before it's over," can be found in Goldman, *The Death and Life of Malcolm X*, 107.

55.	Moses quoted in Euchner, 44; for additional details and documentation, see Clayborne Carson, *In Struggle: SNCC and the Black Awakening of the 1960s* (Cambridge, MA: Harvard University Press, 1981).

56.	Horowitz quoted in Anderson, *Bayard Rustin*, 242; Barry Sheppard, *The Party, A Political Memoir: The Socialist Workers Party 1960–1988, Volume 1: The Sixties* (Chippendale, Australia: Resistance Books, 2005), 96.

57.	The meeting is reported in detail in Arthur M. Schelsinger, Jr., *Journals 1952–2000* (New York: Penguin Press, 2000), 169–172. Schlesinger, an aide to Kennedy, was present at the meeting; Carmichael, 329–330, 331.

58.	Euchner, *Nobody Turn Me Around*, 146. "Unquestionably, the . . . March on Washington movement had accelerated the passage of desegregation legislation at both national and state levels," historian Manning Marable reflected. "It forced the Kennedy administration, and later, the Johnson administration, to align themselves closely behind the moderate civil rights leadership." On the other hand, he adds, "in the long run it also brought about a major shift within the desegregation united front, which ultimately tore the coalition apart." Marable, *Black American Politics*, 96.

59.	Sellers, *The River of No Return*, 65, 66.

60.	I. F. Stone, "The March on Washington," in *The Best of I. F. Stone*, ed. Karl Weber (Washington, D.C.: Public Affairs, 2006), 188, 189.

61.	Mailer quoted in Euchner, *Nobody Turn Me Around*, 179; Baldwin quoted in Anderson, *Bayard Rustin*, 262.

62.	As it turned out, Farmer, along with a number of other CORE activists, was in a south-ern jail and was represented at the march and at the conference by Floyd McKissick.

63.	Flyer, "Conference on the Civil Rights Revolution," Summer 1963, author's private collection.

64.	"Socialist Party Conference on Civil Rights Revolution," *New America*, September 24, 1963, 5.

65.	Stone, "The March on Washington," 189–90.

66.	A. Philip Randolph, "For an Economic and Political Revolution against Racism," *New America*, September 24, 1963, 5, 9.

67.	Cleveland Robinson, *New America*, October 21, 1963, 6, 7.

68.	"Bayard Rustin Summarizes," *New America*, September 24, 1963, 7.

69.	Norman Thomas, *New America*, October 21, 1963, 7; Socialist Party/Social Democratic Federation national committee mail vote (with detailed explanation), August 9, 1963; Minutes, NAC YPSL, August 9, 1963, Tamiment Library.

70. Max Shachtman, "Drive Out Dixiecrats for Jobs and Freedom," *New America*, September 24, 1963, 8, 12.

71. Gary Shapiro, "A Tribute to Norman Hill," *New York Sun*, November 25, 2005, http://www.nysun.com/on-the-town/tribute-to-norman-hill/23503/; also at http://www.socialdemocratsusa.org/oldsite/HillTribute.html.

72. Feldman, "The Making of a Social Democrat," 7.

73. Paul Jacobs and Saul Landau, *The New Radicals: A Report with Documents* (New York: Vintage Books, 1966), 76.

74. Bayard Rustin, Tom Kahn et al., "The Negro Movement: Where Shall It Go Now?" (1964), in Irving Howe, ed., *The Radical Imagination* (New York: New American Library, 1967), 176, 177, 180, 182, 186, 189.

75. Tom Kahn, "Problems of the Negro Movement," in Irving Howe, ed., *The Radical Papers* (Garden City, NY: Anchor Books, 1966), 149.

4. FREEDOM BUDGET FOR ALL AMERICANS

1. See *Brother Outsider: The Life of Bayard Rustin*, http://rustin.org/.

2. Velma Hill, "Bayard Rustin: The Whole Story," *New York Sun*, March 3, 2003; reproduced on the "old site" of Social Democrats USA, http://www.socialdemocratsusa.org/oldsite/VelmaHill.html#top.

3. John Nichols, *The "S" Word: A Short History of an American Tradition . . . Socialism* (London: Verso, 2011), 228.

4. Norman Hill, "Crisis in the Movement," *New America*, November 15, 1963, 3.

5. Thomas J. Sugure, *Sweet Land of Liberty: The Forgotten Struggle for Civil Rights in the North* (New York: Random House, 2008), 375–76; Dona Cooper Hamilton and Charles V. Hamilton, *The Dual Agenda: The African–American Struggle for Civil and Economic Equality* (New York: Columbia University Press, 1997), 147; Paula F. Pfeffer, *A. Philip Randolph, Pioneer of the Civil Rights Movement* (Baton Rouge: Louisiana State University Press, 1990), 286.

6. "A. Philip Randolph Institute Prospectus" in A. Philip Randolph Papers, Library of Congress; also see information on the A. Philip Randolph Institute in Bayard Rustin and Norman Hill, *Seniority and Racial Progress* (New York: A. Philip Randolph Institute, n.d.), 7–11; Jervis Anderson, *A. Philip Randolph, A Biographical Portrait* (Berkeley: University of California, 1986), 314–15; John D'Emilio, *Lost Prophet: The Life and Times of Bayard Rustin* (Chicago: University of Chicago Press, 2003), 397, 414–15; Pfeffer, *A. Philip Randolph*, 291.

7. Martin Luther King, Jr., "Foreword," in A. Philip Randolph, *A "Freedom Budget" for All Americans, a Summary* (New York: A. Philip Randolph Institute, January 1967), 1.

8. Memos from Rustin (12/9/65, 5/24/66, 6/29/66), and Keyserling to Rustin (2/4/66, 4/13/66, 5/5/66, 5/6/66, 5/16/66, 8/5/66, 9/26/66), in Bayard Rustin Papers, Library of Congress. Also see Paul Feldman, "Join Freedom Budget Campaign," *New America*, October 31, 1966, 7; Michael Harrington, *Fragments of the Century, A Social Autobiography* (New York: E. P. Dutton, 1973), 204; D'Emilio, *Lost Prophet*, 430; Daniel Levine, *Bayard Rustin and the Civil Rights Movement*, (New Brunswick, NJ: Rutgers University Press, 2000), 188.

9. Keyserling's intensive involvement not only in drafting and redrafting the Freedom

Budget (four drafts in all), and a summary version of the budget, as well as intensive hands-on efforts in securing endorsers and helping to publicize and campaign for it is evident in three substantial folders of his correspondence from 1965 to 1968 in the Bayard Rustin Papers. David J. Garrow, "Betraying the Dream: That 'I Have a Dream' Day Was Aimed at Economic Justice—Not Simply Desegregation," *Christian Science Monitor*, August 28, 2003, http://www.csmonitor.com/2003/0828/p09s02-coop.html. Also see Donald K. Pickens, *Leon H. Keyserling: A Progressive Economist* (Lanham, MD: Lexington Books, 2009); and W. Robert Brazelton, *Designing U.S. Economic Policy: An Analytical Biography of Leon H. Keyserling* (New York: Macmillan Palgrave, 2001). The 1930s socialist sympathies are quoted and contextualized in Landon R. Y. Storrs, *The Second Red Scare and the Unmaking of the New Deal Left* (Princeton: Princeton University Press, 2012), 159–63.

10. Keyserling to Rustin, 10/19/67, and Keyserling to Greene, 2/24/67, in Bayard Rustin Papers.

11. Keyserling to Editors of *Freedomways*, 12/5/67; and Keyserling to Thomas, 12/21/66. in ibid.

12. Keyserling to Greene, 2/24/67 in ibid.; Keyserling quoted in Helene Slessarev, *The Betrayal of the Urban Poor* (Philadelphia: Temple University Press, 1997), 50; Rustin quoted in D'Emilio, *Lost Prophet*, 432.

13. D'Emilio, *Lost Prophet*, 431–32; "Labor, Rights Groups Back Randolph: Ten-Year Freedom Budget Set Forth to Erase Poverty," *AFL–CIO News*, October 29, 1966.

14. "Review and Outlook: A Poverty of Thought," *Wall Street Journal*, November 17, 1966; "Freedom Budget—Class Struggle," *New America*, November 18, 1966, 3

15. D'Emilio, *Lost Prophet*, 432, 433–34.

16. Ibid., 431–35; Horowitz, 226–27; Eugenia Kemble, "Freedom Budget Mobilizes Broad Coalition Support," *New America*, February 16, 1967, 1, 5; Eugenia Kemble, "Budget Gains Youth Movement at USYC," *New America*, December 16, 1966, 4–5; Charlotte Roe, "Sacramento Conference Backs Freedom Budget," *New America*, April 13, 1967, 1, 5; A. Philip Randolph Institute, "Memorandum on Recent Developments in Support of 'The Freedom Budget for All Americans," April 1967; also Rustin to Barol 1/30/68, both in Bayard Rustin Papers. U.S. Youth Council, *Youth Action on the Freedom Budget,* April 30, 1967, 6, special newsletter also in Bayard Rustin Papers.

17. "Summary of the Freedom Budget and Questions for Discussion" (n.d.); Memorandum to Community Leaders from Bayard Rustin, Re: What you can do about the "Freedom Budget for All Americans" (n.d.); U.S. Youth Council, "Youth Action for the Freedom Budget: A Discussion Outline" (February 1967); *Youth Action on the Freedom Budget,* April 30, 1967; Rustin to Barol 1/30/68. All of these are in Bayard Rustin Papers. Thomas J. Sugrue, *Sweet Land of Liberty: The Forgotten Struggle for Civil Rights in the North* (New York: Random House, 2008), 377.

18. *Youth Action on the Freedom Budget*, April 30, 1967, 5.

19. Ossie Davis and Ruby Dee, *With Ossie and Ruby, In This Life Together* (New York: William Morrow, 1998), 305–6.

20. Charles Euchner, *Nobody Turn Me Around: A People's History of the 1963 March on Washington* (Boston: Beacon Press, 2010), 146–149.

21. Ellsberg was an experienced U.S. State Department military analyst who released to the *New York Times* and other newspapers the Pentagon Papers, a top-secret Pentagon study of U.S. government decision making in relation to the Vietnam War. Daniel Ellsberg, *Secrets: A Memoir of Vietnam and the Pentagon Papers* (New York: Viking, 2002), 274.

22. William Appleman Williams, *The Tragedy of American Diplomacy*, 50th ann'y ed. (New York: W. W. Norton, 2009), 307.

23. Thomas to Rustin (8/31/66); Davis to Randolph (9/4/66); Randolph to Davis (9/14/66), all in Bayard Rustin Papers. Jerome Davis's reference to the 1954 Geneva Agreements referred to formal peace accords that ended the French–Indochinese war, temporarily dividing Vietnam into Communist and non-Communist zones (north and south, respectively) that were to be reunited by internationally supervised elections in 1956 in which the U.S.-backed Diem regime in the south refused to participate.

24. Browne to Randolph (10/26/66); Keyserling to Browne (11/2/66); Thomas to Keyserling (12/14/66); Keyserling to Thomas (12/21/66), all in Bayard Rustin Papers. In addition to teaching economics at Fairleigh Dickinson University, Browne had worked for the U.S. foreign aid program in Cambodia and South Vietnam from 1955 to 1961, and had returned for a visit to Saigon in 1965. He made similar points as those offered by Jerome Davis in an extensive 1965 article that connected opposition to the war with the struggle for civil rights in the first major article opposing the Vietnam War to be published by a black journal, *Freedomways*: see "The Freedom Movement and the War in Vietnam," in *Freedomways Reader: Prophets in Their Own Country*, ed. Esther Cooper Jackson with Constance Pohl (Boulder, CO: Westview Press, 2000), 152–66.

25. See, for example, Paul Feldman, "Landslide LBJ–Vote to Stop Right and Move Left," *New America*, October 18, 1964, 6, 8.

26. See Doug McAdam, *Freedom Summer* (New York: Oxford University Press, 1988); Cleveland Sellers, with Robert Terrell, *The River of No Return: The Autobiography of a Black Militant and the Life and Death of SNCC* (Jackson: University of Mississippi Press, 1990), 94–111; Stokely Carmichael, with Ekwueme Michael Thelwell, *Ready for Revolution: The Life and Struggles of Stokeley Carmichael (Kwame Turé)* (New York: Scribner, 2003), 349–413; Clayborne Clayborne Carson, *In Struggle: SNCC and the Black Awakening of the 1960s* (Cambridge, MA: Harvard University Press, 1981), 111–29.

27. Cleveland Sellers, with Robert Terrell, *The River of No Return: The Autobiography of a Black Militant and the Life and Death of SNCC* (Jackson: University of Mississippi Press, 1990), 108–9.

28. Ibid., 109.

29. Carmichael, 408–9.

30. Jane Stembridge, "Mrs. Hamer," http://www.crmvet.org/poetry/pjane.htm; see also Chana Kai Lee, *For Freedom's Sake: The Life of Fannie Lou Hamer* (Urbana: Illinois University Press, 2000).

31. Barbara Ransby, *Ella Baker and the Black Freedom Movement: A Radical Democratic Vision* (Chapel Hill: University of North Carolina Press, 2003), 338–42.

32. D'Emilio, *Lost Prophet*, 386; Levine, *Bayard Rustin and the Civil Rights Movement*, 165, 169.

33. Eleanor Holmes, "Politics and Protest," *New America*, September 16, 1964, 6. On Eleanor Holmes's involvement in and around the Socialist Party, see Joan Steinau Lester, *Fire in My Soul: The Life of Eleanor Holmes Norton* (New York: Atria Books, 2003), 63, 75, 99, 115, 119.

34. Bayard Rustin, "Politics and Protest," *New America*, September 16, 1964, 6.

35. Ibid., 6, 7.

36. For a useful and informative collection of diverse documents, including from the Johnson administration, edited form a radically critical standpoint, see Marvin E. Gettleman and David Mermelstein, eds., *The Great Society Reader: The Failure of American Liberalism* (New York: Vintage Books, 1967), with material focusing on the War on Poverty on 180–239. A useful summary can be found in Eric Foner, *Give Me Liberty! An American History* (New York: W. W. Norton, 2006), 858–61; and in "Lyndon Johnson's War on Poverty," National Public Radio, January 8, 2004, http://www.npr.org/templates/story/story.php?storyId=1589660. Critical evaluations can be found in Slessarev, 32, 35–38, 46–48; Hamilton and Hamilton, *The Dual Agenda*, 153–167; and Sugrue, *Sweet Land of Liberty*, 356–58, 364–74.

37. Michael Harrington, "New Society with Old Institutions?" *New America*, January 18, 1965, 1, 5.

38. Ibid., 5.

39. Michael Harrington, "Present Limits of the Great Society," *New America*, February 8, 1965, 1, 2.

40. S. M. Miller, "Program Lacks Clear-Cut Goals"; and Paul Jacobs, "A Reconnaissance, Not a War," *New America*, June 18, 1965, 4–5.

41. See, for example, Rachelle Horowitz, "The Harlem Riots," *New America*, August 24, 1964, 2–3; Bayard Rustin, "The Watts 'Manifesto,' " *New America*, September 17, 1965, 6–7; Penn Kemble, "Report on CCAP Conference: Problems of Anti–Poverty Coalition," *New America*, April 22, 1966, 3; Tom Kahn, "Pop Journalism and Myths of the 'New Left,' " *New America*, August 9, 1965, 4, 7.

42. Bayard Rustin, "From Protest to Politics: The Future of the Civil Rights Movement," in *Time on Two Crosses: The Collected Writings of Bayard Rustin*, ed. Devon W. Carbado and Donald Weise (San Francisco: Cleis Press, 2003), 118, 121, 122, 123, 125, 126, 128. The article was drafted by Tom Kahn, according to Rachelle Horowitz's reminiscence of Kahn. Though the assertion often is made that Rustin basically wanted to end protest demonstrations and civil disobedience in favor of electoral action, there is much evidence indicating that this was not his position—including his decision to provide a laudatory Foreword to Martin Oppenheimer and George Lakey, *A Manual for Direct Action: Strategy and Tactics for Civil Rights and All Other Nonviolent Protest Movements* (Chicago: Quadrangle Books, 1965), vii–x.

43. Adolph Reed Jr., *Stirrings in the Jug: Black Politics in the Post-Segregation Era* (Minneapolis: University of Minnesota Press, 1999), 273–74n25.

44. Staughton Lynd, "Coalition Politics or Nonviolent Revolution?" in Jacobs and Landau, *The New Radicals*, 311–312. A later critique involved the assertion: "When blacks won the vote in the South and a share of patronage in the municipalities of the North in response to the disturbances of the 1960s, black leaders were absorbed into

electoral and bureaucratic politics and became the ideological proponents of the shift 'from protest to politics' (Rustin)." See Frances Fox Piven and Richard A. Cloward, *Poor People's Movements: Why They Succeed, How They Fail* (New York: Vintage Books, 1979), 32–33.

45. On indignation over Lynd's critique, see Peter B. Levy, *The New Left and Labor in the 1960s* (Urbana: University of Illinois Press, 1994), 114–15; David McReynolds, "Militant Protest, Then Politics," *New America*, June 18, 1965, 4. McReynolds's ongoing and increasingly futile struggle in the Socialist Party around the question of the Vietnam War is detailed in Martin Duberman, *A Saving Remnant: The Radical Lives of Barbara Deming and David McReynolds* (New York: New Press, 2011), 83–84, 108–10, 112, 121–23, 141, 146–47, 182. Rustin's Madison Square Garden radical pacifist speech against the Vietnam War is now available: Bayard Rustin, "Revolutionary Democracy—A Speech against the Vietnam War," in *We Have Not Been Moved: Resisting Racism and Militarism in 21st Century America*, ed. Elizabeth Martínez, Matt Meyer, and Mandy Carter (Oakland, CA: PM Press, 2012), 34–37; author's telephone interview with Walter Naegle, 11/11/12.

46. Rustin, "From Protest to Politics," 118, 119, 121.

47. Author's interview with Norman Hill, 9/15/12.

48. Hamilton and Hamilton, *The Dual Agenda*, 148, 149. There were, of course, many non-signers who were also supportive. Despite that it was promoted by figures associated with the traditionally anti-Communist Socialist Party–Social Democratic Federation, the Communist Party's national chairman, Henry Winston, responded to the question of whether his party should support the Freedom Budget: "I say without hesitation, Yes. We should do it in the same way that everyone has, from Stokely Carmichael [of SNCC] to Roy Wilkins [of the NAACP] who have endorsed it." He added: "It is basic to the strengthening of Negro-white solidarity" (151).

49. Hamilton and Hamilton, *The Dual Agenda*, 150; Euchner, *Nobody Turn Me Around*, 175–78.

50. Hamilton and Hamilton, *The Dual Agenda*, 128–30.

51. David J. Garrow, *Bearing the Cross: Martin Luther King and the Southern Christian Leadership Conference* (New York: Vintage Books, 1988), 312. By the time King wrote his final book, *Where Do We Go From Here: Chaos or Community?* (Boston: Beacon Press, 2010), his thinking had opened to the idea of preferential treatment: "It is, however, important to understand that giving a man his due may often mean giving him special treatment. I am aware of the fact that this has been a troublesome concept for many liberals, since it conflicts with their traditional ideal of equal opportunity and equal treatment of people according to their individual merits… A society that has done something special *against* the Negro for hundreds of years must now do something special *for* him, in order to equip him to compete on a just and equal basis" (95).

52. Tom Kahn, "Urban League Plan for Middle Class: Preferential Treatment No Answer for Negro Masses—Full Employment Essential," *New America*, February 16, 1964, 4–5. Kahn's erstwhile Shachtmanite comrade, Julius Jacobson, editor of *New Politics*, fiercely polemicized against this position in his 1966–67 essay "Coalitionism: From Protest to Politicking," in *Autocracy and Insurgency in Organized Labor*, ed. Burton

Hall (New York: Transaction Books, 1972), 337–38, explaining, "we support prefer-ential hiring not because it is the ultimate answer but it is at least a small democratic step in the direction of social justice." There is a difference between this, however, and the question of what should be the fundamental strategic thrust in the struggle for economic justice.

53. Levine, *Bayard Rustin and the Civil Rights Movement*, 193; Hill quoted in Helene Slessarev, "The Collapse of the Employment Policy Agenda: 1964–1981," in *Dream and Reality: The Modern Black Struggle for Freedom and Equality*, ed. Jeannine Swift (Wesport, CT: Greenwood Press, 1991), 119.

54. A. Philip Randolph, "Introduction," *A "Freedom Budget" for All Americans* (New York: A. Philip Randolph Institute, 1966), iv.

55. Hamilton and Hamilton, *The Dual Agenda*, 148, 152.

56. Feldman, "Join Freedom Budget Campaign," 1, 7.

57. Ibid., 150, 151; Feldman, "Join Freedom Budget Campaign," 7; Michael Harrington, "Support $100 Billion Freedom Budget," *New America*, December 18, 1965, 2.

58. Kahn, "Pop Journalism and Myths of the 'New Left,'" 7.

59. Jacobson, "Coalitionism: From Protest to Politicking," 342. The history of the Democratic Party is critically surveyed in Lance Selfa, *The Democrats: A Critical History*, updated edition (Chicago: Haymarket Books, 2012).

60. Rachelle Horowitz, "Tom Kahn and the Fight for Democracy: A Political Portrait and Personal Recollection," *Democratiya* 11 (Winter 2007): 248n30.

61. Harrington, *Fragments*, 198; Peter Drucker, *Max Shachtman and His Left: A Socialist's Odyssey through the "American Century"* (Atlantic Highlands, NJ: Humanities Press, 1994), 288.

62. Meany quoted in Paul Le Blanc, *A Short History of the U.S. Working Class, from the Colonial Era to the Twenty-First Century* (Amherst, NY: Humanity Books, 1999), 104: and Archie Robinson, *George Meany and His Times, A Biography* (New York: Simon and Schuster, 1981), 294. Critical surveys of the U.S. labor movement in this period, making sharp distinctions between the trade union apparatus and the work-ing class, are provided in Kim Moody, *An Injury to All: The Decline of American Unionism* (London: Verso, 1988); and Paul Buhle, *Taking Care of Business: Samuel Gompers, George Meany, Lane Kirkland and the Tragedy of American Labor* (New York: Monthly Review Press, 1999).

63. Rick Congress, "Keynesian Palliatives," *New America*, February 27, 1967, 3.

64. By this time, the failure of the Socialist Party to unambiguously build opposition to the war in Vietnam, and its increasing unease or hostility to the deepening radicaliza-tion among 1960s activists, was seriously eroding its influence and membership.

65. Paul Feldman, "A Program for Change," *New America*, February 27, 1967, 3, 4–5. Feldman's call for "a *transitional program*" to generate mass struggle brings to mind Trotsky's use of the term as a program involving demands that make sense to large numbers of workers, and that they are prepared to fight for, but which capitalists and their politicians feel unable to grant, and which consequently forms a bridge from reform struggles to revolution. See Leon Trotsky, *Writings from Exile*, ed. Kunal Chattopadhyay and Paul Le Blanc (London: Pluto Press, 2011), 204–11. It is by no means clear, however, that Feldman was using the term in this way.

66. Rick Congress, "Fails to Attack Roots of Poverty and War," *New America*, April 13, 1967.
67. On the Vietnam War, see Marilyn B. Young, John J. Fitzgerald, A. Tom Grunfeld, *The Vietnam War, A History in Documents* (New York: Oxford University Press, 2002).
68. Harrington, "Support $100 Billion Freedom Budget," 1, 2; Michael Harrington, "LBJ Budget: Not Enough Butter," *New America*, January 23, 1966, 1; and Michael Harrington, "LBJ Budget: Guns Over Butter," *New America*, January 31, 1967, 1.
69. Slessarev, *The Betrayal of the Urban Poor*, 50.
70. A letter from Keyserling to Rustin, dated January 6, 1967, Bayard Rustin papers, states: "A few days ago, I had lunch with Joe Rauh, as we talked about the high need to dramatize the 'Freedom Budget' by some legislative proposal, as many people take these matters more seriously when there is a Bill." The letter describes additional brainstorming between Keyserling and Rauh on how to move the Freedom Budget forward. Although Rustin had his own ambivalences about expressing opposition to the war, and believed it would be counterproductive for civil rights organizations as such to adopt antiwar positions, his most recent biographer cites significant evidence indicating he was supportive of King's opposition to the war. See John D'Emilio, *Lost Prophet*, 413–14, 457–58. When King came out against the war, Rustin, in a public and widely reprinted article on the matter, did not attack the content of his antiwar statements and unambiguously defended his decision to express such views. See Bayard Rustin, "Dr. King's Painful Dilemma," in *Time on Two Crosses*, 184–85. On the other hand, in his polemic against the realignment strategy, *New Politics* editor Julius Jacobson argued angrily that "Rustin is not that much opposed to the war," citing his refusal even to lend his name to antiwar petitions while (according to a 1967 *New York Times* article) publicly attacking Dr. Benjamin Spock, a leader of SANE and a Freedom Budget endorser, for "working along with Maoists and Trotskyites to end the war in Vietnam." See Jacobson, "Coalitionism: From Protest to Politicking," 334–35.
71. Davis and Dee, *With Ossie and Ruby*, 331–32.
72. Randolph, "Introduction," *A "Freedom Budget" for All Americans*, v.
73. Levine, 194, 196, 280n7.
74. Melman's "war budget" comment is quoted in a letter from Penn Kemble to Rachelle Horowitz (11/5/66), and he himself composed a letter (11/1/66) addressed to Benjamin Spock, Norman Thomas, and Irving Howe, and sent to the entire national board of the peace group SANE (of which all four were members), expressing "disbelief and dismay" that they would endorse a document accepting "the military extravaganza." See Bayard Rustin Papers, Library of Congress. Melman included with his letter his article, "Great Society: War, Peace and the Managerial Bent," *Commonweal*, August 5, 1966. His critiques of militarism's destructive impact can be found in his *Our Depleted Society* (New York: Holt, Rinehart and Winston, 1965) and *Pentagon Capitalism: The Political Economy of War* (New York: McGraw Hill, 1970).
75. Bayard Rustin, "Talk on the Freedom Budget" (1967) is available at http://dev.forum–network.org/lecture/bayard–rustin–live–speech–freedom–budget. A more direct comment can be found in Rustin to Irving Howe, 11/10/66, Bayard Rustin Papers.

76. The role of Thomas and other socialists is indicated in Robert Scheer, *How the United States Got Involved in Vietnam* (Santa Barbara, CA: Center for the Study of Democratic Institutions, 1965), 30-33. In the autumn of 1955, Thomas became part of a newly formed group called "Friends of Vietnam," consisting largely of liberals, with some moderate socialists and conservatives. Scheer explains: "The announced purpose of the American Friends of Vietnam was 'to extend more broadly a mutual understanding of Vietnamese and American history, cultural customs, and democratic institutions.' In actuality, it was concerned with the political objective of committing the United States to a massive aid program on Diem's behalf." On Shachtman's evolving orientation on Vietnam and U.S. foreign policy, see Drucker, *Max Shachtman and His Left*, 148, 149, 172, 174-76, 222, 249, 251, 300-304, 307.

77. Thomas to Keyserling, 12/14/66, and Keyserling to Thomas, 12/21/66, Bayard Rustin Papers.

78. This reflected the end of Shachtman's commitment to the "third-camp socialist" position of seeing capitalism and Communism as equally bad. Seeing Communism as worse led him, and a number of his younger followers, to give active support to U.S. Cold War foreign policy.

79. Drucker, *Max Shachtman and His Left*, 302; Fred Halstead, *Out Now! A Participant's Account of the American Movement against the Vietnam War* (New York: Monad/ Pathfinder Press, 1978), 113, 721; "Peace March Helps Debate on U.S. Policy," *New America*, December 18, 1965, 1; Harrington, "Support $100 Billion Freedom Budget," 2; Harrington, *Fragments*, 109-206; Taylor Branch, *At Canaan's Edge: America in the King Years 1965-68* (New York: Simon and Schuster, 2006), 620.

80. Interview with Rustin in James Finn, *Protest: Pacifism and Politics: Some Passionate Views on War and Nonviolence* (New York: Vintage Books, 1968), 330, 339; also see D'Emilio, *Lost Prophet*, 407-39. On Muste's position, see Finn, 193-205, and A. J. Muste, "The Movement to Stop the Vietnam War," in Nat Hentoff, ed., *The Essays of A. J. Muste* (New York: Simon and Schuster, 1970), 503-13.

81. Anderson, *A. Philip Randolph*, 331. In a 1982 interview for a television documentary on the impact of the Vietnam War on the United States, Rustin sought to clarify his position, retrospectively, in this way: "My own views on the war were complicated. . . . My first attitude when the war opened was, yes, as Americans we ought to be in there helping to maintain democracy. But then in a few months I look around and discover that we are attempting to support democracy by relying on dictators and anti-democratic forces which were leading. At that point, my cry became: support the Buddhists and support the trade unions as a third force to let them lead the democratic struggle. Well, this never occurred. At that point, then, I began to feel like many, many other people we better get out of that situation because ultimately we cannot make of it what we would like to make of it. Which is ultimately what happened." WGBH, Interview with Bayard Rustin, 1982, available at http://openvault.wgbh.org/catalog/vietnam-a3b1e1-interview-with-bayard-rustin-1982. Seen through the lens of his later ideological orientation, this seems to create an after-the-fact "neatness" regarding what appears to have been a more complex and difficult process for him.

5. THE POLITICAL ECONOMY OF THE FREEDOM BUDGET

1. For a good discussion of poverty, including definitions, data, and causes, see Lawrence Mishel, Josh Bivens, Elise Gould, and Heidi Shierholz, *The State of Working America* (Ithaca, NY: Cornell University Press, 2012), chap. 7, "Poverty."

2. Unless otherwise noted, data citations and quotations are taken from A. Philip Randolph Institute, *A "Freedom Budget" for All Americans: Budgeting Our Resources, 1966–1975 to Achieve "Freedom from Want"* (New York: A. Philip Randolph Institute, 1966). Hereafter, this is referred to as the Freedom Budget.

3. For some background on the Act, see G. J. Santoni, "The Employment Act of 1946: Some History Notes," available at http://research.stlouisfed.org/publications/review/86/11/Employment_Nov1986.pdf.

4. See Nancy E. Rose, *Put to Work: The WPA and Public Employment in the Great Depression*, 2nd ed. (New York: Monthly Review Press, 2009). We noted in chapter 4 that some critics of the Freedom Budget argued that it was premised on the reformist economics of John Maynard Keynes. Keynes was certainly not a radical, and his economics, laid out in his *General Theory of Employment, Interest and Money*, published in 1936, can be seen as directed at those who wanted to save capitalism during the Great Depression. That is, Keynes showed that a capitalist economy does not automatically move toward full employment, as previous mainstream economists had argued. If some external shock, such as a stock market crash, strikes the economy, the disruption this causes, in terms of failing businesses and unemployment, can make capitalists so pessimistic about future profit prospects that they will not make capital expenditures (on new plant and equipment) no matter how low wages and interest rates on borrowed money are. This failure to invest existing profits will drive down the GDP and employment, and this will lower total wages, making the GDP still lower. The economy might then stabilize with a high rate of unemployment and a good deal of excess capacity for business firms. Keynes said that the only way out of such a dilemma is for the government to spend money—raised by taxing the wealthy and corporate profits and by issuing and selling bonds—on capital projects. This government investment would then raise the GDP, employment, and wages, which in turn would further increase the GDP, and so forth, ultimately allowing the economy to achieve full employment. Keynes was a strong proponent of heavy taxes on speculative incomes, making a distinction between productive capitalists (those whose businesses actually produced useful goods and services) and unproductive capitalists (those who made money by speculating in financial markets). However, he was also a champion of capitalism and believed that it could function in a way that both allowed for profits and full employment.

   Keynes's view of the state, of the willingness of the government to embrace his policies, was naïve, missing the fact that the state is powerfully beholden to the very capitalists he knows have no concern for full employment and the welfare of workers. And today, his distinction between productive and unproductive capitalists sounds foolish. Still, this does not mean that what he said is not true. It is, and his policies have worked wonders in many countries. It is interesting to observe that the countries in which Keynesian economics worked best have been those with strong working-class movements, such as the Scandinavian nations. Even in those, however, capital has always stood ready to roll back the gains workers have made by compelling the government to act in their interests.

Contrary to those critics of the Keynesian outlook of Keyserling and the other economists who built the Freedom Budget, the reformism inherent in Keynes's politics does not mean that the government *can* cause an economic downturn, even a depression, to end. That the government might not do what Keynes said it should certainly does not mean that we should not demand that it do so. The objectives of the Freedom Budget, combined with the radical version of "The Strategy," are radical demands and could galvanize an aroused working class to continue to push for them and expand the list of objectives further.

5.   *The Freedom Budget*, 44.
6.   "Timberline Lodge," *The Oregon Encyclopedia*, http://www.oregonencyclopedia.org/entry/view/timberline_lodge/.
7.   See the masterful four-volume biography of Lyndon Johnson by Robert Caro, which has much useful information on poverty, race, and federal government anti-poverty programs. Robert Caro, *The Path to Power* (1990), *Means of Ascent* (1991), *Master of the Senate* (2003), and *The Passage of Power* (2012) (New York: Alfred A. Knopf).
8.   *The Freedom Budget*, 13–14.
9.   *The Freedom Budget*, 12.
10. *The Freedom Budget*, 19–20.
11. *The Freedom Budget*, Introduction, n.p.

6. DEFEAT OF THE FREEDOM BUDGET

1.   This conception is rooted in long-standing perspectives in the revolutionary Marxist tradition, but it was given a distinctive tag in the 1938 founding program Leon Trotsky developed for the Fourth International. He spoke of *transitional demands* as something "to help the masses in the daily struggle to find the bridge between present demands and the socialist program of revolution," demands "stemming from today's conditions and today's consciousness of wide layers of the working class and unalterably leading to one final conclusion: the conquest of power by the proletariat." See "The Transitional Programme," in Leon Trotsky, *Writings in Exile*, ed. Kunal Chattopadhay and Paul Le Blanc (London: Pluto Press, 2012), 207; and also Paul Le Blanc, *From Marx to Gramsci* (Amherst, NY: Humanity Books, 1996), 73–75.
2.   Martin Luther King Jr., "Where Do We Go From Here?" in Martin Luther King Jr., *A Testament of Hope: The Essential Writings and Speeches of Martin Luther King, Jr.*, ed. James M. Washington (San Francisco: HarperCollins, 1986), 246, 247.
3.   "Estimated Budget [of A. Philip Randolph Institute], September, 1966 through August, 1967"; and Rustin to Meany, 5/3/67, Bayard Rustin Papers, Library of Congress. Meany quoted in Jervis Anderson, *A. Philip Randolph, A Biographical Portrait* (Berkeley: University of California, 1986), 315. Slaiman and Thewell quoted in *Bayard Rustin: Troubles I've Seen, A Biography* (New York: HarperCollins, 1997), 288, 289.
4.   Russell Baker, *Looking Back* (New York: New York Review of Books, 2002), 78, 79.
5.   Martin Luther King Jr., "A Time to Break Silence," in King, *A Testament of Hope*, 240–41, 242.
6.   The relevant works are available online: Lenin's *Imperialism, The Highest Stage*

of Capitalism: http://www.marxists.org/archive/lenin/works/1916/imp-hsc/; and Luxemburg's *The Accumulation of Capital*: http://www.marxists.org/archive/luxemburg/1913/accumulation-capital/index.htm. Also see a useful discussion in Alex Callinicos, *Imperialism and Global Political Economy* (Cambridge: Polity Press, 2009), esp. the consideration of "The Classical Legacy," 25–66.

7. James Finn, *Protest: Pacifism and Politics* (New York: Vintage Books, 1968), 341.

8. Michael Harrington, *Fragments of the Century, A Social Autobiography* (New York: E. P. Dutton, 1973), 196.

9. "You don't have to go to Karl Marx to learn how to be a revolutionary," King insisted. "I didn't get my inspiration from Karl Marx; I got it from a man named Jesus, a Galilean saint who said he was anointed to heal the broken-hearted. He was anointed to deal with the problems of the poor. And that is where we get our inspiration." See *The Autobiography of Martin Luther King, Jr.*, ed. Clayborne Carson (New York: Warner Books, 1998), 351. Herbert Hill, labor director of the NAACP (and himself a former Trotskyist from the Socialist Workers Party), viewed King as "more a mystic than a revolutionary," according to Michael Honey, *Going Down Jericho Road: The Memphis Strike, Martin Luther King's Last Campaign* (New York: W. W. Norton, 2007), 541.

10. Michael Harrington, *Toward a Democratic Left: A Radical Program for a New Majority* (Baltimore: Penguin Books, 1969), 124, 270.

11. Ibid., 186, 188, 218.

12. Harry Magdoff, "Is Imperialism Really Necessary?" in *Imperialism: From the Colonial Age to the Present, Essays by Harry Magdoff* (New York: Monthly Review Press, 1978), 260–261. Miller's co–authors were Roy Bennett and Cyril Allapatt, and their article appeared in *Social Policy* (September/October 1970), 12-19.

13. Paula F. Pfeffer, *A. Philip Randolph, Pioneer of the Civil Rights Movement* (Baton Rouge: Louisiana State University Press, 1990), 290.

14. David J. Garrow, *Bearing the Cross: Martin Luther King and the Southern Christian Leadership Conference* (New York: Vintage Books, 1988), 420.

15. Harrington, *Fragments*, 204.

16. Rachelle Horowitz, "Tom Kahn and the Fight for Democracy: A Political Portrait and Personal Recollection," *Democratiya* 11 (Winter 2007): 227.

17. Fred Halstead, *Out Now! A Participant's Account of the American Movement against the Vietnam War* (New York: Monad/Pathfinder Press, 1978), 275.

18. Harrington, *Fragments*, 204.

19. In a letter to Rustin (7/27/66), AFL–CIO Director of Research Nat Goldfinger, who had been involved in helping to draft the Freedom Budget, wrote: "I notice that among the labor leaders listed [as potential sponsors of the Freedom Budget] are the names George Meany and Andy Biemiller [chief lobbyist for the AFL-CIO]. My suggestion to Lane Kirkland, Executive Assistant to Mr. Meany, is that Don Slaiman and I sign the document, without any signature from Mr. Meany or from any other members of the AFL-CIO staff in the building [AFL-CIO national headquarters]." In Bayard Rustin Papers. Whatever the reasons for this decision, it is clear that neither Meany nor the AFL-CIO as such saw the Freedom Budget as a "fighting issue." Norman and Velma Hill sense, at the very least, an ambivalence related to Meany's not endorsing the Freedom Budget. Authors' interview with Norman and Velma Hill, 9/15/12.

286 / NOTES TO PAGES 158-159

20. Harrington, *Fragments*, 222.
21. Authors' interview with Norman and Velma Hill.
22. Harrington, *Fragments*, 223.
23. One obvious example was Cleveland Robinson of District 65, who had been the treasurer for the March on Washington and was an early consistent opponent of the Vietnam War. There was, of course, the United Electrical, Radio and Machine Workers of America (UE), which had been driven out of the CIO during the early Cold War years on charges of "Communism" but had survived as a relatively democratic and socially conscious organization, and was quite opposed to the Vietnam War. But there were other antiwar forces closer to labor's "mainstream"—Hospital Workers Local 1199, the Packinghouse Workers, the Amalgamated Clothing Workers, Pat Gorman and others in the Amalgamated Meat Cutters and Butcher Workmen, Mike Quill and others in the Transit Workers Union, elements in the United Auto Workers, Joseph Yablonski in the United Mine Workers of America, Tony Mazzocchi of the Oil, Chemical and Atomic Workers, and more.

    Some relevant information on significant antiwar sentiment in organized labor's ranks can be found in the following: Halstead, *Out Now!*, 78, 143, 204, 239–41, 244–47, 248, 359–65, 545, 564, 568, 577–78, 596, 599–600, 609, 610, 612, 651, 673–75; Nancy Zaroulis and Gerald Zaroulis, *Who Spoke Up? American Protest against the Vietnam War 1963–1975* (New York: Holt, Rinehart and Winston, 1984), 157, 266, 333, 359, 365, 369–70, 387; Philip S. Foner, *American Labor and the Indochina War: The Growth of Union Opposition* (New York: International Publishers, 1971).

    On the existence of an alternative labor current to that represented by Meany, brutally marginalized in the early 1950s, see Judith Stepan-Norris and Maurice Zeitlin, *Left Out: Reds and America's Industrial Unions* (New York: Cambridge University Press, 2003); Rosemary Feurer, *Radical Unionism in the Midwest, 1900–1950* (Urbana: University of Illinois Press, 2006); and Ronald L. Fillipelli and Mark McColloch, *Cold War in the Working Class: The Rise and Fall of the United Electrical Workers* (Albany: State University of New York Press, 1995).

    On currents in labor's "mainstream" going in a more radical direction than Meany, see Paul Le Blanc, *Work and Struggle: Voices from U.S. Labor Radicalism* (New York: Routledge, 2011); Roger Horowitz, *"Negro and White, Unite and Fight!" A Social History of Industrial Unionism in Meatpacking, 1930–90* (Urbana: University of Illinois Press, 1997); Burton Hall, *Autocracy and Insurgency in Organized Labor* (New Brunswick, NJ: Transaction Books, 1972); Herman Benson, *Rebels, Reformers, and Racketeers: How Insurgents Transformed the Labor Movement* (Bloomington, IN: 1st Books, 2005); Sol Dollinger and Genora Johnson Dollinger, *Not Automatic: Women and the Left in the Forging of the Auto Workers' Union* (New York: Monthly Review Press, 1930); Moe Foner with Dan North, *Not for Bread Alone, A Memoir* (Ithaca, NY: Cornell University Press, 2002); Les Leopold, *The Man Who Hated Work and Loved Labor: The Life and Times of Tony Mazzocchi* (White River Junction, VT: Chelsea Green Publishing, 2007); Paul Le Blanc and Thomas Barrett, eds., *Revolutionary Labor Socialist: The Life, Ideas, and Comrades of Frank Lovell* (Union City, NJ: Smyrna Press, 2000); Bill Fletcher Jr. and Fernando Gapasin, *Solidarity Divided: The Crisis in Organized Labor and a New Path toward Social Justice* (Berkeley: University of California Press, 2008); and Kim Moody, *US Labor in Trouble and Transition: The Failure of Reform from Above, The Promise of Revival from Below* (London: Verso, 2007).

24. John D'Emilio, *Lost Prophet: The Life and Times of Bayard Rustin* (Chicago: University of Chicago Press, 2003), 438.

25. Finn, *Protest*, 340.

26. Bond quoted in Daniel Levine, *Bayard Rustin and the Civil Rights Movement* (New Brunswick, NJ: Rutgers University Press, 2000), 198; George Breitman, "The National Question and the Black Liberation Struggle," in *Malcolm X and the Third American Revolution: The Writings of George Breitman*, ed. Anthony Marcus (Amherst, NY: Humanity Books, 2005), 140–41. On SNCC's political shift, see Clayborne Carson, *In Struggle: SNCC and the Black Awakening of the 1960s* (Cambridge, MA: Harvard University Press, 1981), 175–306. Rustin's rejection is recorded in "Making His Mark: The Autobiography of Malcolm X" and " 'Black Power' and Coalition Politics," in Bayard Rustin, *Down the Line: The Collected Writings of Bayard Rustin* (Chicago: Quadrangle Books, 1972), 132–39, 154–65. In his 1970 classic *Black Awakening in Capitalist America* (Trenton, NJ: Africa World Press, 1990), Robert L. Allen cited Rustin as offering "the most sophisticated assault" on the black power concept, but went on to add his own critique of the ambiguous, diverse, and sometimes conservative uses to which "black power" and "black nationalism" could be put; see 128–92, 227–31. Relevant to sorting out issues relating to "black power" is Peniel E. Joseph, "The Black Power Movement: A State of the Field," *Journal of American History* (December 2009): 751–76.

27. August Meier and Elliott Rudwick, *CORE: A Study in the Civil Rights Movement 1942–1968* (New York: Oxford University Press, 1973), 5–39, 314–17, 322–24; Anderson, *Bayard Rustin*, 93–95; D'Emilio, *Lost Prophet*, 52–56.

28. Meier and Rudwick, *CORE*, 320, 324–25.

29. Norman Hill to James Farmer, August 16, 1964, copy in Max Shachtman Papers, Tamiment Library.

30. Meier and Rudwick, *CORE*, 292, 310–11, 318–22, 323, 324, 325; Paul Feldman, Sandra Feldman, and Penn Kemble identified as East River CORE members in http://www.corenyc.org/omeka/items/show/113 and http://www.corenyc.org/omeka/items/show/115; McKissick quoted in D'Emilio, *Lost Prophet*, 437.

31. D'Emilio, *Lost Prophet* 438, 450; Michael G. Long, ed., *I Must Resist: Bayard Rustin's Life in Letters* (San Francisco: City Lights Books, 2012), 323, 325–26.

32. Accounts can be found in: Michael Harrington, *Fragments*, 143–165; Tom Hayden, *Reunion, A Memoir* (New York: Collier Books, 1989), 86–92; James Miller, *"Democracy Is in the Streets": From Port Huron to the Siege of Chicago* (New York: Simon and Schuster, 1987), 74–75, 110–17, 126–35, 139–40, 234–35; Maurice Isserman, *If I Had a Hammer: The Death of the Old Left and the Birth of the New Left* (New York: Basic Books, 1987), 202–19; Kirkpatrick Sale, *SDS* (New York: Random House, 1973), 30–34, 60–68, 176–79, 210–13, 237–40.

33. Kazin quoted in D'Emilio, *Lost Prophet*, 439.

34. Paul Le Blanc, "Reluctant Memoir of the '50s and '60s: Part 2," *Against the Current* 135 (July–August 2008), http://www.solidarity-us.org/node/1613.

35. On the factional battleground in YPSL, see Paul Feldman "The Making of a Social Democrat," manuscript for a talk to Social Democrats USA, 2005, http://www.socialdemocratsusa.org/oldsite/feldman1.pdf, 8; Milton Fisk, *Socialism from Below in the United States: The Origins of the International Socialist Organization* (Cleveland: Hera Press, 1977), 34–35; Peter Drucker, *Max Shachtman and His Left: A Socialist's Odyssey through the "American Century"* (Atlantic Highlands, NJ: Humanities Press, 1994), 277, 281, 291–92; Paul Jacobs and Saul Landau, *The New Radicals: A Report with Documents* (New York: Vintage Books, 1966), 55; Josh Muravchik, "Hurray! YPSL Back in Action, Student-Labor Bond," *New America*, September 30, 1966, 4; Martin Smith, "Joel S. Geier: A Life in the Revolution," in *Vive Le Révolution! An Appreciation of Joel Geier*, ed. Candace Cohn (Chicago: Privately printed, 2008), 10–13. Related points emerged in author's interview with Joel Geier (June 30, 2012).

On YPSL membership figures, see Smith, "Joel S. Geier," 8, reporting that eighteen months after January 1961 YPSL membership "grew from roughly one hundred and fifty to eleven hundred"; and Carol Steinsapir, "Year of Growth Sparks Hope at YPSL Convention," *New America*, July 29, 1968, 7, which reports "membership has jumped from 300 to close to 500 in the past year."

On disputes within the Socialist Party, see Drucker, *Max Shachtman and His Left*, 277, 288–89, 305–6; Socialist Party Referendum on Vietnam: 'For Immediate Withdrawal,' Oppenheimer Resolution and 'For Negotiated Settlement,' Thomas Resolution," *New America*, December 1965, 3; "Socialist Party Convention," *New America*, June 30, 1966, 1, 2; Penn Kemble, "Socialist Party Convention: Socialists Set New Course," *New America*, July 29, 1968, 1, 4–5; Paul Feldman, "Democratic Left Strategy Focus of Socialist Debate," *New America*, July 29, 1968, 4–5, 6; plus the following documents from the Max Shachtman Papers, Tamiment Library: Max Shachtman to Michael Harrington, August 20, 1963, referring to "the Draperites, the Mendelsonites, and if I may dare to put this down on paper, the Shuteites" who in his opinion "think only in terms of the little family circle and its problems, real or imaginary, insofar as they do any thinking whatsoever" and constituted "the two-bit faction fighters, the pseudo-Leninists and other psychoceramic elements in the party and above all in the youth." Also see in Max Shachtman Papers, "The Crisis in the SP: Departures from Democratic Socialism" (1967); letter to "Dear Comrade," November 11, 1967 (signed by Robert Alexander, Julius Bernstein. Jim Burnett, Paul Feldman, Alex Garber, Mike Harrington, Tom Kahn, Penn Kemble, Seymour Kopilow, Sally Milstein, Irving Panken, Max Shachtman, Irwin Suall, Joan Suall, Alex Wollod); letter to "Dear member of Local New York," January 28, 1968 (signed by George Aranov, Syd Bykofsky, Abe Friend, Dave McReynolds, Seymour Steinsapir); letter to "Dear Friend," February 23, 1968, signed by Paul Feldman and Penn Kemble, 7 pages; letter to "Dear Comrade," March 13, 1968 (signed by Penn Kemble, Tom Kahn, Irwin Suall, Paul Feldman), 4 pages. Related points emerged in author's interview with David McReynolds (June 23, 2012).

Relevant for the development of a later internal dispute and split from those around Shachtman is Michael Harrington, "Open Letter to the Socialist Party by Michael Harrington," 1971, 9 pages, plus letter from Tom Kahn to Paul Feldman, February 8,

1971, regarding Kahn's "sharp attack" on Irving Howe and *Dissent* magazine at the Socialist Party convention—both documents in the Max Shachtman Papers.

36. "An Open Letter to the Socialist Party by Michael Harrington," 6.

37. By *cadres*, as indicated in chapter 3, we refer to experienced activists, educated in political theory, analytically oriented, with practical organizational skills, who are able attract and train new recruits and contribute to expanding efforts in broader movements and larger struggles. They are essential for creating and sustaining effective organizations, actions, campaigns, and movements.

38. Keyserling quoted in D'Emilio, *Lost Prophet*, 435; see Keyserling to Rustin, October 19, 1967, Bayard Rustin Papers. In the same letter, Keyserling noted: "The first question that inevitably arises whenever I address an audience on the 'Freedom Budget' is, 'What is being done now; we know what was done a year ago,' What am I to tell them?"

39. Anderson, *Bayard Rustin*, 289–90.

40. This is covered in Garrow, *Bearing the Cross*, 573–624, as well as in Taylor Branch, *At Canaan's Edge: America in the King Years 1965–68* (New York: Simon and Schuster, 2006), 629–722; and in Gerald McKnight, *The Last Crusade: Martin Luther King, the FBI, and the Poor People's Campaign* (New York: Basic Books, 1998). The outstanding account of King's efforts on this and especially his involvement in the Memphis sanitation workers' strike is in Michael K. Honey, *Going Down Jericho Road*.

41. Branch, *At Canaan's Edge*, 679.

42. Honey, *Going Down Jericho Road*, 242; Branch, *At Canaan's Edge*, 718–19.

43. D'Emilio, *Lost Prophet*, 370; Honey, *Going Down Jericho Road*, 281, 282–83, 397, 464.

44. Honey, *Going Down Jericho Road*, 464–466, 469, 476–482.

45. Ibid., 501; D'Emilio, *Lost Prophet*, 464–465.

46. Anderson, *A. Philip Randolph*, 345; D'Emilio, *Lost Prophet*, 435; Anderson, *Bayard Rustin*, 290.

47. Bevel quoted in Meier and Rudwick *CORE*, 329.

48. Carson, *In Struggle*, 287–306; Meier and Rudwick, *CORE*, 407–31.

49. C. Vann Woodward, "Introduction," in Rustin, *Down the Line*, xv.

50. Anderson, *Bayard Rustin*, 335, 336, 337; Levine, *Bayard Rustin and the Civil Rights Movement*, 215, 216; D'Emilio, *Lost Prophet*, 471, 474–76, 478. More accurate than saying Rustin was "weary" of the civil rights issue would be to say he had a sense that (a) a partial victory had been won through civil rights legislation of 1964 and 1965, (b) that the fracturing of the civil rights coalition made it impossible to advance the economic justice component of the civil rights struggle. Authors' interview with Walter Naegle, 11/11/12.

51. Long, *I Must Resist*, 465. All of this is elaborated with considerable detail, statistics, and analysis in William Julius Wilson, *When Work Disappears: The World of the New Urban Poor* (New York: Vintage Books, 1997).

52. Manning Marable, *Race, Reform and Rebellion: The Second Reconstruction and Beyond in Black America, 1945–2006*, 3rd ed. (Jackson: University Press of Mississippi, 2007), 115; Julian Bond, Foreword, in Long, *I Must Resist*, xi.

53. This refers to U.S. military interventions overseen by the Johnson administration in the Dominican Republic, the Congo, and Vietnam.

54. David McReynolds, *We Have Been Invaded by the Twenty-First Century* (New York: Grove Press, 1971), 83, 168–69; author's interview with Walter Naegle. On McReynolds's life and struggles, see Martin Duberman, *A Saving Remnant: The Radical Lives of Barbara Deming and David McReynolds* (New York: New Press, 2011).

55. Rosa Luxemburg, *The Letters of Rosa Luxemburg*, ed. George Adler, Peter Hudis, and Annelies Laschitza (London: Verso, 2011), 378, 449; McReynolds, *We Have Been Invaded by the Twenty-First Century*, 81, 169; Rosa Luxemburg, "The Crisis of German Social Democracy (The Junius Pamphlet)," in *Socialism or Barbarism, Selected Writings of Rosa Luxemburg*, ed. Paul Le Blanc and Helen C. Scott (London: Pluto Press, 2011), 204.

56. Van Gosse, *Rethinking the New Left, An Interpretive History* (New York: Palgrave Macmillan, 2005) provides what is perhaps the best-informed and most thoughtful survey of the New Left and the radical "Sixties" as well astheir prelude and aftermath.

57. Harrington, *Fragments*, 197; Isserman, *The Other American*, 266–363.

58. Arch Puddington, "A Hero of the Cold War," *American Spectator* 25/7 (July 1992); Beth Sims, *Workers of the World Undermined: American Labor's Role in U.S. Foreign Policy* (Boston: South End Press, 1992), 46–47; Michael Massing, "Trotsky's Orphans: From Bolshevism to Reaganism," *The New Republic*, June 22, 1987, 18–20, 22; Fernanda Perrone, "Biographical Sketch of Robert J. Alexander," preface to "Inventory of the Papers of Robert Jackson Alexander," Special Collections and University Archives, Rutgers University Libraries 2001, http://www2.scc.rutgers.edu/ead/manuscripts/alexanderf.html.

59. Long, *I Must Resist*, 463, 464.

60. The SDUSA panel discussion "Socialism: What Happened? What Now?" took place on May 1, 2002, and can be found on the old website of Social Democrats USA: http://www.socialdemocratsusa.org/oldsite/MayDayTranscript.html. Also relevant are *New America* former editor Paul Feldman's memoir, "The Making of a Social Democrat," manuscript for a talk to Social Democrats USA, http://www.socialdemocratsusa.org/oldsite/feldman1.pdf (written shortly before he died in 1999), plus a neoconservative memoir by former YPSL leader Joshua Muravchik, "Comrades," *Commentary*, January 2006; reproduced on the website of the American Enterprise Institute, http://www.aei.org/article/society–and–culture/comrades.

It has become common in some circles to argue that "neoconservatism" is rooted in the ideological dynamics of Trotskyism and/or "Shachtmanism," and though there is superficial evidence to make this case, the entire construct has been effectively demolished from the left, with impressive documentation and serious analysis, by Alan Wald in "Are Trotskyists Running the Pentagon?" History News Network, June 27, 2003 (http://hnn.us/articles/1514.html); and "Who Is Smearing Whom?" in History News Network, June 30, 2003 (http://hnn.us/articles/1536.html); and from the right by Bill King in "Neoconservatives and Trotskyism," *Enter Stage Right*, March 22, 2004, www.enterstageright.com/archive/articles/0304/0304neocontrotp1.htm. As of 2013, there are two different entities,organized largely in competing websites, claiming the mantle of Social Democrats USA.

61. Allen, *Black Awakening in Capitalist America*, 273. Cleveland Sellers touches on some of this in his memoir, *The River of No Return: The Autobiography of a*

Black Militant and the Life and Death of SNCC (Jackson: University of Mississippi Press, 1990), 170–277; also see Martin Oppenheimer, "Mobs, Vigilantes, Cops and Feds: The Repression of the Student Nonviolent Coordinating Committee," *New Politics* 14/1 (Summer 2012): 64–74; and Clayborne Carson, Foreword, in *The Black Panthers Speak*, ed. Philip S. Foner (New York: Da Capo Press, 1995), xiii–xvii.

62. Max Elbaum provides an insightful and informative consideration of part of the story in *Revolution in the Air: Sixties Radicals Turn to Lenin, Mao and Che* (London: Verso, 2002). A negative personal survey can be found in Ronald Radosh, *Commies: A Journey through the Old Left, the New Left, and the Leftover Left* (San Francisco: Encounter Books, 2001); and a critical but much more positive personal survey is offered in Peter Camejo, *North Star, A Memoir* (Chicago: Haymarket Books, 2010). Also see Paul Le Blanc, *Marx, Lenin and the Revolutionary Experience: Studies of Communism and Radicalism in the Age of Globalization* (New York: Routledge, 2006), 234–58.

63. Frances Fox Piven and Richard A. Cloward, *Poor People's Movements: Why They Succeed, How They Fail* (New York: Vintage Books, 1979), 254–55.

64. Adolph Reed Jr., *Stirrings in the Jug: Black Politics in the Post-Segregation Era* (Minneapolis: University of Minnesota Press, 1999), 117.

65. For more on the trends indicated here, see Michael D. Yates, *Longer Hours, Fewer Jobs: Employment and Unemployment in the United States* (New York: Monthly Review Press, 1994); Nelson Lichtenstein, *State of the Union: A Century of American Labor* (Princeton: Princeton University Press, 2002), 212–45; Correspondents of *The New York Times, Class Matters* (New York: Henry Holt, 2005). On the global scene, see Kim Moody, *Workers in a Lean World: Unions in the International Economy* (London: Verso, 1997); and Ronaldo Munck, *Globalization and Labour: The New "Great Transformation"* (London: Zed Books, 2002).

7. THE U.S. POLITICAL ECONOMY FROM THE FREEDOM BUDGET TO THE PRESENT

1. See Michael D. Yates, "Oliver Stone, Obama, and the War in Vietnam," *Counterpunch*, January 10, 2013, http://www.counterpunch.org/2013/01/10/oliver-stone-obama-and-the-war-in-vietnam/.

2. *A Freedom Budget for All Americans*, 6.

3. For the basics on the nature of a capitalist economy, see Michael D. Yates, *Naming the System: Inequality and Work in the Global Economy* (New York: Monthly Review Press, 2002). For a fact-filled review of the systematic assault by employers and the state, over the years, on workers' living standards and political rights, see Patricia Cayo Sexton, *The War on Labor and the Left: Understanding America's Unique Conservatism* (Boulder, CO: Westview Press, 1991).

4. A good overview of the connections of the state to the capitalist economy is by David Gold, Clarence Lo, and Erik Olin Wright, "Recent Developments on Marxist Theories of the State," *Monthly Review* 27/5–6 (October and November 1975): parts 1 and 2. Also see Ralph Miliband, "State Power and Class Interests" in his collection *Class Power and State Power, Political Essays* (London: Verso, 1983), 63–78.

5. See Marvin J. Levine, "The Conflict between Negotiated Seniority Provisions and Title VII of the Civil Rights Act of 1964: Recent Developments," *Labor Law Journal* 29/6 (June 1978): 352–63.

6. Robert A. Caro, *The Passage of Power* (New York: Alfred A. Knopf, 2012), in Kindle edition, the passage about Martin Luther King crying is at Location 13909. On Vietnam, see Lloyd C. Gardner, *Pay Any Price: Lyndon Johnson and the Wars for Vietnam* (Chicago: Ivan R. Dee, 1995); Daniel Ellsberg, *Secrets: A Memoir of Vietnam and the Pentagon Papers* (New York: Penguin Books, 2003); Nick Turse, *Kill Anything that Moves: The Real American War in Vietnam* (New York: Metropolitan Books, 2013).

7. Paul M. Sweezy and Paul A. Baran, *Monopoly Capital: An Essay on the American Economic and Social Order* (New York: Monthly Review Press, 1966).

8. An interesting reference work on this period is Ann Fagen Ginger and David Christiano, eds., *The Cold War against Labor*, 2 vols. (Berkeley, CA: Meiklejohn Civil Liberties Institute, 1987). See also Steve Rosswurm, ed., *The CIO's Left-Led Unions* (New Brunswick, NJ: Rutgers University Press, 1992); and Judith Stepan-Norris and Maurice Zeitlin, *Left Out: Reds and America's Industrial Unions* (New York: Cambridge University Press, 2002).

9. See Michael D. Yates, *Why Unions Matter*, 2nd ed. (New York: Monthly Review Press, 2009).

10. For interesting insights on how labor's embrace of cooperation worked out in the automobile industry, see Gregg Shotwell, *Autoworkers under the Gun: A Shop-Floor View of the End of the American Dream* (Chicago: Haymarket Books, 2012). Also see Aaron Brenner, Robert B. Brenner, and Cal Winslow, eds., *Rebel Rank and File: Militancy and Revolt from Below during the Long 1970s* (London: Verso, 2010).

11. An excellent book on "lean production" is Mike Parker and Jane Slaughter, *Working Smart: A Union Guide to Participation Programs and Reengineering* (Detroit: Labor Education and Research Project, 1994). Also see Kim Moody, *Labor in a Lean World: Unions in the International Economy* (New York: Verso, 1997); and Kim Moody, *U.S. Labor in Trouble and Transition* (London: Verso, 2007).

12. See Nelson Blackstock, *Cointelpro: The FBI's Secret War on Political Freedom* (New York: Pathfinder Press, 1988). See also Kenneth O'Reilly and David Galen, *Black Americans: The FBI Files* (New York: Carroll and Graf, 1994); and, with broader historical context, Robert Justin Goldstein, *Political Repression in Modern America, from 1870 to 1976* (Urbana: University of Illinois Press, 2001).

13. On the changing architecture of capitalist production, see Martin Hart-Landsberg, *Capitalist Globalization: Consequences, Resistance, and Alternatives* (New York: Monthly Review Press, 2013).

14. On the Great Recession, the global economy, and the assault on workers, see John Bellamy Foster and Robert W. McChesney, *The Endless Crisis: How Monopoly-Finance Capital Produces Stagnation and Upheaval from the USA to China* (New York: Monthly Review Press, 2012).

8. POVERTY AND ITS ATTENDANT EVILS TODAY

1. The data on poverty in this section are taken from Lawrence Mishel, Josh Bivens, Elise Gould, and Heidi Shierholz, *The State of Working America* (Ithaca, NY: Cornell

University Press, 2012), "Poverty," chap. 7, available at http://stateofworkingamerica. org/subjects/poverty/?reader.

2. The data on unemployment, underemployment, long-term unemployment, etc., are taken from ibid., "Jobs," chap. 5, available at http://stateofworkingamerica.org/subjects/jobs/?reader, and the Bureau of Labor Statistics website: http://www.bls.gov.

3. See Dan Swinney, "Documenting the Social Costs of Unemployment," *Labor Research Review* 1/3 (1983): 48–56.

4. Mishel, Bivens, Gould, and Shierholz, *The State of Working America*, "Poverty," available at http://stateofworkingamerica.org/files/book/Chapter7-Poverty.pdf

5. The wage data in this paragraph are taken from Mishel, Bivens, Gould, and Shierholz, *The State of Working America*, "Wages," chap. 4, available at http://stateofworkingamerica.org/subjects/wages/?reader.

6. Ibid.

7. David Cooper and Doug Hall, "Raising the federal minimum wage to $10.10 would give working families, and the overall economy, a much-needed boost," available at http://www.epi.org/publication/bp357-federal-minimum-wage-increase/.

8. Michael D. Yates, "The State of the Unions," http://cheapmotelsandahotplate. org/2012/11/12/the-state-of-the-unions/.

9. See *Journal of Human Resources* 15/4 (Fall 1980), which summarizes some of the results of the experiments.

10. Jaime Raymond, William Wheeler, and Mary Jean Brown, "Inadequate and Unhealthy Housing, 2007 and 2009," January 14, 2011, available at http://www.cdc.gov/mmwr/preview/mmwrhtml/su6001a4.htm.

11. National Low-Income Housing Coalition, "The Shrinking Supply of Affordable Housing," *Housing Spotlight* 2/1 (February 2012), available at http://nlihc.org/sites/default/files/HousingSpotlight2-1.pdf. The definitions of "extremely low income" and "very low income," as well as the data in each of these sections, is taken from this source.

12. Raymond, Wheeler, and Brown, "Inadequate and Unhealthy Housing, 2007 and 2009."

13. Ibid.

14. Douglas Rice, "Deficit Reduction Deal without Substantial New Revenues Would Almost Certainly Force Deep Cuts in Housing Assistance," November 26, 2012, available at http://www.cbpp.org/cms/index.cfm?fa=view&id=3866.

15. Stephanie Woolhandler and David Himmelstein, "Healthcare Reform 2.0," November 9, 2011, available at http://www1.cuny.edu/mu/forum/2011/11/09/dr-steffie-woolhandler-and-dr-david-himmelstein-on-their-recent-publication-%E2%80%9Chealthcare-reform-2-0%E2%80%B3-in-the-fall-2011-issue-of-social-research/.

16. Elise Gould, "Employer-sponsored health insurance coverage continues to decline in a new decade," December 5, 2012, available at http://www.epi.org/publication/bp353-employer-sponsored-health-insurance-coverage/.

17. "Health Costs: How the U.S. Compares with Other Countries," October 22, 2012, available at http://www.pbs.org/newshour/rundown/2012/10/health-costs-how-the-us-compares-with-other-countries.html.

18. Jonathan Kozol, *Savage Inequalities: Children in America's Schools* (New York: Harper Perennial, 1991).

19. David Noble, *Digital Diploma Mills: The Automation of Higher Education* (New York: Monthly Review Press, 2003).

20. See Diane Ravitch, *The Death and Life of the Great American School System: How Testing and Choice Are Undermining Education* (New York: Basic Books, 2011); Lois Weiner, *The Future of Our Schools: Teachers Unions and Social Justice* (Chicago: Haymarket Books, 2013); and Sarah Knopp and Jeff Bale, eds., *Education and Capitalism: Struggles for Learning and Liberation* (Chicago: Haymarket Books, 2012).

21. Doug Henwood and Liza Featherstone, "Marketizing Schools," *Monthly Review* 64/13 (June 2013).

22. http://www.ssa.gov/oact/STATS/admin.html.

23. For a useful summary of both the benefits of the Social Security system and its solvency, see "Policy Basics: Top Ten Facts about Social Security," http://www.cbpp.org/cms/index.cfm?fa=view&id=3261&emailView=1. Although written in 2005, this essay by Doug Henwood is still pertinent and useful: "Social Security, revisited," at http://www.leftbusinessobserver.com/SocialSecurityRevisited.html.

24. This and the next nine paragraphs are adapted from Michael D. Yates, "The Great Inequality," *Monthly Review* 63/10 (March 2012).

25. Quintile data in this and the preceding paragraph can be found in Carmen DeNavas-Walt, Bernadette D. Proctor, and Jessica C. Smith, *Income, Poverty, and Health Insurance Coverage in the United States: 2010* (Washington, D.C.: U.S. Government Printing Office, 2011), http://census.gov. The data on the income shares of the top 5 percent of households can be found in "Table H2 All Races" at http://census.gov/hhes/www/income/data/historical/inequality/.

26. See Max Fisher, "Map: U.S. Ranks Near Bottom on Income Inequality," *The Atlantic*, September 19, 2011, available at http://theatlantic.com.

27. See "Share of the Nation's Income Earned by the Top 1 Percent," *New York Times*, October 25, 2011, http://nytimes.com. The chart here shows the changing share of the highest 1 percent of income recipients. The data on the share of income growth that went to the richest 1 and 0.1 percent is from Josh Bivens and Lawrence Mishel, "Occupy Wall Streeters Are Right about Skewed Economic Rewards in the United States," October 26, 2011, http://epi.org. On the incomes of the ultra-rich, see Nelson D. Schwartz and Louise Story, "Pay of Hedge Fund Managers Roared Back Last Year," *New York Times*, March 31, 2010, http://nytimes.com.

28. Data in this and the preceding paragraph are from Sylvia A. Allegretto, "The State of Working America's Wealth, 2011: Through Volatility and Turmoil, the Gap Widens," EPI Briefing Paper 292, March 23, 2011, http://epi.org.

29. See Peter Montague, "Economic Inequality and Health," http://huppi.com.

30. John Bellamy Foster, "Capitalism and Environmental Catastrophe," available at http://mrzine.monthlyreview.org/2011/foster291011.html.

31. See "Slavery by Another Name," http://cheapmotelsandahotplate.org/2012/02/23/slavery-by-another-name/.

32. Mishel, Bivens, Gould, and Shierholz, *The State of Working America*, "Income," chap. 2, available at http://stateofworkingamerica.org/subjects/income/?reader.

33. Ibid., "Wealth," chap. 6.

34. See http://www.epi.org/page/-/BriefingPaper288.pdf.

35. See http://www.bls.gov/opub/ted/2011/ted_20110914.htm.
36. Mishel, Bivens, Gould, and Shierholz, *The State of Working America,* "Poverty," chap. 7.
37. See http://www.bls.gov/news.release/empsit.nr0.htm and http://stateofworkingamerica.org/charts/underemployment-by-race-and-ethnicity/.
38. See http://www.epi.org/publication/racial-segregation-continues-intensifies/.
39. See http://www.ecology.com/2013/04/01/us-life-expectancy-mortality-rates/, and for infant mortality, http://www.cdc.gov/mmwr/preview/mmwrhtml/mm6205a6.htm.
40. See http://www.motherjones.com/politics/2011/07/job-crisis-black-unemployment-rates?page=2, and http://bjs.gov/content/pub/pdf/cpus10.pdf.
41. For an excellent set of charts and graphs illustrating GDP growth in the United States, see http://www.tradingeconomics.com/united-states/gdp-growth-annual.
42. See http://www.project-syndicate.org/commentary/the-great-depression-redux-by-j-bradford-delong.
43. See Chrystia Freeland, "Fear of Falling Out of Middle Class Stalks Americans," *Globe and Mail,* April 25, 2013, available at http://www.theglobeandmail.com/report-on-business/economy/fear-of-falling-out-of-middle-class-stalks-americans/article11552575/.

9. TOWARD A NEW FREEDOM BUDGET

1. See http://www.counterpunch.org/2013/04/01/how-to-reduce-unemployment/.
2. For comparisons between the United States and other countries, see http://www.law.harvard.edu/programs/lwp/papers/No_Holidays.pdf.
3. The seminal work is David Card and Alan B. Krueger, *Myth and Measurement: The New Economics of the Minimum Wage* (Princeton: Princeton University Press, 1997). Some local areas have enacted living wage laws. On the great social benefits of these, see Richard R. Troxell, *Looking Up at the Bottom Line: The Struggle for the Living Wage* (Austin, TX: Plain View Press, 2010).
4. On the impact of right-to-work laws, see Elise Gould and Heidi Shierholz, "Average Worker in 'Right-To-Work' State Earns $1,500 Less Each Year," available at http://www.epi.org/publication/average-worker-right-to-work-state/. On U.S. labor law and its many inadequacies, see Michael D. Yates, *Power on the Job: The Legal Rights of Working People* (Boston: South End Press, 1994).
5. Abraham Lincoln, Speech at Hartford, Connecticut, March 5, 1860, in Roy P. Basler, Marion Dolores Pratt, and Lloyd A. Dunlap, eds., *Collected Works of Abraham Lincoln* (New Brunswick, NJ: Rutgers University Press, 1953), 4:8.
6. Chester Hartman, "The Case for a Right to Housing," 1998, available at http://www.escr-net.org/usr_doc/hpd_0902_hartman.pdf.
7. On the problems with Obama's health care law and the advantages of single payer, see Stephanie Woolhandler and David Himmelstein, "Healthcare Reform 2.0," Nov. 9, 2011, available at http://www1.cuny.edu/mu/forum/2011/11/09/dr-steffie-woolhandler-and-dr-david-himmelstein-on-their-recent-publication-%E2%80%9Chealthcare-reform-2-0%E2%80%B3-in-the-fall-2011-issue-of-social-research/.
8. See, for example, information and ideas at the website of Pittsburghers for Public Transit (http://www.pittsburghforpublictransit.org), which is an affiliate of Americans for Transit (http://www.pittsburghforpublictransit.org).

9.   Christina Ergas, "Cuban Urban Agriculture as a Strategy for Food Sovereignty," *Monthly Review* 64/10 (March 2013), available at http://monthlyreview. org/2013/03/01/cuban-urban-agriculture-as-a-strategy-for-food-sovereignty/.

10.   For health and education, see http://www.aft.org/pdfs/americaneducator/spring2011/ Wilkinson.pdf. See also http://www.ncbi.nlm.nih.gov/pmc/articles/PMC2376999/, and Kate Pickett and Richard Wilkinson, *The Spirit Level: Why Greater Equality Makes Societies Stronger* (London: Bloomsbury Press, 2011).

11.   Eric A. Schutz, *Inequality and Power: The Economics of Class* (London: Routledge, 2011). See also Michael D. Yates, "The Great Inequality," *Monthly Review* 63/10 (March 2012), available at http://monthlyreview.org/2012/03/01/the-great-inequality.

12.   Linda Bilmes and Joseph Stiglitz, *The Three Trillion Dollar War: The True Cost of the Iraq Conflict* (New York: W.W. Norton, 2008). For more recent studies by these authors, see http://threetrilliondollarwar.org/

13.   See http://www.pbs.org/newshour/rundown/2012/10/health-costs-how-the-us-com-pares-with-other-countries.html.

14.   See http://www.keepeek.com/Digital-Asset-Management/oecd/education/education -at-a-glance-2012_eag-2012-en.

15.   Andrew Fieldhouse and Rebecca Thiess, "A Technical Report on the Congressional Progressive Caucus Budget for Fiscal Year 2013," available at http://www.epi.org/ publication/wp293-cpc-budget-for-all-2013/. This paper by sophisticated econo-mists at the Economic Policy Institute provides voluminous detail on monies that would be saved with cuts in defense and other socially damaging spending, what progressive programs for employment, education, health care, and others would cost, and how much revenue could be expected with various changes in the tax codes. This paper shows beyond a doubt that what we have proposed in this book is eminently feasible.

16.   See http://www.nytimes.com/2012/11/19/opinion/to-reduce-inequality-tax-wealth-not-income.html?_r=1&.

17.   Sylvia A. Allegretto, "The State of Working America's Wealth, 2011: Through Volatility and Turmoil, the Gap Widens," EPI Briefing Paper 292, March 23, 2011, available at http://epi.org.

18.   See Jesse Eisinger, "The 0.03% Solution to Washington's Budget Problems," http:// dealbook.nytimes.com/2013/02/06/time-to-revive-the-financial-transaction-tax/.

19.   Farrell Dobbs, *Teamster Rebellion* (New York: Monad/Pathfinder, 1972), 71–72; Sol Dollinger and Gernora Johnson Dollinger, *Not Automatic: Women and the Left in the Forging of the Auto Workers Union* (New York: Monthly Review Press, 2000), 131–32; Bruce Watson, *Freedom Summer: The Savage Season of 1964 that Made Mississippi Burn and Made America a Democracy* (New York: Penguin, 2010), 66–68, 105–106, 121, 131–133, 136–139. On the programs of the Black Panther Party, see http://en.wikipedia.org/wiki/Black_Panther_Party#Survival_programs; on the Nation of Islam's substantial economic plan based on collective self-help, see http://www. finalcall.com/artman/publish/Columns_4/article_6680.shtml. Writers for the 99%, *Occupying Wall Street: The Inside Story of an Action that Changed America* (Chicago: Haymarket, 2011). Also relevant is material presented in two volumes by BBC jour-nalist Paul Mason: *Live Working or Die Fighting: How the Working Class Went Global*

(Chicago: Haymarket, 2010); and *Why It's Still Kicking Off Everywhere, The New Global Revolutions* (London: Verso, 2012).

20. For a good examination of the CTU and the 2012 strike, see the articles in the June 2013 issue of *Monthly Review* magazine. Also see Bill Fletcher Jr. and Fernando Gapasin, *Solidarity Divided: The Crisis in Organized Labor and a New Path Toward Social Justice* (Berkeley: University of California Press, 2008); and Paul Le Blanc, *Work and Struggle: Voices from U.S. Labor Radicalism* (New York: Routledge, 2011).

INDEX

31192020472922